# ANCIENT ASTROLOGY
# THEORY AND PRACTICE

# ANCIENT ASTROLOGY
# THEORY AND PRACTICE

*Matheseos Libri VIII*

*by*

## FIRMICUS MATERNUS

Translated

by

## JEAN RHYS BRAM

**NOYES CLASSICAL STUDIES**

# NOYES PRESS
Park Ridge, New Jersey

Copyright © 1975 by Jean Rhys Bram
Library of Congress Catalog Card Number: 75-10865
ISBN: 0-8155-5037-5

Published in the United States by
NOYES PRESS
Noyes Building
Park Ridge, New Jersey 07656

Library of Congress Cataloging in Publication Data

Firmicus Maternus, Julius.
  Ancient astrology.

  (Noyes classical studies)
  Translation of Matheseos libri VIII.
  Bibliography:  p.
  Includes indexes.
  1.  Astrology—Early works to 1800.  I. Title.
BF1680.F5713       133.5       75-10865
ISBN 0-8155-5037-5

*To Susan, Elizabeth, and Margaret*

# PREFACE

Magic, philosophy, science and theology combine in strange ways in the thinking of the last centuries of the Roman empire. For some time the study of these complexities had been one of my main interests. The example of Firmicus Maternus was suggested to me by Professor Larissia Bonfante Warren of New York University.

Firmicus seemed worthy of note for many reasons. He is almost alone as author of works produced both before and after an apparent conversion to Christianity. He was a typical intellectual of his day, having a smattering of literary knowledge yet with a full-blown command of rhetorical devices; at the same time, in his earlier years he was a staunch devotee of individual astrology and rigid fatal determinism, which he combined with the more ordinary philosophical outlook of his period—a mystic blend of Stocisim and Neo-Platonism. He left a lengthy handbook detailing the astrological practices of his day, the only work which has come down to us in its entirety out of numerous astrological treatises written in the Hellenistic and Roman periods, of which only fragments remain. Furthermore, this manual was important not only because it was the first effort of its kind in the Western world, but because it was the channel for astrological lore to the Middle Ages and the Renaissance. Finally, although much attention has been paid to the Christian writings of Firmicus, little study has been applied to his *Mathesis* outside of that by a handful of French and German scholars one or two generations ago.

As a preliminary study of Firmicus, it seemed useful to furnish a translation of the complete manual for the growing number of scholars outside the classical disciplines—researchers who work with social history and the history of ideas, as well as the historical backgrounds of astronomy, mathematics, and astrology.

I am grateful to Professor Warren, not only for calling my attention to this book, but for her constant concern with the progress of the work. I am also grateful to Professor Claireve Grandjouan for her encouragement, to Dr. Tamara Green, Mr. William Mayer, and Mrs. Eirene Christodoulou for their help in verifying and proofreading the text, and to Miss Marjorie Venit, who took great pains with the diagrams. Miss Serinity Young very kindly read the translation and checked it for modern astrological terminology. To Miss Gretchen Clumpner, finally, my deepest thanks for her able deciphering and typing of the entire manuscript.

*Jean Rhys Bram*
*Classics Department*
*Hunter College*

*New York, N.Y.*
*April, 1975*

vii

# TABLE OF CONTENTS

# LIST OF DIAGRAMS

# Introduction

Julius Firmicus Maternus is known to us as the author of two works of the fourth century A.D. The first, *Matheseos Libri VIII* (Eight Books of the *Mathesis,* or Theory of Astrology) stands as the final, as well as the most complete, work on astrology of the Classical world. The other (*De Errore Profanarum Religionum*), written about ten years later, is a bitter attack on the mystery religions from a Christian point of view. Since the astrological work is strongly imbued with pagan philosophical attitudes, we could assume Firmicus was converted to Christianity between the writing of the two works. The second book, however, contains no positive Christian doctrine; it is purely a polemic against the mysteries, which had also been condemned in the *Mathesis*. In his discussion of astrology Firmicus contends that it is a pure and high form of philosophy, far more serious than the usual pagan rites. He bases his argument on the Stoic concept of *sympatheia* which claims that there is an intimate relationship between all parts of the universe, including the stars and mankind.

In Firmicus' own account we hear of two smaller books (*singulares libri*) by him, one on the Ruler of Time *(Math.* IV, 20, 2), the other on the End of Life *(Math.* VII, 7, 14). He also mentions *(Math.* VIII, 8, 14) one he intended to write on the *Myriogenesis,* that is, the influence of individual degrees of the zodiac. No trace of these shorter writings remains.

Doubts as to the single authorship of the *Mathesis* and *De Errore* have been dispelled for most scholars by the careful study of vocabulary and *clausulae* (rhythmic sentence endings) by Clifford H. Moore (*Julius Firmicus Maternus der Heide und der Christ,* Diss. Munich, 1897).

From the internal evidence *De Errore* can be shown to have been written about 346 and the *Mathesis* to have been begun in 334. An eclipse of the sun of July 17, 334 is mentioned in the first book of the *Mathesis*.

No other facts are known about Firmicus Maternus except what appear in his writings. He calls himself a Sicilian and was probably from Syracuse. His style shows the influence of the so-called African Latin, somewhat similar to that of Apuleius, the author of *The Golden Ass*. This style is characteristic of Sicily as well as of Roman Africa.

We learn from Firmicus' own account *(Math. IV, Proemium)* that he had practiced law for many years but finally gave it up for scholarly pursuits. The manuscripts call the author either *Senator, Vir Clarissimus,* or *Vir Consularis*. It is well known that the emperor Constantine was less hostile to the senatorial class than his predecessor Diocletian and in fact greatly increased its numbers, admitting its members to high office and choosing from among them his special followers. Firmicus does not appear to have been of an old senatorial family, so he may have been one of the newly-created senators. There is even a possibility that he was one of the senators created for the new capital at Constantinople, since he opens the *Mathesis* with an account of a long and circuitous journey back to Italy.

No record exists of high administrative or military posts for Firmicus, but he was on friendly terms with his patron, Lollianus Mavortius, a high government official who is mentioned twice by the historian Ammianus Marcellinus (330–395 A.D.) and whose promotions are recorded in a series of inscriptions.

As a Sicilian Firmicus would have been fluent in Greek. Most if not all of the *Mathesis* is derived from Greek sources. The style of both his books shows a thorough grounding in the rhetorical training current in Greek and Roman schools of the time. He takes pains to display his wide, though somewhat superficial, erudition. He had, in other words, a typical gentleman's education.

One may reconstruct that Firmicus, as a wealthy, retired lawyer of senatorial rank, was an upper class litterateur with an interest in philosophy and science, leaning more toward Stoic and Neo-Platonic teachings, as would be fitting for his astrological interests. One must remember that at least from the time of the scientist Ptolemy (second century A.D.) astrology had been linked with the most reputable scientific doctrine, and that fatal determinism was an integral part of Stoic world outlook. The question of how far one should surrender to Stoic determinism had been a subject of high-level philosophic argument from Hellenistic times. The *Mathesis* shows that its author adheres to the extreme position. He fiercely attacks compromisers as well as opponents of his theory and scorns the idea of some philosophers that Fate may control some parts of human life but not others.

## THE MATHESIS

The *Mathesis* can be regarded as a summation of the trends of the fourth century, one of the last great statements of the thoughts and feelings of pagan Rome. In common with all the products of its age, such as the imperial villa at Piazza Armerina on Sicily's east coast, it displays realism and fantasy, magnificence and awkwardness.

Firmicus has browsed superficially through much of the ancient literature, as was expected of an educated man of his period, and he uses every occasion to show his erudition. The writings of the end of the Empire have little urge to originality but show rather a desperate grasping at links with the past. Thus the whole work of the *Mathesis* is composed of snippets of late Hellenistic science and star-lore, much of it attributed to legendary wisdom from the ancient East. The cement holding it all together is also in the fourth century tradition—purple passages embroidering familiar themes from literature and philosophy, built on the strict tenets of the schools of rhetoric. The ideology is a mixture of Neo-Platonic and Stoic with a high moral tone, for this is an ascetic century among pagans as well as among Christians. The passage at the end of Book Two describing the attitudes of a practitioner of astrology could have been written of a Christian prelate as well as a Neo-Platonic philosopher. The old pagan gods appear only as literary flourishes, but there are moving invocations to the only slightly anthropomorphized heavenly bodies, especially to the new Roman supreme deity, the Unconquered Sun.

The first half of the fourth century after the irreparable losses of the third was a time less sophisticated but less turbulent, an age in which the new Rome and newly recognized Christianity gave promise of stability and progress.

This age which took itself so seriously shows only a few writers. It is a period of adjustment, soon to be followed by a last flowering of Latin literature, both pagan and Christian. Later fourth and fifth century authors felt a need to turn into Latin much of the wisdom and poetry which had come to be written more often in Greek in the recent centuries. Firmicus is a forerunner of this trend when he says he intends to put into Latin "for our Romans" the wisdom of the ancients.

Wide-eyed like early fourth century portraits, noble in intent and sometimes in execution, meticulously and rigidly organized in numbers which correspond to the heavenly bodies, the *Mathesis* appears to us as an explicit marker along the history of ideas.

But it is not only for the history of ideas—of his own time and the times he influenced—that we value the *Mathesis*. It also constitutes an extraordinary historical document, not necessarily for Firmicus' own lifetime, since he drew heavily on Hellenistic, often Egyptian or Syrian sources; but as a means of recapturing the thoughts, life styles, ambitions, and occupations of the restless, upwardly mobile people of the eastern Mediterranean between the times of Alexander and Constantine. Neither great literature nor great art nor the carefully recovered pots and pans of a modern excavation can show us as the *Mathesis* does the range of

problems, illnesses, windfalls, and successes of the people history neg-
lects. These are not the tax-crushed, caste-bound populations of the
Theodosian code. They are rather the vigorous, scheming, superstitious
crowds of the back streets of Alexandria and Ostia, the ones we catch a
glimpse of in the *Satyricon* and the columbarian reliefs of the Isola Sacra,
or in the contracts and letters recovered in the late papyri.

Only the mysticism and supernaturalism of the fourth century is
missing in Firmicus. He has no interest in after-life or desire for
miraculous salvation or communication with the "One." He believes he is
coldly scientific in his adherence to fatal determinism. This may be the
secret of his hostility to the mystery religions—they, together with
Christianity, offered a release by miracle from the "wheel of Fate." To
Firmicus fatal determinism is reassuring even when unfavorable, as is the
Stoic doctrine of kinship in all aspects of the universe. Astrology is not
only reassuring in its revelation of immutable natural law, but it is heady
since it promises a way to eavesdrop on cosmic secrets; but only, according
to Firmicus, if one follows all the rules with mathematical rigidity.

Growing as we see it in Firmicus from the intellectual exploration of
the Hellenistic Mediterranean, the security and excitement of the *Mathesis*
were to weather the Christian reassurance of the *City of God.* Despite
official disapproval, it was quietly copied and preserved in monasteries,
re-emerged as one of the first printed books, sparked the astrological
enthusiasm of the Renaissance, and reached us in an age which again
turns to both the reassurance and headiness of philosophies which
promise an understanding of man's place in the universe.

## THE DEVELOPMENT OF ASTROLOGICAL METHODS

Numerous Hellenistic works on astrology were available to Firmicus
as source material. Several—Manetho, Dorotheos of Sidon, Antiochos of
Athens (see list of ancient authors)—have come down to us only in
fragments. One, almost complete, is a kind of diary of a practicing
astrologer of the Near East, Vettius Valens. Almost contemporary with
Vettius was the great work of Ptolemy known as *Tetrabiblos,* a sequel to his
astronomical *Syntagma (Almagest).* Ptolemy's work gives a brief theoretical
background for astrology but does not offer guidance for practice as do
Vettius and Firmicus.

Astrology as Firmicus knew it involved the drawing of horoscopes for
individuals and presenting lifetime predictions based on the configuration of the heavens at birth. It appears to have developed from a
combination of Mesopotamian star observation and Greek mathematics,
possibly in Ptolemaic Egypt. The tendency of the Hellenistic and Roman
periods to attribute the origins of their science and philosophy to various
places in the ancient East led to the listing of such names as Anubis,
Zoroaster, and Asclepius as fathers of astrology.

What was probably one of the earliest manuals of astrological techniques was drawn up in Alexandria around 150 B.C. and given the names of a sixth century Pharaoh, Nechepso, and his scribe Petosiris.

Meanwhile Greek scientists such as Eudoxos (390–340 B.C.) and Hipparchos (190–126 B.C.) were lending to the art of astrology the prestige of their discoveries. Stoic *sympatheia* took in astrology as part of its credo. Star-lore gained a wide audience through the poem on the constellations, the *Phaenomena,* by Aratus (315–240 B.C.). It was based on materials of Eudoxos, commented upon by Hipparchos, translated into Latin by Cicero and by Germanicus, the emperor Tiberius' nephew.

Interest in mathematical astrology reached Rome in the first century B.C. In Cicero's circle of friends Varro and Nigidius Figulus wrote works on the subject, now lost. Although Cicero's teacher, the Stoic Panaetius, encouraged Cicero to argue against the doctrine of Fate, Posidonius, the great Stoic leader, lent his enormous influence to the cause of determinism and astrology. The first emperor, Augustus, skillfully took advantage of a comet he called the *Sidus Julium* (Star of Julius) to promote the catasterism (transformation into a star) of Julius Caesar, "the Divine Julius." Under Augustus and Tiberius an otherwise unknown Manilius published a long poem on the astrological divisions of the heavens (ed. A. E. Housman, Cambridge, 1937).

The friend and confidant of Tiberius, Thrasyllus, philosopher and astrologer, wrote a lengthy work on astrology of which an epitome is known in fragments. He was perhaps the father-in-law of that Balbillus who fulfilled the same post for Nero. The Roman emperors were almost without exception deeply concerned with astrological predictions but, at the same time, for obvious political reasons, encouraged legislation against its practitioners (Frederick H. Cramer, *Astrology in Roman Law and Politics,* Philadelphia, 1954).

At no time had the Empire banned astrological studies, only their practical application in the casting of individual horoscopes, and then only at Rome. Under Augustus' edict of A.D. 11 astrological consultation in regard to the Emperor could be prosecuted as literary treason, as could any other writing about the person of the Emperor.

After the reorganization of Diocletian (284 A.D.) the divinity of the Emperor and his relationship to the heavenly bodies became a matter of doctrine, so that it is not surprising to find Firmicus arguing (*Math.* II, 30) that it is not only illegal but impossible to make a prediction in regard to the life of the Emperor since he belongs to a power higher than the stars.

Within a generation after Firmicus there was a general ban on all kinds of divination within the Empire. Such legislation, however, was enforced only during periods of acute unrest and political turmoil.

## FIRMICUS IN THE MIDDLE AGES

The *Mathesis* of Firmicus is the last work on astrology in the ancient world. The reason for this may be that there was a sharpening of penalties against all non-Christian practices under Constantine and again under Valentinian (375-392). A number of *mathematici* were executed at that time whereas later, under the Theodosian Code (438 A.D.) astrologers were simply ordered to burn their books. Both the persecutions and the book-burning account for the dearth of astrological material in the West for the next five hundred years. Actually there is less evidence for persecution of astrology than for that of heresy and rural paganism. L.W. Laistner ("The Western Church and Astrology during the Early Middle Ages," *Harvard Theological Review,* XXXIV, 1942, 251–75) believes that astrology died out simply because there were not enough literacy and mathematical skill to study the manuals and draw charts.

The first new interest in science and astrology appears at the time of Charlemagne. The Venerable Bede (672–ca. 731) has left a small poem on the zodiac. A note in the library catalog of Regensburg from the tenth century refers to a *Mathesis,* which may be that of Firmicus. He is definitely mentioned in the libraries of St. Maure des Fosses and Bamberg around 1200. The Medieval monks read, copied, and stored the *Mathesis* despite the official disapproval of the Church. Astrology had never been persecuted as severely as the heretical beliefs; it was discouraged, rather, like all exotic doctrine which might run counter to Bible teaching.

Firmicus is also noted in a work called *de Philosophia Mundi* by Honorius of Autun, a widely translated popularizer of the twelfth century. William of Malmsbury, the English historian of the twelfth century, reports that Gerbert (later Pope Silvester II, 999–1003) when in Spain among the Saracens studied "the astrolabe of Ptolemy and Firmicus on Fate." The same author's *de Gestis Pontificum Anglicorum* gives an account of Girard, Archbishop of York, who had sinned by reading Firmicus. Later writers embroidered the story and claimed that the *Mathesis* was found under the pillow of the archbishop at his death so that he was denied Christian burial.

## THE MANUSCRIPT TRADITION

The oldest manuscripts of the *Mathesis* stem from the eleventh century. These contain only Books I to III and part of IV. Of these manuscripts three are in excellent condition and appear to derive from a single French archetype. The end of Book IV and Books V to VII, for which the text is in bad condition, can only be found in manuscripts of the 15th and 16th centuries. There were numerous copies current in the Middle Ages attesting the popularity of Firmicus' work. The first printed edition appeared in Venice, brought out by Symon Bivilaqua in 1497, followed by the Aldine in 1499. In 1894 K. Sittl edited a critical edition of the first half of the *Mathesis*. The complete text, edited for Teubner by W. Kroll, F. Skutsch, and K. Ziegler, appeared in 1913, reprinted in 1958.

## ASTROLOGICAL TERMINOLOGY

Astrological predictions are based on the movements of the planets (seven at the time of Firmicus, including the Sun and Moon). To the naked eyes these are seen to move against, and actually to become part of, the set of twelve constellations called the zodiac which lies along the path of the Sun at an angle to the equator. Although in reality these constellations are of different sizes, it became conventional very early to assume that each was one-twelfth of the circle, i.e., 30 degrees each, the circle having been divided into 360 degrees (duodecimal system) as early as Babylonian times by astronomers (the equal sign theory), and that six are at all times above the horizon.

These planets were believed to be particularly influential when they appear to be in (the ancients said "inhabit") the signs to which they are conventionally allotted as rulers: the Sun and Moon, one sign each, the other planets two each, thus totaling the number twelve. Modern day astrology with its increased number of planets has altered this allotment.

The signs of the zodiac of course were believed to be in constant movement. There was, however, another concept, a set of stationary "houses" also in the shape of a great circle, through which the signs move as if within the framework of something like a bent ladder. Each of the "houses" has a meaning relating to the various phases or attributes of human life: parents, children, careers, death, and so on. The forecast depends partly on whether malevolent or benevolent signs and planets occupy these houses.

What are now called "houses" in English were known in the ancient languages as "places" (Latin *loca,* Greek *topoi*). What we call "signs" were houses or domiciles. When the planets were in the signs which they ruled, the ancients would say that they were in their own houses. One would say in English, "the planet is in its own *sign* in the first *house*."

According to the ancient system the zodiac is divided into quadrants by four points called *cardines* (sg. *cardo*), now known as angles. The one in the East is now called the ascendant; its opposite is the descendant. The highest point is the Medium Coelum (now the Medium Coeli); the lowest is the Imum Coelum. These last two are usually abbreviated to MC and IMC in Firmicus and other ancient writers. In the ancient world the ascendant was known both in Greek and Latin as the *horoscopus*, a word which has come to mean to us the nativity, or chart (Latin *genitura*), that is, a map of the planets, Sun, and Moon at the moment of birth.

A set of geometric relationships among the planets as they appear on this chart is called the "aspects." These can be visualized as chords of a circle joining every second, third, fourth, or seventh sign. The two planets at either end of the diameter of the circle form an aspect known as "opposition." Others form a hexagon (sextile), square, or triangle (trine). Trine and sextile are considered fortunate, square and opposition unfortunate. A "conjunction," that is, the appearance of two planets very close to one another (distant no further than eight or ten degrees — the "orb") is considered another type of aspect. Firmicus, like all other ancient astrologers, did not know that Mercury and Venus can never be more than 28 and 59 degrees respectively from the Sun and therefore cannot form the larger aspects with the Sun.

Each of the seven planets has an "exaltation," a sign usually different from the one it rules, in which it is said to be particularly strong and favorable. Firmicus like the other ancient authors says the planet "rejoices" *(gaudet)* in its exaltation. The sign opposite the exaltation, a place of weakness for the planet, is known as its "fall" or its "debility." "Terms" *(fines, orai)* are fractions of other signs in which the planets are as powerful as in their own signs.

The thirty degrees of a sign are also divided into three decans of ten degrees each which are ruled by various planets in a system of rotation. But in some accounts other than Firmicus' they are ruled by different signs. The concept of the decans may have derived from a very old Egyptian division of the heavens into hours and minutes with special heavenly rulers for each.

Further complications of the heavenly positions are described by Firmicus in the second book. Books III to VII then discuss the meaning and interpretations of this great variety of combinations, providing special examples in some cases. The eighth book contains material known as the theory of the *Sphaera Barbarica*, that is, forecasting by stars and constellations outside the zodiac.

The first book of the *Mathesis* is a defense of the subject, together with detailed discussion of the traditional criticisms of fatal astrology. Firmicus tells us that he has written seven books for seven planets with the eighth as introduction. The first book differs from the other more pedestrian chapters in that it is composed with all the attention to style and in particular to the florid and elaborate rhetoric which could be expected of an able and learned lawyer of aristocratic family and expensive education in fourth century Sicily. The other seven books apparently have been translated literally from the source, but they are often introduced and ended with rhetorical passages. Some of the astrological calculations seem not to be completely understood by the author, but Firmicus occasionally notes that he has made use of this or that technique. He has apparently dabbled in the casting of charts and no doubt discussed the theory with his circle of friends.

## NOTE ON THE TRANSLATION

The 1913 Teubner text as established by Kroll, Skutsch, and Ziegler was used throughout. The sense as a whole is reasonably clear and I have made no emendations, but have omitted the occasional lacunae in the text. The translation tries to reproduce the feeling of Firmicus' two contrasting styles—his polished rhetorical introductions and conclusions as opposed to his plain and plodding enumerations. In neither case, however, is this a word-for-word rendering. Some of the tremendously long rhetorical passages have been cut into several sentences and in the technical descriptions some of the endless repetitions have been compressed while, I hope, retaining both sense and intent. In cases where common Latin usage allows of two or three possible meanings I have selected the one most in accord with Firmicus' time, his customary style, and the usual repertory of astrological vocabulary. The spelling and Latinizations of Firmicus have been kept as they appear in the manuscript, even when they are not consistent. Lacunae are indicated by . . .

Insertions in the text are shown by square brackets.

Notes have been kept to a strict minimum, for quick reference or explanation of unfamiliar terms or concepts. Firmicus, of course, invites the scholar to delightful wanderings through astrological, literary, philosophical, sociological and even archaeological byways, but such excursions are outside the limits set for this translation.

## ACKNOWLEDGEMENTS

My thanks are due to Professor Larissa Bonfante Warren who inspired this project. I am also grateful to Professor Claireve Grandjouan for her encouragement and to Dr. Tamara Green, Mr. William Mayer, Mrs. Eirene Christodoulou, and Miss Karen Snyder for their help in verifying and proofreading the text. Miss Serinity Young very kindly read the translation and checked it for modern astrological terminology. To Miss Gretchen Clumpner, finally, my deepest thanks for her able deciphering and typing of the entire manuscript.

Diagram I.  Symbols of the Signs and Planets.

## SIGNS OF THE ZODIAC

| ARIES | ♈ | LIBRA | ♎ |
|---|---|---|---|
| TAURUS | ♉ | SCORPIO | ♏ |
| GEMINI | ♊ | SAGITTARIUS | ♐ |
| CANCER | ♋ | CAPRICORN | ♑ |
| LEO | ♌ | AQUARIUS | ♒ |
| VIRGO | ♍ | PISCES | ♓ |

## LUMINARIES

| SUN | ☉ | MOON | ☽ |
|---|---|---|---|

## PLANETS

| SATURN | ♄ | VENUS | ♀ |
|---|---|---|---|
| JUPITER | ♃ | MARS | ♂ |
| MERCURY | ☿ | | |

# Liber Primus

1. Some while ago, my dear Mavortius[1], I promised to dedicate this book to you; but for a long time recurrent periods of anxiety and self-doubt interfered with my writing. I was afraid that my slight talent would not be able to produce anything worthy of your ears.

2. When we first met, you had just been put in charge of the Province of Campania—a post you richly deserved—and I was completely worn out from a tedious journey through winter snows. With the ministrations of a true friend you made every effort to restore my enfeebled body.

3. After I was brought back to my former state of health by your soothing care, we spent much time in conversation, discussing our early lives and exchanging literary references.

4. After we had talked over our experiences and our successes, you began to ask me all kinds of questions about the geography of Sicily where I was born and where I make my home. You wanted to know the true explanation of the ancient fables: what really are Scylla and Charybdis, and what is the cause of the tremendous clashing of waters when at fixed times the two seas rush together in the strait. You were curious about the composition of the fires of Aetna: their origin and how they manage to erupt in flames without damage to the mountain. Also you asked about the nature of the lake called Palicus[2] near the Symethus River, which is foul and black from discolored matter but has pale-colored foam and gives out a high-pitched hissing sound.

5. In discussing these and other questions, you also asked me about the wonders of Sicily which you had learned in childhood from the Greek and Roman writers. Finally you shifted the conversation to the globe of Archimedes[3] and showed me the wide range of your knowledge. You described the uses of the nine spheres[4] and the five zones,[5] each with their different coloring. You mentioned the twelve signs of the Zodiac and the

11

effects of the five eternally wandering planets; the daily and the annual path of the Sun; the swift motion of the Moon and its waxing and waning; the number of revolutions it takes to make the greater year,[6] which is often spoken about, in which the five planets and the Sun and Moon are brought back to their original places; it is completed, you said, in the 1461st year.

We went on to the explanation of the Milky Way and the eclipses of the Sun and Moon; why the rotation of the heavens never carries the Dipper to the West or brings it back to the East; which part of the Earth is subject to the North Wind and which to the South; the reason why the Earth itself is in the center and hangs in balance, and how Oceanus, which some call the Atlantic Sea, flows around and embraces the land like an island.

6. You explained all those problems to me, my most illustrious Mavortius, most clearly and simply. That was the point at which I dared to make the rash, impromptu offer to write out for you what the Egyptian sages[7] and Babylonian priests, who are so knowledgeable about the force of the stars, have handed down to us in their teaching about astrology.

7. I was ill-advised to make such a commitment, as I myself have come to learn; and, to tell the truth, I have many times rebuked myself and wished I could take back my promise. But now your encouraging words have strengthened me against my fears and have forced me to carry on the work I so often abandoned in despair.

When you were appointed Governor of the entire East by the wise and respected judgment of our Lord and Emperor Constantine Augustus, you lost no time in demanding what I had unthinkingly promised to do for you.

8. Thus to you, Proconsul and designated *consul ordinarius*[8], we fulfill our promise. We ask pardon if in the light of your great learning and knowledge of literature you expect to find in this book either polished rhetoric, superb organization, or unassailable logic. We have only a small talent and little eloquence and, it must be admitted, a very modest knowledge of astrology. Although troubled by these shortcomings, nevertheless we have undertaken the task of writing this book, my dear Lollianus, in order not to fail you in living up to our exacting commitment.

# I

## [THE OPPONENTS OF ASTROLOGY]

1. At the very beginning of this work it is imperative before we do anything else to answer those writers[9] who are trying to destroy the whole theory of astrology by many different kinds of arguments. These men are carried away by their faith in rhetoric and think they can shatter the whole of celestial science with mere arguments.

I am convinced, and the facts bear me out, that these men are not motivated by their theory, weak and false though it is, but merely by the desire to be in opposition. Arguing with aggressive presumption, they take a position against obvious and clearly-defined facts, facts which we not only discern with our reason, but perceive with our senses and our very eyes.

2. By using far-fetched and extremely theoretical arguments, drawn in the first place from the professional responses of astrologers, these men are trying to creep in, as it were, through an underground passage to undermine and topple the edifice of our science. But the more aggressively they attack, the more various the ways in which they seek to convince us, the more strongly they bolster our faith in astrology.

3. The essential truth of our doctrine is demonstrated by the fact that they struggle against it with such force of argument. This is not surprising since we know how much difference of opinion there is among them about the nature of the gods, and with how many different theories they are trying to destroy the whole force of astrological divination.

Some say there are no gods; others say there are, but describe them as not concerned about the world; some say that they exist and also that they undertake the care and management of all our affairs.

All these thinkers are involved in such a variety of opinions that we should digress too much if we were to list all their views, especially now that we are about to take up another kind of work.

4. Some arbitrarily give the gods physical shape and physical space; they assign them dwelling places and tell many stories about their deeds and lives; they say that all things which are done or planned are governed by the judgment of the gods. Others say that the gods plan nothing, take care of nothing, and have no desire to govern. All these opinions have a certain plausibility which may sway the minds of the credulous.

5. As to ideas about the immortality of the soul, the words of the divine Plato and keen-witted Aristotle are in violent disagreement; their ideas about good and evil are opposed to each other and inconsistent in themselves.

6. Here I think I should leave any discussion of these matters, for we are not concerned with this kind of argument. As a matter of fact, we have not made up our own mind as to what to believe. We have, however, given a brief summary of these disagreements so that the contradictory opinions of those who oppose astrology will become clear to all.

7. And so I would like to evaluate what is said and has been said about the *Mathesis*,[10] but very briefly; we should no longer digress on irrelevant problems.

## II

## [THE ARGUMENT FROM HUMAN TYPES]

1. First, then, they agree on the following remarks about the characters and complexions of mankind:

"If the characters and complexions of mankind are due to the combinations of the planets, and the motions of the planets make up men's traits, as if in painting: that is, if the Moon makes people fair-skinned, Mars red, Saturn black, why is the whole population of Ethiopia black, of Germany blond, of Thrace red-haired, as though the Moon and Mars had no strength in Ethiopia, and Saturn could not produce dark coloring in Germany or Thrace?"

2. As for character, they add, "If Saturn makes men careful, serious, dull, miserly, and silent; Jupiter, mature, kindly, generous, temperate; Mars, cruel, treacherous, and fierce; the Sun, upright, high-minded, and proud; Venus, pleasure-loving, charming, handsome; Mercury, shrewd, clever, excitable, changeable; the Moon, intelligent, distinguished, well-mannered, capable of dazzling people with brilliance, why do certain human groups appear to produce largely one type?

3. "The Scythians are known for monstrous, savage cruelty; the Italians for their king-like superiority; the Gauls are slow-witted, the Greeks frivolous, the Africans tricky, the Syrians greedy, the Sicilians clever, the Asians lustful and pleasure-loving; the Spaniards are absurd with their exaggerated boastfulness.

4. "Therefore Jupiter never softens the rage of the Scythians, nor does the Sun detract from the domineering quality of the Italians. Saturn does not impose gravity on the frivolity of the Greeks; Asian lust is not moderated by the sobriety of Jupiter; nor Sicilian cleverness by Saturn's chill. The greed of the Syrians is not lessened by the wanton influence of Venus, and beneficent Jupiter does not restrain the spiteful talk and deceitfulness of the Africans. The sluggish light of Saturn does not dampen Spanish boasting, nor all-wise Mercury sharpen Gallic stupidity."

5. But their most powerful argument against us is the one in which they say that our art removes all acts of virtue from human control if moderation, courage, wisdom, and justice are ascribed to the planets and not to our will. Whenever anyone breaks the ties of family or community, disregards human laws, gives himself over to cruelty and treachery, he may ascribe his crimes and perverse urges to the judgments of the planets.

6. "If he is unjust, treacherous, spiteful, impious, it is because these vices are brought about by the conjunction of Mercury with Mars! Why do we strengthen our hearts to learn courage, why do we fortify our minds to superhuman steadfastness, why do we, trained in divine doctrine, despise pain and death when we meet the bitter accidents of fate, if praise and rewards come from the Sun in favorable association with Jupiter?

7. "In vain, therefore, we restrain our vices with reason and intelli-

gence; in vain we attempt to control our unlawful desires; in vain we strive for law and moderation if Mercury, influenced by the favorable aspects of the Moon and Jupiter, excites us with desire for that kind of behavior."

8. They even approach individuals with words of this kind: "It is in vain, my good fellow, that you try to choose good and escape evil. Why do you try to fortify yourself with virtuous foresight and conscientious choices if this whole matter depends not on you but on Saturn or Jupiter?

"If this is the case, then, let us despise the gods and destroy the holy rituals in despair and impious rage.

9. "Plowman, why do you call on the gods? Your furrow is made straight without the guidance of your god. You who plant rows of olives in upland plains, you devote young shoots to Liber in vain. Your crops are given or denied by the courses of the planets without the care of any god.

10. "You who publish and confirm the laws, abolish your plebiscites, take down your tablets, free us from harsh punishments. According to the astrologers it was Mercury who made this man a profaner of sacraments, Venus who made that one an adulterer. Mars armed one for the slaughter of men, another to forge documents, still another to mix poisons. Mercury forces still another to wake with magic formulas the souls of those safely at rest, already purged of memory by Lethe's river.

11. "You see there one man inflamed with unlawful desires; another clinging to the embraces of young boys. So much evil we attribute to Mars or Venus.

"One man is struck down at your orders without reason by the hand of the executioner. Another is sentenced by the praetor. If he were forced to sin by the baleful influence of the planets, not by his own desire, you, magistrates, have no cause for punishment. You know we are always forced to commit such crimes by the evil fires of the planets."

12. These and similar arguments they bring together. They ask whether we believe the planets are animate or inanimate. They do that to confuse us, to force us to give an ambiguous solution. Whatever reply we give they turn it to the opposite with their clever rhetoric, twisting our words so that we seem to agree with them.

### III

### [IMPOSSIBILITY OF DEFINITIVE MEASUREMENTS]

1. In all these discussions we admire their cleverness, but we deny their basic premise. Astrology has proven its claims to us by the clear evidence of its forecasts.

2. There are some of these opponents who say that they agree with us to a certain extent. In order to throw the whole doctrine into doubt and despair they say our teaching has great force. But they add that no one can get definite results because of the smallness of the degrees and minutes, the tremendous speed of the stars' orbits, and the inclination of the

heavens. Thus they try to subvert the entire essence of our science by their apparent plausibility.

3. But as for us, though our talent is slight and our words almost ineffectual because of our lack of rhetorical skill, still we must reply. We must refute what they say with the truth of this science, uphold the unchanging nature of the astrological responses, and confirm the teachings of this god-given skill. We ask your pardon, renowned Lollianus, for the fact that what is needed in refuting these arguments is confidence in the truth, not the glitter of rhetoric.

4. First of all I would like to ask this violent opponent of the astrologers whether he has any first-hand knowledge of the science. When he asked for a forecast did he *never* receive true responses? Or did he scorn to listen, in his narrow-minded and violent attitude? Did he expect his ears to be polluted by the responses? Did he throw into confusion with over-excited speech the basic tenets of the whole doctrine?

5. If, when he asked for a forecast, the responses were true and later so proven, why does he criticize what he should wonder at? Why does he falsely attack the divine art?

6. But if, on the other hand, a practitioner who claimed to know the science of astrology gave an arbitrary forecast and was not able to prove his statements, the astrologer's presumption and ignorance must be blamed, and the fraudulence of his forecast. Anyone responsible for casting a shadow on this great art with lying responses deserves every kind of evil fate.

7. But the man who does not want to consult an astrologer, nor hear his responses, who will not adjust his ears to the truth of the forecast, fears the truth will make him change his mind. He is acting unjustly if he criticizes what he cannot grasp with his blunted faculties. Judges are always unjust if they pronounce sentence on cases in which they are ignorant of the facts. No one has a right to be a judge who is influenced in his decision by prejudice or ignorance; also one who does not pass sentence after having examined the case.

8. Therefore, if the accuser is one who had listened to a really well-trained astrologer, and had his responses proven right, then it is through ill-will and love of quarreling that he took up the opposition. But if an ignorant practitioner gave him false responses, then it is not the science which is to be blamed but the deceit and lack of knowledge of the man involved. As for the one who refuses either to hear or to judge, he has no right to make any statement. He is not qualified to criticize what he is not willing to see submitted to test.

## IV

## [DIVINE NATURE OF THE HEAVENS]

1. Certain people would like to dampen our zeal by describing the difficulties of our science. It is true that we deal with knotty problems not easily grasped by a mind which is weighed down and trapped in earthly pollution even though it is formed of immortal fire.

2. For the divine nature, which is maintained by eternal movement when enclosed in the earthly body, suffers a temporary loss of divinity. Its force is blunted by its association with the body and by the constant threat of death. That is why all knowledge which has to do with divine skills is handed down to us in a form hard to understand.

3. We willingly agree with this point of view and are prepared to show how divine matters are discovered only after laborious research. My opponent must admit that the immortal spirit, when separated from the lusts and vices of the body, retains an awareness of its seed and origin. It recognizes its sovereignty and easily reaches with its godlike searching mind all the things which are supposed difficult.

4. Who in the sky sees the path of the sea? Who, by rubbing stones, strikes from them the sparks of hidden fire? Who has learned the power of herbs? To whom does the nature of entire divinity reveal itself but to the Mind which sets forth from the heavenly fire and is sent down to rule the frailty of Earth?

5. It is this divine Mind which has handed down to us the theory and technique of this science. It has shown us the courses, retrogressions, stations, conjunctions, waxings, risings, settings, of the Sun, Moon, and other stars which we call the "wanderers" but which the Greeks call planets. This Mind settles into the frail earthly body and, thanks to its fleeting memory of sovereign soul, recognizes what is taught and hands down to us all knowledge.

6. This is how we can recognize in what sign the planet Saturn is exalted and see how his cold is warmed by another's heat. We can follow his motion every day and every hour. We even predict when he will retrograde and when return to his former station; when the nearness of the Sun spurs on his sluggish course, and when the loss of the Sun's heat slows down his motion. We know how long it will be before he returns to the same degree from which he set out.

7. In the same way this motion can be discovered in the case of the planet of Jupiter as well. Although in a shorter space of time he passes through the twelve signs in a similar motion. Mars, too, blood-colored, fearful with menacing flashes of light, when he approaches Saturn, has his fires moderated by the alien cold. Although his courses are swifter they can be studied in the same way.

8. The daily rounds of Venus and Mercury, too, have been shown to us. They proceed around the Sun at the same speed with only a small

space between, one preceding and the other following, or vice versa. We know when they will appear in the evening, when in the morning, when they are hidden by the orb of the Sun and when, freed from his glow, they shine forth again.

9. How does the course of the Moon appear to you? How wonderful that we can foretell the moment when her light increases and when it wanes. For when she draws near the Sun, either waxing or waning, she lowers her rays as if worshipping the Sun. Then she is born again clothed in her brother's fires and shines with renewed light.

10. Now we learn about a more awesome phenomenon which always strikes ignorant men with fear: when the Sun at midday is impeded by the Moon, as if by some obstacle, and denies his brightness to all mortals. (This, to speak of recent occurrences, was predicted by astrologers for the consulship of Optatus and Paulinus.) Or again the Moon, shadowed by Earth, fails in the same way—a thing we have often seen in the stillness of a bright night.

11. Astrologers have traced all these phenomena and with their mathematical skill have taught us the secrets. Thus I would like to ask you, whoever you are: which do you believe is more difficult, to discover the movements of the stars, as I have just explained they have been discovered—which ones move only on high; which toward the horizon; which travel submerged; which join themselves to the winds and regions of the East, which to the North; how they sometimes retreat, now are hidden, sometimes in direct motion, sometimes retrograde, sometimes sluggish (they always confuse the researcher by the variety of their courses); or is it more difficult afterwards to describe the influence throughout the Earth of these combinations and variations.

12. If you follow this reasoning you must admit that once the course of the stars has been found by mathematical observation, it is easy to see their powers and their spheres of influence. It is always hard to understand those subjects we approach in doubt and fear. We cannot grasp easily with the mind's eye anything for which we are not prepared by earlier training.

13. At first we dislike learning our letters. Set on an unknown road we almost fail at the first step. You see how children learning to do their first sums bend their fingers awkwardly. The man learning to swim fails at first through fear, but after a little while he gains confidence and slips through the waves with easy motion. In all we study—reading, arithmetic, music, and others—eventually we learn with ease, after the path has been made smooth by habit.

14. It is obvious that it is more difficult to understand the movements of the stars than to define their effects. There is no doubt about these movements which we demonstrate to students, first through calculation, then by the evidence of their own senses. Why, then, do you attack the whole Science, when you agree to its basic elements and its subdivisions?

## V
## [REFUTATION OF ARGUMENTS]

1. We must now take up the question of the complexions and characters of mankind. When we have refuted the whole basis of this tricky question, we can approach the awesome secrets of the science itself.

2. "Why," one opponent says, "is everyone in Ethiopia black, everyone in Germany blond, if men's complexions are allotted by the planets?"

3. It is clear that we must fight back with a full reply to overcome the shrewd and tricky statements of false rhetoric. We have restrained our tendency to oratory and rely on truth alone, for we do not wish to capture the ears of our judges by long speeches and the flow of language.

4. First, then, in this community in which we are now living, do all men have the same appearance, though they obviously have the same general shape?

5. I am sure I shall be told that all citizens are quite different, created with a great variety of appearances. If anyone doubts this—which is not likely—let him look around him when the whole population is gathered in one place, as at the theater or political meetings. Let him show me, if he can, any two who seem to have been created with the same limbs or features. Let fathers, brothers, children step forth; although blood relatives, they are seen to be physically different. None can be found so like another that he does not differ in some respect.

6. By this it is shown that our essential nature and the general shape of the naked body are formed from a mixture of the four elements by the skill of the far-sighted Creator. But our individual complexions and our shapes, our character, and our personalities are given us by none other than the constant motion of the planets.

7. For the planets have their own faculties and divine wisdom. Animated by pure reason they tirelessly obey that highest divinity, the ruling God who has organized all things under the rule of law to protect the eternal pattern of creation.

8. No one is so driven by rash impiety as to say that true wisdom exists on Earth where all things are mortal; or to claim that wisdom, reason, and predetermined order do not exist *there*, where everything is immortal forever.

9. Who doubts that by the same law divine Mind is transfused into earthly bodies, that descent is allotted through the Sun, ascent prepared through the Moon?

10. For the divine Mind is diffused throughout the whole body of the universe as in a circle, now outside, now inside, and rules and orders all things. Conceived by self-begetting it is preserved by everlasting fiery motion for the procreation and preservation of all things. It never lays down this duty through weariness but maintains itself and the world and everything that is in the world with its everlasting motion.

11. Out of this Soul the everlasting fires of the stars accomplish the swift completion of their orbits, quickened by the power of the living Mind. They bring part of this Soul to earthly bodies and in turn take it back to the perpetual fires of the great Soul.

12. In this way Immortal Soul endows the frail earthly body with confidence in its power. The individual soul corresponds in every way to its author and source which is diffused through all living things born on Earth and quickens them by divine fire. Therefore, since we are kin to the planets, we should not deprive them of their powers by impious arguments, since we are shaped and created by their daily courses.

# VI

## [ASTROLOGY ENCOURAGES DIVINE WORSHIP]

1. You also claim that we in our profane fury dissuade men from religion and from worshipping the gods. We say that all our behavior is governed by the divine motion of the stars. You are in error; you are contrary to the truth. For we make men fear and worship the gods; we point out the will and majesty of the gods, since we maintain that all our acts are ruled by their divine motion.

2. Let us therefore worship the gods, whose origin has linked itself to us through the stars. Let the human race regard the power of the stars with the constant veneration of a suppliant. Let us call upon the gods in supplication and piously fulfill our vows to them so that we may be reassured of the divine nature of our own minds and may resist in some part the hostile decrees of the stars.

3. Socrates, the man of divine wisdom, taught us we should do this. For when a certain man had pointed out Socrates' habits and desires he replied, "They are as you describe. I recognize them, I confess." And the wisest of men covered his failings by a ready confession. He continued, "All these I have overcome by the power of wisdom and virtue. Whatever vice my body has inherited from its base earthly constitution my divine soul has moderated."

4. It is clear that all we experience comes from the planets that goad us with fiery stings. Even what we struggle against comes from the divine Soul. But as for human laws which punish the sins of mankind, the wise men of old ordained them rightly. They bring aid to the suffering spirit to help the force of the divine Mind cleanse the destructive vices of the body.

# VII

## [EXAMPLES FROM HISTORY]

1. We have now come to the point where we must give a detailed answer to the problem we were discussing about the complexions and

characters of mankind. We have partially discussed the bases of this question and we shall now show that the laws serve the power of the Fates and always do what the Fates decree.

2. We must bring up a further example. Consider the youth at the height of his physical development—rich, innocent, modest. Driven by no private crime, by no anxiety, he has hanged himself. In the case of another, some enemy cut the noose while he was still breathing; he had intended to commit suicide because of the disgrace of his life; but once the noose was untied he was freed for the sentence of the judges. What brought the result of these two cases if not the power of Fate? Another man the judges should have found guilty, a man crushed by weight of evil deeds and convicted by his own conscience, but they freed him from imminent death.

3. Another man, known to everyone as innocent, fell on a drawn sword. One man—upright, sober, modest, whose way of life was always admired—threw himself over a cliff. A just man maintains his life as a wretched beggar while another, stained by well-known crimes, accumulates the highest honors. See how a pirate after the murder of untold innocents gathers his happy children into his bloody embrace. Another, innocent of all crime, is separated from his family by hostility.

4. To what do we attribute all this? Who allows these things to happen? Who has been allowed to have so much power over us? Give us your hand for a little while and hold back from arguments. Soon you may agree that all that stumbling and weak mortality must bear are decided by the chance movements of the planets.

5. What can we say about the honors of the wicked and the flight and exile of the good? See that man, stained by marks of slavery, who covers the filth and disgrace of his family by the consular fasces. Meanwhile one of noble blood is deprived of the honors which are his due. One with no evidence of merit at an early age goes along at headlong speed to every office. Another worn out with old age after an outstanding life is only now starting on a political career.

6. For what reason was the old man held back; what drove the young man to such a lucky career? What but the force which we say belongs to Fate, brought into play by the motions of the stars.

7. What can I say at this point about the condemnation of wicked sins? A while ago you were saying, "Often by general consent we see penalties inflicted on innocent people."

8. A famous man, most wise of the Athenians, who by his life and virtue received the title of "the Wise," was driven into exile by the throw of an unlucky sherd.[11] Or take the case of Socrates. A divine witness attested his wisdom, and his behavior was shaped by the holy teachings of god and man. In the end, overwhelmed by false charges, betrayed, he succumbed to the harsh power of his judges.

9. How many times did Fortune make Alcibiades a general? How

many times an exile? What can we say of such a fate? Alcibiades was
trained by the divine teaching of Socrates and suffered those things for
the sake of the nonmilitary power. Although he always led his army
successfully, he could not turn aside the hostility of Fortune. But some say
he was a captive of depraved desires and it was his arrogant presumption
that led him astray. (Let us forget him in order not to weaken our
argument.) Let us offer instead another example which will force you to
agree.

10. Fate sold out even Plato. It handed over the learning of that godlike
mind to the tyrannical power of Dionysius. But if this were not enough let
us turn to the disasters of Pythagoras. What kind of a man he was
everyone knows. Both men and gods have approved his virtue, knowledge, and wisdom.

11. He taught all subjects, even the most abstract. To finish his training
he learned foreign doctrines and penetrated all the secrets of wisdom. He
was the first or rather the only one while still inhabiting the frail earthly
body to discover the nature and origin of All-Seeing Will and divine
Power. This he did through his wonderful powers of concentration. He
followed that All-Seeing Will all the days of his life. Though his mind was
purged of all dross, though predisposed to virtue in life, yet the harshest
possible decrees of his fellow citizens sent him forth an exile and outcast.

12. Fleeing his fatherland and all Greece he first crossed into foreign
regions. As an exile he lived in Sybaris and Croton. Fortune did not keep
him there for long. He wandered as a fugitive through Locri, Tarentum,
almost every shore of Italy. In the end, together with a crowd of poor
wretches, he was surrounded with raging fire and destroyed.

13. What can you say to that? Do you still deny the power of Fate and
despise the force of the stars? Do you not see the bad end of the good, the
successful acts of the wicked, the destruction of the innocent, the safety of
the guilty? To what do you attribute all this? By whose decrees do you
think all this happened? When Fate determines all this for us, we are
unjust if we still maintain our opposition.

Finally you must answer as all these examples urge you: the guilty one
has sinned because Fate forced him, and the innocent who is condemned
is driven by Fatal Necessity.

14. Let us now turn to an exceptional thinker, Plotinus,[12] in order to
strengthen our case with a recent example. What branches of philosophy
did he not explore? His love of learning brought him distinction, and he
demonstrated his teaching by his own example, not that of others.
Inspired thought came from his mouth as if from a shrine. He was just,
brave, far-sighted, moderate; destined for all the rewards of virtue;
trained for every kind of research into the divine order of the universe.
And he believed he could overcome the attacks of Fortune by reason and
foresight.

15. First he chose for himself a home far removed from the bustle of

human intercourse. There he thought he would be free of Fortune's ill-will and open only to the reward of the divine teaching. Thus he expected that uncorrupted virtue would protect him against all threats of Fortune.

16. Confidently he settled himself in a pure and healthful region and gave himself over to the care and training of his body with the idea that he would leave no point unprotected where savage Fortune might attack. He is said to have chosen the pleasant soil of Campania where the tranquil climate supports the inhabitant with healthful crops. There the temperate climate is in balance between the extremes of winter rigor and summer's burning sun; and all kinds of illnesses are refreshed by the boiling waters of huge springs.

17. Settled there Plotinus despised the outward show of worldly position, thinking the only true honors those of wisdom. The desire for wealth had no hold over him. He thought riches useful only as a means for the trained mind to discover the Author of its origin.

18. You may note that in certain sections of his writing he appears to be lacking in caution and forethought when he attacks the power of Fatal Necessity. He severely reproves men who fear the decrees of Fortune when he claims that the control of our lives is entirely within our own power. He attributes nothing to the force of the stars, nothing to the necessities of Fate, but says everything is in our power.

19. It would be long to list his ideas on every point, the logic he used against the power of Fate and the very force of the stars.

But while he was writing these things he was healthy and unhurt. He never gave a thought to the death of Socrates or Plato. While admiring their mental accomplishments he attributed, one may suspect, their ends to their errors.

20. And yet the power of the Fates took control of him while he was feeling secure in his hostility to them. First his limbs became stiff and his blood became sluggish and congealed. Little by little his eyesight lost its sharpness and his vision failed. Soon after, a malignant infection under his whole skin burst forth. Polluted blood weakened his limbs and his whole body. Every hour and every day small parts of his inner organs were dissolved and carried away by the creeping sickness. A part of his body might be in good condition one moment and the next deformed by the festering disease.

21. His body came to lose its shape, and in a dying body only the mind survived, so that he might be compelled by his own pains, and convinced by true reason, to recognize the power of Fate.

22. What can be said about the well-known death of this man? Why were his virtues—wisdom, moderation, fortitude, justice—not able to free him from the punishment of Fortune? In the end even Plotinus realized the power of Fate and accepted the fiery judgment of the stars.

23. You also know—to return to a more ancient example—what

Miltiades suffered after his victory, what Themistocles had to endure after his triumphs. They were inplicated in scandals of public finance by those very people to whom they had given back liberty.

24. Who stirred up the savage mob against them? Who inflamed such public ill-will that, forgetting all benefits, they struck down these innocent and vigorous leaders? What was it except the force and necessity of Fate, which always conquers?

25. Let us turn, if we may, to a Roman example. That cowardly man—I mean Sulla[13]—stained by every pollution, grew up in the arms of the city scum who make a living by buying and selling shame. With constant success he led his army, was entitled "Felix" (lucky), then caused countless catastrophes to the Republic.

26. Remember how often it ran red with the blood of citizens from the mutilated entrails of the fatherland. Note the countless tablets of proscription he set up and how he was enriched from a parricide's share of blood-stained money. Though it is hard to list all his crimes, we shall tell a few so that we may learn from them the force of Fatal Necessity.

27. Seven thousand of our citizens fell to Sulla's punishment in the middle of the Forum. Believe me, only the necessity of the Fates struck down this multitude through Sulla's hands.

28. What kind of reasonable order is there when a man who never remembered what sex he was, who in old age retained the shameful passions of the body, who was possessed by vices, should govern the Roman Empire? We know that he was indicted in a prefect's petition. Censorinus accused him on well-founded grounds of the spoliation of a province. As an officer in the Cimbric War he deserted the Roman army and his general Marius. Yet this man, polluted by such scandals, was decorated with the authority of regal power, and set our army to despoil us.

29. Allow me to elaborate Sulla's crimes a little longer. My argument will be credited if the whole necessity of the Fates can be illustrated by many types of misfortunes.

30. By order of Sulla, Sulpicius, Tribune of the Plebs, was struck down in an unspeakable punishment. Sulla committed all kinds of cruelty immediately, without any hesitation, and sated his lusts day after day with the blood of citizens.

31. Marius the Younger, a man of praetorian rank, by general consent deserved well of the Republic. On Sulla's order first his legs were cut off; then his arms were loosened from the stump of his torso until they fell off; third, his tongue was amputated, leaving his voice in his throat. In the end, after every part of his body was mutilated, his eyes were torn out. In that small body so many tortures were discovered by the butcher of his father, and his breath was painfully drawn out by many wounds.

32. Perhaps you think only men were attacked by Sulla's fearful atrocity? But in the proscription tablets he wrote the names of women and

mothers of families, too, so that he might exercise his sword on the whole human race.

33. After other races were conquered and the world had been explored to the outermost limits of Ocean, after the minds of all were weakened by pitiable terror, the Roman People itself was forced to serve the evil rule of Sulla. Between the Porcian and Sempronian laws, amidst the groans of all citizens, he posted the third tablet of proscription. Not content with this evil, as a private citizen he murdered Lucretius. Although he had laid down his power, his cruelty lived on.

34. Should I mention the Servilian Lake on which the heads of many citizens floated in a display of his enormous crimes? Even amid the banquet of the gods, officiating at public rites, Sulla looked on the wounds of the Republic. What can be more cruel? He made widows and wretched orphans in the name of public emergency. Against Sulla there was no place for piety, for good faith, for bravery, for foresight.

35. Who now believes that our sins are punished by human or divine law? Sulla feeds on slaughter, he walks amid tyrannical powers, yet there is no divine force to attack his desires. What do you think? What do you decide? Refute what we say! Show us the order of the world! Where are the laws? Where are the judgments? We are forever destitute of judgment, both human and divine, because Sulla committed all these crimes with impunity. Did no whip of angry gods punish his crimes which fed on so many deaths? Those who died through him were deprived even of last rites. Can this be justice?

36. You say the sins of mankind are announced every day to the avenging gods. But in all this Fortune did as she wished. Whatever the Fates had decreed for individuals, these decrees were fulfilled by Sulla's ferocity. And a happy outcome followed him after all these evils. Heaped with distinguished honors he laid down his authority by his own choice. By his order the limbs of the Republic were severed and the blood-stained money was added to the riches of unworthy men; after these evils he enjoyed peaceful security. By unanimous decree of the Senate and the Roman People he was rewarded with a title which implied good fortune and continued prosperity.

37. Who would now deny that our lives are governed by the chance motions of the stars? That man who advanced through every kind of cruelty attained all the rewards of high office. But Marius, after his triumph over Jugurtha and others, after he freed the city of Rone from dangers both foreign and domestic, after purple-clad triumphs, was bound with iron chains. Behold him an exile in the swamps of Minturnae; behold him oppressed in a filthy prison. Observe how as a fugitive he approaches the ruins of Carthage.

38. What god made Marius an exile and Sulla prosperous? The general Aemilius Paullus handed over the supreme command to Marius, who was only a soldier; while Sulla, an officer, deserted the Roman army.

Nevertheless, by judgment of Fortune, the one became an exile and the other prosperous.

39. Scipio, after many triumphs, after the destruction of Carthage and the fall of Numantia, after the blameless deeds of his dictatorship, was killed inside the walls of his own house by the wicked treachery of his servants who broke his neck with their hands.

40. What use to Regulus was his good faith when Fate had laid him low after an unspeakable, pitiful captivity in enemy hands? What other force handed over Crassus and the Roman fasces to the dissolute Persian kings? He had been a hard-working leader and he had the Roman army to support his virtues.

41. After the fifth consulate of Pompey, after many triumphs, on the bank of the Nile a eunuch's sword severed his unconquered neck which had so often been arrayed in royal purple. Who armed the hand of Cato to take his own life? Who betrayed Cicero to the corrupt, effeminate desires of Antony? Those whom Caesar in his clemency had freed from all fear, he afterwards armed for his own destruction.

42. Do you see how everywhere and always Fortune rules? Do you see how various and unstable are the experiences of mankind? The brave are overcome by the cowardly, the inferior bring down the good; justice does not profit the just, foresight always deceives the cautious; the immodest and dissolute are preferred in office to the modest and sober. The zealous are laid low, the wicked are praised, and whatever is a profit to one man deceives another into dangerous imitation.

## VIII

### [THE BELIEF THAT FATE CONTROLS DEATH ONLY]

1. All these events are caused by the movements of the planets and by these various patterns Fortune destroys us. Therefore, with these examples, let us prove the law of Fatal Necessity, not with the flow of words but with provable facts and correct judgment.

2. But there are some who agree with us to a certain extent and admit that Fate and Fortune have a certain power, which they call *himarmene*.[14] But they attribute to it a different character which contradicts the law of the necessity of Fate. Thus they appear to maintain which is possible and not possible at the same time.

3. They claim that this thing which they call *himarmene* is connected to mankind and all living things by a certain relationship. We are so created that after a certain time the course of our life is finished. We are brought back to the divine spirit which sustains us after the dissolution of the body. They claim that we are subject to Fate, that is, to Chance, for attaining the end of life. Thus by the law of Fate they claim one end—that is, dissolution—destroys us and all living beings. But all the things that

pertain to our daily lives they say are in our power. What we do while we are alive belongs to us; only our death belongs to Chance or Fate.

4. I do not know what this different theory accomplishes. I do not know who could be persuaded by what they say. If everyone admits that his end is subject to Fatal Necessity, he prejudges his own argument in this way. He diminishes the power of his argument in the lesser points and concedes it in the more important. With this loose way of arguing he spins an absurd argument. He attributes to Fate the option to punish with death but denies that which is less, the power of controlling human destinies.

5. They claim that once we are created, Fate leads us into the light and opens the doors of life to men arriving for their earthly experience. If the beginning and end of life are set up for us by the law of Fatal Necessity, what else is there which is not in its power, if the beginning and end are decreed by its decrees?

6. See, there is one, his human shape not yet formed, who dies in his mother's womb. In the case of another, although he is formed and already freed from the womb, his vital spirit does not feed on air. Another just wrapped in his first swaddling clothes is deserted by the breath of life when still a wailing infant. One is carried off by weakness when still a child. Another is removed by accident at the age of puberty when, already educated in the traditional learning, he is approaching the period when, as my opponents say, activities are supposed to be under our control. Still another, after too long a life, lacking almost any sense or will, weakened by declining years and foul old age, unwillingly bears his long, tedious burden.

7. Who is it who brings death to one unborn, to another on the first day of life, to the child a little while after, to the youth, to the old man? Let something be discovered which may teach us, which may show us, struggling as we are, the path of truth. Surely it is Fate and the necessity of human death which distributes at its own discretion a time of living to all living things born on the Earth, denies a longer span to some, allows it to others. It makes no sense for one to admit the necessity of Fate and afterwards to deny it. It is a very faulty argument which rebuts in the later part of the discussion what it had admitted in the earlier.

## IX

### [TYPES OF HUMAN DEATH]

1. What can we say of the various kinds of death? One man, when Fate compels, is hanged in a noose. Another is struck by a sword. Others are drowned in seas or rivers. Another, handed over to savage flames, is turned into cinders. One falls off a cliff, another is crushed in the ruins of a falling house. The soul of one is carried off by deadly poison. One is consumed by burning fever. Another, suddenly inflamed by burning blood-vessels, is consumed in a violent heat. One is devoured by rabies

caught unexpectedly from savage beasts. Another, up to then unhurt, suffers an accident. For another the bite of a poisonous serpent contracts his veins in death.

2. These are the different kinds of death which Fate assigns to us. These are the decrees of the planets we set forth a little before. From these come the wretched deaths of famous heroes, the prosperous last days of evil men. Thus the lives of men, each on a different course, are completed, each as Fortune decides. From there, it is agreed, comes the beginning and end of our lives, also all our deeds together, our wishes, our desires, and everything that pertains to the experience of humankind.

3. Let us therefore follow the conclusions of correct reasoning, and concede that nothing is placed in our power, but the whole is in the power of Fate. Whatever we do or suffer, the whole thing happens to us by this same judgment of Fortune.

## X

### [CONCLUSION. INVOCATION TO THE EMPEROR]

1. Now that all these things have been explained—all these things which show the force of Fate and the laws of the decreeing planets—let us return to the question we left in the first part, the one about the complexions and characters of men. When we have settled that question completely, Lollianus, we shall be able to set forth for you what we promised.

2. The question has been asked why in some regions human bodies always turn dark and in others are white. I shall reply with a short disquisition, because on this point many wise men have expressed opinions.

3. In the whole vault of heaven, which is spherical in shape and embraces the earth and sea and all things between, there are five zones. Some of these are homogeneous and others are made up of a mixture of climates.

4. The one in the middle of the five zones is burned by the light of the Sun and is stained with fiery color. The two zones which contain the poles of the universe cling to its sides on the far left and right. They are marked by a pale blue color and are always covered by dark storms, congealed by eternal frost and hard-packed snow.

5. Between these two frozen zones and the fiery one are the two remaining, where a climate of mixed cold and hot has formed a gentle moderation. These are the two zones which produce the whole race of living things on Earth. Through these zones turns the oblique system of the signs (the Zodiac), providing for the rising and setting of all signs forever. Here come and go in regular movement the Sun, Moon, and the five wandering stars which the Greeks call planets. The whole race of

living things comes under the influence of these stars for the everlasting propagation of its kind.

6. The nature of these five zones has produced men of different races, each with their own coloring; but in such a way that there is an appearance of unity, though the bodies of men vary with the radiation of the stars.

7. Whatever race of men lies near the zone which burns with eternal fire, takes on fire from the nearness of its neighbor. These men are permanently dark with the look of burned objects.

8. Those parts which lie next to the icy zones and are deserted by the heat of the Sun endow the men born in their vicinity with a shining white appearance. Yet, even in the regions which produce dark men and those which produce light-colored, the power of the stars is very strong. Each and every man, though his color is uniform, has a different appearance and shape.

9. How would individuals recognize sons, brothers, relatives; how would citizens recognize strangers, neighbors, guests, if the power of the stars did not give separate and different appearances to individuals?

10. Think of the great numbers of the human race. How many wicked crimes could be committed if everyone had the same face! Deceived by the likeness, brother would approach sister as a husband. One man would lead off another man's legal wife in shameless defilement. Men would fight over a son in mistaken conflict. Others would not know the identity of their former slaves. A man of good family might be mistakenly dragged away as a slave.

All this might happen if men did not have different appearances. The stars bring about these differences by their combinations and mixtures of influence.

11. Some blondness has a slight tinge of dark color. The gleam of a little lightness brightens the dark face. A number of colors creep into the hair. The eyes are always colored with different lights. Bodies are sometimes tall, short, slender, broad, heavy, fat. It is the zones which determine who is to be dark and who light. The stars decide the varieties of shape and different mixtures of color.

12. As to the characters of mankind, discussion is unnecessary. Many Asiatics, in fact, almost all of them, show some evidence of modesty and moderation. The frivolity of the Greeks often takes on a serious dignity. The unbridled fury of the Scythians is sometimes tempered by a certain clemency and humanity. The Gauls are growing in thoughtfulness and wisdom. Signs of honest truthfulness improve the tricky Africans. Many Spaniards lay aside the fault of boasting. Sudden generosity has changed the Syrian's greed. It is not difficult to find some stupid men among the clever Sicilians, and the Italians often lose their unrestricted power to rule.

13. We do not need to go far afield or to ancient books to bring you examples. Consider our own Augustus, emperor of the whole world, the

pious, fortunate, far-seeing Princeps. I mean, of course, Constantine the Most Great, son of the Deified Constantine the Princeps, of august and revered memory. He was chosen to free the world from tyrannical government and to crush domestic evils by virtue of his own majesty, so that through him the stain of servitude might be washed away and the rewards of liberty returned to us. He in all his constant battles for our liberty was never deceived by the fortunes of war, a most uncertain thing in human experience. Born near Naissus, he held from his earliest childhood the imperial rule, which he had received under favorable auspices. He maintains the Roman world in continually increasing prosperity by the wholesome moderation of his rule.

14. O Sun,[15] best and greatest, who holds the middle place in the heavens, Mind and Moderator of the universe, leader and Princeps of all who kindle forever the fires of the other stars; and you, Moon, who, placed in the farthest reaches of the sky, shines with holy rays and ensures with your monthly office the continuation of human procreation, ever increased by the light of the Sun; and you, Saturn, who, set in the highest point of the sky, carries the leaden light of your planet in sluggish revolution; and you, Jupiter, dweller on the Tarpeian Rock, who makes the universe rejoice with your benevolent power and who holds the rule of the second sphere; and you, Mars Gradivus, always with your fearful red color, whose home is the third region of the sky; and you two, Venus and Mercury, faithful comrades of the Sun: by virtue of the harmony of your rule, and obedient to the highest god who gives you never-ending lordship, vouchsafe that Constantine the Most Great Princeps and his unconquered children, our lords and Caesars, rule over our children and our children's children through endless ages so that, freed from all misfortune, the human race may enjoy everlasting peace and prosperity.

15. As for us, inspire our fragile nature so that with your protection we may complete these writings which we promised Lollianus, and may set forth in true propositions what we learned from the divine tradition of the wise men.

# Liber Secundus

1. As we begin the writing of these books of the *Mathesis*, we must first organize the material so that those who wish to learn may be trained correctly from the start; for it is not possible to master the true science unless one is firmly grounded in the fundamentals.

2. Our Fronto,[16] who published rules for forecasting by the stars, followed the antiscia theory of Hipparchus:[17] nevertheless, since he was dealing with trained and experienced men, he wrote nothing about the theory nor about basic principles. As a matter of fact, hardly any other Latin authors have written about the principles of this science except Julius Caesar,[18] who produced a few verses which he translated from a foreign work, and Marcus Tullius (Cicero), the chief glory of Roman eloquence, who replied with a few epic verses.

3. Therefore we intend to translate in simple language everything which the Egyptians and Babylonians wrote about this science for those who are in training in forecasting about human fate.

4. But since we have just mentioned the antiscia, we should not pass over this point with pretended ignorance. Fronto copied the theory of antiscia[19] of Hipparchus, according to whom these have no force or influence. There are, it is true, some correct ideas in Fronto about astrology and forecasting, but his treatment of the antiscia is not useful, for he followed a writer who did not hold the correct theory. The true antiscia, as our Navigius[20] proves, are those Ptolemy pointed out after careful research. What their nature is we shall describe in the last part of the work when we show in each case what degree influences another. As to forecasting by the stars, Fronto has written accurately about that, and it is discussed at length in the books and documents of the Greeks. Thus we shall leave aside this discussion and return to the elements of the theory.

31

# I

## THE TWELVE SIGNS

1. The circle of the zodiac[21] in which the twelve signs[22] are fixed and through which the five planets as well as the Sun and Moon direct their courses turns with a slantwise motion.

2. The twelve signs themselves are called by these names: Aries, Taurus, Gemini, Cancer, Leo, Virgo, Libra, Scorpio, Sagittarius, Capricorn, Aquarius, and Pisces. These signs are of different gender, some masculine, some feminine. The masculine are: Aries, Gemini, Leo, Libra, Sagittarius, Aquarius. The feminine: Taurus, Cancer, Virgo, Scorpio, Capricorn, Pisces.

# II

## THE SIGNS OF THE PLANETS[23]

1. Of these twelve signs the Sun and Moon have been assigned one sign each; but the others, the five planets—that is, Saturn, Jupiter, Mars, Venus, and Mercury—have two each, in which they alone have their power and their appointed home.

2. The Egyptians do not name these planets as the Greeks or as we do, for the one we call Saturn the Egyptians call *Faeno*;[24] the one we call Jupiter they call *Faetho*; Mars to us is *Pyrois* to them; the one called Venus by us if *Fosforos* to them; the one we call Mercury they call *Stilbo*.

3. The house of the Sun is Leo, and in this sign he has his home and his power; and that of the Moon is Cancer. Note how fitting it is that while the Sun is the ruler of a masculine sign the Moon rules a feminine one, so that each claims a sign which is suited to its own sex.

4. The other five planets have, as we have said above, two signs in which they exercise their authority. But of these signs which each possesses one is masculine, the other feminine. We shall explain everything in detail so that this may be more clearly understood.

5. Saturn has as his signs Aquarius and Capricorn, of which Aquarius is masculine and Capricorn is feminine. Jupiter has as his signs Sagittarius and Pisces, and of these one is masculine, namely Sagittarius, but Pisces is feminine. Mars has as his signs Aries and Scorpio, of which Aries is masculine and Scorpio feminine. The signs of Venus are Taurus and Libra, of which Libra is masculine and Taurus is feminine. Mercury has as his signs Gemini and Virgo, of which Gemini is masculine but Virgo is feminine.

# III

## EXALTATIONS AND FALLS OF THE PLANETS[25]

1. We must know about exaltation and debility—that is, what is meant by the exaltation of each individual planet, in which it is raised up to a

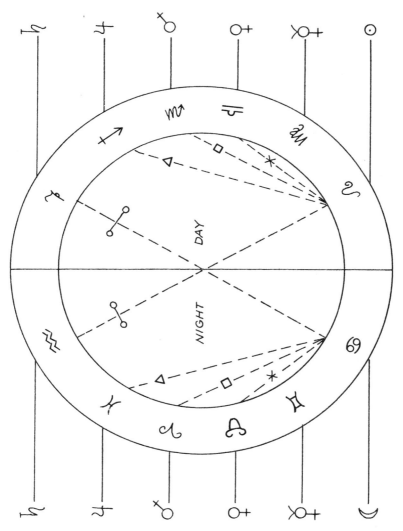

Diagram II. Zodiacal Houses of the Planets.

maximum of its own natural force, and what is its fall, when it suffers loss of that force.

2. When planets are in their own exaltations we say that they rejoice. Whenever in a chart the majority of the planets is in the exact degree of their exaltation, then they indicate the greatest prosperity. On the other hand, men are overwhelmed by catastrophe whenever the majority of the planets is located in the exact degree of those signs in which they lose their power by debility or fall.

3. The former are called exaltations, or favorable places in the chart, because they make those who are born with this configuration fortunate and successful. When they are in their debility or fall—that is, in unfavorable places—they make men wretched, poor, of low birth, and constantly plagued by bad luck.

4. The Babylonians called the signs in which the planets are exalted their "houses." But in the doctrine we use, we maintain that all the planets are more favorable in their exaltations than in their own signs.

5. The Sun is exalted in the nineteenth degree of Aries but is in its fall in the nineteenth degree of Libra. The Moon is exalted in the third degree of Taurus, in its fall in the third degree of Scorpio. Saturn is exalted in the twenty-first degree of Libra, while it is in its fall in the twenty-first degree of Aries. Jupiter is exalted in the fifteenth degree of Cancer, but its fall is in the fifteenth degree of Capricorn. Mars is exalted in the twenty-eighth degree of Capricorn, but is in its fall in the twenty-eighth degree of Cancer. Venus is exalted in the twenty-seventh degree of Pisces, in its fall in the twenty-seventh degree of Virgo. Mercury is exalted in the fifteenth degree of Virgo and is in its fall in the fifteenth degree of Pisces.

6. For this reason the Babylonians wished to call those signs in which individual planets are exalted their houses, saying that Libra is the house of Saturn, Cancer of Jupiter, Capricorn of Mars, Aries of the Sun, Taurus of the Moon, Pisces of Venus, and Virgo of Mercury.

## IV

## THE DECANATE

1. Each sign is divided into three parts, and each part has one decan,[26] so that in each sign there are three decans, each having ten degrees out of the thirty, and over those ten degrees it exercises its power and control. They have infinite power and freedom in indicating the fates of men.

2. In addition, the decans themselves are allotted to individual planets, so that if the planet should be in that decan, even though it is in a strange sign, it is considered as if it were in its own sign. Located in its own decan it accomplishes the same things as when in its own sign.

3. The first decan of Aries belongs to Mars, the second to the Sun, the third to Venus. The first decan of Taurus belongs to Mercury, the second

Diagram III.  The Decans.

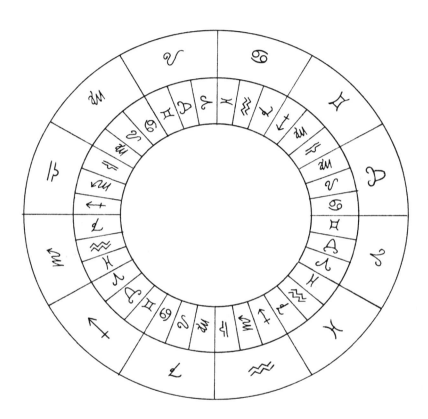

to the Moon, the third to Saturn. Of Gemini the first decan belongs to
Jupiter, the second to Mars, the third to the Sun. Of Cancer the first to
Venus, the second to Mercury, the third to the Moon. Of Leo the first to
Saturn, the second to Jupiter, the third to Venus. In Virgo the first to the
Sun, the second to Venus, the third to Mercury. In Libra the first decan
belongs to the Moon, the second to Saturn, the third to Jupiter. Of
Scorpio the first to Mars, the second to the Sun, the third to Venus. Of
Sagittarius the first to Mercury, the second to the Moon, the third to
Saturn. Of Capricorn the first belongs to Jupiter, the second to Mars, the
third to the Sun. In Aquarius the first decan belongs to Venus, the second
to Mercury, the third to the Moon. In Pisces the first decan belongs to
Saturn, the second to Jupiter, the third to Mars.

4. Some who wish to elaborate this in more detail add three divinities
each to every decan, which they call *munifices*,[27] that is, *liturgi*, so that for
every sign nine *munifices* can be found and every decan is divided into
three *munifices*.

5. Again, the nine *munifices* which they say are allotted to every sign
they divide into an infinite number of powers of divinities. By these they
say are decreed sudden accidents, pains, sicknesses, chills, fevers, and
everything that happens unexpectedly. Through these divinities they say
defective births are produced among men.

6. But this part of the doctrine we must of necessity pass over in this
book. The Greeks also, who tried to reach the secrets of that theory,
stopped at the first stage and left the subject with a certain reluctance. But
now we must return to the doctrine where we left it.

## V

### THE DEGREES OF THE SIGNS

1. Each sign has thirty degrees. A degree is as large a space in each sign
as the Sun and Moon embrace in their circuit.[28] One degree is divided into
sixty minutes.

## VI

### THE TERMS[29]

1. Although the sign itself is the home of a planet, yet the degrees of
this sign are divided among all the planets, and these degrees are called
the "terms" of the planets. These terms the Greeks call *oria* (boundaries).
We must observe these terms carefully; for when a planet is found in its
own terms, it is just as if located in its own sign. We shall explain this
matter in detail.

2. As we have said, Mars is the ruler of Aries; but the terms of Aries are
allotted in this way to the individual planets: from the first to the sixth
degree to Jupiter, from the seventh to the twelfth to Venus, from the

thirteenth to the twentieth to Mercury, from the twenty-first to the twenty-fifth to Mars, from the twenty-sixth to the thirtieth to Saturn. In this way the degrees of Aries are divided.

3. Venus is the ruler of Taurus. But its terms are divided in this way: from the first to the eighth degree Venus has the power over the terms; from the ninth to the fourteenth degree, Mercury; from the fifteenth to the twenty-second, Jupiter; from the twenty-third to the twenty-seventh, Saturn; from the twenty-eighth to the thirtieth, Mars. These planets possess terms in Taurus.

4. Mercury is the ruler of Gemini, but its terms are divided thus: from the first to the sixth degree Mercury holds these terms; from the seventh to the twelfth, Jupiter; from the thirteenth to the eighteenth, Venus; from the nineteenth to the twenty-fourth, Mars; from the twenty-fifth to the thirtieth, Saturn.

5. The Moon is the ruler of Cancer, but the terms of this sign are divided in this way: from the first to the seventh degree Mars rules over these terms; from the eighth to the thirteenth, Venus; from the fourteenth to the twentieth, Mercury; from the twenty-first to the twenty-seventh, Jupiter; from the twenty-eighth to the thirtieth, Saturn. These are the terms in this sign which the planets rule.

6. The Sun is the ruler of Leo, but the terms are divided thus: from the first to the sixth degree Jupiter possesses the terms; from the seventh to the eleventh, Venus; from the twelfth to the eighteenth, Saturn; from the nineteenth to the twenty-fourth, Mercury; from the twenty-fifth to the thirtieth, Mars. To this extent are the terms of that sign divided among the individual planets.

7. Mercury is the ruler of Virgo, but the terms are divided thus: from the first degree to the seventh Mercury possesses terms; from the eighth to the seventeenth, Venus; from the eighteenth to the twenty-first, Jupiter; from the twenty-second to the twenty-eighth, Mars; from the twenty-ninth to the thirtieth, Saturn.

8. Venus is the ruler of Libra, but its terms are divided thus: from the first to the sixth degree Saturn possesses terms; from the seventh to the fourteenth, Mercury; from the fifteenth to the twenty-first, Jupiter; from the twenty-second to the twenty-eighth, Venus; from the twenty-ninth to the thirtieth, Mars.

9. Mars is the ruler of Scorpio, but its terms are divided thus: from the first degree to the seventh Mars possesses terms; from the eighth to the eleventh, Venus; from the twelfth to the nineteenth, Mercury; from the twentieth to the twenty-fourth, Jupiter; from the twenty-fifth to the thirtieth, Saturn.

10. Jupiter is the ruler of Sagittarius, but its terms are divided thus: from the first degree to the twelfth, Jupiter holds terms; from the thirteenth to the seventeenth, Venus; from the eighteenth to the twenty-third, Mercury; from the twenty-fourth to the twenty-seventh, Saturn;

from the twenty-eighth to the thirtieth, Mars.

11. Saturn is the ruler of Capricorn, but its terms are divided thus: from the first degree to the seventh, Mercury holds terms; from the eighth to the fourteenth, Jupiter; from the fifteenth to the twenty-second, Venus; from the twenty-third to the twenty-sixth, Saturn; from the twenty-seventh to the thirtieth, Mars.

12. Saturn is the ruler of Aquarius, but the terms are divided thus: from the first degree to the seventh Mercury holds terms; from the eighth to the thirteenth, Venus; from the fourteenth to the twentieth, Jupiter; from the twenty-first to the twenty-fifth, Mars; from the twenty-sixth to the thirtieth, Saturn.

13. Jupiter is the ruler of Pisces, but the terms of this sign are divided thus: from the first degree to the twelfth, Venus holds terms; from the thirteenth to the sixteenth, Jupiter; from the seventeenth to the nineteenth, Mercury; from the twentieth to the twenty-eighth, Mars; from the twenty-ninth to the thirtieth, Saturn.

## VII

## THE CONDITIONS OF THE PLANETS

1. Now that we have described the terms, we must explain which stars rejoice by day and which by night, and whose condition they follow.

2. The ones which rejoice by day are: the Sun, Jupiter, and Saturn. Thus Jupiter and Saturn follow the condition of the Sun. Therefore, in diurnal charts, if they are in favorable positions, they indicate good fortune. Venus, Mars, Mercury, and the Moon rejoice by night. Therefore Venus, Mars, and Mercury follow the condition of the Moon. Favorably located in a nocturnal chart they indicate good fortune, unfavorably in a diurnal chart, the greatest evils.

3. If Venus and Mars aspect the waning Moon in a nocturnal chart, the waning Moon indicates all kinds of prosperity and good fortune. But if a full or waxing Moon comes into aspect with Venus or Mars, it brings about the greatest catastrophes and stirs up enormous ill fortune. Venus is adverse to the waxing Moon because they conflict with each other.

4. Let it suffice to have stated these things briefly in this book dealing only with the basic principles. Everything about the Moon as well as about the other planets will be set forth most fully in the following books.

## VIII

## MATUTINE AND VESPERTINE PLANETS

1. The five planets, that is, Saturn, Jupiter, Mars, Venus, Mercury, are either matutine, vespertine, *occiduales* (setting), or *absconsae* (hidden, i.e., by the Sun's rays). These the Greeks call *afaneis* (hidden), *synodicae* (in conjunction with the Sun), or *acronyctae* (at nightfall). How they came to

have such characteristics and why they are given their names we shall now explain. Matutine planets are those which in their rising precede the Sun. Vespertine or evening planets are those which in rising follow the rising of the Sun. *Absconsae*, or hidden ones, are those which the Sun's orb conceals (heliacal rising). *Acronyctae* are those which rise when the sun sets.

2. When these positions of the planets are favorable and when they are harmful we shall deal with in the later books, for we have not brought this up without a reason. To sum up, however, it should be stated that nearness to the Sun is harmful to all planets. Certain astrologers, however, claim that Mars is favorable when setting, when he is overwhelmed by the rays of the Sun, for in being subservient to the Sun he loses his natural malefic qualities.

3. We must also know in what conditions the matutine star rejoices and in what the vespertine star rejoices, for they are protected in a favorable position whenever they precede the Sun. Some planets located with a morning rising rejoice in company with the Sun. For the divine power of the Sun is protected by very favorable influences whenever he is accompanied by the morning rising of planets. But those planets become weakened whenever they follow after the Sun in an evening rising. Those placed in the light of the Moon are protected by its greatest influence when in any aspect they precede its rising.

4. We must further show what is effected by a combination of rising planets in a chart when the planets become matutine, when they are vespertine, and how many degrees of distance from the Sun it takes to make a planet matutine.

## IX

### BY HOW MANY DEGREES
### PLANETS BECOME MATUTINE OR VESPERTINE

1. When the planet of Saturn is fifteen degrees distant from the Sun, that is, when it has risen before the Sun, it is matutine. In the same way the planet of Jupiter is matutine when it precedes the rising of the Sun by a distance of twelve degrees; Venus by eight, and Mars also by eight. Mercury preceding the Sun by eighteen degrees becomes matutine. On the other hand, they are vespertine when they follow the rising of the Sun by the same number of degrees.

## X

### THE NATURE AND CHARACTERISTICS OF THE SIGNS

1. We must now explain about the nature of the twelve signs, their appearance, essential qualities, their principles and risings.

2. Aries (the Ram) is a masculine sign of the zodiac, equinoctial, solstitial, dominant, fiery, aggressive, four-footed, sensual, with lascivious

eyes, restless, impulsive, passionate, lustful. It is the sign of Mars, in which the Sun is exalted in about the nineteenth degree, with Saturn in its fall around the nineteenth degree, aspected in trine to the Sun by day, by night to Jupiter.

3. This sign is called equinoctial or solstitial because in it the hours of the day and night have equal measure, which the Greeks call *tropicon isomerion* (equinoctial tropic). For when the Sun is in Aries it makes the hours of the day and night equal, so that the day has twelve hours and the night also. This sign is called *Crios*[30] by the Greeks for the reason that when the Sun is in this sign it judges, so to speak, between night and day, which in Greek is *crinein* (to judge); and because the Sun located in that sign, between summer and winter, is in turn judged.

4. The sign is called tropical because when the Sun is located in that sign it makes the spring season, for spring begins when the Sun has entered the first degree of this sign . . . . . . . . [lacuna][31]

5. Pisces (the fishes) are a feminine sign, dual, damp, watery, double-bodied, fertile, scaly, spotted, curved, silent, mutable; one fish turns to the South, the other to the North. They are the sign of Jupiter, in trine with Venus by day, with Mars by night, exalted with Venus about the twenty-seventh degree, in debility with Mercury about the fifteenth degree. This sign is under the influence of the north wind.

## XI

## THE RISINGS OF THE SIGNS[32]

1. Now that we have discussed the genders and shapes of the signs and discussed their nature carefully, just as has been handed down to us by the learned Greeks, we must show in the following chapter after how many years each particular sign rises in the charts.

2. All the planets attain their maximum power of prediction and exercise their particular force when the signs in which they are located are rising. But these rise at different times and days according to the regions of the earth's surface. What signs rise in which regions at what times we shall show in the following table.

3. In the first region, in the area of Alexandria, or in the second, in the area of Babylonia, and in all other regions which lie near to these, the signs rise in this period:

| | | |
|---|---|---|
| Aries | rises in the 20th year. | |
| Taurus | " " " 24th | " |
| Gemini | " " " 28th | " |
| Cancer | " " " 32nd | " |
| Leo | " " " 36th | " |
| Virgo | " " " 40th | " |
| Libra also | " " " 40th | " |
| Scorpio | " " " 36th | " |

| | | | | | |
|---|---|---|---|---|---|
| Sagittarius | " | " | " | 32nd | " |
| Capricorn | " | " | " | 28th | " |
| Aquarius | " | " | " | 24th | " |
| Pisces | " | " | " | 20th | " |

4. In the region which is near Rhodes and in other adjacent regions:

| | | | | | |
|---|---|---|---|---|---|
| Aries | rises in the | | | 19th | year. |
| Taurus | " | " | " | 23rd | " |
| Gemini | " | " | " | 27th | " |
| Cancer | " | " | " | 32nd | " |
| Leo | " | " | " | 36th | " |
| Virgo | " | " | " | 40th | " |
| Libra also | " | " | " | 40th | " |
| Scorpio | " | " | " | 36th | " |
| Sagittarius | " | " | " | 32nd | " |
| Capricorn | " | " | " | 27th | " |
| Aquarius | " | " | " | 23rd | " |
| Pisces | " | " | " | 19th | " |

5. In the region of the Hellespoint and adjoining regions:

| | | | | | |
|---|---|---|---|---|---|
| Aries | rises in the | | | 17th | year. |
| Taurus | " | " | " | 22nd | " |
| Gemini | " | " | " | 27th | " |
| Cancer | " | " | " | 32nd | " |
| Leo | " | " | " | 37th | " |
| Virgo | " | " | " | 42nd | " |
| Libra also | " | " | " | 42nd | " |
| Scorpio | " | " | " | 37th | " |
| Sagittarius | " | " | " | 32nd | " |
| Capricorn | " | " | " | 27th | " |
| Aquarius | " | " | " | 22nd | " |
| Pisces | " | " | " | 17th | " |

6. In the region of Athens and the surrounding regions:

| | | | | | |
|---|---|---|---|---|---|
| Aries | rises in the | | | 18th | year. |
| Taurus | " | " | " | 23rd | " |
| Gemini | " | " | " | 27th | " |
| Cancer | " | " | " | 32nd | " |
| Leo | " | " | " | 36th | " |
| Virgo | " | " | " | 41st | " |
| Libra also | " | " | " | 41st | " |
| Scorpio | " | " | " | 36th | " |
| Sagittarius | " | " | " | 32nd | " |
| Capricorn | " | " | " | 27th | " |
| Aquarius | " | " | " | 23rd | " |
| Pisces | " | " | " | 18th | " |

7. In the vicinity of Ancona and surrounding regions:

| Aries | rises in the 15th year. |
|---|---|
| Taurus | " " " 21st " |
| Gemini | " " " 27th " |
| Cancer | " " " 32nd " |
| Leo | " " " 38th " |
| Virgo | " " " 44th " |
| Libra also | " " " 44th " |
| Scorpio | " " " 38th " |
| Sagittarius | " " " 32nd " |
| Capricorn | " " " 27th " |
| Aquarius | " " " 21st " |
| Pisces | " " " 15th " |

8. In the zone of Rome and its surrounding regions:

| Aries | rises in the 17th year. |
|---|---|
| Taurus | " " " 22nd " |
| Gemini | " " " 27th " |
| Cancer | " " " 32nd " |
| Leo | " " " 37th " |
| Virgo | " " " 42nd " |
| Libra also | " " " 42nd " |
| Scorpio | " " " 37th " |
| Sagittarius | " " " 32nd " |
| Capricorn | " " " 27th " |
| Aquarius | " " " 22nd " |
| Pisces | " " " 17th " |

9. These are the risings of the signs in which the individual planets are advanced to their greatest dignity.

## XII

## WHICH SIGNS ARE SUBJECT TO WHICH WINDS[33]

It is appropriate for us to know which signs are subject to which winds, for this knowledge is very necessary to us in forecasting by the stars. To the north wind are subject the signs Aries, Leo, Sagittarius; to the south wind Taurus, Virgo, Capricorn; to the *afeliotes* (Greek, east wind — "wind from the sun"), which we call the east wind, Gemini, Libra, Aquarius; to the south-west wind, which the Greeks call *libs*,[34] Cancer, Scorpio, Pisces.

## XIII

## THE DUODECATEMORIA[35]

1. Now I shall briefly set forth what you want to know about the

duodecatemoria. Some people think that from these the whole essence of the chart can be found and they claim that whatever is hidden in the chart can be revealed by the duodecatemoria.

2. What these are will be shown by example. Of whatever planet you wish to compute the duodecatemorion, multiply its degree by twelve, and however much that comes to, divide it among the thirty degrees of the individual signs, beginning from the sign in which the planet is whose dudecatemorion is being sought. In whatever sign the final number falls, that shows you the degree of the duodecatemorion. But in order that you may understand more clearly we shall give this example.

3. Say the Sun is in Aries at five degrees and five minutes. Twelve times five makes sixty, and twelve times five minutes makes sixty minutes. Sixty minutes make one degree, and therefore one arrives at sixty-one degrees. You give Aries, in which we said the Sun is, thirty degrees, and thirty to Taurus; the duodecatemorion is found in the first degree of Gemini.

4. Consider therefore whether the full moon happens to send a duodecatemorion by day toward the terms of Mars or whether, when waning, she sends one into those of Saturn, or whether Mars on the descendant sends one toward Venus, or Venus into those of Mars.

5. The favorable influence of Jupiter fails when, because of the weakness of the sign, or a shift of a degree or decan or condition, his favorable influence is hindered. But so does the unfavorable influence of Saturn grow stronger when he receives power to harm from the quality of the house, of the terms, of the decan, of the sign, or of the condition. In a similar way this holds true for the other planets.

6. One thing, however, should be noted: however favorable the influence of the planet of Jupiter might be, if it be under the attack of Mars and Saturn, surrounded with hostile influences, it is not able to resist them alone. For men would be immortal if the favorable influence of Jupiter were never overcome in their charts. But since God the Creator has made man in such a way that his physical substance is dissolved after a limited span of life, it is necessary to restrain Jupiter, who affords health-giving protection to the life of man. The dangerous and malevolent powers of the unfavorable planets must persist with increased hostility, so that the compound of the body can be dissolved.

## XIV

## THE EIGHT HOUSES[36]

1. Now we must give our attention to the cardinal points and houses; for when we have carefully searched them out we discover how each facet of a man's life is determined. But, meanwhile, a general view. A little later, when we come to the books about forecasting by the stars, we shall show in detail the way in which the individual houses may be exactly located. For

now, the student is being trained in general theory so that, having acquired a good general conception of the subject, he may more confidently approach the more recondite details of the chart.

2. Now that the house itself has been located we must consider what its nature is: in what sign, in whose terms, and what planets influence it, and to what extent. One must especially note who is the ruler of the house itself, that is, of the sign: in what house it is placed; or in what kind of a sign it is; or in what terms. These are data which must be carefully collected. Also whether it is influenced by favorable planets or attacked by unfavorable. Now let us return to a general description of the houses.

3. In general the House of Life is in the sign in which the ascendant is located; of Expectation of Inheritance and Wealth in the second house from the ascendant; of Brothers and Sisters in the third; of Parents in the fourth; of Children in the fifth; of Health in the sixth; of a Spouse in the seventh; of Death in the eighth. Beginning from the ascendant we have listed all the houses by name: Life, Expectations of Wealth, Brothers and Sisters, Parents, Children, Health, Spouse, Death.

4. As we said before, let this be enough to explain in general terms the basic elements of this discipline. Later we shall take care to explain by means of a detailed analysis of their degrees exactly how the influence of these houses is revealed. But now you must clearly understand that what we said about the charts of men is true as well in those of women: what the planet of Venus shows for a wife the planet of Mars shows for the husband.

## XV

## THE CARDINAL POINTS OF THE NATIVITIES

1. In the nativity there are four cardinal points: Ascendant, Descendant, *Medium Caelum* (Zenith), and *Imum Caelum* (Nadir), which the Greeks usually call by the following names: *Anatole* (East, Sunrise), *Dysis* (West, Sunset), *Mesuranima* (Meridian, Zenith), *Ypogeon* (below the Earth).

2. The rising is the degree of the Ascendant . . . . The Descendant is opposite it. The Greeks call it *Diametrium Dyticon* (Western Opposite).

3. In order that you may understand more easily, compute, starting from the degree of the ascendant through the other signs, 180 degrees; and in whatever sign the 181st degree is found, in that sign or section of the chart is located the descendant, or setting.

4. The *Medium Caelum* is the tenth house from the ascendant, but sometimes also the *MC* is found exactly in the eleventh sign from the ascendant. In order to understand this more clearly, compute, starting from the degree of the ascendant, through the other following signs, 270 degrees, and in whatever sign the 271st degree is found, this is allotted to the *Medium Caelum*, which the Greeks call *Mesuranima*.

5. The *Imum Caelum*, which by the Greeks is called Ypogeon, is located in the fourth house from the ascendant. In order to understand this more

Diagram IV.  The Eight Houses.

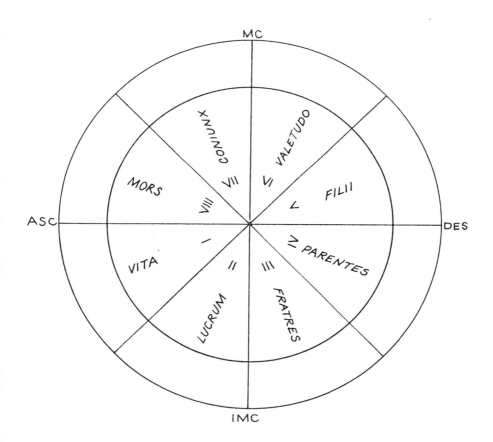

Diagram V.  The Cardines (Angles).

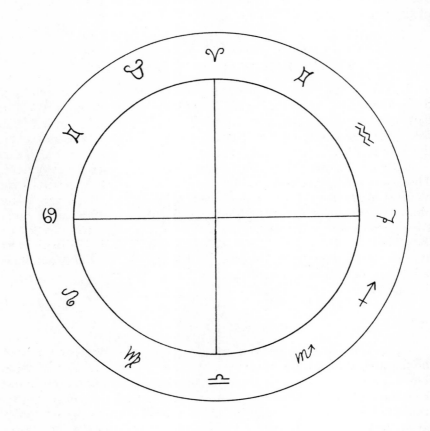

| TROPICS | ♈ | ♋ | ♎ | ♑ |
| SOLIDS | ♉ | ♏ | ♒ | ♌ |
| DOUBLES | ♊ | ♍ | ♐ | ♓ |

clearly, compute from the degree of the ascendant 90 degrees consecutively, and where the 91st degree falls, there the *IMC* is located. These are the four cardinal points of the nativity and the forecast.

6. These are the four cardines (angles) of the chart. We must always observe them carefully so that we may set forth the most correct revelation of the whole pattern of destiny.

## XVI

### THE FOUR FOLLOWING (FAVORABLE) HOUSES

1. After these four cardinal points, that is, after the ascendant, descendant, MC, and IMC, there is another set of four points in the nativity which are also of following and favorable power. These are Dea, Deus, Bona Fortuna, and Bonus Daemon, which by the Greeks are called thus: *Thea, Theos, Agathe Tyche, Agathos Daemon*.[37]

2. Dea is the third house, that is, the third sign, from the ascendant. This house, as we have said, is called that of *Thea* by the Greeks. Deus is the name of the house which is diametrically opposite this house, that is the ninth from the ascendant. This house is called *Theos* by the Greeks. Bona Fortuna is located in the fifth house from the ascendant and is called by the Greeks *Agathe Tyche*. The Bonus Daemon is located diametrically opposite this house, that is, the eleventh house from the ascendant. This house is called *Agathos Daemon* by the Greeks.

## XVII

### UNASPECTED HOUSES

1. The remaining four houses are all feeble and debilitated because of the fact that they are not aspected to the ascendant. The first of these remaining four houses, however, which is located in the second house from the ascendant, is called the Gate of Hell, or the *Anafora* (rising up from the Underworld). The house which is diametrically opposite to this house, that is, the eighth from the ascendant, is called the *Epicatafora* (casting down into the Underworld). The last of the four are those of Mala Fortuna and Malus Daemon. Mala Fortuna is located in the sixth house from the ascendant but the Malus Daemon in the twelfth from the ascendant. But Mala Fortuna is called *Cace Tyche* by the Greeks, and Malortuna is called *Cace Tyche* by the Greeks, and Malus Daemon, that is, the twelfth house from the ascendant, the Greeks call *Cacodaemon*.

## XVIII

### THE SEQUENCE OF EACH HOUSE

1. Now we ought to know which of these twelve houses precede and which follow, that is, which are the first houses, which the second, so that

we may investigate everything in the most careful way.

2. The ascendant precedes the descendant, the *Medium Caelum* comes before the *Imum Caelum*. The eleventh house, that is, the Bonus Daemon, comes before the Bona Fortuna; the ninth house, that is, Deus, before the third place, that is, Dea. *Anafora*, that is, the second place, is before *Epicatafora*. The eighth from the ascendant, Mala Fortuna, that is, the sixth from the ascendant, is before the Malus Daemon, that is, the twelfth from the ascendant.

3. All these positions must be learned so that when we come to forecasting by the stars, putting all the data together and working out our conclusions, we may prove them well-grounded.

## XIX

## THE MEANING OF THE TWELVE HOUSES

1. We must now explain in detail the meaning of the twelve houses, beginning with the ascendant, so that, when everything is described in order, all confusion will be cleared up.

2. The first house is the place in which the ascendant is located. In this house is to be found the life and vital spirit of men; from this house the basic character of the entire nativity is determined. This house, from the point of the chart in which the ascendant is, radiates its influence through the following thirty degrees. It is also the first cardinal point (angle) and the cornerstone and basis of the whole nativity.

3. The second house from the ascendant is located in the second sign, begins from the thirtieth degree from the ascendant, and extends its influence through the next thirty degrees. This house shows increase in personal hopes and in material possessions. But it is a passive house and not aspected to the ascendant. Therefore it is called the Gate of Hell, because it is not in any way aspected to the ascendant.

4. The third house, which is the third sign from the ascendant, begins at the 60th degree from the ascendant and stops at the 90th. From this house we will predict everything that concerns brothers and friends. Dea is the name of this house; but it is also the house of travelers. This is the first of the houses to be joined to the ascendant by a weak aspect. It can be seen to look back at the ascendant in sextile aspect.

5. The fourth house from the ascendant, that is, the *Imum Caelum*, is located in the fourth house from the ascendant which begins at the 90th degree and reaches the 120th. This house shows us family property, substance, possessions, household goods, anything that pertains to hidden and recovered wealth. This is also a cardinal point of the nativity, in that it is called *Imum Caelum* which is in opposition to the *Medium Caelum*. This house is in very powerful aspect to the ascendant because it influences the ascendant in square aspect and is influenced by it in square.

6. The fifth house is located in the fifth house from the ascendant and

Diagram VI. The Twelve Houses.

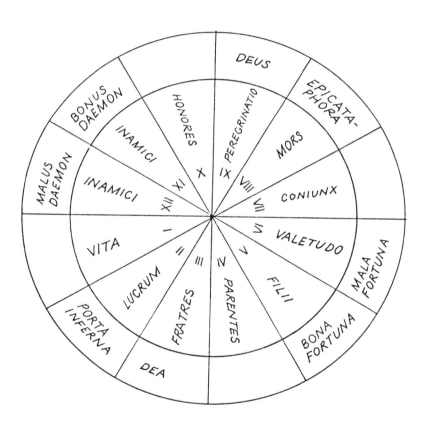

begins at the 121st degree from the ascendant and reaches the 150th. From this house is discovered the number of children and their sex. It is called Bona Fortuna because it is the house of Venus. This house also has a powerful aspect with the ascendant and sometimes the *Medium Caelum* is located in opposition to this house. The house is aspected very powerfully to the ascendant, namely, in trine.

7. The sixth house is located in the sixth house from the ascendant at the 150th degree from the ascendant, and extends to the 180th. In this house we find the cause of physical infirmities and sickness. This house is called Mala Fortuna because it is the house of Mars. This is also a passive house because it is not aspected to the ascendant. But sometimes the unfavorable influence is removed from this house if a planet in this house is in favorable aspect to another planet in the tenth house from the ascendant.

8. The seventh house, located in the seventh house from the ascendant, begins at the 180th degree from the ascendant, reaches to the 210th, and stops there. Its beginning is located in the 180th degree. In this house is another cardinal point of the nativity. We call it descendant or setting but the Greeks, as we have said above, call it *Dysis*. This cardinal point is opposite the cardinal point of the ascendant. From this house we shall inquire as to the nature and number of marriages. But this house is aspected most detrimentally to the ascendant for it is in opposition.

9. The eighth house is located in the eighth house from the ascendant. It starts from the 210th degree, extends to the 240th, and stops there. This house is called *Epicatafora*. It is, however, a passive house, since it is not in aspect to the ascendant. From this house is discovered the kind of death. But it is necessary for us to know that no planet rejoices in this house except the Moon, and then only in nocturnal charts. If the waxing Moon is found in this house in a nocturnal chart, and if she is not in aspect to any unfavorable planets, and if Jupiter is in trine or sextile aspect to her in her own sign or in the sign of Venus or Mercury or Jupiter, or in the terms of any of these planets, this portends the greatest good fortune and riches beyond measure, great glory of material power and outstanding recognition in worldly position.

10. The ninth house is located in the ninth sign from the ascendant. The length of this is from the 240th degree and it reaches to the 270th. It is also the house of the Sun God. In this house we find the social class of men. It also has to do with religion and foreign travel. This house is importantly aspected to the ascendant in trine aspect.

11. The tenth house is located in the tenth sign from the ascendant. It begins from the 270th degree and reaches to the 300th, and stops there. This place is the first in importance and has the greatest influence of all on the angles. This house we call the *Medium Caelum*, and the Greeks the *Mesuranima*, for it is located in the middle part of the universe. In this house we find life and vital spirit, all our actions, country, home, all our

dealings with others, professional careers, and whatever our choice of career brings us. From this house we easily see the infirmities of the mind. The influence of this house is aspected to the ascendant very powerfully, for it can be seen to be in square aspect to the ascendant.

12. The eleventh house is located in the eleventh house from the ascendant. This house starts at the 300th degree and extends to the 330th. It is called the Bonus Daemon or *Bonus Genius*, by the Greeks *Agathos Daemon*. The *Medium Caelum* is often found in exact conjunction with this house. It is, furthermore, the house of Jupiter, and not indifferently aspected to the ascendant; it can be seen to be in sextile aspect.

13. The twelfth house is constituted in the twelfth house from the ascendant. Starting from the 330th degree it extends to the 360th. This house the Greeks call *Cacos Daemon*; we call it Malus Daemon. From this house is easily determined the nature of enemies and the character of slaves. Also we find defects and illnesses in this house. But it is a passive house because it is not aspected to the ascendant. It is, moreover, the house of Saturn. The Sun gives definite information about the father in the nativities of both men and women, the Moon about the mother, Venus about the wife, Mars about the husband.

## XX

## THE NAMES OF THE TWELVE HOUSES, WHAT PLANETS ARE ALLOTTED TO THEM AND WHAT ARE THEIR PREDICTIONS

1. Now that we have spoken about the characters, names, and nature of the twelve houses we must briefly show the meaning of these same houses. Let us begin with the ascendant, which marks the beginning of the other houses.

2. It will be useful to name the houses in this order: Life, Hope, Dea or Brothers, Parents, Children, Health, Spouse, Death, Deus, *Medium Caelum*, Bonus Daemon, Malus Daemon. Through these names and houses the character of the entire nativity can be found. When you look at it carefully and put together all the information, notice which planets rule the individual houses.

3. Look carefully to see which planets are nocturnal and which are diurnal, as well as the kind of influence the favorable and the unfavorable planets have on individual houses.

4. For when the benefic planets are in aspect, whether in conjunction, in trine, or in sextile, all the things which we have mentioned turn out well.

5. But if, without influence of an aspect from the benefics, only malefics are aspected to the same house, either in conjunction or square or opposition, there is danger of frequent disaster and misfortune.

6. But if both benefic and malefic planets are in aspect, then the good

fortune is diminished, the bad fortune is mitigated, and the whole character of the house is evened out.

7. Note also what planet is located in the house or the terms of which particular planet and, if your planet is located in the house of another, look at the ruler of that house to see which house of the chart it is in, whether it is on the first cardinal point of the chart or in the second house or in a passive house; and inquire into its exaltation and fall, as well as into the sign in which it rejoices and in which it is dejected.

8. For if the ruler of the sign is well located, that planet about which we are inquiring also shares in a part of the good fortune of the host's joy. But if the ruler of the sign is dejected in any way, that planet about which we are inquiring, even though placed in a fortunate house, will be hindered by the dejection of that other planet which is the ruler of the sign.

9. This also you can easily observe from human behavior. If you enter anyone's home by invitation and the master of the house has just been blessed with an increase in good fortune, you too become a participant in his good fortune, for you share in the happiness of the good fortune of your host. But if the host is suffering from miserable poverty and is embroiled in the wretched accidents of misfortune, you make yourself also a partner in his grief and trouble, and the adversity in which you share overwhelms you too.

10. This is also true of the planets who are rulers of the signs.

11. Find out too, if the chart is diurnal, how many planets in the chart are in exaltation by day and how many rejoice by night. For if the planets which rejoice by day are in important houses in a diurnal chart, and are found on the first cardinal points, they portend the greatest increase in good fortune. But if the planets which we said rejoice by night are in the important houses or cardinal houses in a diurnal chart, they indicate unending misfortune and constant catastrophe.

12. We should observe this also in nocturnal charts, but with the order of influence in reverse.

13. If all these things are carefully noted, and if you take into consideration the influences of the benefic and malefic planets, the force of the houses, and the powers and degrees of the signs, giving them equal weight, then you can easily set forth a description of the whole man from his first beginning to his very last day, all his life and expectations, his brother and sisters as well as parents and children, health, spouse, death, social class, deeds, offices, foreign travel, home, possessions, character of friends and enemies, scandals, and dangers.

14. Meanwhile we have said enough about this in a book dealing with basic principles. But when we come to forecasting by the stars we shall describe everything first in general, then with technical interpretation, and explain everything in simple language, so that no doubt or hesitation may stand in the way of the practice of the art of forecasting.

## XXI

## TYPES OF NATIVITIES

1. This too we should know, that an average chart is that which has a single planet on its own sign, located in an important house of the chart. The man who has a chart with two planets, each in its own sign, is blessed with moderately good fortune. Fortunate and powerful beyond the usual is the one who has three; and he could be near to the gods in happiness who has four planets, each located in its own sign. More than this number the character of the human race does not allow; while on the other hand, he who has no planet in its own sign will forever be unknown, of low-born family, and doomed to a miserable life.

## XXII

## THE ASPECTS:[38] TRINE, SQUARE, SEXTILE, OPPOSITION, AND THE UNASPECTED

1. Among the most important things which we must discuss are the mathematical principles, that is, the nature of the aspects of opposition, trine, square, sextile, and the unaspected, and which is the right trine, the left trine, the right and left sextile.

2. In opposition to Aries is Libra, and to Libra, Aries. Scorpio is the opposition of Taurus and Taurus of Scorpio; and all the other signs in the same way. But so that you may find these not only with the eye but by calculation, we will show this in a simple example: from one sign to another which is the seventh sign, this is opposition. This is always an unfavorable and threatening sign.

3. Trine is the fifth sign from the one where we start, as will be shown by example: from Aries to Leo is a trine aspect, from Taurus to Virgo, and so on through all the signs, whichever is the fifth sign, that is trine.

4. We must know too which is a right and which a left trine. The right trine is that which is back of the sign from which we begin, the left trine is the one ahead. So, for instance, the right trine of Aries is Sagittarius, the left is Leo, and in the same way the right trine of Leo is Aries and the left, Sagittarius. This is how in all other signs, too, you look for the trine. This is a prosperous and a fortunate aspect.

5. The square aspect is the fourth sign from the sign in which we begin, as is shown by this example: the sign of Cancer is the square of Aries, and Libra of Cancer, and Capricorn of Libra, and Aries of Capricorn.

6. But which is the right and which the left square you will find in a similar way to that which we described for the trine. For whatever is in back, that is a right square; the left square of Aries is Cancer, the right is Capricorn, just as in all other squares; what is in back is right and what is ahead is left. This is also a threatening sign and full of adverse influence.

7. The sextile aspects are the same as the trine, but less powerful. The sextile is the third sign from the one in which we begin, so that the Gemini (Twins) are in sextile aspect of Aries. Which is the right and which is the left sextile you will find just as the others, but lest there be any question of this, too, we shall give examples: the right sextile of Aries is to Aquarius, the left Gemini. Just as in the other signs, the one going back is right, the one in front is left. But those sextiles are more powerful which have between them a tropical or a bi-corporeal sign, while those separated by solid signs are weak.

## XXIII

## HOW THE ASPECTS ARE CONNECTED TO THE ASCENDANT

1. Now we must explain briefly why we have said that certain houses are aspected to the ascendant but others turn away from it. These last we have called "passive" or "alien."

2. All signs are of necessity mutually aspected. Why we have said this you can soon learn. We have explained that all signs have 30 degrees. If you put all these together twelve times, you arrive at the number of 360 degrees, which are divided among all the bodies of the signs, so that these signs are respectively aspected to each other by the nearness of the relationship. Whichever add up to 360 degrees by the addition of a whole number of degrees joined together, these are related when their sum is added up.

3. We have described how the sextile aspect is related to the ascendant and to other points. We have stated before what sextile is, and now we shall describe it in particular. If you take 60 degrees from the ascendant, that will be the side of the sextile. If then you take 60 six times, so that the total of 360 degrees is reached, each of these is mutually aspected.

4. Trine is the fifth house from the ascendant and from any other point, whether it be right trine or left. We have said that it is most powerfully aspected to the ascendant and to other houses. We shall explain briefly how this comes about. If we start from the first degree of the ascendant and count off 120 degrees we find this house. If then we take 120 degrees three times we get a total of 360 degrees. This is the way each house is aspected to the ascendant, and all trines are aspected to each other in this way.

5. We have also said that quartile is very strongly aspected to the ascendant. I shall briefly show the calculation for this connection. Setting out from the degree of the ascendant we stop at 90 degrees. Then, multiplying this by four, we reach the total of 360 degrees. The number of 90 degrees multiplied by four adds up to the sum of 360 degrees, and is therefore called a square. This is the calculation for all squares.

6. Oppositions, too, as we have said, are aspected to the ascendant, but I shall explain the calculation of the aspect as well. Starting from the first

Diagram VII. The Aspects.

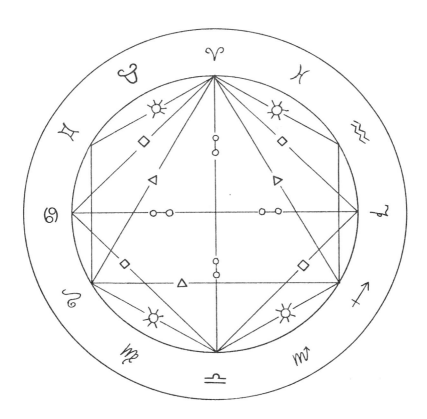

degree of the ascendant we arrive at 180 degrees and stop. Therefore, if we multiply the number of 180 degrees by two, we get a total of 360 degrees. Because therefore the two—that is, 180 taken twice—give the sum total of 360 degrees, these houses are very strongly aspected to each other. This is the calculation for all oppositions.

7. When instead the houses are so placed that their degrees, when multiplied by two, three, or four, do not make up the total of 360, they are not at all aspected to the ascendant or to any other signs. And, because of this, whatever sign is found outside of this number is called passive and *ableptum*.

## XXIV

### WHICH PARTS OF THE BODY ARE ALLOTTED TO WHICH SIGNS[39]

1. We must explain what parts of the body the twelve signs control, for this is very useful for forecasting from the stars, especially when you wish to find the house of health or of defects. The head of man is in the sign of Aries, the neck in Taurus, the shoulders in Gemini, the heart in Cancer, the breast and stomach in Leo, the belly in Virgo, the kidneys and vertebrae in Libra, the sex organs in Scorpio, the thighs in Sagittarius, the knees in Capricorn, the legs in Aquarius, and the feet in Pisces. In this way all parts of the human body are divided among the signs.

## XXV

### FORECASTING THE LENGTH OF LIFE

1. Now we must explain the following subject: which stars portend how many hours, months, years of life—more if the stars are well located, fewer if badly situated.

2. When you look carefully at the Giver of Life, that is, the ruler of the chart, and you see in what house it is located, and in what kind of a sign, and in what degrees, and you also consider the ruler of the sign in which the Life-Giver is situated, in what sign and in what house and in what degree it is, and to what extent the Giver of Life and the benefic planets are aspected to the Sun and Moon, you will easily be able to delineate the whole character of this life. For, if the Life-Giver is situated in a good house, in a good sign and in good degrees, a healthy number of years is portended, especially if Jupiter in a diurnal nativity, or Venus in a nocturnal nativity, is in favorable aspect to the Giver of Life.

3. If Saturn is the Giver of Life and is favorable, he decrees 57 years; but if he portends evil he decrees 30 years, or 30 months and 12 hours.

4. If Jupiter is the Giver of Life and is favorable, he decrees 79 years, but if unfavorable 12 years, or 12 months and 12 days and 12 hours.

5. If Mars is the Life-Giver and is favorable, he portends 63 years; if unfavorable 15 years, or 15 months, 15 days, and 12 hours.

6. If the Sun is favorable he decrees 120 years; if unfavorable 18 years; if moderate 45 years.

7. Venus, if she decrees favorably, 84 years; if unfavorably 8 years, 8 days, 12 hours.

8. Mercury, if he decrees favorably, 108 years; if moderately 79 years; if unfavorably 20 years, or 29 months, 20 days, 20 hours.

9. If the Moon decrees favorably, 84 years; if unfavorably 25 years.

10. If the Ruler of Life or the Giver of Life, that is the ruler of the nativity, is in his own house or in his own exaltation or in his own terms, and if planets in his own condition exert a favorable influence on him, that is, are favorably aspected to his position, and those stars themselves which influence him are well placed, then a larger number of years is portended. But they indicate an average age if the Giver of Life is in his own terms or in his sign or in his rising while the ascendant is in Libra.

## XXVI

## THE RULER OF TIME[40]

1. The Greeks call the Ruler of Time *Chronocrator* (Greek: ruler of time). But the Sun controls the beginning of time in diurnal charts and divides it with the other planets; in a nocturnal chart, the Moon. Do not accept any other theory, for this is accepted by everyone.

2. Thus when the Sun is the Ruler of Time he holds dominion for ten years and nine months (129 months). In a similar way the Moon, when she becomes Mistress of Time, will hold it for ten years and nine months.

In a diurnal chart, first of all, the Sun is allotted ten years; second, the planet which is found in the second house of the chart as one goes through the signs; thirdly, the planet coming after the second; and in a similar way the others. But so that you may understand more clearly we give this example:

3. If in a diurnal chart the Sun is found in Aries, it itself will be ruler of a ten-year period, and also in whatever other sign it might be found. Then, whatever planet is in Taurus, that planet will be in second place, and the one after Taurus, that one will be in third; and thus with the others. In the nocturnal nativity we shall do the same thing, beginning with the Moon.

4. But whichever planet is allotted the ten-year period, although it is ruler of the entire time, nevertheless it divides the whole stretch of the ten years with the other planets, beginning with himself and afterwards giving to those who are placed in order, first giving to the one of these found in the second place, according to their order in the chart.

## XXVII

## THE ALLOTMENT OF TIME[41]

1. We shall briefly show how much life span is allotted. The Sun receives 19 months, the Moon 25 months, Saturn 30 months, Jupiter 12 months, Mars 15 months, Venus 8 months, Mercury 20 months.

2. What this distribution of time means we shall show in the books on forecasting by the stars, also what one star portends when it takes over time from another. All things, good or bad, which happen to us, we connect with this calculation of time. The end of life will be found in this way and the character of the entire nativity, and everything which the order of the planets portends.

3. We find the year with a very easy calculation; for it always begins from the ascendant, and the first year will be the one in which the ascendant is located, the second in the second sign, the third in the third, and thus for the others in order. Some obtain this same result in a diurnal chart from the Sun, at night from the Moon. And this is also possible.

## XXVIII

## THE DIVISION OF THE YEAR

1. The days of the entire year, too, are divided among individual planets. To what extent they are divided, and from where they begin, I shall take care to show.

2. I shall point out when illnesses, foolishness, when profit or loss, when joys and griefs may be expected. For when benefic planets control the days we are freed from all evil. When malefic, then we are attacked by sudden misfortunes.

3. In whatever sign the beginning of the year is located, the ruler of this sign controls the first days, and after him come the others, just as they are located, one by one. I shall therefore show how many days each planet is allotted and this, too, I shall illustrate: the Sun, 53 days; the Moon, 71; Saturn, 85; Jupiter, 30; Mars, 42; Venus, 23; Mercury, 57.

4. In this span of days we are able to find everything that happens to us. But first look carefully at the character of the sign and the house. For if they are well situated, are allotted time, either months or days, and are favorable, they portend everything good. But if a malefic planet controls time, either months or days, and is badly situated, it portends misfortunes according to the character of the house.

## XXIX

## THE ANTISCIA

1. The antiscia should be dealt with at this point because we introduced them a little earlier; in this way nothing may seem to have been

Diagram VIII.  The Antiscia.

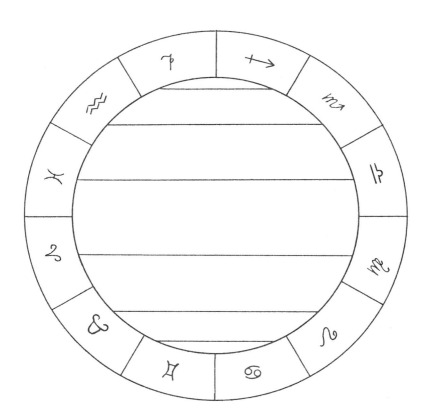

overlooked in this account of principles.

2. The antiscia of the Greeks have been handed down by tradition. I do not wish anyone to think that this topic has not been discussed by the Greeks. For even Ptolemy[42] followed no other theory but that of the antiscia. Antiochus,[43] when he said that indeed Libra did not see Aries because the Earth was in the middle, as if through a mirror reached the theory of the antiscia. Dorotheus of Sidon,[44] on the other hand, a very wise man who wrote about forecasting by the stars in very accurate and learned verses, explained the calculation of the antiscia in clear terms in his fourth book.

3. Now I shall briefly describe how the antiscia[45] are related. The beginning of the antiscia is either from Gemini and Cancer or from Sagittarius and Capricorn. Let us therefore begin our explanation from Gemini and Cancer. Gemini (the Twins) send antiscia toward Cancer and Cancer toward Gemini; Leo toward Taurus and Taurus toward Leo; Virgo toward Aries and Aries toward Virgo; Pisces toward Libra and Libra toward Pisces; Aquarius toward Scorpio and Scorpio toward Aquarius; Sagittarius toward Capricorn and Capricorn toward Sagittarius. If again we begin from Sagittarius and Capricorn, in the same way they stop with Gemini and Cancer. All these we must now consider with careful inquiry so that our respectable profession should not at any time be dishonored by fraudulent lies in forecasts.

4. What we have said about the antiscia is not enough unless we list in detail which degrees emit influences to which other degrees, and receive them in turn. It is necessary to note that no degree influences the 30th degree, nor does the 30th degree send antiscia to any other degree. This example which we have given from Gemini and Cancer pertains to the antiscia of all the signs: the first degree of Gemini send antiscia toward the 29th degree of Cancer, and the 29th degree of Cancer in turn sends antiscia toward the first degree of Gemini.

5. This example which we have given of Gemini and Cancer applies to the antiscia of all the signs: the first degree of Gemini sends antiscia toward the 29th degree of Cancer, and again the 29th degree of Cancer sends antiscia toward the first degree of Gemini; the second toward the 28th and the 28th toward the second; the third toward the 27th and the 27th toward the third; the fourth toward the 26th and the 26th toward the fourth; the fifth toward the 25th and the 25th again toward the fifth; the sixth toward the 24th, again the 24th toward the sixth; the seventh toward the 23rd and the 23rd toward the seventh; the eighth toward the 22nd and the 22nd toward the eighth; the ninth toward the 21st and the 21st again toward the ninth; the tenth toward the 20th and the 20th again toward the tenth; the 11th toward the 19th, the 19th again toward the 11th; the 12th toward the 18th, the 18th again toward the 12th; the 13th toward the 17th, the 17th again toward the 13th; the 14th toward the 16th, the 16th again toward the 14th; the 15th toward the 15th, again the

15th toward the 15th; the 16th toward the 14th, the 14th again toward the 16th; the 17th toward the 13th and again the 13th toward the 17th; the 18th toward the 12th, the 12th again toward the 18th; the 19th toward the 11th, again the 11th toward the 19th; the 20th toward the tenth, again the tenth toward the 20th; the 21st toward the ninth, again the ninth toward the 21st; the 22nd toward the eighth, again the eighth toward the 22nd; the 23rd toward the seventh and again the seventh toward the 23rd; the 24th toward the sixth, the sixth again toward the 24th; the 25th toward the fifth, again the fifth toward the 25th; the 26th toward the fourth, again the fourth toward the 26th; the 27th toward the third, the third again toward the 27th; the 28th toward the second, the second again toward the 28th; the 29th toward the first, again the first toward the 29th.

6. In this way Gemini and Cancer send each other antiscia. For a degree, from whatever degree it receives an antiscium, sends an antiscium from itself to that degree. Thus Taurus and Leo send an antiscium against each other, thus Virgo and Aries, Libra and Pisces, Scorpio and Aquarius, Sagittarius and Capricorn.

7. In order that this may be more clearly understood, that is, what sign sends antiscia toward what other sign, I have written out all the degrees in detail so that all difficulties may be cleared up: toward whatever degree, therefore, the first degree sends an antiscium, from there it receives an antiscium itself in turn: likewise the second, and so with the others. We have therefore written out the degrees of Gemini and Cancer and it is well that this serve also as an example in the case of degrees of other signs and of these signs which degrees send, as we have said, an antiscium toward each other.

| | |
|---|---|
| I | XXVIIII |
| II | XXVIII |
| III | XXVII |
| IIII | XXVI |
| V | XXV |
| VI | XXIIII |
| VII | XXIII |
| VIII | XXII |
| VIIII | XXI |
| X | XX |
| XI | XVIIII |
| XII | XVIII |
| XIII | XVII |
| XIIII | XVI |
| XV | XV |
| XVI | XIIII |
| XVII | XIII |
| XVIII | XII |

XVIIII ........................................... XI
XX .................................................... X
XXI .......................................... VIIII
XXII .......................................... VIII
XXIII .......................................... VII
XXIIII .......................................... VI
XXV ............................................... V
XXVI .......................................... IIII
XXVII .......................................... III
XXVIII .......................................... II
XXVIIII .......................................... I

8. Thus Taurus toward Leo and again Leo toward Taurus; Aries toward Virgo and again Virgo toward Aries; Pisces toward Libra and again Libra toward Pisces; Scorpio toward Aquarius and again Aquarius toward Scorpio; Sagittarius toward Capricorn and again Capricorn toward Sagittarius.

9. Thus if, in computing the chart, some of the planets are not in aspect, it must be asked whether they are connected to each other through the relationship of the antiscia. For when they send an antiscium in such a way that they are in aspect through the antiscium, in trine, square, sextile, or opposition, they portend just as if they were thus located in the normal arrangement, and all of these various influences fit together in the final calculation. When you do this you will easily be able to find out everything which is looked for in men's destinies. For there is a theory underlying the nature of the antiscia which is strengthened by universal agreement; this theory I shall take care to explain to you at another time.

10. How much the force of the antiscia counts and how effectively the theory of the antiscia works you will be able to learn from this nativity[46] which we are about to give: this man had a chart with the Sun in Pisces, the Moon in Cancer, Saturn in Virgo, Jupiter in Pisces in the same degree as the Sun, Mars in Aquarius, Venus in Taurus, Mercury in Aquarius in the same degree as Mars, the ascendant in Scorpio. The father of this native after two consecutive consulships was sent into exile, but the native himself was exiled for the crime of adultery and suddenly brought back from exile, was first chosen for the administration of Campania, then the consulship of Achaia, but afterwards was made proconsul of Africa and Prefect of Rome.

11. Any man not knowing the theory of the antiscia, if he saw the Sun with Jupiter in the same degree in the fifth house from the ascendant— that is, in the house of Bona Fortuna—would have foretold a father fortunate, prosperous, powerful, and so on, and the same thing for the native himself. Concerning his exile and the constant plots against him he would have been able to foretell nothing unless he turned his attention to the theory of antiscia.

Diagram IX. Chart of Albinus, I.

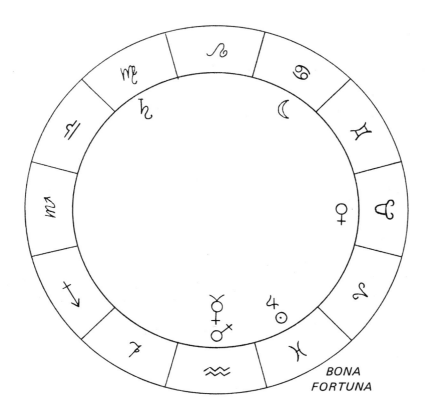

BONA
FORTUNA

12. You remember that we said that Pisces sends an antiscium toward Libra and Libra again toward Pisces. And so the Sun and Jupiter, located together in Pisces, send an antiscium toward Libra, in this sign in which it is out of dignity and debilitated and in the twelfth house of the nativity, that is, the *cacodaemon*; this shows a humble origin of the father's family and for the father himself a scandalous exile. But Jupiter, whose force and power the influence of the antiscium transferred from the sign of Pisces to the sign of Libra, located in the twelfth house, that is, of the *cacodaemon*, through the antiscium excited a great many enemies against the father, and against the native himself, and made them win.

13. Consider another thing which indicated exile for the father. Saturn, located in Virgo, was in opposition to the Sun, and received the Sun's antiscium from the opposition; for, located in Virgo, he sent an antiscium toward Aries. This antiscium, located in Aries, and the antiscium of the Sun, which was sent against Libra, were thus brought into opposition to each other, and brought it about that he was sent into exile because the antiscia of Saturn and the Sun were in opposition to each other.

14. As to why the native himself became an exile and why he became an adulterer (this was the crime of which he was accused), that is shown by this calculation. We have said that Cancer sent an antiscium toward Gemini. Therefore the Moon, located in Cancer, sent an antiscium toward Gemini, and that antiscium Mars, located in Aquarius, received from the right side; and Mars is malefic whenever he receives light from the waxing Moon, from either side. This man, first afflicted with many bodily infirmities, was later made an exile.

15. But Mars himself, located in Aquarius, sent an antiscium toward Scorpio, which is the sign in which the ascendant was located. First located in the *Imum Caelum*, he attacked the degree of Life, that is, of the ascendant, with violently hostile influence. Then he received the antiscium of the Moon, located in Gemini in full trine aspect; thirdly, his antiscium settled on the degree of the ascendant. Fourthly, this antiscium of Mars, which had been sent toward the ascendant, was aspected in trine to the Moon, located in Cancer.

16. And so the waxing Moon, attacked from all sides by the many influences of Mars, made this man, weakened in body, finally an exile. And if Jupiter, located in Pisces, had not been aspected in trine to the ascendant, he would never have been freed from his exile; and if he had not been aspected in trine to the Moon in his exaltation (for the exaltation of Jupiter is in Cancer), the native would have died a violent death. We have however, described how the benevolence of Jupiter fails in this way in the first degrees because of this reason, that on the third day the Moon, located in Leo, when in fullness of light, sets herself up in opposition to Mars. For this day, that is, the third, is very important in the nativity.

17. But what configuration caused that man to become an adulterer, this also I shall explain: Mars, located in Aquarius, sent an antiscium

Diagram X.  Chart of Albinus, II. (Pisces sends an antiscium
toward Libra, and vice versa.)

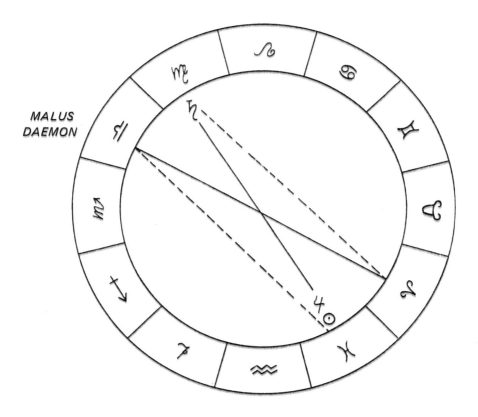

Diagram XI.  Chart of Albinus, III. (Cancer sends an antiscium
            toward Gemini.)

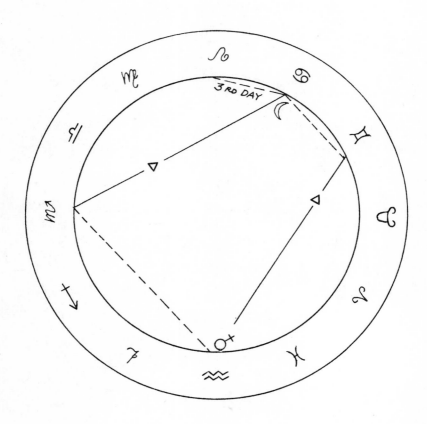

Diagram XII.  Chart of Albinus, IV. (Mars sends an antiscium
toward Scorpio.)

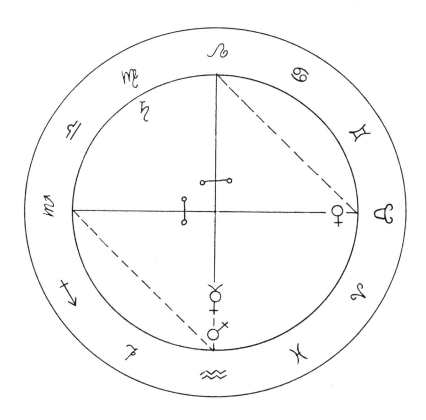

toward Scorpio; thus the antiscium of Mars found Venus located on the descendant in the chart; for Venus is unfavorable and indicates many calamities if in declination, located in the descendant, she is afflicted by a hostile aspect from Mars. And again, the antiscium of Venus, sent toward Leo, was in opposition to Mars, located on the *Imum Caelum* in Aquarius; and from the *Imum Caelum* Mars, without counting the antiscium, was related to Venus in square aspect. In all these ways, therefore, through themselves and through their antiscia on the chief cardinal points of the nativity, Venus and Mars, either in opposition or in square, attacked each other with hostile aspect. This configuration caused the native to be accused of adultery.

18. But Mercury, located in Aquarius, without aspect to Jupiter, was located in the sign of Saturn, and Saturn in the sign of Mercury—their signs are in mutual reception—and this made the native knowledgeable of arcane literature. But because Venus sent an antiscium toward Leo from Taurus, that is, toward the house of the Sun, and on the *Medium Caelum*, for those crimes she caused the Emperor to pass sentence on him.

19. The full Moon, located in her sign in the ninth house, decreed the greatest honors for him, especially since she has the first place in decreeing honors in a nocturnal chart according to the power of her condition. Such learning and knowledge are also decreed by Mercury and Saturn when their signs are interchanged, so that his eloquence and oratorical style can be compared to that of ancient writers.

20. Whose chart this is, my dear Lollianus, you know very well. Putting all these things together you will discover how much force there is in the antiscia. If anyone follows up this topic with careful study the trend of his forecast will never fail him while he is studying the fate of men.

## XXX

### LIFE AND TRAINING OF AN ASTROLOGER

1. Now you, whoever you are who try to read these books, since you have received the whole knowledge of this divine science and are now endowed with the secrets of the stars and have learned the first principles of the art, shape yourself in the image and likeness of divinity, so that you may always be a model of excellence. He who daily speaks about the gods or with the gods must shape his mind to approach the likeness of divinity.

2. Therefore study and pursue all the distinguishing marks of virtue and, when you have trained yourself in these, be easy of access, so that if anyone wishes to consult you about anything, he may approach you without fear. Be modest, upright, sober, eat little, be content with few goods, so that the shameful love of money may not defile the glory of this divine science. Try with your training and principles to outdo the training and principles of worthy priests. For it is necessary that the acolyte of the

Sun and Moon and the other gods, through whom all earthly things are governed, should so educate his mind always that it be proved worthy by the attestation of all mankind.

3. See that you give your responses publicly in a clear voice, so that nothing may be asked of you which is not allowed either to ask or to answer.

4. Beware of replying to anyone asking about the condition of the Republic or the life of the Roman Emperor. For it is not right, nor is it permitted, that from wicked curiosity we learn anything about the condition of the Republic. But it is a wicked man and one worthy of all punishment who, when asked, gives a response about the destiny of the Emperor, because the astrologer is able neither to find out nor to say anything. You must know that even the *haruspices*, [47] as many times as they were asked by private citizens about the condition of the Emperor, and wanted to answer the one who consulted them, always disturbed the entrails which were intended for this purpose by tampering with the arrangement of the veins and cartilages.

5. In fact no astrologer is able to find out anything true about the destiny of the Emperor. For the Emperor alone is not subject to the course of the stars and in his fate alone the stars have no power of decreeing. Since he is master of the whole universe, his destiny is governed by the judgment of the Highest God, since the whole world is subject to the power of the Emperor and he himself is also considered among the number of the gods whom the Supreme Power has set up to create and conserve all things.

6. This consideration also makes things difficult for the *haruspices* because, whatever divinity is invoked by them, since it is of lesser power, is not able to explain the character of the greater power which is in the Emperor. For all free-born men, all classes, all the rich, all the nobles, all the officials, all powers serve him; endowed with divine authority and immortality he is numbered among the first ranks of the gods.

7. Therefore, if anyone asks anything about the Emperor, I do not want you to disturb him with a harsh and stern answer, but convince him with persuasive words that no one can discover anything about the life of the Emperor so that, warned by your arguments, he may put aside his madness and his wrong intention. Nor do I wish you to give a report, if anyone asks you anything wrong lest, after he has received the death sentence because of his forbidden desires, you should seem to have been the cause of his death. This is foreign to the purpose of a priest.

8. Have a wife, a home, many sincere friends; be constantly available to the public; keep away from all quarrels; do not undertake any harmful business; do not at any time be tempted by an increase in income; keep away from all passion of cruelty; never take pleasure in others' quarrels or capital sentences or fatal enmities. Employ peaceful moderation in all

your dealings with other people; avoid plots; at all times shun disturbances and violence.

9. Bind your friends' loyalty to you with strong ties; be careful to keep
your honesty uncorrupted in all your activities; never stain your self-
respect by becoming a false witness. Never ask interest on money lest you
accumulate an increase in income from the needs of others. Do not give or
take an oath, especially if it has to do with money, lest the divine protection
of the gods appear to be asked by you for money.

10. To erring men, especially those bound to you by ties of friendship,
show the right road of life so that, trained in your principles, they will
easily avoid the errors of life. Never be present at nocturnal sacrifices,
whether they are held publicly or privately. Do not bring forecasts to
anyone by stealth, but openly, as we have said before, and in the sight of all
exercise the discipline of this divine art.

11. In drawing up the chart I do not wish you to show up the vices of
men too clearly, but whenever you come to such a point, delay your
responses with a certain modest reticence, lest you seem not only to
explain but also to approve what the evil course of the stars decrees for the
man.

12. Keep away at all times from the enticements of the shows, lest
anyone think you are a patron of this kind of thing. For the priest of the
gods must be apart from low, base pleasures.

13. When you have equipped your mind with the characteristics and
protections of virtue, approach with confident boldness of mind this book
as well as the following books which we have written on forecasting from
the stars. But if your mind has strayed in any way from these principles
which we have laid down about human character, see that that you do not
approach the mysteries of this doctrine with a perverse instinct of
curiosity or sacrilegious rashness.

14. Do not entrust the secrets of this religion to the sinful greed of
men's minds; for one should not initiate souls of depraved men into the
holy rituals. This divine science cannot at any time adhere to a mind
captured and stained by wicked greed, and it always sustains the greatest
loss when it is defamed by improper intentions.

15. Therefore be pure and chaste; and if you have separated yourself
from all kinds of wicked activity which destroy the spirit; and if the desire
for the right way of life has freed you from any suspicion of crime, and if
you conduct yourself as one mindful of the Divine Seed, approach this
work and commit to memory the following books. In this way, having
attained the true knowledge of this divine art, when you calculate the
destinies of men and chart the course of their lives, you will be directed
not only by your readings but also by the conclusions of your own
reasoning. Thus your own divinely inspired ideas may be of more profit
to you than the traditions of the written word.

# Liber Tertius

1. We propose to translate into propositions the entire literature of the *Mathesis* so that the system developed by the divine predecessors may be fully introduced to eager learners.

2. In the first place, my dear Lollianus, we must be aware that God the Creator, copying nature, has made man in the image of the universe, a mixture of four elements—fire, water, air, and earth—so that a well-proportioned combination might produce the living being as a divine imitation. With his divine skill he so composed man that the whole force and essence of the elements is collected in that small body. In this way he prepared a lodging for the divine spirit which descends from the heavenly Soul to maintain the mortal body. This spirit, though fragile, is nevertheless a likeness of the spirit of the universe.

3. Thus man, like a tiny universe, is sustained by the everlasting fiery movement of the five planets and the Sun and Moon.

4. Those divine men, altogether worthy and admirable, Petosiris and Nechepso, who approached the very secrets of divinity, also handed down to us the birthchart of the universe in order to show us that man is made in the likeness of the universe according to those same principles by which the universe itself is ruled; and that he is sustained forever by those same everlasting fires.

## I

## THEMA MUNDI[48]

1. Petosiris and Nechepso in this doctrine followed Aesculapius and Hanubius. To them Most Powerful Mercury entrusted the secret. They set up the birthchart of the universe as follows: the Sun in the 15th degree of Leo, the Moon in the 15th degree of Cancer; Saturn in the 15th degree

of Capricorn; Jupiter in the 15th degree of Sagittarius; Mars in the 15th degree of Scorpio; Venus in the 15th degree of Libra; Mercury in the 15th degree of Virgo, and the ascendant in the 15th degree of Cancer.

2. By this they wished to prove that the fates of men are arranged in accordance with this birthchart, the conditions of the planets, and the influence they exert on the chart, just as is related in the book of Aesculapius which is called *Myriogenesis*.[49] Thus nothing in the individual charts of men should seem different from the birthchart of the universe. Let us see to what extent and with what aspect each planet influences the luminaries—the Sun and Moon.

3. Saturn first relates himself to the Moon, for he follows the condition of the Moon. He follows the condition of the Moon because, located in a feminine sign, he receives in opposition the rays of the Moon, also in a feminine sign. But when that same Saturn makes a transition to the sign of Aquarius, he relates himself to the Sun, also in opposition, and is in the same condition as the Sun. For then he and the Sun are in masculine signs.

4. In the same way, when Jupiter is located in Sagittarius, he is in a masculine sign and, aspected in trine to the Sun, he relates himself to the condition of the Sun. For this reason, located in a masculine sign as the Sun is also, he follows the power of the Sun. But when he makes the transition to Pisces he is related to the Moon for, himself in a feminine sign, he is in trine to the Moon in a feminine sign.

5. In the same way Mars, located in Scorpio, a feminine sign, is aspected to the Moon in trine. But when he comes to Aries he transfers his aspect to the Sun; for, located in a masculine sign, he relates himself in trine aspect to the Sun.

6. But this situation is changed in the case of Venus. When in Libra, a masculine sign, she is in square aspect to the Moon. But when she makes the transition to Taurus, a feminine sign, she comes into square aspect with the Sun.

7. They argued, however, that the planet of Mercury is common in the above-mentioned chart because it is not in any aspect to the Sun or Moon, nor is it related to the Sun or Moon in any way, but rejoices with the Sun by day if in a morning rising and with the Moon by night in an evening rising. They believed that all this should be observed in the charts of men, and they thought men's fate could not be discovered unless these influences had been investigated.

8. But these wonderful inventions should not deceive any man. One should not think that the wise men made up the birthchart of the universe without reason. We shall explain everything in detail so that the secret will be clear to all.

9. There was no birthchart of the universe; for it did not have any certain day of origin. There was no one there at the time when the universe was created by the plan of the divine Mind and foreseeing Will. Human reason has not been able to conceive or explain the origin of the

Diagram XIII. The Thema Mundi (Birthday of the Universe).

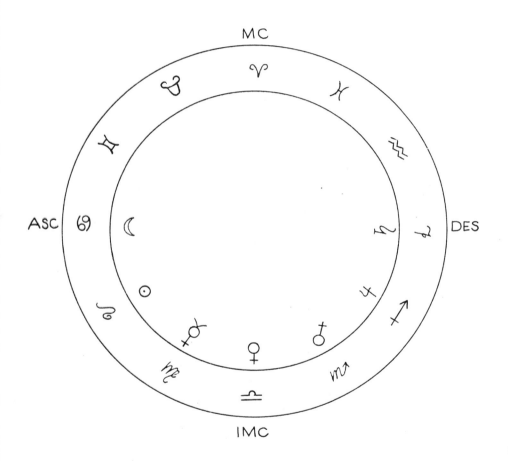

universe, especially since the Great Year[50] of the return of the stars to their places after fire and flood is supposed to happen only after 300,000 years. The apocatastasis (the return of the stars) happens only after these two events—that is, the flood which follows the destruction by fire. For nothing which is burned can be reborn unless the hardened dust of the ashes is mixed with water to produce the renewed fertility of all procreative seeds.

10. The divine wise men of old invented this birthchart of the universe so that it would be an example for astrologers to follow in the charts of men. Therefore I would like to explain the rationale of that divine story.

11. With good reason they located the Moon in such a way that she would first be related to Saturn and would give over to him the rulership of time. For in the beginning the universe was rude and uncultivated; crude men had just taken the first unfamiliar steps toward enlightenment. This rude and rustic time was allotted to Saturn so that human life in its beginning should seem to harden itself by uncivilized ferocity.

12. After Saturn, Jupiter received the rulership of time, with the idea that the roughness of early times should be left behind and mankind be given a more cultivated mode of life. But in the third place the Moon joined herself to Mars, and gave him the rulership of time so that human life, entered on the right path and already instructed in civilization, might learn arts and skills.

13. After Mars, Venus received control of time; in this period training in learned speech and training in the individual sciences encouraged the education of mankind. The wise men wished this period to belong to Venus so that men would be protected by a joyful and healthgiving divinity.

14. But the final period they thought should be given to Mercury, to whom the Moon related last. For the human race was now purified of crude habits and had learned skills and sciences. Different institutions and customs arose, and wickedness and evil appeared. At this time men invented and handed down wicked crimes. For this reason it was thought that this time should be allotted to Mercury.

15. And so, from events which actually occurred in the history of mankind, the hypothetical birthchart of the universe was put together with allegorical meaning. It has been handed down to us as an example to follow in the charts of men. So that we may not seem to have left out anything we shall explain how it can be proved that man was created in the image of the universe.

16. We have said, and there is universal agreement, that the apocatastasis takes place through fire and flood. The essence of the human body at the end of life's course is dissolved in a similar way; either through the natural burning of the heat of fevers or through a flood of humors. Thus it is either burned by fiery heat or dissolved by too much liquid. The wisest practitioners of the medical arts tell us that the natural end of the human

body comes about by liquids which destroy the heat of the body or by the predominance of heat when the inward blood dries out and dies. Thus Creating Nature composed men in every way in imitation of the universe. Whatever dissolves and reforms the essence of the universe also dissolves and reshapes man.

17. We must now explain why they began the twelve signs with Aries. In the book of principles that question could not be discussed until the birthchart of the universe had been explained. Otherwise the explanation might have been confusing to beginners.

18. In the chart of the universe, which we have said was invented by very learned men, the MC *(Medium Caelum)* is found to be in Aries. This is because frequently—or rather, always—in all charts, the MC holds the principal place, and from this we deduce the basis of the whole chart, especially since most of the planets and the luminaries—the Sun and Moon—send their influence toward this sign.

19. We must now define what the individual planets indicate when they are located in the houses of the chart. Some may think these matters have been discussed too generally, but this has been done so that the intelligence of the astrologer-in-training may pick it up easily and not be confused. Furthermore, much will be discussed in detail in this book. The planets will be seen to have their own characteristic strength if they are located exactly in their own houses.

## II

## SATURN

1. Saturn, when located by day on the ascendant, will bring the native to birth with a great cry. The one born will be the eldest of all children or, if any is born before him, that one will be separated from the parents. That god always, by day, on any of the angles, will make the native the first-born or the first to be reared, or he destroys those born before. But he makes the natives themselves boastful and full of pride.

2. If Saturn is on the ascendant by day and Mars is on another angle or the anafora (sign before) of an angle, this indicates many evils—immense danger and loss of inheritance. But often, if there is no benefic planet in a favorable location in aspect to them, or if Mars receives the influence of the waxing Moon, this will make for a violent death.

3. But if Saturn is located by night on the degree of the ascendant, the native will be hindered by the greatest weariness and will always be oppressed by hard labor. Some will be allotted occupations around water, but of such a kind that they will always be worn out by hard work.

4. When Saturn occupies the second house from the ascendant, he indicates serious illnesses and great reverses of fortune. The native becomes the murderer of his wife and children, a frequent agitator of great public disturbances, and he wastes his maternal and paternal

inheritances. He is slow in all his activities and suffers from constant bodily afflictions.

5. If Mars is on any of the angles or is in opposition or square aspect to the Sun or the waxing Moon, this will make wretched paupers, their bodies burdened with daily toil.

6. Saturn in the second house by day will slowly and gradually provide an increase in income. The natives themselves he makes withdrawn, recluses, poor in mind, always denying that they own anything. Some will get their living from watery professions or business having to do with liquids.

7. Saturn in the third house makes the natives slow, sluggish, seeking no kind of income. If he is with the Moon and Mercury in this house the natives will be stupidly malicious, ready with sacrilegious words against divinity. They will always lose their possessions and be thieves, but the kind who never make a profit from their thievery. If Mars is in aspect to them in any way he will make informers, sycophants, evil malicious people, always destined to an evil death.

8. Misers, hoarders of gold and silver are those who have Saturn by day in the fourth house. By night in this house he makes them waste their paternal inheritance, and he indicates an early death for the father. He also causes serious illnesses and horrible chills for the natives and always brings ill repute in early years.

9. If Saturn is in conjunction with the Moon or in opposition or square aspect to her, this will make the native sterile. It forces him to adopt strangers as his children or to have strangers as guardians for his wards. It deforms his body with constant illness and hidden pains, makes the mother a widow at an early age, and brings the native constant pains in the stomach and serious illness from women.

10. Saturn in the fifth house, if by day, will make kings and leaders, very powerful men. But if the Sun is on the degree of the ascendant and Saturn comes into conjunction with the waxing Moon, continual good luck and great power are indicated. But if Jupiter and not the Sun is on the ascendant, this will make magistrates of lesser degree and governors of individual states; it will also make masters of great income so that from their own resources they can support others. But if neither Jupiter nor the Sun is on the ascendant and Saturn in the fifth house comes into conjunction with the waxing Moon, this will give wealth and inheritance. But the native will often be without a wife and will involve himself in unworthy sexual alliances.

11. If Saturn is in the fifth house by night, he allots a portion of good fortune over a period of time, but he produces a man slow in all his activities and makes his courage undependable. The waning Moon in conjunction with Saturn indicates some loss of inheritance and of whatever has been accumulated in life.

12. Destruction of the entire inheritance is indicated by Saturn in the

sixth house. He always makes a bad prediction in this house. He brings illnesses, especially if the waning Moon is in conjunction with him or in opposition or square aspect. This will produce men who are unlucky, unstable, of bad repute, never able to settle in one place.

13. But if, when Saturn is in the sixth house, Mars is in opposition or square aspect to him or in conjunction with him, this will produce hidden pains in the body, dysentery, and consumption; if there is no influence of a benefic planet the native will die of these diseases.

14. Saturn in the seventh house, that is, on the descendant, if in a morning rising and in a diurnal chart, will be favorable and will grant great possessions, but only when the threshold of old age is reached. In this house he allots an extended old age and makes the native a guardian of money. But he predicts hidden pains in the body, hemorrhoids, or painful contractions of the muscles.

15. If Saturn is in this house in an evening rising, he makes boils around the anus and hemorrhoids, especially if Mars is in aspect. The natives are rheumatic and often have abscesses. They are always grieved by the very painful condition of their wives.

16. Saturn in the eighth house, if by day, allots an increase in income over a period of time. If he is in the house or the terms of Mars, he indicates for some an inheritance from the death of strangers.

17. But if he is in this house by night the inheritance will be lost. If the Moon is in opposition or square aspect, this is a bad portent; it is also bad if Saturn is in this house, the Moon is in the house of Saturn and in aspect as before. If Mars is in any aspect to the Moon thus located with Saturn, a violent death is indicated. But if Mars is in this position and Jupiter is in favorable aspect to the Moon and Saturn, the prospect is for favorable expectations in life; but the natives will always be insecure as to the affections of their wives.

18. Saturn in the ninth house will make famous magicians, renowned philosophers, or temple priests noted for their reputation for magic. According to the nature of the signs he also makes seers, diviners, and astrologers. These are always outstanding in their responses. Some carry on the rites of temples or are in charge of rituals. Sometimes they become long-haired philosophers or interpreters of dreams.

19. Saturn in this house by night indicates wrath of the gods and hatred of emperors, especially if the waning Moon is moving toward him in any way. But greater evils are predicted from gods and emperors if Mars from any direction is in aspect to Saturn and the Moon.

20. Emperors, generals, and praetorian prefects are the indication of Saturn in the tenth house, that is the MC. If Saturn is on the MC by day and in his exaltation with the Sun on the ascendant, this will make respectable farmers of good character, but wealthy, whose holdings are near the sea, rivers, or lakes. It will also provide large income, great glory, and inheritance from important persons, especially if Mars is not in

aspect. But if Mars is strongly aspected he will diminish this good fortune.

21. Saturn by night on the MC indicates misfortunes: loss of inheritance, no marriage, no children, especially if he is in the house or terms of a malefic planet. But if a benefic planet, that is, Venus or Jupiter, is in favorable aspect to Saturn thus located by night, those things which were denied will be given in another way. But in general, Saturn by night on any angle indicates the greatest evils. He destroys wives and children and always predicts grief from loss of relatives.

22. If Saturn in this house comes into aspect with the waning Moon, the native will be so burdened with poverty that he scarcely will have daily bread, especially if the waning Moon is in a feminine sign. But if Saturn comes into aspect with the waxing Moon, this indicates an unstable life; the native will not have one single course of life but constant change.

23. Mercury in aspect to Saturn in the tenth house will give sharpness of mind and a long life, especially if he is the ruler of the chart or the giver of life. But if these functions are taken over by some other planet, subtract 30 from the allotted years. Greater evils are indicated if Saturn is in opposition to the ruler of the chart or to the Giver of Life, especially if Mars is in opposition or square aspect to Saturn. For this will make paralytics, clownish hunchbacks, crooked dwarfs, hermaphrodites, and the like, all in accordance with the nature of the signs.

24. If the Moon, moving away from Saturn in the tenth house, comes into aspect with Mars in a nocturnal chart, this will make madmen who are depressed and sluggish. Saturn located on the tip of the horn of the waning Moon in a nocturnal chart makes consumptives.

25. Moderately good fortune is the indication of Saturn in the eleventh house. When an important promotion is destined for the native, he will receive the same position his father had, but only after his thirtieth year. Before his thirtieth year whatever he achieves will be lost; he will not attain position or possessions until after his thirtieth year.

26. Saturn in the twelfth house indicates an uprising of slaves or crises on account of slaves. He may also reduce the native to slavery. Great illnesses are indicated and serious afflictions, especially if the Moon is in any aspect and no benefic planet is on any angle. But if a benefic planet is on any of the angles, the evils we described will be mitigated. All these will be lighter if Saturn is in this house by day, but stronger if by night.

27. When Saturn is located in these houses, carefully observe his degree so that you may find in what house and in which terms the duodecatemorion is; from this information you may discover the whole power of Saturn.

## III

## JUPITER

1. If Jupiter is found exactly on the first angle, that is, on the

ascendant, especially in those signs in which he rejoices or in his own house or terms or in his exaltation, he will make the native high-born, famous, always ruling great states, perhaps the first ten of the great states. He will also make him, according to the computation of the chart, virtuous, charming, benevolent, cheerful, rich, especially if Jupiter is in this house by day and no malefic planet is in aspect. But if a malefic planet is in aspect, this whole prediction is to a certain extent diminished.

2. Jupiter by night on the ascendant will make the native first-born among his brothers; or it will destroy one born before, or send him to regions far away from his parents, so that the native will have first place in his father's house. He will be carefully nurtured and his parents will have great prosperity. If Jupiter is in this house by night and a malefic planet is in aspect, all paternal and maternal inheritance will be wasted.

3. Jupiter located on the angles will always make the native first-born or will destroy the older brother, as we said, so as to make the native occupy first place in his father's house. The waxing Moon in any aspect to Jupiter on the ascendant, by night or day, will make great administrators, in charge of states or important affairs.

4. Inheritance from strangers or adoption by strangers is indicated if Jupiter is in the second house. Great riches and possessions are also predicted if Mercury is in aspect in a favorable position. But if Mars or Saturn are in aspect from any direction, this will change the native's status and transfer him from respectable to dishonorable occupations. His life will be constantly changing, at one time abounding in riches, at another oppressed by poverty.

5. Jupiter in the third house is neither good nor bad but always a balanced mixture, so that sometimes possessions are lost and sometimes unexpected riches are attained.

6. Very important judges, legislators, or interpreters of the law result from Jupiter in the fourth house. He also makes breeders and lovers of livestock; also those to whom the most important public duties are entrusted, according to the quality of the signs. The natives are sent here and there on frequent journeys at the order of generals or heads of state. They are friends of princes, in charge of public affairs, and are the type who commit themselves to the protection of the gods and ask help from them. To them with frequent signs the gods show the right road. Many who have Jupiter in this position foretell the future or hold positions, often the highest, in temples. Some find treasure according to the nature of the signs. In this house Jupiter always indicates a fortunate old age until death.

7. Jupiter in this house makes the father high-born and famous but destroys the native's income around middle age and then restores it again. The native is sluggish in his relations with women and separated from the affection of his children. In this house by night Jupiter makes men of moderate income, but who become more fortunate in course of time.

8. Jupiter in the fifth house indicates great increases in prosperity. In his own house, terms, or exaltation, or in the house of the Sun, he makes the native honored in important public affairs. If Mars is in favorable aspect, this will indicate generals with power of life and death. If Mercury and the Moon are in any aspect, without Mars, this will make agents or account-keepers for kings. But Venus alone in aspect from any direction will make them immoderately fortunate. But if Jupiter is in conjunction with Mars, as we said above, the native will be outstanding in regal power and all his pronouncements will be accepted as if from holy writ. The one who has Jupiter in this house will have a strong body and healthy bones.

9. If Jupiter comes into aspect with the waxing Moon, this will create men of almost divine and immortal nature. This happens when the Moon is moving toward Jupiter. It is difficult to observe this. If Jupiter is in the north and the waxing and full Moon comes into aspect moving from the east (with Jupiter in his own house or exaltation or in signs in which he rejoices), the result is unconquered generals who govern the whole world. This is especially true if the Sun in his exaltation is in trine aspect to Jupiter. For Jupiter rejoices by day when aspected by the Sun or Saturn, especially if he is in a morning rising.

10. If Jupiter in this house is in aspect to the waning Moon, this will make men of decent character, raised to the honor of moderate positions, never suffering from poverty. But if the waxing Moon is in aspect to Jupiter in this house, this will make administrators, consulars, often regularly elected consuls, especially in a diurnal chart. Mercury in aspect indicates a long life; he will provide children of both sexes, or twins, especially if he is the ruler of the chart or of the ascendant or of the sign in which the ruler of the chart is located. But if Jupiter is in a nocturnal chart in opposition to the giver of life (for Jupiter does not rejoice in a nocturnal chart), subtract 12 years from the allotted span of life.

11. If in a nocturnal chart Mars or Venus or the Moon are in unfavorable aspect to Jupiter, the native will suffer the greatest afflictions according to the nature of the signs. If Jupiter is in human signs, the native will be oversexed and driven by insane desires to monstrous loves, behaving like women. In four-footed signs, they will be hunters and lovers of wild beasts who delight in lonely forests and are involved in continual troubles. Jupiter in earth signs makes gardeners or men wishing to know more than is allowed about human nature. In watery signs he makes fishermen and those who make their living around rivers, swamps, seas; they are hard-working and live from their own skills.

12. If Jupiter is in the fifth house in a nocturnal chart with Mars, Venus, and the Moon opposed to him, and if the Moon is moving away from him, this indicates a changeable kind of life with frequent periods of misery. The misfortune will be somewhat lessened if the receding Moon is in aspect to Venus. But if the receding Moon is in aspect to no planet, the greatest misfortunes, difficulties, and miseries are indicated. If the

receding Moon in some way comes into opposition or square aspect to Mars, this indicates a violent death, according to the nature of the signs. For if Mars is in opposition to the receding Moon in a nocturnal chart, quarrels, dangers, and struggles are indicated—always with an inferior. By night in this sign Jupiter often predicts dire catastrophes.

13. The greatest evils are indicated by Jupiter in the sixth house; for he will expose the native at birth, especially if he is the ruler of the sign in which the ascendant or the MC is; this is especially true if it is a nocturnal chart and he is in opposition to the Sun, Saturn, or Mars, and in square aspect to the waning Moon or in the same sign with her.

14. But if he is in aspect to the waxing Moon without unfavorable aspect of any other planets, the evil is to a certain extent lessened. In this house he makes goldsmiths and those who adorn clothing with gold thread; sometimes also silversmiths. But even with these arts he often indicates reversals of fortune. For this house, the sixth, has its own special allotment of evil, and whatever planet is in that house acquires great force for forecasting evil from the nature of the house.

15. Jupiter in the seventh house, (that, is, the descendant) in a diurnal house indicates wealth and a happy old age. By night he changes drastically the house of marriage and children. For the native will lose a beloved wife and see the deaths of children. Late in life, however, he will receive an increase in income, not very large, but enough to keep him from want.

16. Jupiter in the eighth house often destroys income, makes great enemies, and often stirs up revolutions among the people. He involves the natives in evil activities and makes them lower class. They voice stupid hostilities, are unreasonable, with a temper which almost amounts to insanity. All this is especially true if there is a malefic planet on one of the angles. But if in this house Jupiter has Mercury with him or in trine aspect to him, or the waxing Moon in favorable aspect, this will make administrators or account-keepers for kings or royal heralds. But they will die at an early age.

17. Jupiter in the ninth house in a diurnal chart will make interpreters of the gods, able to foretell the future. Some will follow the profession of priests, others will have duties in temples. But sometimes this combination indicates losses and fevers of the mind. Jupiter in this house by night makes dreamers of false dreams who often tell lies about the gods. He also makes those who promise some hope to themselves from drawing lots and who think they are divinely inspired by this activity.

18. Jupiter in the tenth house (that is, the MC) by day makes heads of public business, leaders of important states, men on whom great honors are conferred by the people, anxious to be conspicuous for popularity. They always enjoy a good living. Some carry on the affairs of great men and emperors; others receive rewards and prizes throughout their lives.

19. Jupiter in this house indicates the greatest good fortune if no

malefic planet is on the IMC. But if one is, whatever honor or wealth was accumulated in early life will be diminished, wasted, or completely destroyed in later life, unless the descendant is strengthened by a benefic planet. But if Jupiter is in the tenth house by night, he makes the natives honorable in character but easily cheated, and their inheritance is often quickly wasted.

20. The greatest good fortune and great fame—consular or proconsular power—result from Jupiter in the eleventh house, if the Sun and Venus are in favorable aspect and if the full Moon (moving away from the east, while Jupiter is in the north) is in aspect, that is, if she is on such a course as was described in connection with the fifth house.

21. In a nocturnal chart all this is diminished and loses effect. If Mars is in unfavorable aspect in the eighth house, all honor or position which was gained will be changed in a wretched reversal of fortune.

22. Greater misfortunes are indicated by Jupiter in the twelfth house. He always makes enemies who frequently exercise power to hinder the native's activities, especially if a malefic planet is on the ascendant. Mars on the descendant will bring about a violent death.

23. The evils will be greater and the calamities stronger if the Sun and Saturn are in opposition to Jupiter. The natives will be wretched and poverty-stricken if the waning Moon is in opposition to Jupiter in this position by night. But if neither the Sun nor Saturn are in opposition and hold favorable locations in the chart and the waning Moon is not moving toward Jupiter, this will make skilled craftsmen. They will either be workers in gold or mosaic, silverplaters, or silversmiths. If Venus is in favorable aspect they will be sought out and praised for their skill.

24. Always look carefully at the duodecatemorion of Jupiter so that you may discover his strength from it.

## IV

## MARS

1. Mars on the ascendant in a nocturnal chart and in a masculine sign will make soldiers. In a morning rising without aspect of Jupiter he will make them dark-complexioned, rather tall, willing to give more than their income allows. They appear to be lavish and their activities are always in the public eye.

2. But if by night the ascendant is in the house of Mars and in a masculine sign and, of course, Mars is in that same sign and in conjunction with Jupiter or in favorable aspect to him, this will make leaders in war to whom the entire army is entrusted and power of life and death. At their coming states and provinces will tremble. They will be brave, serious, fortunate; their anger only evoked by great wrongs. But Mars in this house does not allow wife or children to be cherished with warm affection.

3. Mars on the ascendant by day makes men bold, clever, emotional;

wanderers, unstable in every way; never able to complete what they propose; whatever they undertake flows from their hands and their inheritance is wasted. They also lose their whole livelihood, their wives and children; nothing is saved from their paternal inheritance which they lose at an early age.

4. If Jupiter from his own house, terms, or exaltation is in trine to Mars in this house, these evils are to a certain extent alleviated. But I myself know, as I have often discovered in computing charts, that many who have Mars on the ascendant have been sent into exile but are now good and diligent government officials.

5. Mars in the second house, if by day, indicates great evils and great misfortunes, especially if he is in a morning rising. The native will be estranged from his parents and his home, always wandering in foreign countries. But if the waxing Moon is in opposition or square aspect, this will make him sluggish, weak, apt to be wounded by weapons. He will be weakened by cold or injured by animals. Some will be exposed as infants; others will be taken captive or dragged into slavery. They are always in great trouble and ferment of mind. But if Jupiter from his house or his terms is in favorable aspect, they escape all danger, are redeemed from captivity, and are brought back from slavery to freedom. But sometimes they will lack the necessities of life.

6. If Mars is found in this house by night, he makes soldiers or athletes but entraps them in constant dangers. There will be similar dangers if Jupiter and Venus, as we said above, are in favorable aspect.

7. Fame is indicated by Mars in the third house but only after the greatest toil. The native will desire the goods of others, be envious of all, and will have evil knowledge of a certain very grave crime. But if Jupiter is in the seventh or eleventh house there will be, after great suffering, a post in government service with great opportunity for income.

8. Jupiter in aspect to Mars in the third house indicates a ruling position with greatest power and honor. The native will be superior to all of his rank. If Mars in this house is in his own house, terms, or exaltation and Jupiter is in aspect, this will make men in charge of river banks, officers in charge of dredging rivers and supervising levees, generals, vicars, praetorian prefects, and often holders of "imperium."

9. Mars in the fourth house, that is, on the IMC, if by night will make soldiers. They will have difficulties and will be retained in desert regions or will be trainers or keepers in charge of wild beasts. Sometimes they will overthrow emperors or judges according to the nature of the signs; and they will waste their inheritance and possessions. Mars also indicates wounds, failures, losses by death. He allots either one son or none. The natives will be hindered in all activities.

10. Mars in this house by day weakens the whole body. He makes the natives sluggish, epileptic, liable to wounds from weapons, sickly, the type whom women always attack and who have trouble with women. Whoever

receives anything from them will always be without gratitude.

11. If the Sun is in opposition, square aspect, or conjunction with Mars in the fourth house, the evils will be greater and more frequent. The natives will be madmen if with this combination the ascendant is in the house of Mars or in the Part of Fortune[51] or the house of desire or of the Daemon.

12. Mars in the fifth house if by night, in his own house or terms or exaltation or the house or terms of Jupiter, or if Jupiter is with him or in possessions, and all manner of good fortune. Honors will be decreed by the people and friendship offered by powerful men or great administrators.

13. If the waning Moon is in favorable aspect to Mars in this position with Jupiter, this will make powerful, fearsome leaders to whom the greatest armies are entrusted, with power of life and death. But if the Moon is moving away from him and Venus is in trine aspect, the natives will be fortunate and rich, gaining glory for themselves; they are always pleasing in bodily appearance.

14. If Mars is in the fifth house by day, he will destroy inheritance, frequently change dwelling places, and always detain the native in strange regions and involve him in serious dangers. But if Jupiter or Venus are in trine or sextile aspect or in conjunction with him, the native will gain great profit from the inconveniences of his journeys and will be quickly recalled to his own land.

15. It is a combination to be feared if Mars in this house by day has the waxing Moon in opposition; for this indicates the greatest suffering and occupations which are almost like slavery. If the native appeared fortunate before, now he will always be subject to some foreign power. He will be an assistant to great judges but a victim of accusations, revolts, riots, losses, and frequent dangers; he will have weakness of some part of the body and such debility that with burning fever he will come close to insanity. Also prison, chains, arrests are indicated unless Jupiter aspects the Moon, which is in opposition to Mars or is in aspect to Mars himself, and thus alleviates these misfortunes. For whenever Jupiter is in aspect to Mars and the Moon thus located the natives are in the greatest danger. But when they are despairing of all help Jupier suddenly frees them. Mars in this house also denies offspring if the influence of Jupiter is lacking.

16. Mars in the sixth house indicates many evils. He will be harmful to children and make illnesses and many reverses in life, according to the nature of the signs. In crooked signs he makes for an early death and sometimes produces cripples or hunchbacks. In this house all kinds of afflictions are indicated if Mars is located exactly in the sign.

17. Mars in the seventh house, that is, on the descendant, indicates the greatest evils and enormous perils. He will make the natives suffer as criminals and murderers, be defendants accused as discoverers of new

crimes; or they will be torturers, executioners, or informers. If while Mars is on the descendant he aspects his own house in opposition, he will not make a violent death (for Mars never attacks his own house); but the native will be short-lived if the ascendant and the Moon are aspected by Jupiter. But if the ascendant is not in the house of Mars he makes the natives short-lived, especially if he is in aspect to the full Moon on the ascendant or the MC (that is, in square aspect or opposition).

18. Mars in the seventh house, that is, on the descendant by night or day makes for a violent death according to the nature of the signs. He indicates this evil more strongly in alien signs for then he predicts pains, lacerations of the body from a fall, or death; or he has the native thrown into prison, or condemns him to deadly misfortune.

19. In nocturnal charts Mars indicates painful fevers from all kinds of activities; often he inflicts wounds that become infected so that they have to be cauterized by a hot iron. He produces hidden pains in the body, especially if he himself is the ruler of time or if he shares the rulership of time with the full moon.

20. If, when Mars is in the seventh house, Saturn is either on the ascendant or the MC, or if the full Moon is moving toward Mars or the waning Moon to Saturn, this indicates deadly catastrophes. The native will encounter accusations, chains, prisons, condemnations on capital charges. Or he is forced to meet wild beasts, is thrown over a precipice, or severely wounded in domestic plots, or killed by bandits. Or he is drowned in a shipwreck. All these are decided by the signs. For if Mars is in an earth sign the native is forced to meet wild beasts; in fixed signs he is crushed by ruins or thrown over a precipice; in watery signs he perishes in a boat; in human signs he is killed by a sword.

21. If the Sun is in opposition to Mars[52] or in conjunction with him or is on another angle, the native will be burned alive. Thus Mars in this house destroys man in every way. Before the last day of his life the native will have activities connected either with fire, weapons, or violence of some kind, or torture or homicide. Mars in the seventh house most violently persecutes the house of wife and of children.

22. Mars in the eighth house by day either denies inheritance or strips it away in proscription. If he has the Sun and Moon in opposition he indicates blindness. Alone in this house he predicts poverty, difficulties, fevers, riots, revolutions, dangers.

23. But if the Moon is on the anafora of the ascendant, that is, in the second house from the ascendant, with Mars himself and Jupiter in no aspect to Mars or to the ascendant, this will make a violent death, but according to the quality and nature of the signs. In human signs the native is killed by a sword; captured by pirates, bandits, or domestic slaves he is struck with a sword and dies. Or he is executed by the sword after being convicted of a crime. Often the Moon, thus located without influence of Venus or Jupiter, makes gladiators who perish in a cruel death in view of

the populace. But in earth signs they die in desert places after being involved in many various dangers. In four-footed signs they will be torn apart by beasts. If Mars is in watery signs with the Moon in the second house, as we said, the native will be drowned in lakes or the sea, or killed by pirates. In fixed signs he perishes by falling off a precipice. In fiery signs he is burned up.

24. Those who have Mars in the eighth house by night will be intelligent, shrewd, and involved in dangers. They will be engaged in well-known public activities but suffer violent death, or a sudden one, such as happens to apoplectics. But if Jupiter is in aspect to Mars in this house or is together with him, these evils are to a large extent lessened.

25. If Jupiter is on the ascendant but Mars himself in the house of Jupiter, and Venus favorably aspected to Jupiter and in opposition to Mars, all these deadly calamities are to a great extent changed. For fevers, accidents, and wretched misfortunes brought about by Mars in this and other houses are always alleviated by favorable aspect of Jupiter or Venus.

26. Mars in the ninth house will be favorable in regard to life and fame. And if Jupiter is on the ascendant he makes the natives happy and has them win whatever they seek. If Mars is in the ninth house by night and Jupiter is on the ascendant, this indicates great power of administration and right of the sword, and it makes leaders of armies. Often, however, thus located he indicates difficult journeys.

27. If Mars in the ninth house is in the house of Mercury or Venus, he makes learned and famous orators. But if he is in his own house or the house of Jupiter, or his exaltation, and Jupiter is not on the ascendant, the natives will be violent toward the gods and despise all kinds of oaths. They will be feared by all demons and at their approach depraved spirits will flee. They free possessed men, not by force of words, but only by their appearance. Any violent demon, either of air or earth or from the underworld, who shakes the body of a man—at the order of that man he flees, and is terrified by his pronouncements. These men are called exorcists. The native who has Mars in the ninth house will thus easily be able to free suffering mankind from all malevolent demons.

28. Mars in the tenth house, that is, on the MC, in a nocturnal chart, if in a masculine sign, in his own house or exaltation or in the house or exaltation of Jupiter, will involve the natives in dangers and some kind of deception; nevertheless they will be generals, leaders, masters of life and death, or tribunes, feared by states and provinces.

29. But if Mars in the tenth house is on the MC by night and receives the aspect of the approaching Moon, and if Jupiter is on any angle and he himself in his own house, exaltation, or terms, this will make powerful generals, masters of the whole earth. But if there is no aspect of Jupiter and he is not found on any angle, this will nonetheless make military men, officers or tribunes, leaders of minor rank in great provinces or minor posts, holding the power of life and death.

30. But if Jupiter is on one of the angles and Saturn on another with Mars, as we said, the natives will be kings, emperors, extremely powerful and feared, involved in dangers, overturners and founders of states, but shortlived. Some perish in a bad end. They may lose their lives and position in foreign countries under an alien power.

31. But if Mars on the MC is found in a feminine sign in his own house or that of Jupiter by night, this will nevertheless make the natives highly honored. By night in a feminine or masculine sign he denies the possibility of children.

32. But if Mars is found by day in the tenth house, he will produce men who are active but hindered in all their activities. He also indicates great losses, including that of inheritance, and has the native proscribed or condemned. For some he indicates the burden of travel, on others he imposes great poverty, still others he forces to flee into exile. Some perish on the journey or in exile.

33. Mars in the eleventh house indicates many good things: increase in income and popularity with the people. Often he bestows the marks of highest office if, while he is thus located with the waning Moon, Jupiter is in trine aspect or in conjunction with them. In that case the indication is for judges with the power of life and death.

34. Great illnesses are indicated by Mars in the twelfth house. He involves the natives in wretched weakness and stirs up frequent plots among slaves. He makes the natives the type slaves wish to harm, often through inventing scandals. Sometimes the natives are in prison or suffer fevers, anxieties, losses, and perils. But all these are alleviated if Mars is found in a nocturnal chart.

35. In all charts we should hope that Venus and Jupiter should be in aspect to Mars in any way from any house. For then the attacks of Mars are weaker, mitigated by the other planets. We should also hope that Mars not hold any angle of the chart by day; for thus located by day he threatens the native in many ways. Mars, Saturn, and Jupiter by day on different angles indicate violent deaths or suicides.

36. But if Mars is on any angle by day and Venus on another, this will wear out the natives with constant illicit love affairs; it also makes them wife-murderers and suicides. But Mars and Mercury on different angles by day will produce stomach disorders and condemnations of some kind. If Mars is on one angle and the Sun on another, this will always have the native consumed by fire.

37. If the waxing Moon is in similar aspect to Mars from any angle, this will make violent deaths and destroy the mothers in a painful death. But if the Moon is not in aspect, nor any other planet, while Mars is on any angle by day, this indicates severe illnesses and disabilities. Mars always rejoices when in aspect to Venus and the waning Moon; for we have shown in the book of principles, as you may remember, that these three planets are of one condition.

38. If Mars is on any angle and Mercury on another, this indicates danger without limit. Whatever is evil in human affairs—the whole of it is predicted by the mutual aspect of these two planets. We must also remember that Mars on any angle by day denies offspring. If the house of children is in his sign and he himself on an angle, because he is the ruler of that house he will deny offspring. But if the house of children is in another's house and the ruler of that house is in opposition or square aspect to Mars, this also denies offspring.

39. If Mars is the Giver of Life by night, he indicates great length of life. If by day in a diurnal chart, he will make the natives perish in the first days of life. But if another is the Giver of Life and Mars is in opposition or square aspect to him, this diminishes the allotted life by 15 years. If the moon is located at the midpoint of Mars and Saturn, this weakens or amputates some part of the body, depending on the kind of sign the Moon is in. If Mars is in aspect to the waxing Moon in opposition or square aspect, this will make the native die at birth or be exposed.

40. In order to assess the power of Mars more accurately, carefully observe his duodecatemorion and the terms of the duodecatemorion.

# V

## THE SUN

1. The Sun on the ascendant will make trouble in regard to brothers and sisters. Located in a masculine sign in his own house or in his exaltation and in aspect to benefic planets, he indicates high office. But if malefic planets are in aspect, this to a great extent weakens the eyes. But because we have said he foretells the greatest good fortune, we must explain everything in detail.

2. Located on the ascendant by day with Saturn, the Sun will make emperors or kings. But if his strength is slightly impeded, he will make consulars, proconsulars, and regularly-elected consuls. If Mars is in aspect to or in conjunction with the Sun, this indicates generalship and imperial powers, but together with ill-will, danger, impediment, contests, and difficulties.

3. If the Sun is on the ascendant by day, Jupiter on any angle, Mars on the MC in a masculine sign, and the full Moon on any angle or on the anafora of an angle, the native, although not a lord or king, will have power throughout the whole world.

4. But if Mars is on the descendant, and the Sun and Jupiter are located as we said, and the full Moon is together with Mars on the MC or in the eighth house, this indicates a violent death for those natives who are kings or administrators or they will be captured and destroyed in an evil death according to the nature of the signs. But sometimes they will simply be deposed from their position and lose all power.

5. If Mars is not with the Moon, as we said, but is alone on an angle or on the anafora or catafora of an angle and the Sun on the ascendant, this will nonetheless make the natives who are kings and administrators captives, violently killed, or deposed with great disgrace. But also if the Sun is on the degree of the ascendant and Saturn on the MC, in a similar way this will make kings and powerful administrators.

6. If the Sun and Saturn are located as we have described, and Mars is in the second or eighth house with the full Moon on another angle or in the second or eighth house with Mars, this will make a violent death, exile, or captivity for the natives who are kings and administrators. But if the Sun is alone on the ascendant in the signs we said (it is necessary for you to remember this), Mars on the anafora of the Moon, the Moon on another angle or the anafora of an angle, this also will cause a violent death for the kings and administrators or have them deprived of their positions.

7. If Mars is not in aspect to this combination but Jupiter is either with the Sun or on any angle or on the anafora or catafora of an angle, the natives will govern the whole world, overturning and raising up states. But if Mars is in aspect to the Sun, Moon, and Jupiter, or with them or on an angle or the anafora or catafora of an angle, an evil death for the native will result. This also indicates illnesses and afflictions and types of death, but these are decided according to the parts of the body which we have said are divided among the signs.

8. If all the planets are located as we have just described and also Saturn is on the anafora or catafora of an angle, the natives will not have as much power as we said. Nevertheless they will be men of great influence: famous judges, officers, or tribunes of legions. They will be successful and feared but will not continue in their positions and powers. They will either be made captive, be driven into exile, or die a violent death.

9. In general the Sun on the ascendant will make the natives high-born and noble. If Jupiter, Venus, and Mercury are on other angles, this will make great men who inherit prosperity from their parents. From early life they will increase in possessions and prosperity so that they will always be free from poverty.

10. If Saturn is in trine or sextile aspect or in conjunction with all these planets, continual good fortune is indicated. If to this whole combination Mars is in conjunction, opposition, or square aspect, this will produce great judges holding power of life and death; but also rapacious thieves who out of greed seize the goods of others. These men, after the greatest depradation, rapine, and enormous thefts, become exiles and die a violent death.

11. If the Sun is on the ascendant by night, the native will be born into a lower class family. If Saturn or Mars is in opposition or in square aspect or in conjunction with the Sun, this destroys older brothers, but it also wastes the inheritance of the native, destroys his livelihood, and ruins all his activities. The Sun on any angle always weakens all older brothers or

makes the native the first born among all brothers.

12. The Sun in the second house will make the natives seek a livelihood through their own efforts. They will be agreeable and respectable throughout their lives. But it makes them sluggish, of small energy, and hindered in many ways. All their lives they will be anxious and fearful.

13. If Venus and Jupiter are in trine or sextile aspect or in conjunction with the Sun, this indicates sudden increase in possessions—not a small one. It will lead humble and oppressed men to high position in public life. But this occurs together with great suffering, difficulties, and voluntary loss of wealth. Therefore, whoever has the Sun thus located should never seek for anything or dare to do anything, since he knows that the Sun will impede all his activities.

14. The Sun in the third house indicates an evil death; it also makes the natives sickly, but respectable and serious in counsel. They will carry on public business, be administrators of states, or managers of the imperial treasury if Jupiter and Mercury are in favorable aspect. But they will marry and have children late in life.

15. The Sun in the third house, if in his own house or exaltation or in the house or exaltation of Venus, Jupiter, or Mercury, will make pious worshippers of the gods who on their own account dedicate images to the gods or who by order of leaders or judges take charge of the building of temples. In other signs, as we have said, the Sun makes humble servants or slaves working in temples.

16. If Saturn and Mars are in any aspect or together with the Sun, this produces treacherous perjurers, miserable because of constant accusations of this crime. They will be gluttons, frequenters of secret dens of vice, and will be free with sacrilegious words against the gods. They will be disturbed by constant burning anxieties.

17. Death for the father, ruin for the whole family, and loss of the entire inheritance is the prediction of the Sun in the fourth house if Mars and Saturn are in any aspect to him. For the native himself there will be difficulties, troubles, and reverses. But he will have a fortunate old age with the greatest prosperity. He will, however, be uncertain about the affection of his wife.

18. Those who have the Sun in the fifth house are agreeable and successful and win all their desires, largely through the help of friends. If Venus is in conjunction with the Sun[53] in this house or in sextile aspect, the native will win prizes, gain consular rank, and be honored by the people. Malefic planets together with the Sun in this house are not able to exercise their malevolence because of the natural benevolence of this house. It is, however, harmful to children. If the Sun is alone in this house, the good fortune is less and there will be harm to children and much grief over accidents and deaths of offspring.

19. Many misfortunes are indicated by the Sun in the sixth house. He will always be harmful and bring long, serious illnesses. Mars on the

ascendant indicates public office but also wounds from weapons. The father in this case will die an evil or quick death, or be condemned on some charge, and the whole inheritance be lost if there is no planet in the tenth house, that is, on the MC. If any planet is in the tenth house (the MC), this will make the natives immensely wealthy and have them succeed to the great good fortune of their fathers. But if there is no planet on the MC, and Jupiter and Venus are with the Sun in the sixth house, the evils we described above are alleviated and the misfortunes hindered.

20. The Sun in the seventh house indicates great afflictions and illnesses, especially if Mars and Saturn are with him or in any aspect. The illnesses follow the nature of the malefic planets. Mars causes fevers and fiery sicknesses, and Saturn, chills and vicious humors. If the Moon is with the Sun or on the ascendant or the MC, high position and great power are indicated, especially if she is in her own house or exaltation, or the house of Jupiter, or if the Part of Fortune is located (with most careful measurement) on any angle.

21. Jupiter on any angle together with this combination makes kings and emperors, but good and benevolent characters. They will be brave, temperate, successful: they will be leaders and governors, conquerors of provinces and states. But if in addition Mars and Saturn are in the second or the eighth house all honors, positions, and posts are lost, either through enemy tribes, personal enemies, or competitors. There is also indication of captivity, exile, or suicide.

22. Mercury together with the Sun in the seventh house or on any other angle, either in a morning or an evening rising, produces writers with great knowledge of literature. But Saturn in aspect to this combination makes evil, malicious characters and students or writers of obscure books.

23. The Sun, Saturn, and Mercury together in this house by night produce stone workers, corpse-washers, funeral organizers, or guardians of tombs.[54] Also they produce herdsmen—cowherds, shepherds, trainers of horses, swineherds, and the like—according to the nature and power of the signs. If Venus is in the seventh house with these other planets, or if she is in the sixth or the twelfth house, this makes eunuchs or shrewish women who never couple sexually with men or, if they do, do not conceive or give birth.

24. If Mars is in aspect to them in any way or with them in the seventh house, the result is hermaphrodites in whom a double nature is joined. If the Moon is with them or in any aspect, this will make castrates who amputate their virility with their own hands. It also makes pimps who hire out prostitutes for their profit.

25. All this is accomplished if no planet on the MC relieves this evil influence. If a planet is on the MC, all these misfortunes are lessened. But if Mercury is with Saturn in the second, fifth, or eleventh house, and the Sun with them, the natives are malicious in all their acts, either lawyers or

scribes learned in the law, shorthand writers, gardeners, or water commissioners.

26. If Mars is in any aspect to all these planets located as we have described, the natives will be public executioners, jailers, or prison guards, or prison officials trained to beat prisoners with whips, and similar professions.

27. None of the above happen if Jupiter and Venus are in aspect or together with the other planets in the seventh house. The influence of Venus and Jupiter will produce priests, sacrificers, those in charge of sacred rites, breeders of animals for sacrifice, or temple officials, sometimes very important ones.

28. The same predictions are in force for all these planets located together in the twelfth house. In this case the natives will be slower in temperament but will attain power and fame. All these planets indicate the same in the sixth house if there is another planet on the MC. If the Sun is found alone with Mars on any angle in the seventh house or the fifth or the eighth or the eleventh, this indicates skill connected with fire and iron or the manufacture of some hard material. The Sun and Mars together on the angles always signify manufacturers of this kind.

29. The father will die early if the Sun is in the eighth house. Mars or Saturn together with him or in opposition or square aspect makes the natives hostile, raving, delirious, or suffering from stomach disorders. These weaknesses follow the nature of the signs.

30. Serious illnesses and weaknesses are also predicted if the full Moon, Mars, and Saturn are in opposition to the Sun in the eighth house or together with him. The head is burdened with malevolent humors and with persistent conditions arising from humors; epilepsy and madness follow. Or the natives have lapses of memory and are confused in speech. They may suffer from spotted leprosy, impetigo, consumption, dropsy, or elephantiasis. Some will be cripples, hunchbacks, paralytics, or have important parts of the body amputated. These afflictions are determined according to the nature of the signs. This combination of planets has the same effect in the second, sixth, eighth, or twelfth houses.

31. All these afflictions have the possibility of cure if Jupiter and Venus are in any aspect, especially trine, or are in conjunction or are in aspect to the Moon. If, however, a malefic planet comes into aspect with the Moon moving toward him, the illnesses will be lifelong. The only recourse then is the help of some divinity.

32. Mercury in sextile aspect or together with these planets in the eighth house cures the illnesses with medicine or incantations, especially if the waxing Moon is in aspect to Jupiter or waning to Venus. But if the Moon is with Mercury and benefic planets are in trine or sextile aspect, the natives flee to the gods and remain there demanding remedy. But if Jupiter and Venus are in dejected houses (with the combination we described above), the natives will be madmen possessed by demons and

involved in such constant calamities that they perish in a violent death.

33. Natives who have the Sun in the ninth house make images of the gods or worship divine images; or they decorate the gods, design their temples or write hymns and praises of the gods. They make ostentatious display of holy songs and gain fame and honor from this activity. The father will be fortunate, but both the native and his father will have many changes in life. If a benefic planet is on the anafora of the MC the good fortune will be derived from journeys. If a malefic planet, however, is on the MC there will be many difficulties on the journeys, ending in a painful death.

34. The Sun in the tenth house, in his house or the house of Jupiter in a diurnal chart, or in his exaltation, makes kings, generals, governors, consuls or proconsuls—all of whom inherit their position from their father.

35. These positions are achieved only after struggles, dangers, or ill-will if Mars is on any angle. If Mars is on the descendant in aspect to the full Moon on any angle, the native, whether king, general, consul, proconsul, or governor, will be an exile and a captive.

36. The captives and exiles will die a violent death if Mars is in the second or eighth house and the full Moon in opposition, square aspect, or conjunction with him. On the other hand, the power of these kings and generals will be extended throughout the world if Mars is not in the house we mentioned, but Jupiter is on one of the angles or the catafora of an angle, and the full Moon is on another angle in aspect to Jupiter.

37. In general the Sun on the MC makes the parent of high rank and honorable, especially if a benefic planet is in aspect. The aspect of malefic planets diminishes this prediction. Also in general the Sun on any angle with Mercury will produce literary men educated in various kinds of letters, carrying on different kinds of literary activities. If Jupiter is in aspect, they will become teachers of kings because of their literary talents. Mercury will accomplish this even if he is far from the Sun, as long as Mercury and Saturn are not in aspect and Venus and Jupiter are favorable.

38. When the Sun is in the eleventh house, the natives and their fathers are fortunate and hold high position; their prosperity increases over time. The good fortune is even greater if Jupiter is with the Sun or in trine aspect to him or Venus is with the Sun as a morning star or in sextile aspect as an evening star; for all these honors are obtained through the goodwill of friends. If malefic planets are with the Sun or in aspect to him, they do not affect the high position but are constantly harmful to the house of children.

39. Slavery, captivity, early death of the father, and total loss of inheritance can be expected from the Sun in the twelfth house; also afflictions and serious illnesses. If a benefic planet is found with the Sun, this will nevertheless make for great loss of status. If a malefic planet is

with the Sun, illnesses and afflictions are indicated, and perpetual slavery.

40. Look carefully at the duodecatemorion of the Sun and its terms so that the teaching of this book may not lead you into any error.

## VI

## VENUS

1. Venus on the ascendant by night will make men of divine intelligence, friends of emperors and powerful men, entrusted with the management of their affairs. They will be important and respectable orators according to the nature and quality of the signs. Venus in human signs will make the natives chief priests, robed in purple and gold, able to foretell the future. They will be handsome and charming if no malefic planet is in aspect.

2. If Mercury is in aspect to Venus or in conjunction with her, the indication is for crowns or wreaths as prizes in contests; the natives will be musicians, widely acclaimed.

3. Venus in fixed signs or those with small voice[55] in a nocturnal chart will make devoted friends of emperors, who make and invent things that please royalty; they cater to royal luxury and receive great riches from these occupations. In earth or watery signs she makes manufacturers of perfumes, weavers of magnificent textiles, or successful dyers. In four-footed signs the natives are animal lovers in charge of the king's herds; they are also well-born, famous, and of good character.

4. Venus on the ascendant by day makes the natives oversexed, unchaste, of ill repute. They will be linen weavers, embroiderers, or artists in paints, dyers, innkeepers, or tavern-keepers. Saturn in aspect to Venus in any way will make the natives effeminate, homosexuals, or engaged in sedentary activities. Venus on the ascendant promises a wife at an early age. Saturn, however, in strong aspect produces castrates, or weavers, or inventive workers in colors. Jupiter in favorable aspect will make them managers of royal weaving.

5. Natives who have Venus in the second house in a nocturnal chart will be designers of important crafts. They will become very wealthy but over a period of time; be charming, agreeable in love affairs, but often victims of scandal.

6. Those who have Venus in this house by day will have great reverses of fortune and also late marriages; they will have law suits over another woman. Some will be several times widowed. If the Sun or Saturn are in opposition, square aspect, or conjunction with Venus the natives will be sterile, never successful in sexual activity, will never marry, and always be lovers of boys. The misfortunes are less if Venus is in the house or terms of Saturn, Mars, or Mercury.

7. Venus in the third house is favorable if Jupiter is in any aspect. She predicts a wife from a temple, a priestess or the daughter of a priest. If

Mercury is with Venus the natives themselves will be prophets, temple attendants, or in charge of rituals.

8. Those who have Venus in the fourth house suffer destruction of inheritance, frequent loss of wives by death, and only with difficulty achieve their goals. Mercury in aspect makes adulterers and also has the natives proscribed for maladministration, public or private.

9. By night in this house Venus brings public approbation over a period of time and friendships with great men. The natives will be handsome, charming, lacking nothing, even in youth. But they will suffer from some kind of mental or emotional affliction according to the nature of the signs. In tropical or double signs they will suffer from death of wives, court sentences, law suits brought by women or over women. In fixed signs the wives are agreeable, are greatly loved by their husbands, and bring great fame and possessions, except for the sign of Aquarius. For, if Venus is found in this sign in the fourth house, with the Moon either in opposition or square aspect or conjunction with her, the natives will be sterile, not able to engender children, never enjoy conjugal life, and always prefer intercourse with boys.

10. Those who have Venus in the fifth house are honorable, benevolent, and easily attain their goals. They are crowned with wreaths as prize winners. Jupiter in any aspect makes them famous and ennobled. Mercury in conjunction with Venus provides promotions in life but with much ill fame. The natives will be victors in all contests and win prizes, be powerful in all their activities, and know how to foretell the future. They will be familiars of famous men; gain great possessions from wives or other women, or advance in their position through the patronage of women. In the course of time everything will turn out well for them.

11. If the waxing Moon is in aspect they will achieve fame and high position, but at the expense of ill-will. They will be responsible men never accused of lying. They will not be willing to give or take an oath in a case which is obviously true. But Venus together with the Moon causes suspicions, quarrels, or conflicts with wives.

12. Venus in the sixth house, by day or night, if there is no planet on the MC, indicates wives who are low-born: widows, sickly, and not agreeable to men. If a woman has Venus in this house she will suffer great difficulty and danger in childbirth. She will frequently abort or have the foetus lacerated in her womb and brought forth by physicians.

13. If another planet is on the MC in a nocturnal chart, the natives will be charming and well-mannered. Women will always be agreeable to them and bring them good fortune. They easily attain their goals. But if Venus is alien to the angles, and malefic planets are in strong aspect to the Moon located on the angles, the native will be exposed by parents or die immediately after birth.

14. If Venus in the seventh house is in her own house by night, she predicts a happy old age, but a late marriage and children only with

difficulty. Great scandal over love affairs is indicated according to the nature of the signs. If she is in tropical, scaly, or mutable signs, and Mars is with her or in opposition or square aspect, the natives are oversexed, impure, and of ill repute.

15. If Saturn is in opposition, in square aspect, or conjunction with Venus, located as we have said with Mars, women who have this combination make love unchastely to other women. These vices will be stronger if this combination occurs in Capricorn or Aries.

16. Venus in the eighth house by day provides a wife late in life, one who is either low-class, a widow, sterile, or deformed with unusual ugliness. If Mercury is with Venus and a malefic planet in opposition, square aspect, or conjunction, inheritance is wasted or stripped by proscription. Death will come to the native through gonorrhoea, that is, a seminal flux, or from contractions, spasms, or apoplexy. But if Venus is found in this house by night, she indicates riches and good fortune through the death of women. Death for the native is quick and without any suffering.

17. Constant attacks by some demon are indicated by Venus in the ninth house. The natives go around sordid and unkempt or stay in temples prophesying, claiming that they are announcing the will of the gods. Often they are interpreters of dreams. These effects are stronger if Saturn is in aspect.

18. In this house by night Venus makes holy men, worshippers of the gods, involved in sacred rites. Some have duties in and around temples. But if Mars and Saturn are in opposition, square aspect, or conjunction great misfortunes through women are indicated. Women are always displeasing to the native, especially if this combination is found in tropical signs.

19. If Jupiter is in trine or sextile aspect or conjunction with Venus, the natives will be loved by women. They will be handsome, charming, easily attain their goals, and dominate their wives. Some are guardians or administrators for women. Others have posts in palaces or houses of the powerful, making things which are useful for the care of women: from this they receive advancement and great increase in income.

20. But if Mars is in opposition or square aspect to Venus in this house, especially if he is on one of the angles, the natives will have enemies and see the sad deaths of children. They will be enemies to their children because of adultery or impure sexual behavior. If Jupiter is in square aspect or conjunction with Venus and Mercury, or if Saturn is in opposition, or if Saturn, Venus, and Mercury are together in this house, the natives will be sterile, lovers of boys, and for this vice involved in homicides or other dangerous crimes. If a woman has this combination she will always imitate the behavior of men.

21. Venus in the tenth house, that is, on the MC, predicts great fame, good fortune, and prizes of wreaths. In this house with Mercury she will

make the natives clever, inventors of theories, easily attaining their wishes. If Saturn and Mars are in no kind of aspect but she herself is a morning star, this results in public musicians honored by the populace. But if Saturn is in any kind of aspect, they will have a bad reputation and never achieve first rank in the skills from which they make a living, but always be in second place. They entrust their affairs to the care of strangers. Mars strongly aspected to Venus in this house or in conjunction with her makes well-known cases of scandal.

22. A woman with Venus in this house will be oversexed, addicted to all kinds of pleasure—a prostitute who sets herself up in business or lets herself out to a pimp. But all these things are accomplished according to the nature and quality of the signs. In mutable, tropical, or scaly signs, or in the house of Saturn, the native will have a bad reputation forever and will commit unnatural acts in a variety of ways. But if Venus in this house is in a feminine sign and the waxing Moon, also in a feminine sign, is in aspect to Mars, this will make eunuchs, castrates, or hermaphrodites who do what women are accustomed to do when driven by extraordinary lust.

23. Venus in the eleventh house, if she is an evening star and aspected in any way to Mars and Saturn, will make the natives sterile, unable to engender children; only with difficulty will they attain the state of matrimony. Venus often makes them lovers of boys or of women from the stage; or they become managers of houses of prostitution, especially if she is in tropical signs. As to their income, it will grow step by step, and advancement will come through the protection of friends. They will be handsome and agreeable. If Venus receives the influence of the approaching Moon, this will make the natives affluent and extremely powerful, destined for great fame and entrusted with great powers. Sometimes they will become one of the first ten men of noble states.

24. But if Venus is a morning star while in this house and in the same way receives the influence of the Moon, she will make the natives powerful at an early age and men to whom great power is entrusted, so that by their merits they become friends of great men and emperors. To the last day of their lives they will have grace and beauty. These effects will be more definite if Mercury is in any aspect to the Moon and Venus or if he is found with them in the same house.

25. The native with Venus in the twelfth house will be tormented with constant pain and grief for the sake of women. If Mars and Mercury are in strong aspect, they will have trouble with slave women over sexual problems. Venus overheats the mind and incites base loves. Some natives join themselves to slave women in marriage, others associate with prostitutes on their own marriage couch and for this reason are denied offspring.

26. Venus in this house by day indicates destruction and dreadful death because of women, according to the nature and quality of the signs. For she has diverse powers of prediction which are difficult to discover. Just as

a creative artist portrays the outline of the limbs with the mixture of his colors, and with his blended paints brings out the definite shape of the body, so the combined influence of the planets and their mutual effect on each other depict the fates of men.

27. Logic proves that what we have said is true. For when Venus is located as we have described, and if Saturn is in any aspect, this produces minds involved in perverse vices, not successful in any normal human activities, especially if the combination of Venus and Saturn is found in a nocturnal chart. But if Venus in this house is aspected to Jupiter, the native is freed from the evil described above. For then he attains an increase of income through his own efforts and is free from taint of vice, if, however, the Moon is not in opposition.

28. But if the Moon *is* in opposition the natives will be objects of serious scandal as lover of boys or for being overly promiscuous in pursuit of women. That combination indicates incest and debauchery. They are forced to intercourse with sisters, stepmother, daughters, or daughters-in-law. Nevertheless from that incest great profit accrues to them and some advancement in position.

29. Venus, in conjunction with or in square aspect to the Moon, always indicates illicit loves or scandal with consequent ill fortune. This combination makes the natives monsters of impure desires or objects of scandal for incestuous relations. Either, as we said above, they have sexual relations with their own sisters or, if with non-relatives, with two sisters together; or with daughters or mothers, daughters-in-law or the wives of stepsons, or with children or relatives of sisters.

30. A woman who has Venus in this combination will be involved in promiscuous sexual pleasures, an object of scandal and accused of incest. For she has intercourse either with brothers, sons, parents, nephews, sons-in-law, uncles, maternal or paternal; or she will call two brothers to her bed. Some women seek to imitate masculine behavior.

31. This effect will be stronger if Venus and the Moon are in tropical, mutable, scaly, or double signs and still more violent if Mars or Saturn are in opposition or square aspect, or together with Venus and the Moon; or if the Moon and Venus are found in the house of Saturn or Mars or in the signs of Mercury, or if one is located in the sign of Mercury and the other in aspect as we have described.

32. Good fortune is indicated by Venus as an evening star in a favorable sign, in a nocturnal chart, if she is in favorable aspect to Mars. She bestows fame, power, and great riches in this position. But many great evils are predicted if she is in any aspect to Mars by day. For Venus rejoices by night if she is in aspect to the Moon, Mars, and Mercury; then as long as she is in a nocturnal chart with favorable aspect, she predicts the greatest good fortune.

33. All right-thinking astrologers believe that Venus with the Sun in the twelfth house is very unjust. She always makes bad predictions when

associated with the Sun. She does not rejoice when with the light of the Sun; whatever appears evil and wretched in human affairs, this Venus indicates when she is with the Sun. But she rejoices when she is behind the Sun in a morning rising. Then whatever good fortune she has predicted from favorable position is now increased.

34. But if she is the ruler of the ascendant and the ruler of the whole chart and also the Giver of Life, located in good signs and favorable houses, she bestows a very long life. But if the ruler of the chart or of the ascendant or the Giver of Life is another planet and opposed to her, from the allotted time of life she subtracts eight years. In this situation she indicates vices but not tainted with serious scandal.

35. Also in the case of Venus, look for the duodecatemorion and its terms so that you may discover in every way the secrets of the chart.

## VII

### MERCURY

1. Mercury located exactly on the ascendant in signs in which he rejoices, in a daytime chart, makes philosophers, teachers of the art of letters, or geometers: often he makes those who measure heavenly phenomena or study them so that they can contemplate the presence of the gods, or men skilled in sacred writings. Often he makes orators and lawyers, especially if in this house he is in his own sign or in other voiced signs.

2. If either the Sun, Saturn, or Jupiter are in aspect to Mercury in this house, he will make great men crowned with wreaths for being famous in sacred matters. He also makes men to whom the most important business of emperors is entrusted. But if Mars is in opposition or square aspect or together with Mercury on the ascendant, the native is attacked by a variety of continual evils. These evils cannot be identified or defined. If Mars is in trine aspect to Mercury in this house, this involves the natives in reputable and prosperous professions.

3. Mercury on the ascendant in a nocturnal chart makes men of divine sensibilities, easily attaining their wishes. They are sober and respectable in character, in charge of such activities as farming, construction, tax collecting, money-changing, or lending at interest. In this house by night Mercury also makes them interpreters of emperors or powerful judges. But all these are indicated according to the different qualities of the signs.

4. Mercury in the second house in a morning rising makes the natives of humble class, of criminal disposition, with no knowledge of letters, destitute of all means of livelihood. But if Mercury is an evening star and in a nocturnal chart, he will make money-lenders or managers of others' money. In a diurnal chart he makes students of language skilled in

difficult writings, unwilling to compare their own nature with that of other men. For they are fond of all things which have not been handed down by tradition. They are wretched in life and always wear themselves out with various troubles.

5. If Jupiter is in any aspect or conjunction to Mercury in this house and the Moon in favorable aspect, the natives will be great and famous but always subordinate to others, never attaining the first place. Nevertheless they will be in charge of great undertakings and have at their disposal royal facilities, will be managers of royal treasures and journeys. But all this good fortune is finished in a short space of time.

6. Mercury in the third house will make priests, magicians, healers, astrologers, men who through their own efforts discover things not handed down by tradition. They are intelligent, fortunate, easily taking part in any kind of activities. If Jupiter is in trine or sextile aspect, or together with Mercury, this indicates high intelligence and great and divine counsel. Mars in any aspect to Mercury and Jupiter in this position will make agents of kings, famous leaders, powerful administrators, to whom the royal income is entrusted. They will overcome all obstacles with their courage and good fortune.

7. Natives who have Mercury in the fourth house (the IMC) are sharp of mind, in charge of public activities, erudite in many kinds of learning. If Mercury is in a morning rising they will be teachers of certain secret arts. But if Mars and Saturn hold other angles, that is, in opposition or square aspect to Mercury, this produces indictments, condemnations, and prison terms. But if Mercury is in an evening rising this will make goldsmiths or gold miners, teachers of certain secret arts, or those who appear learned in computing and calculating: or they will be in charge of wrestling schools.

8. Mercury in the fifth house makes misers of gold or other money who through their own foresight make great use of their resources or those of others. They will be in charge of great riches. They seem to be of good and divine character. Great length of life is also predicted and many children.

9. But Mercury in an evening rising in this house will not allow money to be saved in any way. Whatever gold, silver, or other property was entrusted will be dissipated in profuse outpourings. The natives are in some kind of administrative post, or, in accordance with the signs, teachers, geometers, or astronomers who measure the stars. They may also be managers of wrestling schools or leaders of wrestlers.

10. If Mercury in this house comes into aspect with the waxing Moon, the man's whole body will be marked with white spots or he will be involved in afflictions and illnesses according to the nature and quality of the signs. The waning Moon with Mercury in this house indicates the most disgraceful sicknesses and will often make the native turn away from the right path of life in monstrous attacks of madness.

11. Mercury in the sixth house will pile up the greatest prosperity for the native either from his facility in speech or from law or business or as a gift of the gods, especially if another planet is found in the tenth house while Mercury is in the sixth.

12. Mercury in a morning rising, in a nocturnal chart, in the sixth house makes interpreters, fishermen, bird catchers, or sculptors, if another planet is in the tenth. If there is no planet in the tenth house the natives will be malicious authors of evil counsel, thieves who enviously desire others' goods and who rejoice at the accidents of others; informers who persecute their relatives and neighbors with bitter hatred; sluggish and mentally short-sighted men displaying all kinds of malevolence.

13. But if Mercury is in an evening rising in this house he will make the natives intelligent, sober, secretive; in charge of such activities as money-changing, granaries, storehouses, or construction, and from these professions they will gain much profit. If Mercury receives the influence of the Moon moving toward him, he will make scribes of judges or of high officials or of the Senate, or (men) who are made teachers by the emperor or are ordered to manage at their own discretion the affairs of their superiors. This is especially true if the Moon or some other planet is in the tenth house.

14. Those who have Mercury in the seventh house, that is, on the descendant, in a diurnal chart are always burning with sexual desires and are involved in serious vices. They will be the lovers either of boys or young girls. They are allotted debased women for wives and often undertake the care and guardianship of men of ill repute. But this is in accordance with the nature of the signs. For Mercury in this house in signs in which he does not rejoice—that is, in the signs of Mars or Saturn or in others in which he is humiliated—will make pimps and whoremasters, soiled by the scandal of that ill fame. If Mercury is with Mars or if Mars is in opposition or on the MC in this house a short life is predicted. The natives will be consumptives, fugitives, exiles, or condemned prisoners.

15. Mercury by night in the seventh house makes caretakers for rich women, who attain the greatest good fortune through love affairs. They are also discoverers in mathematics or music or in different kinds of writing or obscure languages. I have personal knowledge that Mercury in this house has often produced jugglers.

16. Mercury in the eighth house in an evening rising by day makes the natives sluggish, never wishing or daring to do anything, always hindered in difficult undertakings, stupidly malicious and never successful. If Mercury in this house is in the sign or terms of Saturn, he makes the natives deaf; especially if he is also aspected to Saturn in some way.

17. But in an evening rising in this house by night, the natives will inherit a stranger's property or find hidden treasure. They will be lucky but weak in body and worn out with long-continued illnesses. In a morning rising in this house he predicts an indefinite increase in

possessions and the greatest enterprises. Some are faithful and dependable guardians of various activities or constructions or inheritors of another's wealth.

18. Those who have Mercury in the ninth house without influence of another planet are quarrelsome, contentious arguers, claiming that they themselves know whatever is suggested to them, malevolent, and never able to finish anything carefully.

19. Mercury in this house in a morning rising makes priests, *haruspices,* augurs, astrologers, astronomers, physicians, and such as gain their livelihood from that kind of skill. These predictions are stronger if Mercury is protected by a benefic planet. For then he makes the natives lucky, with great powers and all good fortune. But if malefic planets are in unfavorable aspect the natives will be impious, irreligious, spoilers of temples, indicted and condemned; always in flight in alien lands or oppressed by sentence of exile.

20. Mercury in this house in an evening rising will make priests, magicians, physicians, craftsmen of such talent that they gain their livelihood from these skills and learn through their own efforts whatever is not handed down to them by tradition.

21. Natives who have Mercury in the tenth house in a morning rising are admirable and famous in all activities. If Jupiter is in trine or sextile aspect in a diurnal chart, they will be given great powers, handling the business of great states or of emperors or powerful men—faithful, benevolent, wise, sober. Venus in aspect to Mercury in this house in a nocturnal chart will have the same effect as Jupiter in a diurnal chart. But if Mars is in opposition or in square aspect, the natives are persecuted, going and coming, by various difficulties. Because of this they will often be exiles or sentenced in some other way. The Moon in any aspect to Mars will produce violent death.

22. Mercury in an evening rising in the tenth house will make travelers who constantly change their place of abode and will also involve them in public business. Watery activities are indicated if Saturn is in opposition or in square aspect from any degree. Then duties will be either near rivers, lakes, or the sea. Illnesses and weaknesses from abundance of fluids is also predicted.

23. Mercury in the eleventh house will make the natives intelligent and effective in all kinds of professions, men to whom important enterprises are entrusted. Higher positions are indicated if Jupiter is in favorable aspect to Mercury.

24. Mercury in the twelfth house will make the natives intelligent. In a morning rising he involves them in important affairs or makes them administrators of public business so that even if others are endangered by these affairs they themselves will have a prosperous outcome. In an evening rising Mercury in this house will make the natives stir up or discover important enterprises. Wise men, not without reason, have

noted this house and have made it the house of child-bearing.

25. The sixth house is compared to the twelfth so that all planets in these houses have sluggish action. But Mercury in this house will make learned men of letters, orators, geometers, teachers. They constantly sell their orations or defenses or come to the aid of men in trouble with the protection of their oratory and free them from danger. They seem to be more intelligent than all others and have great learning. This happens only when Jupiter is in aspect, or Mercury is not attacked by malefic planets.

26. If Mars is in opposition or square aspect or in conjunction, this will make informers, misers, and malicious tricksters, also malevolent poisoners. Through these activities they incur serious charges. Or they will be condemned as forgers. For they falsify records of public deeds and for this are condemned to death. There is also danger through slaves or because of slaves.

27. The waxing Moon in aspect to Mercury and Mars in this house will produce violent death, but by sentence of the court. If the Sun is found with them without aspect of Jupiter the native will be burned with flames. But all these things are indicated according to the nature of the signs.

28. But since we have said that Mercury joins himself easily to other planets and indicates good with good planets and evil with evil, we must explain what he indicates with individual planets. He indicates greatest good fortune, for instance, if with Jupiter and the Sun in favorable houses, but direst calamities if found with Mars by day. By night the situation is reversed. He is favorable with Venus, the Moon, and Mars, but with the Sun he indicates the grestest evil and misfortune. To show this more clearly we must explain every detail. But first look carefully at the duodecatemorion of Mercury and the terms of the duodecatemorion so that you may find the secrets of the chart.

## VIII

### MERCURY AND THE SUN

1. Mercury together with the Sun on the ascendant by day will make powerful kings and leaders; but if found together in this house by night they make the fathers of low class and low occupation. The natives will work for the government but in obscure and wretched jobs according to the nature and quality of the signs.

2. Mercury with the Sun in the second house indicates an increase in possessions and control of some kind of activities.

3. In the third house they produce *haruspices,* dream interpreters, physicians, priests, augurs, astronomers, astrologers; those who predict the future and whose skill and training are well-known.

4. In the fourth house, that is, on the IMC, Mercury with the Sun

makes the natives of low class, skilled in secret and illegal arts but sober and honest. If they are together in this house one must especially investigate what sign they are in and who is the ruler of the sign. For Mercury is particularly dangerous in this house if it is the house of Saturn.

5. Natives who have Mercury with the Sun in the fifth house will be high-born and accomplish everything easily. But they are involved in dangers, do not have continual good fortune, and easily deceive others.

6. Mercury with the Sun in the sixth house makes the natives low-born or slaves, sluggish, involved in troubles; their fathers are unknown or they are orphans. If no other planet is found in the tenth house, they never accomplish anything. But if another planet is found, they attain riches, high position, and fame, especially if a benefic planet is in the tenth house.

7. Mercury with the Sun by day in the seventh house will entrust the natives with power and great affairs, but they will perish by a violent death. If found thus by night the natives will suffer many evils, laboring and seeking daily bread by low-class occupations. Their skills will be sordid or filthy or of a dreadful odor or requiring constant wakefulness, such as the occupations of tanners, leather makers, fullers, wool workers, millers, cooks, and the like. The natives themselves will have stomach diseases or other illnesses at an early age.

8. Those who have Mercury with the Sun in the eighth house will be sickly, easily cheated, often mad, and suffer violent death.

9. Mercury with the Sun in the ninth house will make exorcists whose arts free men suffering from possession of demons. They attain great profit from those skills.

10. If Mercury is together with the Sun in the tenth house, that is, on the MC, if in a sign in which he rejoices or in his exaltation by day he will make the natives masters of the whole earth, or by their own merits put in charge of many of the greatest and most powerful provinces, especially if Jupiter is in favorable aspect.

11. An increase in good fortune over a period of time is indicated by Mercury with the Sun in the eleventh house.

12. Mercury with the Sun in the twelfth house will make paupers or wretched slaves. They always perish on a journey.

## IX

## SATURN AND MERCURY

1. Those who have Mercury and Saturn together on the ascendant in a diurnal chart will be misers, lawyers, men skilled in the law, or scribes; but they will be sluggish and quickly fail. If the chart is nocturnal the natives will be captives or handed over to be slaves of powerful men. If Saturn and Mercury are in a feminine sign they will make eunuchs, impotent men, base, degenerate, disreputable, immodest male prostitutes.

2. Saturn with Mercury in the second house in a diurnal chart will make botanists or physicians who bring health to mankind. They will be rich and famous from their activities. Often, according to the quality of the signs, they will be orators or agents of powerful Men. If it is a nocturnal chart they will be madmen, naked beggars, or temple slaves. Often they will be accused and taken into custody. They are frequently in mourning, lacking children, afflicted in some part of the body.

3. Mercury together with Saturn in the third house will make divers who raise water from wells, gardeners, managers of small estates; corpse-washers, funeral managers, watchers of dead bodies, or door-keepers of tombs.

4. In the fourth house these two will produce students or teachers of secret or illegal skills, but wicked, who seek their daily bread from evil arts. Some will be condemned or in prison. All these predictions vary according to the signs and the positions of other planets.

5. Frequent change of dwelling is indicated by Mercury with Saturn in the fifth house. Natives will be in charge of grain markets or storage of grain and other such places or in charge of pearls, perfumes, or metals. They may also be sculptors of sacred images.

6. Mercury and Saturn in the sixth house make the same prediction. If Mercury and Saturn are found by day in this house, the natives will be knowledgeable in many skills. They wish to know everything which pertains to human affairs; are truly malevolent and envious, and are involved in afflictions and illness. Mercury and Saturn by night in the sixth or twelfth houses will make authors of false writings, criminal, malevolent, poisoners. They are always in great trouble and great evil. If it is a diurnal chart, if Mars is in square aspect or opposition, they will be involved in unescapable evil and punished by public death.

7. Those who have Mercury and Saturn together in the seventh house, that is, on the descendant, will inherit from women and be great lovers of women. They will be burning with desire for great enterprises. But if the two planets are found in this house by night, the natives will be miserable in all life experiences, owing enormous debts, also weak and afflicted with illnesses. They will be malicious; some will be accused and taken into custody.

8. Mercury with Saturn in the eighth house predicts an increase in possessions and position over a period of time. Some inherit after the death of a stranger. But they will suffer from bladder stones or illness of the stomach. Saturn and Mercury in this house by night make the natives sluggish and wrinkled; also paupers or proscripts. They will die by sentence of the court if the waning Moon is moving toward Saturn or the full Moon toward Mars.

9. Prophets, dressers of holy statues, or carriers in divine ceremonies are indicated by Mercury with Saturn in the ninth house.

10. Mercury with Saturn in the tenth house, that is, the MC, will make

inheritors of a stranger's money or important inventors. Sometimes they will be scribes or agents of powerful men. If a benefic planet is in aspect they will be orators of divine talent, teachers of the art of oratory or men of letters employed by some great power; or they will be masters of the census or students of the heavens. Some keep records; others are teachers or students of obscure languages.

11. Mercury with Saturn in the eleventh house means the same as in the fifth.

12. Mercury and Saturn in the twelfth house mean the same as in the sixth.

# X

## MERCURY AND JUPITER

1. Mercury together with Jupiter on the ascendant in a diurnal chart will make the natives famous and glorious, in charge of states or the first ten in great states; or they will be judges who restore the law to provinces and states and who always delight in just processes of law. In this house by night they make overseers or managers of business, sometimes scribes of powerful men, or keepers of records, accounts, storehouses. They will be clever and talented and achieve the greatest good fortune because of their keen intellect.

2. Mercury and Jupiter together in the second house in a diurnal chart will make heirs of a stranger's money or children adopted by strangers. They will be managers of many institutions and stored goods and in the course of time achieve great increase in possessions. In a night chart the natives will be somewhat stupid, not enjoying constant good fortune, and frequently deceived in the course of life.

3. Those who have Mercury and Jupiter together in the third house will be successful and renowned magicians; hymnwriters, or carriers for the gods or guardians of temples, or those who initiate men into cults or managers of sacred contests; diviners who predict the future by messages from the gods. These same predictions are made by Jupiter and Mercury together in the eleventh house.

4. Those who have Mercury and Jupiter together in the fourth house make discoveries in mathematics or in machines. They also undertake the care and guardianship of children or women. Some discover something by chance; others find their way to hidden treasure and from this gain great happiness.

5. Jupiter and Mercury together in the fifth house, both by day and by night, indicate the same thing in a similar way. High position and many powers are predicted for the native in the course of time. They will be successful in all their activities and easily attain their goals. The same is predicted by the two planets together in the eleventh house.

6. Jupiter and Mercury together in the sixth house by day and night

indicate the same things in the same way if they are in a morning rising. They make the natives sensible men, successful in business affairs. They will be in charge of law suits, business affairs, certain contests, or religious rites. In the last case they will find great opportunities in the revenues of the gods, especially if some other planet is located in the tenth house while Jupiter and Mercury are in the sixth.

7. But if the Moon is moving in such a way that she comes into aspect with these two planets when she is in the tenth house, the natives will be affluent, controllers of much money, and receive high interest from their holdings. They will be fortunate and happy; have the affairs of kings under their control; be managers of the royal treasury or the privy purse, or in charge of provinces or states.

8. If no planet is found in the tenth while Mercury and Jupiter are in the sixth, the natives will be mediocre in life, inheritance, and profession. But if it is a nocturnal chart they will be interpreters, fishermen, augurs, or sculptors. Or they will be weighed down with laborious tasks and servile occupations or involved in squalid or odorous crafts such as that of fullers, leather workers, shoemakers, millers, wool-workers, and the like.

9. Mercury together with Jupiter in the seventh house, that is, the descendant, by night and day indicate the same things. Great good fortune in this case comes from women. The natives are in charge of public works, or chiefs of states or tribes, or the first ten in states. They have a long life and a happy old age, are of good counsel and habits, and always desire useful things. But these predictions are diminished in a nocturnal chart if Saturn is in square aspect, opposition, or conjunction with Mercury and Jupiter in this house.

10. A mediocre life is indicated for those who have Mercury with Jupiter in the eighth house by day. A livelihood is derived from some kind of discoveries. Some natives are of ill repute in youth but in the course of time receive a moderate increase in income. With Mercury and Jupiter in this house by night they either discover something from which they make great profit or inherit a large income. In the course of time they achieve the greatest good fortune. Nevertheless they are sluggish and weak in body.

11. Mercury and Jupiter together in the ninth house mean the same as they did in the third house.

12. Mercury with Jupiter in the tenth house indicates great activities and great powers according to the computations of the chart.

13. Mercury with Jupiter in the eleventh house mean the same as they did in the fifth house.

14. Mercury with Jupiter in the twelfth house, if in a morning rising, will make scribes of kings or of the Senate, or secretaries chosen by princes to be caretakers of great states. But they often offend someone and in later life meet with misfortune or, if it is a nocturnal chart, with a violent death. In a diurnal chart they continue in their positions and duties and

do not often act offensively. Mercury as an evening star in this house with Jupiter makes the activities more sluggish and indicates misfortune. Some natives are engaged in laborious tasks for the government.

## XI

## MERCURY AND MARS

1. If Mercury and Mars are found together on the degree of the ascendant in a diurnal chart, they will make the natives spit up blood or suffer from stomach trouble. They are short-lived and unlucky. They will be condemned either from some experience with women or from illicit loves or secret writings or forgery. This may lead to a violent death.

2. Together on the ascendant by night these two planets make men in charge of great religions, generals, heralds, or guards, and followers of emperors; or great administrators to whom the outcome of battles brings great good fortune. By night if Saturn is in opposition or square aspect they are involved in dangers and are often cheated. They are hindered in all their activities, for Saturn in this position makes men inert, without skills, weighed down by every burden of misfortune.

3. Mercury and Mars in the second house in a diurnal chart will make the natives exposed,[56] or, if they are nursed, makes them fugitives in some way; they will frequently be exiles, sometimes captives, and often stripped of possessions by proscription. Some are involved in serious illnesses or afflictions. Others die a violent death if Mercury and Mars are in aspect to the full Moon. But if the planets are found in this house by night, the natives are timid, malicious, obscure, of evil mind, not bold, easily cheated in all their dealings. But their occupations are varied. They will be either publicans, tax collectors, or spies. Some become insane.

4. Those who have Mercury with Mars in the third house make their living from fire or occupations concerned with iron. They will be able to predict the future, spend much time in temples. But they are fearsome to others in everything they do, even if they know nothing and do nothing. In the course of time their fortune increases.

5. Mercury with Mars in the fourth house, that is, on the IMC, will make the natives sluggish and humble in all occupations and fortune. They are involved in constant hostilities either with parents or relatives, or make great plots against their relatives. They will be professional witnesses and from this occupation will incur many dangers and finally arrive at poverty and humiliation. When this happens to them they will become leaders or followers in illegal practices or as accessories be caught and sentenced by the court. Some who are involved in these calamities are oppressed by long-drawn attacks of illness, especially if Mars and Mercury in this house are in opposition or square aspect to the Moon. But if the Moon is with Mars and Mercury in this house by night, the natives will be

tribunes, generals, powerful administrators, but will perish in a violent death.

6. Those who have Mercury with Mars in the fifth house will be brave and manly, unconquered athletes in all contests. They will live in various pleasant places and get a living from public funds or the privy purse. In all contests they will be superior to and feared by their adversaries.

7. Mercury and Mars together in the sixth and twelfth houses indicate the same things in a similar way. By day in this house they indicate afflictions and illnesses. The natives will be arrested, will be familiar with prisons, and will be condemned by some kind of sentence; or they are sought after and indicted on false charges. Slaves or servile men are brought as witnesses against them, and they perish under great torture with violence and atrocity, especially if Mercury and Mars are in aspect to the Moon in any way.

8. But if Mercury and Mars are found by night in the sixth or twelfth houses, the natives will be involved in debts and interest payments to usurers. They will have violent emotions and be cheated by embezzlers; be sluggish in all occupations and suffer serious accusations and ill will from slaves or on account of slaves. Some are crucifiers of slaves or wear out their own slaves by famine, torture, disease, or constant toil. They never continue in one occupation but are constantly changing from one to the other.

9. Mercury together with Mars in the seventh house, that is, the descendant, by day compels the natives to kill their women or wives with their own hands, or they kill themselves or another because of a woman or because of monstrous desires in love. They will be imprisoned and condemned for some such crime.

10. In general, those who have Mercury together with Mars in this house become involved in death or homicide, according to the nature and quality of the signs. They become rioters, bandits, assassins, pirates, or the like and, apprehended for these crimes, are punished with a severe sentence.

11. If it is a nocturnal chart, they will be cheated by unjust acts of a woman, or be married to a shrew and have children from her, or be always involved in important afflictions.

12. Those who have Mercury with Mars in the eighth house are never able to attain their desires, are always in danger, and lose altogether their whole inheritance. Some will be insane and raving, others are thrown into prison, condemned, and often meet a violent death.

13. If it is a nocturnal chart the natives make some kind of a living from evil skills and practices; day by day they grow more wicked. They will be thieves, housebreakers, or steal what was entrusted to them on credit; or they are planners or executors of wicked crimes. Mercury together with Mars produces torturers, executioners, betrayers of their own people; they make much gain from these activities but they suffer a violent death

with severe torments, or they die from insanity.

14. Mercury together with Mars in the ninth house makes impious, unjust perjurers; but even with that defect they become servants of the gods. But also they despoil and strip the gods they serve and prey on temple gifts. Mercury and Mars indicate these things especially if they are far from the influence of the Sun or if, on the other hand, they are in the terms or the house of the Sun. The effects will be stronger if the full Moon is in opposition or square aspect.

15. The natives are wretched and unsuccessful if they have Mercury and Mars in the tenth house. They will take delight in constant sea voyages and will be fond of gymnasiums. They sell their lives for the sake of some vice to powerful men or kings. The kind of vice they practice will be in accordance with the nature of the signs.

16. Mercury together with Mars always locates the native in public business, administration, or public professions, but they never remain long in these professions. They are either arrested, accused, and sentenced, or oppressed by false accusations. From such misfortunes their possessions are so dissipated that they are at the mercy of usurers.

17. If Jupiter is in any aspect to Mars and Mercury in this house or if he is found together with them, the natives will be great in all activities and occupations. They are in charge of important affairs and in a similar way lose their income and seek another. If Venus is in any aspect or is found with Mercury and Mars, she makes managers for emperors in charge of the public revenues or the privy purse; they are logical reasoners, accustomed to handle important affairs.

18. Mercury with Mars indicates many different kinds of occupations and administrative posts. If the planets are located in the house of Mercury or in his terms, the natives are fond of the gymnasium or are athletes in public games. In the signs or terms of Mars they become fighters, lovers of arms, soldiers, hunters, caretakers of wild beasts, heralds or couriers of kings. But if Mercury and Mars are in the house or terms of Venus they become linen-workers, weavers of tunics, craftsmen with feathers, dyers, perfumers, or jewelers. But in the house of Jupiter or his terms they make the natives tribunes in charge of regions or states; in the house of Saturn or his terms they involve the natives in wicked crimes and evil occupations; they become torturers, executioners, butchers, informers, betrayers of their own people. But if Mars and Mercury are in the house of the Sun or Moon, the natives will be metal-workers, sculptors in brass or iron, manufacturers of leather hides, making their living from fire and iron. The change of signs indicates professions of this varied kind.

19. Those who have Mercury with Mars in the eleventh house always perish in battle. They are lovers of the gymnasium, others of arms, but all are brave in counsel and attain great success.

20. Mercury with Mars in the twelfth house has the same meaning as in the sixth.

## XII

## MERCURY AND VENUS

1. Mercury with Venus on the ascendant in a diurnal chart will produce shield bearers or protectors of emperors who would guard the safety of the prince by their own death. Or they are ordered to manage at their own discretion royal money or treasures, and they are the kind to whom administrative duties are always entrusted. They will be musicians, dancers, composers of music; teachers, orators, men of letters, or writers of law or mathematics.

2. By night in this house they make the natives sharp, talented, easily attaining their goals. They will gain prize-winning wreaths, be in charge of sacred rites, or be bearers of sacred images, and will receive advancement over a period of time. They may be skilled in harmony or in charge of royal letters; their oratory and speech will be full of grace and charm.

3. Mercury with Venus in the second house will make the natives transact much business and be occupied in important activities over a long period of time. They are pleasant and charming in life and character, but oversexed and alcoholic. If Mercury is in a morning rising in this house the natives will seek a livelihood through their own efforts, but be fortunate, well-educated, and have some musical training.

4. If he is in an evening rising with Venus in this house, this indicates great opportunities and in the course of time allots great income and good fortune. The natives will be chiefs of states, administrators of laws, entrusted with control of the greatest provinces. Some discover something which is the beginning of their fortune; others receive a large inheritance.

5. Mercury with Venus in the third house will make victors in sacred contests, priests, prophets, dressers of the gods; or those who carry on important duties in temples, in charge of sacred rites; or managers or chiefs of states or ambassadors of good character, to whom the state with confidence entrusts its projects.

6. Those who have Mercury with Venus in the fourth house will be experienced magicians; philosophers who study the heavens, or cure suffering mankind, or who are of service to mankind in some way. If Mercury is in a morning rising with Venus in this house, this will bring the native out of slavery to freedom, and from a low station to splendor and high rank. But they will undertake the defense of wretched women, or old or slave women, or maidens under their guardianship, and will get into trouble in various ways for these actions. Their occupations and activities are governed by the nature and quality of the signs.

7. Mercury with Venus in the fifth house indicates the greatest good fortune over the course of time. The natives attain great rewards and gifts from women or wives and are familiars of powerful men.

8. Those who have Mercury with Venus in the sixth house make a

living from accounts or records, business computations, or teaching, or from revenue of the gods. If another planet is found in the tenth house, the natives will get a wife only with difficulty; they will be oversexed and because of this incur a certain amount of scandal.

9. If Mercury is found in a morning rising with Venus in this house in a nocturnal chart, the natives will sleep with slave women or widows or prostitutes and marry them. They will have servile occupations around water if no planet is found in the tenth house. But if a planet *is* found in the tenth house they will seek many things through their own efforts; for they will be travellers, salesmen, sea-captains, sailors, or goldsmiths.

10. Mercury in an evening rising with Venus in this house makes the natives intelligent, talented, musicians or machinists, or dyers of colors, or merchants of perfumes, jewels, or pearls. Some will be dealers in ointments or discoverers of medicinal drugs. They will often be workers in metal and will make great profit from this activity.

11. Mercury and Venus together in the seventh house indicate hidden illnesses. They cause liver trouble, madness, melancholia, or diseases similar to these. The natives will always be strangers to the affection of their wives and be of ill repute in the last period of their lives.

12. Great riches from women or wives are indicated by Mercury with Venus in the seventh house by night. Also great honors and good fortune, especially if Mars and Saturn are not in aspect in any way. If they are in aspect the prediction turns out to the contrary.

13. Those who have Mercury with Venus in the eighth house in a diurnal chart are ineffectual and accomplish nothing. They will always suffer and be involved in troubles; weak in mind and body, they achieve matrimony only with difficulty; they will be sterile and have no children. They will die of convulsions, a flux, apoplexy, or madness.

14. But if it is a nocturnal chart the natives will inherit a stranger's money or care for a stranger's property; they will be respectable, kind fathers of families, they will receive many things from women or wives. Some will discover something which will bring them income. They will have a sudden death without pain or torment.

15. If Mercury is in a morning rising with Venus in this house, the natives will know or teach many things or be discoverers who easily attain their goals and who in process of time receive increase in possessions.

16. Those who have Mercury with Venus in the ninth house will marry, will have advancement to positions of power; they will seek a livelihood from some kind of temple duties. They will be priests or diviners or haruspices, astrologers, augurs, magicians, or those who explain omens.

17. Public activities are indicated for the native who has Mercury and Venus in the tenth house. They will be honored by peoples and states but will incur ill repute from the behavior of their wives. In a morning rising, Mercury in this house with Venus will make musical composers, but

destined for the stage or public performances. They will be unfortunate in regard to marriage; for they will have prostitutes, public women, actresses, or disreputable women for wives; some will be lovers of boys, involved in licentious vices.

18. Those who have Mercury with Venus in the eleventh house carry on business with women or are entrusted with many possessions by women. Afterward they will be involved in reverses or great losses.

19. Mercury together with Venus in the twelfth house by day will make lovers suffering from the affliction of love, well-known for these difficulties. They will be informed against and sentenced for these troubles. It will make them perish in a violent death. In a nocturnal chart there will be many persecutions by unworthy women; or they are driven by lustful instincts to prostitutes. They will work at mechanical arts and in this profession appear to be occupied in many worthy activities. But they frequently fall from their position and are often cheated in their business or profession.

## XIII

## THE MOON

1. The Moon on the ascendant in a nocturnal chart, if she is full and in signs in which she rejoices, indicates the greatest good fortune. She makes the native advance before his brother, deservedly, at an early age. By day she makes captains of great ships.

2. But if Mars and Saturn hold any angle when the Moon is on the ascendant, that is, if they are in opposition, square aspect, or conjunction with the Moon, this will make pirates noted for their fierce cruelty and bestiality or judges in inaccessible places. If no benefic planet is in aspect to this combination the natives will be exposed; no time of life is predicted. They perish immediately in a violent death.

3. The Moon in the second house in a nocturnal chart will make the native famous and involved in well-known activities, but luxurious, given to voluptuous pleasures. They gain a greater income over a period of time.

4. But if she is found in this house by day, she either destroys the parents immediately or divides the native from them, or separates the parents by dissolving the marriage. She also diminishes the inheritance in various kinds of loss. Some, with the Moon in this house, are involved in constant journeys and divide their activities among many places. They will be subject to some alien power. If the Moon is waning in this house and Saturn is on the degree or in the sign of the ascendant, this indicates blindness from sudden wounds in the eyes. Mars on the degree or the sign of the ascendant will make pains in the joints, also hemorrhages and other illnesses.

5. The Moon in the third house will make the native's mother low-class

or tainted with some kind of scandal. If she has Jupiter with her in this house the native will be supported on public funds or by the privy purse. Mercury in aspect to this combination will make attendants on some great goddess, or priests of a powerful religion, or managers of public business. If the Moon is with Venus, this indicates occupations connected with paints, perfumes, wine, or flowers.

6. If the Moon is found in this house in a nocturnal chart with Saturn, the natives will be sluggish and never reach their goals. They incur the anger of the gods by uttering sacrilegious words. If the Moon is found in this house by day with Mercury and Mars, the natives will be sacrilegious, despoilers of temples, unjust, impious, and murderers.

7. If the Moon is in the fourth house, that is, the IMC, by day, the mother will be low-class and be survived by her husband. If Saturn is on another of the angles and Venus on the descendant, the mother will be taken captive at some time and made a slave. But the full Moon in this house by night will make the mother rich and provide constant increases in income to the native.

[Houses five through eight are missing].

8. The Moon in the ninth house forces some to cultivate rites of the most important religions. Others carry on business for women. But if the Moon is in this house by day, this will make travellers of humble class whose lives are disturbed by dangers and difficulties. Some exercise servile or low-class duties in temples, especially if a malefic planet is in aspect to the Moon in this house.

9. If the Moon is found in the tenth house, that is, on the MC, in a nocturnal chart in signs in which she rejoices or is exalted, if she is waxing and protected by a favorable aspect of Jupiter, this will make the greatest emperors and most powerful governors with power of life and death. Also she produces regularly-elected consuls. If she precedes or follows the MC but is nevertheless situated in nearby houses or degrees, she will produce generals, tribunes, and administrators. In general, if the Moon is located in the same sign as the MC, she indicates great power and good fortune. But if in this position she is moving toward Saturn, or if Saturn is on another angle, this often indicates enmities and misfortunes.

10. The Moon by day on the MC makes the native mediocre in life and in all occupations. He is cheated in various ways. If the Sun is on the ascendant in his own house or exaltation or in the house of Jupiter, this will make governors of the most important provinces or states, or proconsuls, much feared in their administration. If Jupiter in this combination protects either the Sun or the Moon or both, this makes most powerful emperors, just and fortunate, universally regarded with terror.

11. The Moon in the eleventh house indicates the same as in the fifth house.

12. The Moon in the twelfth house in a nocturnal chart indicates a short span of life. But if Jupiter and Venus or one of the two is on the ascendant,

this indicates some kind of power and good fortune. If Mars and Saturn or one of the two is one the ascendant, this indicates serious misfortunes, serious accidents, illnesses, and afflictions for the native and his mother.

13. The Moon in the twelfth house with nothing on the ascendant indicates loss of inheritance, miserable occupations, and journeys. In this house by night she will make the native unhappy, low-class or born from a low-class or slave family, always suffering, and occupied in wretched tasks. Their body or mouth is foul with horrible odor. They are often cheated and in danger and contract some kind of illness from travel.

14. Look carefully at the duodecatemorion of the Moon and its terms. For whatever is concealed in the chart in the general combination of the planets is made obvious in the duodecatemorion and its terms. If you wish to set forth the whole essence of the forecast from the duodecatemorion you will not be deceived. The Babylonians attribute all the forecast to the duodecatemorion; but Ptolemy to the antiscia, and we to both.

## XIV

## THE MOON IN THE PART OF FORTUNE

1. If the Moon is found in the Part of Fortune[57] and moving toward Jupiter or together with him, this indicates leadership, governorship, fame, and good fortune. If Venus is in the Part of Fortune or the Moon is moving toward Venus, the natives will have grace and charm.

2. But if the waxing Moon in the Part of Fortune is moving toward Mercury or is together with him, she makes the natives fortunate, powerful, very intelligent. Through their good fortune and intelligence they attain honors and position, fame and large possessions. But if the waning Moon is moving toward Mercury in the Part of Fortune or is with him, illness, afflictions, and ill fortune are indicated.

3. If the Moon is in the Part of Fortune in a daytime chart and is moving toward Mars or is with him, the natives are suffering and wretched, seeking their livelihood from fire, iron, or some hard material. If this happens in a nocturnal chart the indication is for military power and leadership in war. Also it indicates athletes, according to the nature of the signs. They will be in charge of others because of their courage.

4. If the waxing Moon in the Part of Fortune is moving toward Saturn or is with him, this diminishes paternal and maternal inheritance. The mother is either a widow, or afflicted with illness, or destined to die an evil death. The natives themselves are miserable and hard-worked in early life, but fortunate at a later age.

5. If the waxing Moon is moving toward Saturn by day or is with him, the native will be orphaned by death of parents and forced to waste his inheritance, but in the course of time he receives good fortune and prosperity. A waning Moon in the Part of Fortune by night indicates the

same thing, but if by day the waning Moon is moving toward Saturn or is with him, the prediction is for sickness, affliction, misfortune, proscription, and evil death.

6. But if the Part of Fortune is found in the tenth house, that is, on the MC, or in the eleventh in which the MC is often found; and if the waxing Moon is there, moving toward Saturn or with him; and if the Sun is on the ascendant, this will make the natives fortunate, blessed, noble, with the greatest power. But it also indicates afflictions and illness.

7. If the Sun is not on the ascendant but the Moon is with Saturn or moving toward him, this indicates the same as above. But if the waxing Moon is moving toward the Sun or is with him, this indicates powerful leaders and judges. If Jupiter is in aspect in any way the prediction is for imperial power.

8. If the waning Moon in the Part of Fortune is moving toward the Sun or is with him, the natives will be of humble position early in life and easily cheated. But in the course of time they achieve fame, wealth, and very high position.

9. Whenever the Moon is found in the same degree with the Sun in the Part of Fortune or in other houses or signs in conjunction with the Sun, and does not free herself from association with the Sun, she involves the native early in life in dangerous and low-class occupations; but in the course of time, after serious losses, she predicts the possibility of winning wealth.

10. In all charts you must first observe the course of the Moon; not only on the first day on which the native begins the first steps of life, but with care the third day; notice what planet the Moon attaches herself to and with what aspect; toward whom and from whom she is moving. For on the third day the new-born infant absorbs his first nourishment. Thus, on the third day one must observe whether the Moon is diminished or full of light, and to what extent benefic and malefic planets are in aspect. For the third day, like the first, determines everything and in the same way. If this information is carefully collected we will never be confused or disturbed in explaining the fates of men. If anything seems to have been left out in this explanation we shall discuss it in our fourth book.

# Liber Quartus

1. Those like myself who work up legal defenses become involved in quarrelsome contests and, so to speak, dog-eat-dog confrontations. From these pursuits I have gained nothing day after day but an accumulation of risks and an enormous burden of ill-will. For I have constantly found myself opposing aggressive characters—either those who delight in pointless mischief, or who exploit strangers from motives of greed, or who terrify miserable men with fear of the courts. In this profession I could only rely on my steadfast faith in the right, but I earned only malevolent envy and stormy perils.

2. Therefore I have deserted the law to avoid being enmeshed in ever increasing plots and dangers. Struggling as I was for the welfare of strangers, and despising profit from my legal efforts, my adversaries raged against me without respite and pursued me with bitter hostility. Meanwhile I was resisting with no other means than the uncorrupted and faithful defenses I was preparing for my suffering and troubled clients.

3. Thus I am now set at leisure from legal contests, have put off the snares of treacherous enemies, and given up the occupation of stealing, or rather of banditry. Freed from all care, my mind purged of the vices which I acquired from contact with evil men, separated in every way from earthly experience, I have engaged in writing these books for you, Lollianus, so that I may apply myself to heavenly and divine thoughts.

4. In the first place, in this book will be explained what we promised at the end of the third, that is, all the shapes and appearances of the Moon—her aspects, her defluxions, and whatever pertains to her power. Also we shall discuss the Part of Fortune and that of the Daemon, the ruler of the chart, which the Greeks call *oecosdespotes* (master of the house), and I shall explain the effects of all of these. I shall also show the meaning of full

and empty and of masculine and feminine degrees. The Moon will again occupy us in the last section.

5. We have written in these books all the things which Mercury and Hanubius[58] handed down to Aesculapius;[59] which Petosiris and Nechepso explained; which Abram,[60] Orfeus,[61] and Critodemos[62] wrote, and all the others knowledgeable in this art. We have collected and edited these theories, compared different opinions, and now present them to all the Romans. This science has appeared difficult to some because of the limitations of the Latin language; but I have endeavored to explain it in true and clear propositions.

## I

## [POWER OF THE MOON]

1. We promised that we would explain in this book all the courses of the Moon; also what she predicts, and in what way. The whole essence of the human body is related to the power of that divinity. For after life-giving breath has entered the completed human being and the spirit of the Divine Mind has poured itself into the body, the Moon by her courses maintains the shape of the already formed body. Therefore we must carefully observe the movements of the Moon in order to explain the whole essence of the human body.

2. The human being would not be able to exist unless his body had been formed with strong protection. They are wrong who maintain that the only knowledge of the life and spirit of man is found in the birth chart—that is, in the ascendant and the MC. It is true that the essence of life and spirit *will* be found in these places, but we must also diligently observe the courses of the Moon as well as the ascendant and the MC.

3. God the Creator of man, when with his unique skill he formed the living being, bound the immortal soul to the earthly body. The soul, poured inside and fastened by the force of necessity, governs and serves the fragile mortal body.

4. The soul will not have a perfect receptacle and will not be able to show its divinity unless the body has been strengthened for its reception. Thus the soul and body, mutually sustaining each other by the strength of their own natures, show that man is composed of an earthly and a divine nature in one perfect form and shape.

5. We must know how the Moon undertakes the care of the human body and what has been allotted to the power of the Moon. For we feel in our bodies the increases of the waxing Moon and the losses of her waning. The innermost parts of the human grow when the Moon grows, and when she begins to lose light they languish, fatigued in body; when she grows again, their power of growth comes flooding back.

6. The whole essence of the earthly body is governed by the power of the Moon. Since she is located in the lower regions of the heavens, because

of her nearness she has been allotted power over the Earth and all the bodies animated by the breath of the Divine Mind. She maintains her course with infinite variety and runs with speed through all the signs, joining herself to all the planets. From different elements she builds up the human body, once conceived, and dissolves it again into its elements.

7. In any chart the degree in which the Moon is located must be carefully observed. We must diligently study how the Moon carries herself around and how she joins herself to the other planets. The first day of life and the third have the same meaning. The seventh and eleventh through the Moon show the whole substance of life.

8. Both the ruler of the chart and the giver of life are found from the positions of the Moon; likewise the last day of life. Also the ruler of time, whom the Greeks call *chronocrator,* is shown to us by the Moon together with the Sun. For in nocturnal charts she herself undertakes the beginning and rulership of time, in diurnal charts, the Sun. We shall explain the uses of this in later books.

9. We have described many forms of the Moon in the book of principles; now we must go over them briefly. For all difficult problems should be explained more than once to make them easier to understand.

10. The Moon is either *synodic* (in conjunction with the Sun), full, *dichotomous* (half), *menoides* (new), or *amficyrtous* (gibbous). As she changes from one to the other she completes the month of light. Thus we must carefully observe the changing appearance of her various shapes, computing the chart on the first and on the third day; also her aspects; which planet she moves toward and away from; and with whom she associates herself in second aspect after the first; with whom she comes into aspect as she approaches; when she moves on high, or when lower down; what planets she aspects either in trine, square, or opposition; when and toward what planets she moves when full, or when waning; in which of her conditions she aspects the different planets; when she comes into conjunction with the Sun. All these we must study so that we may attain the full science of forecasting.

## II

### THE MOON AND SATURN

1. If the waxing Moon is in aspect with Saturn or moving toward him, this indicates widowhood for the mother and constant grief for the house of women. The natives themselves have occupations in temples and lose their entire inheritance. But in the course of time they gain it back through their own efforts.

2. If the waning Moon is in aspect to Saturn, the parents will be low-class or slaves, or immersed in poverty and misfortune. Some will have mothers who are sickly or meet a violent death in early years. Or the natives themselves will be weak and sickly, short-lived, and die some kind

of evil death, especially if the Moon is found on important places of the chart, that is, if she is in aspect to the ascendant.

## III

### THE MOON AND JUPITER

1. If the waxing Moon is in aspect to Jupiter or is moving toward him, the natives will be fortunate, famous, and rich; masters of many great estates and wide possessions. They predict the future either through their own divine gifts, through messages from the gods, from oracles, or skill in an ancient art. If, however, Mars is in opposition or square aspect to this combination, these predictions will be lessened and great danger to life is predicted.

2. But if the waning Moon is in aspect to Jupiter, the natives will be adopted; or exposed, and later returned to their parents. They seek income by their own efforts, and over a period of time receive advancement and achieve power and fame. These things only come about if Mars is not in opposition or square aspect to the Moon, either waxing or waning.

3. But if Mars is in aspect, the natives will be exposed and be oppressed by perpetual slavery or will be born of a slave or a sickly mother. Or they themselves will be afflicted in some part of the body and oppressed by weight of misfortune, especially if Mars is in aspect in a daytime, or Saturn in a nighttime, chart; but if Saturn, then the Moon must be waning.

## IV

### THE MOON AND MARS

1. If the waxing Moon is in aspect to Mars or is moving toward him in a nocturnal chart, the natives are impetuous and violent, often involved in dangers, but liable to be cheated in various ways; their life is devoted to the greatest dangers but they are successful and efficient. They are given to a military life or athletic competitions, especially if they have the Moon and Mars in important houses. Nevertheless they will be afflicted and suffering. Their mothers are either sickly or destined for a violent death.

2. If it is a diurnal chart and the Moon is in aspect to Mars in this way, some part of the body will be amputated. Some have trouble with the eyes; others have afflictions of the stomach; or they are short-lived and suffer a violent death. But all these predictions come about according to the nature of individual signs; and according to the different situations of the angles, and the anaforas of the angles, and according to those signs which we have said are alien (not in aspect) to the ascendant.

3. For in the signs which are alien to the ascendant, that is, in the sixth or twelfth, if the waxing Moon is in aspect to Mars, the inheritance is

decreased; the parents separated; or the parents are killed and the native becomes an orphan and is oppressed with misery. Some have the body cut with a sword; others suffer such wounds that they can only be cauterized by fire. They practice occupations which have to do with iron and fire. Some become soldiers, held in continual military service. If the Moon in the eleventh, second, eighth house, or on the ascendant is carried toward Mars by day, she indicates pains in the side, a short life, and a violent death.

4. But if it is a nocturnal chart and the Moon is moving toward Mars in the houses we listed, the natives will be great, fearsome, and powerful, conquering important states; especially if the Moon is found on the first angles.

5. But if she is found in important houses by day, paternal inheritance is wasted and the parents themselves are afflicted and suffer violent death. The natives will be public craftsmen or soldiers but suffering illnesses and afflictions, often great peril, and violent death.

## V

## THE MOON AND THE SUN

1. If the Moon is moving toward the Sun and is in any kind of aspect to him, the natives will be miserable and unfortunate, victims of dangers and every kind of demotion. Sometimes they will be spastics or contorted with afflictions and illnesses; others will be epileptics, deprived of reason, or insane.

## VI

## THE MOON AND VENUS

1. If the waxing Moon is moving toward Venus or coming into aspect with her, the parents will be noble, raised up to the highest power. But the natives will be separated from parents and suffer as wretched orphans. They will, however, attain high position, be well-known, successful in all their activities, and easily attain their goals. They are handsome and charming and attain the highest position, but all over a period of time.

2. But if the waning Moon is moving toward Venus, she indicates high position, greatest honors, and trappings of great power. The parents bestow great fortune on the natives from an early age. But they will be constant objects of scandal.

3. The Moon moving toward Venus in any of her shapes always indicates extraordinary sexual vices and constant scandal. The natives are unchaste and impure, always burning with immoderate desire for women's love; often incestuous desire drives them to immoral connections.

For they seduce sisters, nieces, daughters-in-law, wives of step-sons, or step-mothers; or they corrupt the father's or the uncle's concubine and are indicted for these deeds, especially if Mars is in opposition. If it is a diurnal chart and the Moon on the angles is moving toward Venus, but Mars is on the descendant or the MC, they will perish by the sword because of the crimes we have described.

4. But if a woman has the Moon moving toward Venus, she will always be of nervous and shrill temper; she will be driven to promiscuous love affairs; and will always burn with impure passion and conceive illicit, incestuous desires. She makes love either with brothers, sons, nephews, or uncles; entices a step-father to her marriage couch, or corrupts other close relatives or friends. Venus makes some women shrews, especially if located in tropical, mutable, double, or scaly signs with the Moon moving toward her. These passions are stronger if Mars or Saturn is in opposition or square aspect to the Moon or to Venus. The evils will be greater if Venus and the Moon are in the house of Saturn or Mars, if there is no favorable influence of Jupiter, and if Mars or Saturn are in opposition or square aspect.

## VII

## THE MOON AND MERCURY

1. If the full Moon is moving toward Mercury or is in aspect to him, the natives will be intelligent and talented; orators displaying the greatest eloquence, especially if Mercury is in favorable houses or signs or in his own degrees, and Jupiter is in trine aspect to him. For then the natives for their own merits win great prizes for literature and eloquence. With the power of their eloquence they are able to calm the fury of raging men or of light-minded people confusedly stirring up revolution. They know mathematics and music and regularly exercise at the wrestling field. The secrets of the heavens and of divine philosophy are known to them and on some occasions they are allotted fame and important leadership.

2. But if Jupiter is in aspect as the Moon moves toward Mercury, the natives will be in charge of the privy purse or the public treasury, or will be managers of the money of foreign countries.

3. The waning Moon moving toward Mercury will make the natives malevolent, criminal, unstable in desires, undependable, always hesitating, and never able to make up their minds; they constantly change their occupations and deny money entrusted to them, desire to reveal hidden things, or lay information about confidences given them; they are impostors and deceivers; they associate with thieves and house-breakers or themselves engage in these activities. They are weak in body, sluggish, afflicted with vicious humors.

## VIII

## IF THE MOON IS MOVING TOWARD NOTHING (VOID OF COURSE)

1. If the Moon is so located that she is moving toward nothing (void of course), is in aspect to no planet, and there is no benefic planet on the angles, this will make paupers destitute of all necessities, without means of daily life. They beg for a living and are always in need of a stranger's help to sustain life. They will always be inferior to their parents; and their bodies sickly. They suffer from infected wounds or malignant humors under the skin which attack their joints, especially if the Moon, "running through a vacuum," which the Greeks call *cenodromon* (empty course), is in opposition or square aspect to Mars or Saturn on the first or third day, or if malefic planets are on the angles.

2. If in this situation the Moon is aspected by benefic planets, the natives will be stripped of everything, be worn out with constant toil, seeking a livelihood with labor and sweat. As soon as they come near to good fortune, even from the highest step she casts them down again. Sometimes she leads them to the top but does not allow them to grasp good fortune. For when the Moon is void of course she involves the early years in wretched misfortunes. But after she has for a time troubled the body and mind and ruined their youth with many crimes, dragged them here and there in miserable journeys, then she bestows good fortune equal to the mishaps of youth.

3. But if the Moon, moving through a vacuum, comes into aspect with Mars or Saturn, she will produce unfortunate epileptics or lunatics, oppressed by various kinds of bad luck from the beginning of their life to the end. The natives will be miserable paupers, barely covered by ragged clothing, guardians of tombs; or they will be punished by perpetual imprisonment.

## IX

## [PHASES OF THE MOON]

1. We have carefully explained the aspects of the Moon and now we turn to another kind of interpretation, namely that of the Moon herself: we would not wish to overlook anything in these detailed discussions, especially since the whole essence of life is influenced by the course of the Moon.

2. If the waxing Moon, moving away from Saturn, comes into aspect with Jupiter or is moving toward Jupiter, the natives will be wealthy, generous, famous, noble, ruling great people or great states. To some is allotted large inheritance, to others treasure, to still others important gifts.

3. Nothing of the kind is indicated by the waning Moon in this situation; then she makes caretakers to whom private affairs are entrusted; who travel for business; or they become sea-captains, ship-owners, or tax collectors; or those who exercise their profession around water and thus win a modest living.

4. If the full Moon, moving away from Saturn, comes into aspect with Mars, she indicates illnesses and afflictions and an early death. If she is waning, she predicts torments of a long-drawn-out illness for the mother and an evil death with vomiting of blood. The natives themselves are miserable orphans, or weak and sluggish, or are separated from parents by dissension.

5. Both paternal and maternal inheritance is wasted and frequent sword wounds are predicted, such that they have to be cauterized by burning. There will be continual pains in hidden parts of the body; a large part of life spent in suffering, and finally a violent death in one of various ways. They may die from drowning or by burning, hang themselves, or kill themselves with a sword.

6. Enormous ill fortune and great catastrophes are indicated by the Moon moving away from Saturn toward the Sun. The natives will be lunatics, madmen, epileptics, or suffer from dropsy or elephantiasis. These evils are persistent and continue to the last day of life.

7. If the waxing Moon is moving away from Saturn and comes into aspect with Venus, the natives will be great, noble, powerful, lucky, wealthy, but savage and passionate, and for that reason will suffer from serious scandal. But the waning Moon in this situation indicates illicit, depraved love affairs or base professions, long continued. Nevertheless she will make the natives seek and obtain great fortunes, great power, and good luck.

8. The waxing or full Moon moving away from Saturn into aspect to Mercury makes the natives obscure, secluded, silent, students of secret and illegal writings, or involved in celestial religions, or experienced in interpretation of the stars. They will be managers of affairs, public teachers of the liberal arts, orators of outstanding eloquence, or well-known physicians.

9. But if the Moon is waning she either impedes the sound of the voice, deafens the ears, or weakens the body. She makes the natives melancholy, jaundiced, suffering from spleen, consumptive, dropsical; and painfully binds the humor in the veins into a narrow passage.

# X

## [THE MOON MOVING FROM JUPITER]

1. If in a nocturnal chart the waxing Moon, moving away from Jupiter, is carried toward Mars, great power is predicted: control of great

states and regions. But it also indicates anxieties and dangers. The natives will not be free from afflictions and illnesses but will be the type who endure these things easily, especially if Mars is found in important houses of the chart. But if Mars is in dejected houses, this indicates skills pertaining to fire. The natives themselves are low-class and humble; suffer illnesses and afflictions and often an evil death.

2. But if the waxing Moon is moving away from Jupiter toward Mars by day, the natives will be exposed, be slaves, or wretched beggars. They will suffer illness and afflictions, slavery which is like captivity, and lose their life in a violent death.

3. If it is a nocturnal chart, the natives will be famous and important. Mars found in important houses will make leaders or judges entrusted with the highest power. But Mars in dejected houses will make soldiers or athletes who make a living for themselves by fire or sword; or he will make physicians or surgeons.

4. The waning Moon in this situation wastes paternal and maternal inheritance, destroys the parents when the native is young, and imposes the burden of extreme beggary. Some suffer bitter pain; some become slaves, sometimes captives, often dying a violent death, especially if Mars is on one of the angles or its anafora or catafora. For then the effects we have described will be much stronger.

5. Loss of paternal and maternal inheritance is also indicated by the Moon moving from Jupiter toward the Sun. The natives are also estranged from parents and sent on long journeys. Some are exiles, others fugitives; some slaves or disgraced captives, especially if the Sun or the Moon is found in the house of Saturn or Mars.

6. If the waxing or full Moon is moving away from Jupiter toward Venus, the parents will have great position and power; but the native will be estranged from them or early become an orphan; nevertheless, for him power, fame, and high position are indicated, but all over a period of time. Great good fortune also is gained through wives. These men are handsome, pleasing, and charming, and obtain power through their grace and charm.

7. The waning Moon moving from Jupiter toward Venus, in important houses, indicates infinite good and increasing fortune. For it indicates high positions, powers, consular rank, and great positions of power handed down from the parents and obtained in early life; also great riches and good fortune from wives and other women.

8. The full Moon moving from Jupiter toward Mercury makes judges of good counsel, respectable, kingly, famous; they may also be managers of the privy purse, chiefs of religious rites, or interpreters of law. From these occupations they obtain great riches and their good fortune continues throughout their lives.

9. But if the Moon is waning in this situation, the natives seek their livelihood from literature, from teaching, business, or from granaries.

Some obtain some kind of inheritance; others make discoveries; others refuse to return what has been entrusted to them so that from this treachery they lay the foundation for a fortune.

10. If the waxing or full Moon moves from Jupiter toward Saturn, the natives will be adopted by strangers or be themselves the fathers of alien children, or tutors or guardians of minors. Some are forced to find their exposed children after a period of time. They will be involved in humid or watery occupations, be constantly wandering on journeys, or gain a livelihood from commerce.

11. But if the Moon is waning in this situation, the natives will be exposed or slaves; or they will endure miserable captivity, illnesses, or other afflictions so that their whole life is consumed in the bitterness of pain and they suffer an early and wretched death. In a nocturnal chart they meet a violent death.

## XI

## [THE MOON MOVING FROM MARS]

1. Afflictions and illness, a short life, and a violent death are indicated by the Moon moving from Mars toward the Sun. Some die on a journey or in foreign lands.

2. The waxing or full Moon moving from Mars toward Venus makes adulterers, passionate lovers, always troubled by sexual desires and dangerous adventures. They will practice arts, either of painting, perfumery, or work with jewels or pearls; often they will become dyers or merchants in metals, according to the nature and quality of the signs. Or they may be innkeepers, or prepare things necessary for food and drink in a successful business.

3. But if the waning Moon is moving from Mars toward Venus, the natives will be successful, blessed, lucky, and rich. They will either seduce women or carry off rich but foreign-born wives and gain fortune from them. Through women they reach high office, especially in a nocturnal chart. But in a daytime chart the natives are involved in a variety of occupations and are often attacked by scandal for their sexual activities and are always excited by desire for promiscuous love affairs.

4. Soldiers and athletes, sometimes famous, are produced if the full Moon is moving away from Mars toward Mercury in a nocturnal chart. Some are in charge of well-known public offices; but they will be malevolent and have increasing desire for every kind of crime. They will be executioners or government spies. But if the full Moon is in this position by day, this indicates convictions and sentences at court, deportations by sentence of the judge, and a violent death.

5. The waning Moon in a daytime chart moving from Mars toward Mercury indicates monstrous greed. The natives will be bandits who will be caught in their crimes and suffer harsh penalties. Others will be

crushed by a falling house or driven from the correct course of life by insanity. A nocturnal chart makes prison guards who gain income from this occupation, lovers of ships or of sports, or hunters of four-footed animals. But they will suffer afflictions and constant danger.

6. The waxing or full Moon moving away from Mars toward Saturn will make the natives slow and sluggish. Nothing will turn out well for them and they never attain their desire. Their mother is either a widow, sickly, or afflicted, and may finish in an evil death. They suffer losses of inheritance and constant misfortunes.

7. The waning Moon moving from Mars to Saturn predicts famines, illness, and sickness; it produces insanity, hemorrhoids, lameness, paralysis, hunchbacks, a short life; or, if none of these, then a violent death. Or the mother and father suffer afflictions and a violent death.

8. If the waxing or full Moon is moving from Mars toward Jupiter in favorable houses, this predicts leaders of armies, imperial rulers fearsome in every way, rulers of provinces and states. They will be extremely wealthy; easily gain their desires, and are victors in all conflicts.

9. But if the Moon is waning, the natives will be destined for some kind of public contest and will always have a reputation for respectability. They may be famous soldiers with constantly increasing good fortune and frequent opportunities for advancement. Nevertheless they will have hidden afflictions and frequent illness.

## XII

### [THE MOON MOVING FROM THE SUN]

1. In a diurnal chart the Moon moving from the Sun to Venus will make the natives sterile, not able to generate offspring, who only with difficulty have intercourse with loved spouses. They marry wives who are either sterile or old women or slaves; or they themselves are sterile and seek the base love of boys; for this reason offspring are denied them. They will be entangled in monstrous sexual vices and base desires; always involved in servile pursuits and occupations; excessively seeking gain. They win a livelihood through their own efforts and in the course of time attain increase in good fortune.

2. If the Moon is moving from the Sun toward Venus by night, this indicates many wives, important activities, and great opportunities. The natives will be pleasing and friendly, rich and famous, and hold high and powerful positions. Their luck will be the best, especially if Saturn is not in opposition or square aspect to any of the planets involved. Even then the same good fortune is indicated if the combination occurs in favorable houses.

3. The Moon moving from the Sun to Mercury by day predicts dangers in life and occupations, and predisposition to bad character. The

natives deny the gods with monstrous sacrilege. Also they refuse to return what has been entrusted to them.

4. But the Moon in this situation by night makes public record-keepers who get a living from some kind of writing. They will be publicly rewarded for this activity and will be universally considered best in their field. If Jupiter is in trine aspect, they often undertake the management of their state. They will be discoverers of obscure writings or of wisdom, or, given to celestial rites, learn the secrets of the gods; or they work with hidden or illicit writings. Some find hidden things; others obtain an inheritance, but only if Mars and Saturn are not in aspect.

5. If the Moon is moving from the Sun toward Saturn by day, inheritance is lost; natives are estranged from parents or orphaned. In the course of time, however, they achieve good fortune and large possessions.

6. But if the Moon is moving from the Sun to Saturn by night, in addition to loss of parents and inheritance, long and difficult journeys are predicted. Also harsh afflictions, serious illnesses, or dangerous and violent events.

7. If the Moon is moving away from the Sun toward Jupiter by day, the native inherits high position and good fortune from his parents. Some will govern important states or regions, and they will be fortunate beyond the usual.

8. But if this occurs by night, the natives gain their position by themselves. They travel constantly; are cheated in early youth, but achieve fame and suitable income in later life.

9. The death of parents is predicted by the Moon moving from the Sun toward Mars by day. Often the parents suffer violent death. They themselves are blinded or have some diseased part of the body amputated or, if none of these is the case, die at an early age, often by a violent death.

10. The Moon in this situation by night makes the natives violent and cruel, given to dangerous criminal activities, or suffering in illnesses and afflictions. Nevertheless a public career, military duties, or athletic activity is predicted, accompanied by great fame, especially if Mars and the Moon are found in important houses. But if they are in dejected houses without influence of a benefic planet, this decreases inheritance, makes the natives orphans, humble in life, sickly, and afflicted, and finally suffering a violent death. Their professions will have to do with fire, iron, or other metals and involve continual hard work.

## XIII

### [THE MOON MOVING FROM VENUS]

1. If the full or waxing Moon is moving from Venus toward Mercury, the natives will become defenders or caretakers of noble women and will receive some sort of protection from women. Or they will be dyers, or

workers in perfumes or pearls; sometimes musicians, physicians, or managers and trainers of athletes. They are continually active in sexual affairs and are pleasing and agreeable in love.

2. But the waning Moon in this situation indicates afflictions, unchastity, and sickness. It predicts a variety of professions: orators, lathe-turners, plasterers, sculptors, painters, druggists, caterers, or those who provide exotic pleasures and delights.

3. If the full or waxing Moon is moving from Venus toward Saturn by night the natives marry an old wife or a public prostitute or one of their relatives: from their marriage they obtain promotion and high position.

4. If the chart is diurnal, the natives are noted for vicious sexual activities and, for this, are attacked by frequent scandal. They lead a low-class, unstable, slave-like life as masters of prostitutes or pimps. But if the chart is that of a woman, she will be a public prostitute who gains a livelihood by selling her body in a public place.

5. The waning Moon moving from Venus toward Saturn in a nocturnal chart makes the natives sterile, eunuchs, castrated priests, hermaphrodites, or driven by desire to act the part of women. They will be short-lived or die a violent death.

6. By day the waning Moon in this situation makes the natives weak and afflicted with malignant humors. They will have laborious activities around water; for they are forced to draw water from deep wells, or ordered to clean sewers or wells; or they will be gardeners, but poor; sailors or water carriers; fishermen or divers.

7. These activities change according to the quality of the signs. They may be cowherds, ox-herds, horse-tenders, shepherds, or cleaners of stables; or they may be guardians of tombs, or corpse-washers. All these are indicated according to the variety of the signs and houses. We have written fully about this variety in other works on astrology.

8. Great and powerful nobles, rulers of states, are produced by the Moon moving from Venus toward Mars in a diurnal chart. But some will be raised up by the protection of women; they will be pleasing and handsome, lovers of women, and will attain all their desires in love affairs.

9. But if the waning Moon is moving from Venus toward Jupiter, this will provide financial help from individual women; and fame and good fortune will be passed on from parents to natives at an early age; some will receive an inheritance, others will discover means for the greatest profit or hold honored office in temples.

10. If the full or waxing Moon is moving from Venus toward Mars in a diurnal chart, this predicts a calamitous outcome to love affairs so that the natives are thrown into prison, sentenced, and die a violent death. Some are robbed, others are subjugated by a foreign power or led into captivity, according to the nature of the signs.

11. But if the full or waxing Moon is moving from Venus toward Mars by night, this makes artisans, aggressive and clever but sickly. If the Moon

is waning, they will be fearsome and powerful and will, with their courage and power, subdue great regions, especially if Mars or the Moon is on the ascendant or in the fifth house. But if this combination is in other houses, it makes soldiers, artisans, or athletes involved in constant dangers.

12. The waning Moon moving from Venus toward Mars by day indicates loss of inheritance, afflictions, illness, and misfortunes. Some natives become exiles or fugitives or slaves. Some it destroys in early life. For the sake of a woman or because of some love affair, it often produces plots, dangers, convictions at law, or a violent death.

13. If the Moon is moving from Venus toward the Sun, this alienates the natives from parents or makes them orphans. They will have trouble in life and income; will be unchaste and have sexual vices. But as soon as they leave the period of youth they obtain an increase in income and whatever they desire.

## XIV

## [THE MOON MOVING FROM MERCURY]

1. The full Moon moving from Mercury toward Saturn by day makes the natives either stammerers, deaf, or impeded in speech. They will be occupied either in keeping accounts, in teaching, or business affairs, travelling, or in interpretation of words; they always study heavenly secrets. Some gain their living from the care of water works or prisons.

2. But if the full Moon moves away from Mercury toward Saturn by night, the natives will have laborious occupations around water as laborers who hire out their bodies, carrying loads on their back or shoulders. Some end in prison, condemned by the court, and die in squalor, unkempt of hair and deformed, especially if malefic planets are in aspect to this combination.

3. But if the waning Moon is moving from Mercury toward Saturn, the result is ragged paupers sunk in direst need. Others serve in temples or prophesy. Many are madmen, suffering sacred illnesses; or they are epileptics or have pitiable convulsions.

4. By night the waning Moon moving from Mercury toward Saturn makes the natives exposed; or they will be unfortunate slaves or captives. They will also be afflicted or ill, and in early life condemned on some charge. If none of these is the case they suffer a violent death.

5. The Moon moving from Mercury toward Jupiter will make the natives great and powerful, entrusted with papers and secrets of emperors; or faithful managers of royal treasures. Many become teachers or messengers of kings, but also sometimes temple attendants, prophets, or priests. All these gain great wealth and honors from their occupations.

6. But if the waning Moon is moving from Mercury toward Jupiter, they will be keepers of public records or recorders of loans and interest,

agents of the government or of the privy purse, or judges in private law cases. From these occupations they will gain great wealth and honors. Some will receive an inheritance; others discover hidden treasure. Still others are entrusted with others' money and keep it without taint of fraud, so that they gain great fame.

7. The full or waxing Moon moving from Mercury toward Mars in a diurnal chart makes the natives sacrilegious, perjurers or forgers. Or they will be burglars, thieves, pillagers of temples, or bandits and killers. They will be caught in these crimes, thrown into prison, and suffer a violent death for these crimes.

8. But in a nocturnal chart they will be generals or military tribunes, fearsome tyrants, or rulers of states. They never continue their position but always make mistakes in using their power. Some become fugitives, others will go into exile, still others will die a violent death, especially if Mars and the Moon are found in important houses in the chart.

9. But if this happens in dejected houses, the crime of parricide is indicated. For then the natives murder their sons, brothers, or parents in monstrous greed and fury; or they strangle relatives or defile their marriage couch with blood of a slaughtered wife. In every way they rage with homicidal madness. But these events vary according to the difference of the signs and houses. Their death will always be violent or a public execution: it will be incurred because of slaves or condemned men or prisoners.

10. The waning Moon moving from Mercury toward Mars by day will make the natives forgers, evil-doers, or house-breakers; or thieves and familiars or receivers of robbers. For these crimes they are imprisoned and condemned by a harsh sentence. Some become public executioners or legal scribes; or men in high office or their assistants; or sometimes prison guards.

11. The waning Moon moving from Mercury toward Mars in a nocturnal chart produces soldiers, arms-keepers, or athletes in contests. They will be successful, well-known, and inspire fear.

12. But if this combination occurs while Mars or the Moon are on the ascendant or in the fifth house, the prediction is for a violent death. In other houses afflictions, illnesses, and dangers are indicated and laborious occupations involving wakefulness and violence. But all this varies according to the difference of the signs.

13. If Mars is in a mutable or tropical sign, when the Moon is moving away from the Sun, or Mercury is in the signs of malefic planets or moving toward Mars in opposition or square aspect, or if she is near him and in aspect, this will make furriers, leather-workers, shoemakers, cooks, brass workers; all of these using iron and fire. But if this combination is in the sign of Venus, this will make linen workers, dyers, plasterers, or tavernkeepers. In the houses of Mars or Mercury it makes lovers of arms and of the gymnasium or managers of public business, and in the house of

Jupiter, tribunes or generals in charge of great legions, or officers of states or provinces.

14. If this combination is in the house of Saturn, wretched and criminal occupations are predicted; for it will make torturers, executioners, informers, hunters of wild beasts, or snake-charmers who hunt serpents. Some will be masters of wild animals, fishermen, or bird-catchers. Some laboriously raise water from deep wells or work in the wilderness or in gardens. They may be ship-owners, sailors, sea-captains, builders, stone-cutters, corpse-washers, or undertakers. For in this combination with Mars the forecasts are of many different kinds.

15. Those who have the Moon moving from Mercury toward the Sun will be retarded in mind, impeded in speech, or deaf. They will be wretched paupers, wanderers, or travellers, who never have a settled home. But these misfortunes are lessened over a period of time and after early youth they acquire some protection in life from various occupations.

16. The full Moon moving from Mercury toward Venus in a nocturnal chart indicates high position, famous activities, and great good fortune. Some she makes fluent orators, others poets, endowed with divine gift of song. Or they will be in service to the gods or to emperors, with great honor. From the recommendation of women or in certain female occupations they will gain power and fortune because of their grace and charm.

17. But the full Moon in this situation makes discoverers of paints or colors or medicines, or workers in precious stones; or they work with their own skill on costly tunics; play the organ or act in pantomimes. Some are trained in dancing or singing. But they never have great opportunities and live a mediocre life, oppressed by need. In the course of time their prospects improve. They are always involved in some kind of sexual activity or vices and from this become objects of scandal.

18. But if the Moon by night is waning, the natives are rich, powerful, great rulers, governors of states or regions, especially if the Moon is free of the Sun's influence and found on the ascendant. This is also true if Venus in the same way is free of the Sun's influence, in the house we mentioned, and in the path of the approaching Moon. If this combination occurs in other houses, the natives will be respected, will carry on important affairs, and seek their livelihood through their own efforts.

19. If the waning Moon by day is moving toward Venus on the MC or in the tenth house, victory in sacred contests is indicated. The natives will be builders of temples or consecrators of shrines, or they will be temple attendants or chief priests, with important duties.

20. This combination in other houses makes natives of mediocre talents working in metal. Or they may be furriers, perfumers, or polishers of precious stones, or those who paint gems with different colors; or sculptors or image makers, or temple musicians. Some study heavenly

lore and know the secrets of the skies. They easily learn hidden and secret lore and make their living from this.

## XV

### [PHASES OF THE MOON]

1. If the waxing or full Moon is moving away from Saturn toward nothing but is running through a vacuum, she causes loss of inheritance, estranges the natives from parents, or makes them orphans in early youth. They will be sluggish and involved in long journeys.

2. If the Moon in this situation is waning, she causes continual cold around the stomach, which the Greeks call *psychrocoilium* (cold belly). Or the natives suffer from phlegm, spleen, dysentery, consumption, suppression of urine, and are tormented by hidden pains from these afflictions. These sicknesses are indicated according to the quality of the signs.

3. The full Moon moving away from Jupiter toward nothing makes impoverished wanderers who in course of time lose all good fortune. But if the Moon is waning, she makes captives, oppressed all their lives with the burden of slavery. Some will be sickly or have a short life.

4. The full Moon moving away from Mars toward nothing wastes inheritance and destroys parents, imposes some kind of affliction on them, or causes an evil death. To the natives themselves she predicts death from wild beasts or from a fall from high places; some die of public execution.

5. But if the waning Moon is in this situation, the natives are separated from family or parents, lose their inheritance, undertake laborious skills having to do with iron and fire, or become unfortunate soldiers.

6. The Moon moving away from the Sun toward nothing will make paupers, unhappy wanderers or travelers, engaged in servile occupations. Some begin in occupations which they like and make some progress, but the Moon makes them give up in despair. In process of time this difficulty is mitigated and the unhappy outcome is changed; weight of poverty is left behind, a small income is accumulated, and they find other occupations.

7. The waxing Moon moving from Venus toward nothing makes the natives sexually passive, never able to hold the love of their wives; they take pleasure in incestuous embraces. But they will be naked paupers who earn their living by carrying burdens on their shoulders. If the Moon is waning, the paupers will always be vicious and base, burdened with weight of misery or given to dishonest and wretched occupations.

8. If the full Moon is moving away from Mercury toward nothing, she will make orators, physicians, musicians, grammarians; and those who

study the courses of the stars. Or they carry on the business of money lenders and obtain fame and fortune, but only after a period of time.

9. The waning Moon in this situation indicates illness from body humors or serious dangers from water; some she injures in mind, some in speech, others in the ears; but all these are illiterate; others will prophesy, but in temples; some become guardians of temples and still others servants or assistants in temples.

## XVI

## [OTHER INDICATIONS OF THE MOON]

1. Now all the effects of the Moon's swift course must be set forth so that we may appear to have explained everything both in general and in detail.

2. The Moon in aspect to Saturn makes unfortunate parents; to Mars she indicates low birth for both parents and misfortune for the father. If she is moving from Mars to Saturn so that she is between the two, she indicates the affliction of the sacred illness. But if she is moving from Saturn to Mars, she indicates the same, but moderately. She predicts that affliction for a woman if Saturn is in aspect. She makes madmen if she approaches Mars or Saturn in any shape, if Venus and Jupiter are not in aspect. If Venus and Jupiter *are* in aspect all the misfortunes described above are lessened.

3. The native will be fortunate and more than fortunate with all kinds of good luck and honor if the Moon is in signs in which she rejoices, without unfavorable aspect of Mars or Saturn, but in aspect to either Venus or Jupiter. The Moon rejoices on the ascendant or in the fifth or eleventh house if in aspect to Venus or Jupiter. Also in the eighth house in a nocturnal chart and in signs in which she rejoices, with aspect of Venus and Jupiter, she indicates the greatest good fortune.

4. Whatever house you wish to study in the chart, whether of character, nurture, birth, parents, brother, marriage, offspring, or last day of life, carefully observe the course, aspects, and waxing and waning of the Moon and her elongation[63] and her exaltation.

5. We must beware in every chart that the Sun does not come into aspect with the approaching Moon. For, after receding from opposition to the Sun, she feels her light waning as she hastens to the synodic position; in whatever shape she is she indicates destruction for everyone, according to her form. For if her influence is strong she indicates great evils and misfortunes; if her influence is moderate the misfortunes are lessened.

6. If she approaches the Sun when waning and, attaching herself to his orb, disappears from human sight, then she indicates more powerful evils and all kinds of calamities, according to the forecasts which we described

in the preceding part of this book.

7. But if, freed from conjunction with the Sun, she approaches Saturn, this indicates great good and prosperity. But if she joins herself to Jupiter in a similar way, good fortune beyond all measure is predicted. The native who has this occurrence in his chart will be fortunate beyond measure.

8. If she is found with Mars, as we said, she indicates ill fortune and, according to the nature of the signs, a violent death. But these evils are lessened if Mars is in a feminine sign. If the Moon is in aspect to Venus on the MC or the IMC, she indicates a fortunate marriage, especially if there is no aspect of Mars. But if she is in aspect to Venus in other signs, the prediction is for a good life but marriage with a relative.

9. If Mars is in aspect, he indicates illicit love affairs and unhappy passions. If the Moon is in aspect to Mercury, this indicates infinite vices and unheard-of evils. Therefore we must pray that the Moon should not be in aspect to Mercury.

10. If the waning Moon by night comes into aspect with Saturn while he is retrograde or stationary, great calamities follow. According to the nature of the signs and the power of the houses a violent death is predicted. Saturn in a feminine sign mitigates these evils somewhat.

11. If the Moon comes into aspect with Jupiter by night, the native will have an abundance of good things. Also with Mars the prediction is for great good fortune. The fortune will be greater if Mars is in a straight course (not retrograde). Predictions will be for a good marriage if she comes into aspect with Venus on the MC, or in the fifth or the eleventh house, or on the ascendant, if Saturn is not in any aspect. The fortune will be even better if Venus is retrograde from the important houses. Then she will not be harmful but may make many consumptive. Good predictions are stronger in a nocturnal chart, but indications of evil stronger in a diurnal.

12. Now that we have carefully explained the course of the Moon, let us turn to the discussion we promised in this work, namely, the explanation of Fortune. We cannot explain the essence of Fate unless that place is carefully investigated. We must consider the Part of Fortune with as much care as all the other points in the chart; I shall point out easily how it is discovered. When you find it, observe the combinations and aspects of all the planets and then you will be able to understand the uses of the Part of Fortune.

## XVII

## THE PART OF FORTUNE AND ITS EFFECTS

1. In any nocturnal chart count the signs from the Moon to the Sun; in a diurnal chart, from the Sun to the Moon. Take the number of signs and,

starting with the ascendant, count them off. The last number shows the sign of the part of Fortune.

2. This is the general computation which we have included so as not to seem to have left anything out. There is a more detailed way of computing the Part of Fortune and it is the one you should follow in all charts: if you do you will be able to give the true explanation of all the houses.

We shall explain all these things more clearly when we come to the *Sphaera Barbarica;* [64] the divine Abram and wise Achilles [65] endeavored to discuss this with the most correct computation. But we are about to speak about the Part of Fortune, which is found in this way:

3. In a diurnal chart begin from the degree of the Sun and count all degrees to the Moon, including the one she is in. Taking that number begin from the degree of the ascendant and, numbering on the right side, allot 30 degrees to every sign. The last degree is that of the Part of Fortune.

4. In a nocturnal chart do the same but count from the degree of the Moon to that of the Sun.

5. The Part of Fortune shows the quality of life, the amount of inheritance, and the course of good and bad fortune. Also love and the affection of men toward women, the effects of child-care, and all desires. It shows the fatherland in an easy way. Abram called it the Place of the Moon.

6. Therefore observe who is the ruler of the sign and of the degree of the Part of Fortune, that is, in whose terms the Part is; also in what house each ruler is, whether on first or second angles, in favorable or dejected houses, in their exaltation or fall; whether each ruler is in aspect to the Part of Fortune and if they, on the angles, are in aspect to each other.

7. When you have carefully investigated all this, then observe who is the ruler of the degree of the Moon (in a nocturnal chart) or of the Sun (in a diurnal chart) and see if this ruler is in aspect to the Part of Fortune. If one planet is found to be the ruler of all these degrees and is favorably located in signs in which he rejoices, or in his exaltation, or his own house, this indicates a lucky chart. If this planet is well located with the Sun and Moon and in aspect to the Part of Fortune, still greater good fortune is indicated by the multiple aspect. If the Part of Fortune is on one of the angles in aspect to the Moon, this indicates even greater good fortune.

8. But if there is not one ruler of the sign of the Part of Fortune and of its terms and of the terms of the Sun and Moon, the one which has the greatest power should be the most important in the forecast; if this one is benefic and in favorable signs, in his exaltation or in his own house, or on first angles and in aspect to the Part of Fortune, a great and noble chart is indicated.

9. That prediction holds if the planet is exactly on the angles. But if it is only roughly located on the angles the indication is for a mediocre chart.

The native will not be lucky beyond measure nor oppressed by want. But if both are well located—the ruler of the sign and of the terms of the Part of Fortune and in favorable signs—that is, in which they rejoice or in which they are exalted, or in their own houses and located exactly on the angles—they predict such great good fortune that the native is close to emperors in every way. But if they are found only roughly on the angles the indication is for a modest increase in good fortune.

10. If the ruler of the sign of the Part of Fortune and the ruler of his terms, and the ruler of the terms in which the Moon is, are well located, in their exaltation or in their own houses or in signs in which they rejoice or on first angles, they will make emperors whose rule extends throughout the whole world and whose power is so great that it approaches that of the gods.

11. But if, of the stars we have mentioned, none is favorably located, that native will be oppressed by ill fortune to the end of his life. Observe especially the MC and the sign which is the anafora of the ascendant; if none of the stars we have mentioned is favorably located, look whether a benefic planet, following the power of its own condition, is on the MC or in the anafora of the ascendant. If one is so found, the preceding evil is alleviated in process of time. But if all the planets we have mentioned are badly located and there is no benefic planet on the MC or the anafora of the ascendant, the chart will show unending bad fortune. But observe carefully the duodecatemorion of the Part of Fortune so that the meaning of the chart will not escape you.

## XVIII

## THE PART OF THE DAEMON

1. We find the Part of the Daemon in the following way.[66] (We have included it in this book because Abram called it the Part of the Sun and it is not right that it should be separated from the Part of the Moon.) This is the way to find it: in a diurnal chart count the degrees of every sign from the Sun to the Moon and, beginning from the ascendant, distribute these degrees to every sign. In whichever sign the last degree falls, that is the Part of the Daemon. In a nocturnal chart count from the Moon to the Sun and proceed in the same way.

2. This place is also called the essence of the soul; from this place we find professions and material goods; it shows the affection of women toward men. But also this place shows the fatherland clearly. Observe, therefore, what benefic and what malefic planets are in aspect to this Part and you will thus set forth the forecast according to the influence of individual planets.

## XIX

## THE RULER OF THE CHART

1. You must carefully observe the ruler of the chart,[67] whom the Greeks call *oecodespotes*. He himself controls the sum of the whole chart and from him the individual planets take their power of forecasting. If he is well-located—in signs in which he rejoices, or is exalted, or in his own house, and the chart is of his condition, and he is not attacked by malefic planets or lacking protection of benefic—he predicts all good things, according to the quality of his nature and the whole number of the years of life. But if he is impeded by malefic planets or deserted by benefic, then he languishes and his efficacy is weakened.

2. I shall explain this with all the information from the ancient scholars so that you can find the ruler of the chart. Some have said that the ruler of the chart is the planet which is located in favorable houses of the chart, in his own house or his own terms. But others have figured from the Sun and Moon, arguing that the ruler of the chart is the one in whose terms the Sun and Moon are found, that is, the Sun in the daytime and the Moon at night. There is some point to this theory. Others say that the ruler of the chart is the ruler of the exaltation of the Moon. Still others maintain that the ruler is the one whose sign the Moon enters after she has left the one in which she is found at the birth.

3. We follow this last method and it is universally approved; but consider everything we have said carefully. We shall instruct you with an example.

4. Suppose the hour of birth has the Moon in Aries. The next house the Moon would be in would be Taurus; and Venus is the ruler of Taurus. It is the same with the other signs. But we must note that neither the Sun nor the Moon can be the ruler of any chart. For as rulers of the whole they disdain individual rulerships. Therefore, if the Moon is found in Gemini on the day of birth, then neither Cancer, for that is the house of the Moon, nor Leo, which is the house of the Sun, can show the ruler of the chart. When she has crossed Cancer and Leo and comes to Virgo, then she shows the ruler of the chart. Mercury is the ruler of Virgo so he becomes the ruler.

5. *SATURN.* If Saturn is the ruler of the chart, is favorably located, and has been allotted the rulership by the waxing Moon, he will make the natives proud, arrogant, honored, respectable, serious, of good counsel. Their work is respected in judgment and they fulfill all their duties correctly and prudently. They will, however, always be at odds with wife and children. They will be distant, not much occupied with self; taking little food but enjoying drink. These men are of moderate size, pale, sluggish; they will have stomach trouble and vomit easily, be attacked by malignant humors, and constantly a prey to internal pains. They will be malevolent, anxious, hard-working, troubled in mind; always making a

living in connection with water.

6. If Saturn as ruler of the chart is in his own house or terms, or in the house or terms of Jupiter or of the Sun, in a diurnal chart, the indication is for high position, fame, and every type of good fortune which is in the power of the houses. If he is in the house or terms of Mars, or in the house of the Moon, the natives will be unhappy, hard-working, poor, low-class, obscure, and suffer constant grief.

7. These evils are greater if it is a nocturnal chart and the waning Moon allots the rulership of the chart. Then the native is partly or completely bald, his eyesight is bad, or his eyes are constantly running. They also will have lung disease, dropsy, gout, epilepsy, or will be spastics, especially if the ruler of the chart, in dejected signs or degrees, is in aspect to the waning Moon.

8. But if benefic planets are in favorable aspect to Saturn when he is ruler of the chart, the illnesses we have listed will be cured, either by the protection of some god or by a competent physician. If a malefic planet, however, attacks Saturn, the evils we have described will increase. The native may die from the sicknesses brought about by bodily humors. Or they die in watery or humid places or in hidden and unknown places. Saturn as ruler in the house or terms of Mercury makes malevolent poisoners or perjurers, hostile to both parents and brothers.

9. *JUPITER*. Those who have Jupiter as ruler of the chart are always trustworthy, of high spirit, and are impelled toward great deeds. They spend more than their resources or their inheritance allows. Commanding in all their acts, noble, famous, honorable, lovers of luxury, cheerful, desiring to please in every way, large eaters, faithful friends, they are simple and friendly to all; successful and accustomed to do everything well.

10. Their body is of middle size but well-formed, handsome, and they are light-complexioned. Of beautiful eyes and head, with long flowing hair; firm of step. Their life will be glorious and filled with good fortune and they attain all their desires. Their activities turn out well, and they are protected by the influence of great men; they always love their wives and children and their sons are successful, so that they reap much deserved respect from the position of their sons. Their illnesses come from stomach trouble, from wine and from indigestion; death comes from high living, hemorrhoids, or sexual intercourse.

11. When Jupiter is ruler of the chart you must carefully observe the same things you did with Saturn and the other planets. To give you one example which will instruct you with the rest: if Jupiter is the ruler of the chart and holds one of the first angles, either in his own house or his exaltation, or his terms, or in the house or exaltation of the Sun, and if it is a diurnal chart with influence of benefic planets; and if the full Moon is moving toward Jupiter; and Mars does not hold any angle and is not in opposition to Jupiter or the waxing Moon, this chart shows every indication of good fortune.

12. But if Jupiter is in signs or terms in which he is dejected, or in sluggish houses, and if he and the Moon are attacked by the unfavorable aspect of malefic planets, the native will lack strength and be deprived of all powers; there is nothing great in his chart and not a whole number of years of life. For if malefic planets are in opposition or square aspect, according to their strength they subtract from the decreed number of years.

13. *MARS*. Mars as ruler of the chart makes the natives fierce, unconquerable, active, quarrelsome, bold, involved in dangers, violent, but liable to be deceived in various ways. They are gluttonous and digest food easily; brave, just, fiery. They have red hair and bloodshot eyes, commanding ways, always seeking positions of power. Their occupations have to do with iron and fire. They are monstrously bad-tempered, never get on with wives, children, or friends, and are envious of others' possessions. Afflictions come from iron and fire—that is, cuts and burns; they often fall from high places and break their arms and legs. They will have a sudden and violent death.

14. If Mars is in aspect to the full Moon, the native will die a captive of bandits or be accused and handed over to public authorities; or, persecuted by informers, he will be sentenced to punishment. If there is influence of the Sun, he will be publicly burned. These predictions are stronger in a diurnal chart if the ruler of the chart is on the first angle or on the MC or the descendant, and the full Moon on another angle in malefic aspect to Mars, or if she is full when she allots the rulership to Mars.

15. In a nocturnal chart if Mars is in the house of Jupiter or Saturn, or in their terms, or in his own house or terms, or in the fifth or eleventh house, or on the MC or the ascendant and in aspect to the waning Moon; or the waning Moon has allotted him the rulership of the chart; and if Jupiter is in trine to the angles, this will make powerful, fear-inspiring generals or tribunes, ruling great regions and many states, entrusted with the control of the whole world.

16. But if Mars is on the descendant and all else is as we have just described, he makes for a violent death. Mars on the descendant always means a violent death, but the kind of death is according to the nature of the signs, as shown in the third book. If, however, he is located in the terms of Jupiter or favorably aspected by Jupiter or Venus, this dampens the heat of his malevolence.

17. *VENUS*. Venus as ruler of the chart will make men lovable, cheerful, talkative, wasting time in constant play, amiable, pleasing, passionate lovers, faithful friends, pious, and just. Their bodies will be tall and light-skinned. Their eyes are always shining with the light of sexual desire; their hair is long and lightly curly, or carefully trimmed around the head with tight curls. They digest all foods easily but take little, are fond of drink, and have strong sexual desires. They will be noble and

worldly and always surrounded by music.

18. All these predictions are according to the quality of the signs. Venus as ruler of the chart in dejected signs produces makers of musical instruments or painters who paint the whole figure. In favorable houses she makes the natives famous, crowned with diadems or gold wreaths, discoverers of sacred teachings. Also she binds women to men and men to women with close bonds of affection.

19. As an evening star she helps women, as a morning star, men. For this reason they say the power of Venus is two-fold. For she will make the native fertile, rejoicing in many offspring, gaining great joy from daughters. She makes illnesses concerned with natural and necessary functions; but predicts famous and glorious deaths. But when she is ruler of the chart you must carefully observe, as with the other planets, the combination of the planets and the power of her condition.

20. For in a nocturnal chart in the fifth or eleventh house or on the MC, in her own house or terms or in her exaltation, and if the rulership has been allotted by the waning Moon; if Jupiter favorably located is in trine aspect, or if the waning Moon is moving toward her without influence of Saturn, gold robes and consular power are indicated.

21. But if Mars is in trine to that combination, in addition to those powers, proconsular and imperial power are predicted, especially if Mars is in his own house or terms, or in the house or terms of Jupiter or in his exaltation, and if Venus is free of the Sun's rays.

22. But if Mercury is found either in his own house or terms or in his exaltation, or in the house or terms of Venus, and is in favorable houses, this will make great and famous poets. In a diurnal chart the prediction is almost the same but a little weakened. But in a nocturnal chart, if Saturn is located on the angles or in favorable houses, and in unfavorable aspect to the combination or in aspect to the waning Moon, the whole of what we promised is hindered.

23. If on the other hand Venus, as ruler of the chart, is found in dejected or sluggish houses, or in the house or terms of Saturn; and the waning Moon on one of the angles is moving toward Saturn by night, or, full, by day toward Mars, the natives will be impure, unchaste, over-sexed, involved in continual calamities, objects of scandal for their amorous desires or criminally prosecuted for illicit sexual habits; or they will be accused of the crime of adultery and for this reason become famous cases of violent death, especially if Mars on the descendant is in threatening aspect to Venus.

24. *MERCURY*. Those who have Mercury as ruler of the chart are clever, talented, students of all things, modest; they desire to learn the secrets of all skills. If Mercury is in his own house or terms or in his exaltation, or in the house of Venus or in trine aspect to her, he makes poets, orators, famous for pleasing fluency of speech.

25. But if Mercury is found in the house of the Moon, the natives are

eloquent but their speech is not pleasing. But in the house of Saturn, if Jupiter and Venus are in favorable aspect and either he himself or Jupiter is on one of the angles or in the third house, this will make men dedicated to certain religious rites, knowledgeable in secrets of magic, astrologers, astronomers, *haruspices*; they seek the secrets of all religions and of heaven itself. The duties of ambassadors are often entrusted to them. They are faithful to relatives and friends; just and pious, prudent in counsel, free of all hint of extravagance.

26. If Mars is in square aspect to Mercury, and Mercury is in the third house in human or voiced signs, and in favorable aspect to Jupiter, and Jupiter is on the ascendant or the MC, this will make orators of outstanding talent who obtain everything through their own efforts.

27. If Saturn in favorable houses in a nocturnal chart aspects that combination, this will cause plots, dangers, accusations, crises, and scandal. If Mars is found on the descendant in aspect to Saturn and the full Moon, the native will die by the sword, accused of such wrong-doing as illicit religious rites or counterfeiting money.

28. Mercury as ruler of the chart makes the body of medium size and graceful, the face slender and pale, the eyes truly beautiful. The natives take little food and drink and gain their whole livelihood from literature; because of their writing or their learned speech they are chosen ambassadors. They delight in the obscure writings of secret religions.

29. Mercury makes the natives teachers of grammar and oratory or interpreters of philosophy; they easily carry on commerce and establish good credit for lending and borrowing. These men accumulate substance by their own efforts, are abstemious fathers of families; are just, think little of themselves; are isolated from public uproar and god-fearing in all religions.

30. If Mercury is in the house of health and illness and in aspect to malefic planets, he indicates affliction by bodily humors; if the Moon is badly located the natives will be spastics, madmen, or epileptics; death will come to them from water or bodily humors.

31. We must remember, as we said before, that the Sun and Moon never accept the rulership of the chart. But if they are located with the rulers of the chart or in favorable aspect to them, in the houses or terms of the rulers of the chart, they indicate much from their own nature; although others may be the rulers of the chart there is much influence in the forecast from favorable aspect of the Sun and Moon. And so I shall briefly explain what the Sun indicates when in conjunction with the ruler of the chart. How long a space of time each indicates singly I have shown in the book of principles.

32. *THE SUN WITH THE RULER OF THE CHART.* If the Sun is in conjunction with the ruler of the chart, together with other things which the ruler contributes, these also are indicated according to the power of his nature: the Sun makes men full of responsibility but raised up with

inflated pride, wise, moderate, humane, pious; they always respect their fathers. The Sun makes them tall and handsome of body; their hair, shining and yellow. They are tillers of the field, seeking income through their own efforts; successful, intelligent; always enjoying watery regions.

33. They fulfill all their duties with the greatest honesty but are never loved by wife or children. They have afflictions of the eyes and other parts of the body; and often are burned by fire. Death comes to them violently in foreign places, sometimes by execution. The Sun increases the time of life, if, well-located, he holds the terms of the ruler of the chart and if he is not in aspect to malefic planets.

34. *THE MOON WITH THE RULER OF THE CHART.* If the Moon is in conjunction with the ruler of the chart, together with the other things which the ruler contributes these also are indicated according to the power of her nature: the Moon makes men stable, appointed to high position, respected, large of body (but the type of body is indicated by the signs), corpulent but truly handsome; they enjoy food but take little drink. Their life is changeable so that their income is being constantly increased or diminished. The Moon holds them in watery places.

35. They are always loving toward wives, children, and mothers, but separated from the affection of their father. If a malefic planet aspects the Moon, affliction of the eyes is indicated; there may also be wounds of the eyes, or the eyesight obscured by a discharge. The body is marked by a series of white spots or by leprosy, or is deformed with contractions or weakened by tremors. Death from malignant humors is predicted. The influence of benefic planets alleviates these evils.

36. When the ruler of the chart is discovered from the course of the Moon, we should not examine it in isolation but consider it in combination with all the other planets. For when one planet is in aspect or conjunction with another, in accordance with its nature it increases and diminishes everything else. The effects of the ruler of the chart come from the influence on him of other planets and from the power of the houses and the signs.

37. Therefore, if the ruler is malefic his influence is alleviated by favorable aspect of benefic planets. The thoroughgoing evil of his malevolence is changed and, although he is prepared to be harmful, through the influence of the good planets he becomes almost helpful, especially if surrounded by all the favorable planets. Unlucky planets' influence is also mitigated by the sign or the house.

38. And if there are many planets which offer helpful protection, the ruler himself receives from them good will and a better forecast if he reverses his harmful power through the influence of good planets. For then serious misfortunes are turned into prosperous activities, the accused and condemned are freed; then a god cures illnesses and all evils are repressed at their beginnings.

39. But if a malefic planet is alone in its predictive force, then by

necessity it exercises its fierce power against the native. Thus again benefic planets, if they are not hindered by threatening aspect of the malefic, would predict high position and good fortune; but if they are attacked by a threatening aspect they are not able to fulfill their promise.

40. Thus we must always carefully observe the mixtures and combinations of aspects; for otherwise the whole substance of fate will not be explained. We must diligently observe when a benefic and when a malefic planet obtains rulership of the chart and whether it is in favorable or sluggish houses and in its own house or exaltation. From all of these, together with the nature of the signs and houses and the conditions, whether nocturnal or diurnal, you will be able to set forth the most certain and true forecast,showing who holds the sum total of the chart, the end of life, and the whole substance of the forecast.

## XX

## THE CLIMACTERIC YEARS

1. When you begin to draw up the chart and collect all the data, there is nothing more important to investigate in the beginning than the time of life and the power of the ruler of the chart. For often, even though certain planets are well located, the ruler of the chart indicates a short span of life; the whole of what the well-placed planets had predicted is changed by an early death.

2. You must therefore carefully compute the time of life from the Sun and Moon, the degree of the ascendant and, what is most effective, the ruler of the chart. All these things, although briefly discussed in this work, are explained in detail in the single book which we wrote for our Murinus[68] on the *Ruler of the Chart* and the *Chronocrator*. Therefore, the ruler of the chart must be diligently sought out because we find from him the span of life which is divided among the different planets.

3. Aside from other climacteric periods, seven and nine years and their multiples through all life in hidden ways affect men with various dangerous crises. Thus the 63rd year which is the multiple of the two numbers is called the *androclas* (man-weakening). Since the course of both numbers comes together in the 63rd year, this is a period of great danger. If the periods of seven and nine years which the Greeks call *ebdomadici* and *enneadici* indicate severe dangers for men, how much more does the 63rd year which is the multiple of the two. For this reason it was called *androclas* by the Egyptians, because it breaks and weakens the force of men.

4. Therefore, among all the other dangers of the chart which are indicated by malefic planets in accordance with the anaforas of the signs and with the nature of their threatening aspect, these dangers we must also carefully observe: we must note those of the seven and nine-year periods. We must know at what time of life the crisis threatens and what

benefic planets are in aspect to the Moon and the rulers of time and of the chart.

5. If Jupiter and Venus on the ascendant are in favorable houses and aspect the Moon and the rulers of time and the chart, by their protection men are freed from threatening dangers.

6. But there is not one kind of danger. It may come from accusations, information, plots, ship-wrecks, journeys, sentences of the court, loss of possessions, sickness, sexual desires, weakness of body, wild beasts, ruined buildings, quicksand, or precipices.

7. Therefore, when you have discovered the nature of the danger observe, as we have said, the ascendant and the Moon, whether aspected by benefic planets; also the rulers of time and the chart; then you can see how imminent danger and death may be avoided.

8. You must observe the planet that is the author of the danger, that is, the ruler of time, what house, sign, and degrees it is in when it predicts danger and to what extent it is aspected by benefic planets. For if this planet is well located, with benefic aspects, the threat is lessened. But if not, and its harmful power is intact, it involves the native in such inextricable miseries that danger and death cannot in any way be avoided.

## XXI

## OCCUPATIONS

1. Now we must learn which planets determine the occupations of men and what those occupations are; then we must observe what house that planet is in. Mars, Venus, and Mercury determine occupations for men. The one in any chart which determines the occupations is the one on the MC or in right or left trine to the MC, or on other angles.

2. If Mars is in position to determine the occupations and is favorably located, in aspect to benefic planets in a nocturnal chart, he predicts arms, leadership, and fame; power of the sword and trappings of the highest position, insofar as the whole forecast makes this possible. At any rate, he indicates famous and noble skills connected with iron and fire which make the native widely known and acclaimed. In sluggish or dejected houses and in signs in which he does not rejoice Mars predicts respectable skills, but obscure.

3. If benefic planets are in aspect to Mars in this location, considerable fame and income result from the occupations he has determined. But if not benefic but malefic planets are in aspect, the natives will be in subordinate, laborious jobs and spend more than they earn.

4. If Venus determines occupations and is in her own house or terms, or on the ascendant or the MC, or in the fifth or eleventh houses—for she also determines occupations from these houses—and if it is a nocturnal chart, she indicates important occupations and great fame, especially if

Jupiter is in trine aspect to her or the waning Moon is moving toward her. In that case she has such power that the native may be compared to kings or emperors.

5. Then she predicts gold crowns and consular robes or proconsular powers; she will make—according to the measurement of the chart—rulers of the games or governors of Asia, high priests of the provinces, always honorable and famous throughout the world, pleasing, amiable, handsome, just; everything they wish turns out well, and much good fortune comes to them from women or wives.

6. But if Venus is in alien houses or terms, she indicates honorable and civilized skills: she produces goldsmiths, gold-platers, workers in gold leaf, silver-smiths, musicians, organists, or painters. But if she is found in dejected houses, she will make inn-keepers, tavern keepers, cooks, perfumers, makers of wreaths for festivals and sacred occasions, and things needed for pleasure.

7. In general, benefic planets in conjunction with, or in trine aspect to, the giver of professions indicate fame, nobility, and great opportunities for good fortune. The amount of good fortune is in direct proportion to the number of benefic planets.

8. If there are no benefic planets in aspect, the prediction is for a low position in life, subordinate occupations, laborious work, and constant ill repute. But if malefic and benefic planets are equally in aspect, then both sides do what they can in proportion to their nature. Those whose aspect is stronger will have the greater influence.

9. If Mercury determines occupations and is in favorable houses—just as we said in the case of Venus and Mars—and in his own house, terms or exaltation, he determines everything according to his nature. He makes either kings, judges or royal account-keepers, or teachers of emperors, or similar occupations according to the nature and power of the signs and the aspects. He also makes orators, chief physicians, astrologers, astronomers, *haruspices*—all according to the power of the signs.

10. In fixed signs he produces important judges or record keepers; in tropical signs he indicates occupations having to do with translation and money-changing; in equinoctial signs, public officials; in double signs he makes the natives intelligent, talented inventors, astronomers, and the like.

11. In general we must remember that when Mercury determines the occupations, and there is a benefic planet in aspect, this will result in great fame and fortune and authority. A malefic planet in aspect indicates a wretched life and bad reputation. The nature of the planets in aspect makes a great difference in these predictions.

12. If Mars is in aspect he makes bold, adventurous leaders, quick and active, easily deceived, but never in the power of another. Saturn produces characters who are gentle, tall, silent, proud, who do everything with dissimulation. You must look for this kind of thing with the two other

planets so that you can form a true forecast from all the data. Thus you will delineate the characters of men just as in painting so that all the traits of the body and the hidden effects of personality can be discovered.

## XXII

### EMPTY AND FULL HOUSES[69]

1. I am now about to explain fearful secrets which the revered ancients left wrapped in obscurity so that they should not come to the ears of the profane. Give this your full attention, with a calm mind, so that you may understand easily what I am about to say.

2. We said in the book of principles that each sign has three decans. These decans have great divine power and by themselves determine all good and bad fortune. Nechepso, the most just emperor of Egypt and a truly good astrologer, by means of the decans predicted all illnesses and afflictions; he knew which decan produced which illness and which decans were stronger than others. From their different nature and power he discovered the cure for all illnesses, because one nature is often overcome by another, and one god by another.

3. There are 36 decans in the whole circle of the zodiac and they are divided among the twelve gods, that is, the twelve signs. There are three decans to every sign, but their power does not extend to all 30 degrees of each sign. In every sign decans possess certain degrees and not others. Those they possess are called "full"; those where they have no power, "empty."

4. Those natives who have in their chart the Sun, Moon, and all five planets in full degrees will be elevated like gods with the protection of the greatest majesty. But it is never possible in human charts to have the ascendant, the Sun and Moon, and five planets in full degrees. Those who have one planet in full degrees will be mediocre; those who have two will approach a certain amount of good fortune; three, good fortune beyond the ordinary; with four they reach royal happiness. Beyond that it is not possible for human charts. But those who have neither the ascendant nor any planet in full degrees will be always wretched, destitute paupers involved in every kind of ill fortune.

5. Thus you must diligently observe this possibility in all houses and all planets. If the ascendant is in full degrees, the natives will be very strong in vitality, courage, animal spirits, type of body, and power of authority. Those who have the ascendant in empty degrees are small of body, depressed in mind, weak in bodily strength, always subservient, serving more powerful men, and lose the initiative in all business affairs.

6. In a similar way the MC in empty degrees predicts lack of success, but in full degrees indicates everything strong and valid which the house is accustomed to predict. The same is true of the Part of Fortune, the ruler

of the chart, and the one who determines occupations. For all these, even though located in favorable houses, if not in full degrees lose their power. But if they are in full degrees they more firmly guarantee everything they promise.

7. I shall explain the full and empty degrees so that the secrets of that theory may not be open to criticism. I shall include the names of the decans in order, beginning with Aries, so that you may know everything we promised. The full degrees are those in which you will find the names of the decans.

8. I. *Aries.* In this sign there are twelve full and 18 empty degrees, as follows:

|     |       |         |       |          |
| --- | ----- | ------- | ----- | -------- |
| I   | locus | degrees | III   | empty    |
| II  | locus | degrees | V     | *Senator* |
| III | locus | degrees | IX    | empty    |
| IV  | locus | degrees | IV    | *Senacher* |
| V   | locus | degrees | V     | empty    |
| VI  | locus | degrees | IV    | *Sentacher* |

9. II. *Taurus.* Taurus has 20 full and ten empty degrees as follows:

|     |       |         |       |          |
| --- | ----- | ------- | ----- | -------- |
| I   | locus | degrees | III   | empty    |
| II  | locus | degrees | VII   | *Suo*    |
| III | locus | degrees | II    | empty    |
| IV  | locus | degrees | VIII  | *Aryo*   |
| V   | locus | degrees | V     | empty    |
| VI  | locus | degrees | V     | *Romanae* |

10. III. *Gemini.* There are in Gemini 18 full and twelve empty degrees:

|     |       |         |       |          |
| --- | ----- | ------- | ----- | -------- |
| I   | locus | degrees | VII   | *Thesogar* |
| II  | locus | degrees | II    | empty    |
| III | locus | degrees | V     | *Ver*    |
| IV  | locus | degrees | III   | empty    |
| V   | locus | degrees | VI    | *Tepis*  |
| VI  | locus | degrees | VII   | empty    |

11. IV. *Cancer.* Cancer has 19 full and eleven empty degrees:

|      |       |         |       |          |
| ---- | ----- | ------- | ----- | -------- |
| I    | locus | degrees | VII   | empty    |
| II   | locus | degrees | VI    | *Sothis* |
| III  | locus | degrees | II    | empty    |
| IV   | locus | degrees | IV    | *Sith*   |
| V    | locus | degrees | II    | empty    |
| VI   | locus | degrees | IX    | *Thiumis* |
| VII  | locus | degrees | I     | empty    |

12. V. *Leo.* In the sign of Leo there are 21 full and nine empty degrees:

| | | | |
|---|---|---|---|
| I locus, | degrees | VII, | *Craumonis* |
| II locus, | degrees | IV, | empty |
| III locus, | degrees | III, | *Sic* |
| IV locus, | degrees | VI, | empty |
| V locus, | degrees | X, | *Futile* |

13. VI. *Virgo.* Virgo has 14 full and 16 empty degrees:

| | | | |
|---|---|---|---|
| I locus, | degrees | V, | empty |
| II locus, | degrees | V, | *Thumis* |
| III locus, | degrees | II, | empty |
| IV locus, | degrees | VI, | *Tophicus* |
| V locus, | degrees | VI, | empty |
| VI locus, | degrees | IV, | *Afut* |
| VII locus, | degrees | III, | empty |

14. VII. *Libra.* In the sign of Libra there are 19 full and twelve empty degrees:

| | | | |
|---|---|---|---|
| I locus, | degrees | V, | *Seuichut* |
| II locus, | degrees | VI, | empty |
| III locus, | degrees | VIII, | *Sepisent* |
| IV locus, | degrees | III, | empty |
| V locus, | degrees | VI, | *Senta* |
| VI locus, | degrees | III, | empty |

15. VIII. *Scorpio.* In the sign of Scorpio there are 16 full and 14 empty degrees:

| | | | |
|---|---|---|---|
| I locus, | degrees | III, | empty |
| II locus, | degrees | V, | *Sentacer* |
| III locus, | degrees | VI, | empty |
| IV locus, | degrees | VI, | *Tepisen* |
| V locus, | degrees | II, | empty |
| VI locus, | degrees | V, | *Sentineu* |
| VII locus, | degrees | III, | empty |

16. IX. *Sagittarius.* In the sign of Sagittarius there are 23 full and seven empty degrees:

| | | | |
|---|---|---|---|
| I locus, | degrees | IX, | *Eregbuo* |
| II locus, | degrees | III, | empty |
| III locus, | degrees | VII, | *Sagon* |
| IV locus, | degrees | IV, | empty |
| V locus, | degrees | VII, | *Chenene* |

17. X. *Capricorn*. In the sign of Capricorn there are 13 full and 17 empty degrees:

| | | | |
|---|---|---|---|
| I locus, | degrees | VII, | empty |
| II locus, | degrees | III, | *Themeso* |
| III locus, | degrees | V, | empty |
| IV locus, | degrees | IV, | *Epiemu* |
| V locus, | degrees | V, | empty |
| VI locus, | degrees | VI, | *Omot* |

18. XI. *Aquarius*. Aquarius has 19 full and eleven empty degrees:

| | | | |
|---|---|---|---|
| I locus, | degrees | IV, | empty |
| II locus, | degrees | V, | *Oro* |
| III locus, | degrees | IV, | empty |
| IV locus, | degrees | VI, | *Cratero* |
| V locus, | degrees | III, | empty |
| VI locus, | degrees | VIII, | *Tepis* |

19. XII. *Pisces*. In the sign of Pisces there are 13 full and 17 empty degrees:

| | | | |
|---|---|---|---|
| I locus, | degrees | VI, | empty |
| II locus, | degrees | VI, | *Acha* |
| III locus, | degrees | III, | empty |
| IV locus, | degrees | V, | *Tepibui* |
| V locus, | degrees | VI, | empty |
| VI locus, | degrees | II, | *Uiu* |
| VII locus, | degrees | II, | empty |

20. That most true and immutable theory the ancients left wrapped in obscurity so that it should not come to the notice of everyone. The great Petosiris touched on it only lightly; not that he was not familiar with it (for he had arrived at all hidden secrets), but he did not want to divulge it lest his work should lose its divine character. Therefore, when you have collected all your data, look carefully at the individual planets and houses and note which of them are in empty degrees. For only then will you be able to explain the whole forecast.

## XXIII

### [MASCULINE AND FEMININE DEGREES]

1. Now I shall explain masculine and feminine degrees. We must know which degrees in all signs are masculine or feminine. From these degrees it is discovered whether it is a masculine or feminine chart. There

are 197 masculine and 163 feminine degrees. I shall set forth in detail which are which.

2. In Aries the first to the seventh are masculine, the eighth to the twelfth feminine, the 13th to the 16th masculine, the 17th to the 22nd feminine, and the 23rd to the 30th masculine.

3. In Taurus the first to the seventh are masculine, the eighth to the 17th feminine, the 18th to the 30th masculine.

4. In Gemini the first to the 17th are masculine, the 18th to the 23rd feminine, the 24th to the 30th masculine.

5. In Cancer the first and second are masculine, the third to the seventh feminine, the eighth to the tenth masculine, the eleventh and twelfth feminine, the 13th to the 18th masculine, the 19th and 20th feminine, the 21st to the 27th masculine, the 28th to the 30th feminine.

6. In Leo the first to the fifth are masculine, the sixth and seventh feminine, the eighth to the 15th masculine, the 16th to the 26th feminine, the 27th to the 30th masculine.

7. In Virgo the first to the seventh are feminine, the eighth to the twelfth masculine . . .

8. In Libra the first to the fifth are masculine, the sixth to the tenth feminine, the 11th to the 21st masculine, the 22nd to the 28th, feminine, the 29th and 30th masculine.

9. In Scorpio the first to the fourth are masculine, the fifth to the tenth feminine, the eleventh to the 16th masculine, the 17th to the 19th feminine, the 20th to the 27th masculine, the 28th to the 30th feminine.

10. In Sagittarius the first and second are masculine, the third to the fifth feminine, the sixth to the twelfth masculine, the 13th to the 24th feminine, the 25th to the 27th masculine, the 28th to the 30th feminine.

11. In Capricorn the first to the eighth are masculine, the ninth to the twelfth feminine, the 13th to the 19th masculine, the 20th to the 30th feminine.

12. In Aquarius the first to the ninth are masculine, the tenth to the twelfth feminine, the 13th to the 19th masculine, the 20th to the 30th feminine.

13. In Pisces the first degree to the tenth are masculine, the eleventh to the 20th feminine, the 21st to the 23rd masculine, the 24th to the 30th feminine.

14. Now that we have explained everything carefully, this book hastens to its end. But because at the beginning of the book of principles we wrote much about the course of the Moon and closed the book in the same way, so the beginning and end of this book should be dedicated to the most powerful divinity of the Moon. I shall therefore explain what the Moon signifies when located on the angles so that we may turn to other secrets in the fifth book.

## XXIV

## THE MOON WITH OTHERS ON THE ANGLES

1. If the Moon is located with the Sun on the ascendant in signs in which she rejoices or is exalted, or in her own house and free of the Sun's rays, she makes the parents famous and fortunate. She does the same located with the Sun on the MC. But on the descendant or on the IMC together with the Sun she makes them servants, wretched and humble, either slaves or beggers.

2. If Mars is in threatening aspect to the Moon thus located, or in opposition to the Sun and Moon, this indicates severe afflictions to the body and frequently blindness. If Mars is in conjunction with the Sun and Moon, he not only strikes down the parents with misery but indicates a violent death.

3. If the Moon is in conjunction with Saturn on the ascendant, this will make the natives first-born or first to be reared, but the mothers will be wretched widows, or work in temples and suffer serious illness. She indicates the same also on the MC if she is found with Saturn in this place.

4. The Moon on the descendant and on the IMC makes the mother oppressed with wretched slavery, but the natives themselves captives or separated from parents; these things are determined by the quality of the signs.

5. If the Moon is found in conjunction with Jupiter on the ascendant, she makes the mother high-born and noble, but the natives themselves are involved in religion and know the future. They also will be famous and noble. This is true of the Moon in conjunction with Jupiter on the MC.

6. But on the descendant or the IMC, in conjunction with Jupiter, the father's resources are destroyed; but afterwards from friends or relatives another inheritance is obtained. But in all charts you must observe the power of the houses and degrees, as we have so often said.

7. If the Moon is in conjunction with Mars on the ascendant, the mother is sickly and forced to take many journeys. Either the eyes or the stomach of the native are weak. If it is a diurnal chart, the native is weak in the whole body or has some part amputated. This is also true if the Moon is in conjunction with Mars on the MC. But on the descendant or the IMC together with Mars, they leave the fatherland and are detained in foreign lands.

8. If Mercury is found with them, the natives will be bandits, pirates, homicidal killers, despoilers of temples, sacrilegious, always accused of crimes, and for this suffer public punishment. But all things, as we have said, are determined by the quality of the signs.

9. Also if Saturn is in aspect in any way, the natives will be thrown into custody or suffer prison, so that they are always unshorn and unwashed. They will be in such want that they beg aid from enemies; some end their life in prison. But if Jupiter is in aspect they become temple servants.

10. If the Moon is found in conjunction with Venus on the ascendant or the MC, she will make the natives famous and noble, wielders of great power. On the descendant or the IMC, the family of the mother is humble but the natives never lack anything in life. They are, however, always objects of scandal in early life. In all signs and houses, if the Moon is found with Venus it makes husbands of two sisters, or wives of two brothers, or joins relatives in marriage.

11. If the Moon is found in conjunction with Mercury on the ascendant or the MC, the natives will be famous for their literary gifts, high-born, and acceptable for any high position. But if on the descendant or the IMC, the natives will carry on the business of lending and borrowing or account-keeping. This is enough for us to have said briefly in this last part of the book. We have put this matter last so that it can be easily remembered.

## XXV

## [CONJUNCTIONS AND DEFLUCTIONS OF THE MOON]

1. We must now show you how the Moon recedes and how she is joined; phenomena which the Greeks call *synafas* (junction) and *aporroicas* (defluction). For in all signs she recedes from many and is joined in aspect to many. For whenever she is found in the sign or terms of some planets she is always in a state of receding from their house and entering into the next house.

2. Observe therefore if the ruler of the terms aspects her and from what house. Observe the planet whose sign she enters in the third place—for that also has power in the forecast—and pass on to the last degrees of that sign, so that you will be able to find everything which pertains to the Moon's significance.

3. You must notice that in all signs when the Moon possesses the last degrees she does not indicate anything; for she is impeded by the sign she is meeting. Again when she is in the first degrees of a sign and receding from no one, then only the effects of the aspects must be considered. All the power of the sign she has just passed through is left behind at the boundary which is between signs, and another meaning is allotted in the first degree of the next sign.

4. This is exact conjunction and defluction of the Moon. In general we deal with signs as a whole. But in our work we have to deal also with details. Therefore we insist, again and again, that whenever you draw up a chart take into account the whole body of the data and put the whole together from the aspects of the individual planets, carefully observe the power of the houses and signs, but also compare the nature of the signs and the quality of the houses; observe the conditions of the planets and their courses, together with the phases, conjunction, and defluctions of

the Moon. If you have done all this you will be able to put together a true forecast.

5. Now the work is carried over into the fifth book so that everything may be explained in detailed forecast and we may continue to the chapter on the *Sphaera Barbarica*.

# Liber Quintus

[PRAEFATIO]

1. We have laid the foundation for our promised treatise, Mavortius, and the mature work has grown step by step. I have explained in easy language everything which seemed difficult and involved in obscurity. Your capacious intelligence, kindled by your burning enthusiasm, should by now have imbibed the message of the preceding books. With the help of the favorable influence of the stars you will now reach the divine secrets and be able to discover and interpret the fates of men.

2. But the reader expects more from us; the propositions of the preceding books anticipate more information. Thus, so that I may not deceive the eager mind with false promises, I shall cast off sloth and proceed to complete the secrets of the Mathesis. I would not wish to lose your attention in the midst of the explanation of the theory. And so we are presenting you with the full work which we promised.

3. But, lest the work be left bare of divine protection and lie open to the attacks of the hostile, let us begin with an invocation: Whoever Thou art, God, who by day keeps in motion the course of the heavens, who perpetuates the floods of the sea in their changing motion, who supports the solidity of the Earth on the immovable strength of its foundation, who refreshes toil-worn bodies with nightly sleep and who gives back again the renewed pleasure of the longed-for light, who strengthens the body's weakness with infusion of the Divine Mind, who fertilizes all the works of his hand with the health-giving breath of the winds, who with unwearied constancy deepens the waters of fountains and streams, who with the changeless cycles of the days brings back the varied seasons, Sole Governor and Chief of all, Sole Emperor and Lord, to whom the entire force of the heavenly powers is subservient, whose Will is the essence of finished creation; by whose unbreakable laws the organized nature of the world had imbued all things with eternity, Thou, Father of all and at the

same time, Mother,[70] Thou Father and Thine own Son, bound together by the chain of fate, to Thee we stretch out hands in prayer, Thee we worship with trembling supplication.

4. Pardon us that we are attempting to explain the course of Thy stars and their meanings. May it be Thy power, whatever that may be, which guides us to that interpretation. With purified soul, freed from earthly contacts and all taint of sin, we have written this book for Thy Romans in order that this subject may not be the only one which the Roman genius has not pursued.

5. And you, courses of the everlasting stars, and also Moon, mother of human bodies; and you, chief of the stars, who from the monthly courses of the Moon takes away her light and likewise returns it, Sun, best and greatest, who day after day order all things above all things with the rule of thy majesty, through whom, by divine decree, immortal soul is imparted to all living things, who alone opens the door of the realms above; at whose will the disposition of the fates is arranged; pardon us if with subtle speech we have reached the secret of thy power; not the impious desires of a sacrilegious soul drives us to this inquiry, but a mind infused with divine inspiration. Our purpose is to convey to the temples of the Tarpeian Rock whatever the divine ancients of Egypt brought forth from their shrines. Vouchsafe to me, therefore, the protection of your power, and strengthen with your majesty the timidity of my soul, lest I be deprived of your protection and fail in my promised work.

# I

## [THE SIGNS]

1. The signs of the zodiac, my dear Mavortius, have their own nature even without the presence of any planet. They have great power of forecasting and in many charts this is sufficient, even when bare of planets. But this effect is found only on the angles. I shall give an example so that you may understand more clearly.

2. If the ascendant is found in Aries, the MC in Capricorn, the descendant will then be in Libra and the IMC in Cancer. I shall explain in a general way what this situation indicates. When the ascendant is in Aries this has great predictive force for early youth; it denies the possibility of brothers; or out of many brothers it preserves only one. Also it weakens the native himself with pain or disease. His reputation is threatened; his paternal inheritance is at one time dissipated and again restored. To some the native will appear as a protector because of his excessive generosity, but to others his lavishness will be displeasing. His help will be given to ungrateful recipients. Life experience for him will be changeable and he will contend with constant headaches.

3. If the MC is in Capricorn, the indication is for some kind of fame.

The native will be surrounded by humble flattery; he will be put in charge of some kind of affairs or writings, provide many people with their daily needs, and supply what is necessary for foreign powers. He will be clever in many important undertakings, and have the secrets of obscure rites entrusted to him. He will penetrate the secrets of the heavens, if Mercury is in aspect to this point (the MC) in any way, or is on it.

4. The third angle, that is, the descendant, also claims for itself the power of forecasting. If it is found in Libra, the life of the native will be passed in royal houses or in the midst of public activities. But his life will be varied with a number of changes, so that bad luck will always follow good, and vice versa. Spiteful ill-will will attack his reputation, especially if Jupiter is not in trine to the ascendant or on it. If he is *not* in one of these positions, the misfortunes will be greater.

5. The fourth angle is the IMC; it will always be in Cancer if the ascendant is in Aries. This will make the natives famous and winners of prizes. Statues and portraits will be decreed for them if Jupiter from the ascendant aspects the IMC or is on it. Some of those closest to the native will be enemies, either on their own account or because of some relative. The natives themselves will be unkempt and squalid, but will always be supplied with friends, especially if Jupiter is on one of the angles.

6. If the ascendant is found in Taurus, the native will be worn out with many kinds of suffering; whatever he achieves in early youth he will always lose; but afterwards will regain it again. He will see his enemies laid low. If the MC is in Aquarius he will always have friendly ties with men more powerful than he; and will lead his life in the midst of public activities; his occupations will be around water; he will never be attacked by hostile accusations; will have both increases and losses in his possessions.

7. The descendant in Scorpio will make the native prudent in all life experiences; he will supply resources for foreign needs and will lose his first wife by accident or death. But if the chart is a woman's, she will lose her husband, and also her son. The IMC in Leo will make the natives seek a livelihood through their own efforts. By various kinds of trickery they obtain great property; and this will keep them in the ranks of the fortunate. But all this is determined by the calculation of the chart.

8. If the ascendant is in Gemini, the native will suffer in the first part of his life, but help will always come to him from his parents. He will learn heavenly secrets, and be linked to great men in faithful friendship; but will lose his inheritance. The MC in Pisces indicates a life spent in watery places and occupations having to do with water. An income will be received from foreign investment and either power or income will be divided between two states.

9. If the descendant is in Sagittarius the death of either brothers or relatives will come about through the native himself, and he will suffer great anxieties throughout his life. He will have enemies, lose his country

and wander in foreign travel. Afterwards returning to his father's gods he is restored to their protection. The IMC in Virgo makes him suffer constantly in early age, but indicates good fortune in later life. All this comes about according to the calculation of the chart, which you must always take into consideration.

10. The ascendant in Cancer always makes the natives sharp in intellect, but the kind who accomplish everything very slowly. They are sober and learned, but inclined to violent anger, and they commit evil acts under the influence of rage; otherwise they are strong and tolerant, and their anger, though easily aroused, is just as easily softened. They make a living from government or royal occupations, and many people are forced to flatter them for various reasons. Saturn, on or aspected to the ascendant in Cancer, indicates a violent death, great ill-health, or deaths of elder brothers.

11. The MC in Aries involves the native with powerful men; affords him his daily living from foreign investments. He will always be seeking possessions and luxuries. But his resources will be constantly in a state of flux, so that as often as he loses, he will gain the whole back again. The descendant in Capricorn indicates attacks from hidden ill-will which are, after many difficulties, harmonized in a peaceful settlement. The native will be clever and quick-thinking, but will suffer some kind of pain and great mental anguish.

12. The IMC in Libra indicates many sufferings, government duties or public affairs, or loss of inheritance. The native will be second in command in his occupation and will be indispensible to his superiors. He will be able to earn a living from literary pursuits and be entrusted with hidden secrets. He will be the eldest among all male children, will arrive at extreme old age and be honored by a notable funeral; but if Venus is found in the second house, a daughter will have a long life, if the ruler of the chart is well-located and favored by benefic planets.

13. Many toils and dangers are indicated by the ascendant in Leo, but great fame throughout life . The native will be freeborn, have unlimited power and never use his power for evil; he will secure his possessions by his own efforts, and attain power of command. If Mars is on the ascendant or the Sun in opposition or square aspect, this altogether denies the possibility of children. Jupiter in one of these locations indicates one daughter.

14. The MC in Taurus predicts a life in a public place or a temple. Also marriage with a widow, or a woman seduced by or subject to another, or in a servile condition, or an old woman, or an object of public shame. The native will be greatly honored by a powerful man, will be knowledgeable in all things and have a great increase in good fortune.

15. But the descendant in Aquarius indicates a life of ups and downs; in some cases, there will be popularity and approval. If the IMC is in Scorpio, the native will be in charge of certain projects. But if Mars is in any aspect

to this point, he will be in some kind of custody, but a loose kind. If Mars is in a morning rising, he will be a soldier, or in charge of arms, or will spend time in foreign places, or be cut down in a sudden or violent death.

16. The ascendant in Virgo predicts many toils and anxieties. But also a gift of prophecy either through dreams, casting of lots, or messages from divinity. The native will be involved in illicit activities through aggressive desire for women, but only until the rising of the sign is accomplished. He will be cheerful and gentle, with a true need for friendship. Grief for some kind of loss clings to him. He will be learned, always seeking the secrets of all doctrines and will retain closed in his heart what he has learned. He will have a reputation for simplicity, but acquire great possessions through his gift for learned speech, or from the accomplishment of his duties, or from moving into another's place, from religious activities, or from his own virtue.

17. The MC in Gemini indicates an income from public or sacred occupations, but only at the threshold of old age. The native will be a cultivator of the gods and religious rites, obeyed by a large number of citizens, a seeker after hidden things, knowledgeable in many skills and systems. In the last age of life he will be pointed out for his upright and correct life.

18. The descendant in Pisces makes the native popular, clever, involved in many activities, skilled in all kinds of contacts, and always well-born. He will travel in many lands, be known to many people who fawn on him. If the IMC is in Sagittarius he will be fortunate and his income will be from his possessions, and many will fawn on him. He will give thanks to the gods for his good fortune and will be entrusted with sacred duties. The prosperity of his children will gladden him; grief for lost children will be lightened by the happiness of more offspring. He will be skilled in all art, learned, and famous for his good fortune.

19. The ascendant in Libra predicts sickness and dangerous involvements. A crowd of enemies will always be ready to attack; and there will be constant law-suits in well-proven cases. The native will be devout, a worshiper of the gods, but his life will be varied. He will, however, be unconquered, seem inferior to none, and be famous. But the house of children will be ambivalent for him; some of his children will not survive. His judgment will always be correct, and he will be a servant of heavenly rites.

20. The MC in Cancer predicts famous deeds. The native will be maintained in religious or government office, and in extreme old age will attain fame, so that the last period of his life will be marked by high position. He will be extremely wealthy in old age and gradually over a period of time will attain all good fortune. He will get children late and have one son; but if Jupiter is in aspect to this point in any way, he will be gladdened by numerous fortunate progeny.

21. The descendant in Aries means a livelihood from watery occupa-

tions or watery places; also constant danger, continual anxiety, and some crisis in the desert, but riches are attained through frequent voyages. The native will have a hidden weakness; but in old age the greatest good luck will come to him. His wife will suffer from madness. The IMC in Capricorn will make prosperity fluctuate for various reasons. Whatever he has acquired he will lose, and what he has lost, will gain again. But his whole income will be gained through his own efforts, so that in the last period of life he will have the greatest prosperity. He will be forced to adopt a son from a strange family or get children from a low class woman.

22. Those who have the ascendant in Scorpio are clever, bad-tempered, and active in early youth, but encounter many kinds of misfortune in life. But afterwards, if Jupiter is in aspect in any way, they will attain fortune, power, and happiness; they will be famous and protected by the gods and will partake of the rites of sacred or heavenly religion. By their own wish they will travel into another region or state. They will be elevated in mind, sharp-witted, and have a fondness for eloquence. Variety will always be pleasing to them. Because of friends they will always be meeting troubles or dangers; and after much grief from loss of children, they will again be gladdened by offspring.

23. Leo on the MC makes life laborious with toil and sweat. The native will be in the power of a more powerful man, either for position or for food. He will have a position of power and will increase the amount of inheritance. He will be flattered by many and will give much of his resources to others. If the descendant is in Taurus there will be many enemies who will be overcome in a variety of ways. But the native will be driven to sexual activities and suffer some kind of scandal. He gains income, then loses it again. As many times as he loses it, he always recovers it. If the IMC is in Aquarius, he will live near water or have a living from water. Whenever he is useful to some, they will always be ungrateful.

24. The ascendant in Sagittarius indicates many enemies, and gain from an unexpected source. The native will be detained in foreign countries, and will sail on a large river or a large sea. He will be involved in public affairs, and will make his living from water or watery places, will acquire many skills and different kinds of learning, will be prudent, intelligent, knowledgeable in all things. If the MC is in Virgo, he will be selected for great advancement and placed over many. A crowd of listeners will follow his orders and many will have their subsistence through him, but they will be ungrateful.

25. The descendant in Gemini indicates sons and grandsons, but only in old age. The native will be able to bear all grief calmly and intelligently and despise all losses. Some read secret writings and point out sacred and heavenly things. They will be prudent, intelligent and just, and always entrap their enemies with hidden trickery. If the IMC is found in Pisces, this indicates occupations in watery places. The native will be famous and noble, responsible for all things entrusted to him; but he will be estranged

from his wife or family. If Jupiter is in any kind of aspect, a wife will be easily won and matrimonial ties will be pleasant, but the wife will be known for promiscuity or adultery.

26. If the ascendant is in Capricorn, the native will always show pure affection for his friends. He will be tricky and happy and will lack nothing for his subsistence. He will travel; those he helps will always be ungrateful. He will be likeable, but of small mind; he will annoy the gods with long-winded prayers, but his resources will be plentiful. He will be involved with passionate women but will be the kind who curses them once his pleasure is fulfilled. The secrets of sacred rites or a foreign way of life or a hidden religion will be known to him.

27. The MC in Libra makes the native pious, learned, of good repute, and endowed with pleasing speech. He will keep his vows to the gods, and be free of needs and dangers. His activities will be prosperous in the beginning, but he will later be overcome with evil deeds. Good fortune will come from the misfortune of others, and a profit from another's death, or from some ancient or unknown relationships.

28. If the descendant is in Cancer, the native will have great trouble from relatives and will be involved in great danger. If the IMC is in Aries he will make great mistakes. After trouble, a restful life will be allotted him, but his life will be changeable. At one time he will be on the highest step of honor, the next cast down from his position. The wife and first son will be seriously ill.

29. If the ascendant is in Aquarius, whatever the native attains will be lost and ruined; whatever he seeks he will lose again, but whatever he has lost he will regain easily. He will do favors for many and help them with means of subsistence, but they will always be ungrateful. He will be in great danger so that his life is despaired of, but he will be freed by protection of the gods. Many men will attack him with fierce hatred. He will work with divine or religious writings and will be known to many for his good deeds. If the MC is in Scorpio he will be brave, but his life will be troubled with harsh experiences.

30. He will travel from one place to another and, if he is low-born, will carry on servile occupations; but afterwards, affairs will turn out prosperously for him. He will have misfortunes in early life concerning wife and children, but later fortune will come to him from the notice of others. If the descendant is in Leo, he will quarrel with his wife; he will be married to an old or an unworthy woman, or one who has been detected in various love affairs; and he will be plotted against by his own people. Enemies will rise up against him suddenly but he will overcome them with his courage and strength.

31. If the IMC is in Taurus, the native will be great and a familiar of many powerful men; he will have fame, and control the income of many; and have many projects entrusted to him because of his upright character. He will die oppressed with weight of old age, if the ruler of the chart

follows the condition of Taurus, if it is located in favorable houses, and if it is in exact aspect as to sign or degree, and decrees the number of years.

32. The ascendant in Pisces makes the native talented, intelligent, faithful, friendly. He will be in charge of affairs, but in such a way that he will always be someone's subordinate. Enemies will be easily overcome. Fame will come from some long-continued business; in the course of time he will attain high position and great good fortune, and he will be famous for his many journeys.

33. If the MC is in Sagittarius, the native will be involved in many mistakes and various kinds of danger. He will be skillful in all confrontations and will have more than moderate conflicts with powerful personalities. Because of a certain individual, he will meet hidden attacks and will lose the whole of what he possessed at first. He will manage other peoples' affairs, and be a firm friend. But he is always driven by visual attraction to sexual promiscuity.

34. If the descendant is in Virgo, the native will be prudent and will furnish subsistence for foreigners. He will be a faithful guardian of secrets, will make many friends by his protection of them, and will attain great riches. His friends will often be ungrateful, but he will be tied with bonds of love to his wife, though she herself will often be ungrateful to him. He will suffer severe grief through misfortune of wife and children.

35. The IMC in Gemini indicates hidden pains, weakness, and great ill fortune. But good luck will come later, and what is lost will be returned in a sudden discovery of riches, so that he will possess resources which fulfill all his needs, and death will come to him in old age on a journey. But in this the ruler of the chart must be consulted.

36. Some readers may think that these are just general remarks, but there is real substance in them. For the individual signs make all these predictions with their own power. If you read the *Myriogenesis* of Aesculapius[71] which he claimed Mercury had revealed to him, you will find that from individual minutes, without any help of the planets, the order of the whole chart can be explained. For the ascendant, located in individual minutes, explains the whole order of life most clearly and obviously: its appearance and experiences, kinds of danger, and the first day of life. Since the individual sign consists of 30 degrees and 1800 minutes, the location of the ascendant in one minute describes the entire fate of men.

37. The divine Aesculapius, sprung from a divine race and taught by the revered power, left the renowned theory which is embodied in this work. Because of our mortal and earthly nature we do not deserve to be taught by such teachers. Therefore we shall follow the footsteps of divine men, and write only what has been handed down by tradition.

38. But, my dear Lollianus, do not look for the theory of *Myriogenesis* in this book. When our meager talent with the help of favorable powers will have finished this book, then I will write for you in twelve other books the

secrets of that teaching. But now we must continue, or we will never arrive at the *Myriogenesis*. First we must learn the basic principles.

## II

## [THE ASCENDANT]

1. We have described in general what the angles indicate. Now we shall explain in more detail the effect of the ascendant located in the terms of the planets. You should note attentively what we say and commit it to memory. Otherwise you will not be able to interpret the fates of men.

2. If the ascendant is found in the terms of Saturn, this will make the natives always sluggish and slow, with thoughts hidden in deep silence; they are wicked and malevolent, alien to all grace and charm; their plans are slow to take effect; their hostility is turned against everyone and their anger is long-continued. If Saturn himself is found exactly on the ascendant, he will deny brothers, or he will strike down all brothers and sisters so that the native will never have nieces and nephews.

3. If Jupiter is found in the terms of Saturn together with the ascendant, he will make the natives severe, avaricious, and unclean; in their whole life they avoid happiness, pursue servile occupations and attitudes, and give over all their possessions to another by right of gift. If Mars is found in those degrees, he will make the natives cruel and criminal, possessed by malice. They hire themselves out for various evil deeds. But their malice and criminal tendencies can never be hidden and their evil doing is uncovered by their rashness.

4. The Sun in those terms makes the natives moderate in character, but prepared for every poisonous evil; always leaving their projects unfinished. Venus in these degrees will involve them in sordid love affairs, and make them always passionately desire strange things. Mercury in those degrees will make them sordid in all experiences, often involved in miserable crises because of crime and frequently in prison. The full or waxing Moon in those degrees makes the natives empty in mind and body. But if she is waning she fouls the whole body with malignant humors, or produces dropsy, or makes the natives deformed, pale, or insane.

5. The ascendant in the terms of Jupiter indicates all characteristics of virtue and wisdom. If Jupiter himself is found in his own terms, he will make the natives large in spirit, but fierce and cruel. If Saturn or Mars is found in those terms in a diurnal chart, they will be treacherous, and never keep their promises. They pretend to have wisdom, or think themselves wise; but they hold a low and squalid place in life. Jupiter by day in these terms somewhat alleviates this misfortune.

6. If Venus is in these terms, the natives will be characterized by all kinds of good deeds, but will never have a successful marriage. They will be benevolent and reap the rewards of their good deeds in continual

prosperity. Mercury in these terms will make men of good character, alien to all malice, with a clear intelligence, thinking deeply about everything. The Moon in these terms indicates all kinds of good fortune, especially good physical health which overrides affliction and illness. The Sun in these terms indicates the same as the Moon.

7. Those who have the ascendant in the terms of Mars are always marked with a sharp mind. Saturn in these terms makes them similarly sharp, but given to frequent rages. Mars in this place by day drives them, with depraved greed, to all manner of crime; they will be rash, involved in constant misfortune and forced to toil for a living. But in a nocturnal chart they will be brave, cruel, greedy, and irreligious, and inclined to destroy the property of others.

8. The Sun in these terms makes clever men who both lay traps and are caught in them. Venus, thus located, always indicates the passion of adulterers. They take pains with their own good looks, are said to be charming and to win much profit from friendships with men. Mercury in these terms will make aggressive murderers. They are intelligent, but given to sexual license and drunkenness; they are generous and spendthrift, never display good judgment, pay for their expenses without forethought or order, and prefer illicit love affairs with boys.

9. The Moon in this position makes men who spy out their enemies in various ways, but are also detected by them. They are weighted down with toil, and suffer serious wounds from iron or fire. But the full Moon in a diurnal chart makes them strong in body. The waning Moon by night makes them strong and robust in body, but constantly traveling. A violent death is always indicated for these men.

10. Those who have the ascendant in the terms of Venus will be musicians or lovers of music. They will be kind, benevolent, merciful, wishing to help all men. In a diurnal chart they will hold high office, be friends of powerful men or emperors, and have prosperous men or emperors, and have prosperous offspring.

11. Those who have Saturn in these terms in a diurnal chart hate women and marriage. If it is a nocturnal chart, they will be impure and unchaste, not able to accomplish normal sexual intercourse, but trapped in monstrous unnatural vices. They will be in trouble from the changing nature of their plans and will be hated by all respectable people. Jupiter in these terms will make them gentle, sensual, luxury-loving, never cruel in any way, moderate in all their activities. They will be famous artisans and hold high positions in temples.

12. Mars in these terms in a diurnal chart indicates riots, a life disturbed by revolutions or troubles, and dangers because of women. They will be musicians, organ-players, poets, sculptors, or artificers or mechanics of subtle and intricate arts; they will definitely be talented. Mars, if found in those terms in a nocturnal chart, indicates marriage with a powerful high-born woman who brings with her enormous wealth. But the native

will be tortured by painful anxieties.

13. If the Sun is found in these terms, all occupations will turn out prosperously, but marriage will be quarrelsome. The Sun indicates profit and friendship with powerful men. Mercury in this position will make the natives lustful, but intelligent and of good character. They will be pleasing, lovable, and learned; astronomers, grammarians, divine poets whose songs have grace and charm, or gifted orators; their speeches or poems will be praised by posterity.

14. The Moon in these terms will make artisans of excellent taste or popular sculptors. This is true in a daytime chart. But in a nocturnal chart, she indicates occupations around water, such as fishing, but far from human society. The natives will be jealous, but otherwise benevolent, and will accomplish everything with a balanced moderation.

15. Those who have the ascendant in the terms of Mercury will be literary men, learned, correct in judgment, who faithfully carry out their entrusted duties. They will be made caretakers or governors of states, responsible administrators, or governors of the treasury. If Mercury is found in his own terms with the ascendant, he will make astronomers, astrologers, or *haruspices* who foretell the future. They will always be famous and well-known in every way.

16. Saturn in these terms will make the natives bitter, unhappy, silent, moderate in speech, good keepers of secrets; they always work hard, make progress slowly, and have a bad reputation with the people. For they will be poisoners, burning with continual rage, and using every kind of poison, but vindicated either by chance or their own deserts. They are accustomed to foretell the future through dreams, but are rash in their counsels.

17. Jupiter in this place will make physicians or men so skilled in law that the affairs of powerful men hang on their intercession. They will be popular, but frequently involved in adultery. If they are born during the night, they will be famous and reputable administrators or notaries. They will be respectable to the end of their lives.

18. Mars found in these degrees in a diurnal chart will make the natives wicked, malevolent, constantly fighting, cruel, rash, softened by no feelings of humanity, loud and shameless; they are insane with rage, spit on everything in a mood of vicious satiety, are fickle, easily persuaded to change their views—cheats, killers, given to every kind of crime. But in a nocturnal chart these evils are somewhat alleviated.

19. The Sun in these terms will make the natives famous and high-born. They will be well-known and popular throughout the whole state, and they will hold many positions. And if Mercury himself is with the Sun (and the ascendant in his own terms), the natives will be known for fulfilling their duties responsibly and for great uncorrupted wisdom.

20. Venus in these degrees indicates the same as Mercury in the terms of Venus. She will make the natives great, fortunate, attractive, attaining

everything easily, happy, learned, elegant, lovers of music. With their gift of oratory, they are able to persuade the multitude to whatever they wish. Or they may be well-known poets. All these obtain good fortune from others' mischance. But if the Moon is in the terms of Mercury with the ascendant, in a daytime chart, this will produce artisans with outstanding skills. In a nocturnal chart she indicates facility in all the arts; the natives will be clever, knowledgeable, and chosen for all kinds of occupations. They are often traveling merchants or, for various reasons, move from place to place. They never show their feeling and despise all outward show of grief.

## III

## [SATURN IN DIFFERENT SIGNS]

1. We have described in detail what the ascendant indicates; now we shall explain what is signified by the planets located in individual signs. I shall discuss this in detail so that a malicious reader may not be able to say to you that we have left anything out.

2. Saturn in Aries in any chart indicates evil and unfortunate events in early life, and hindrance to all activities. Also, by the time Saturn has finished his first orbit, that is 30 years, the native will have lost all or most of his paternal and maternal inheritance. But in the course of time another inheritance will be bestowed on him.

3. These natives will be sluggish; they will meet serious dangers every seventh or ninth year and be overwhelmed by them, unless they are freed by the influence of a benefic planet, and if Saturn himself is ruler of the chart. They will quarrel in early life with wives; their wives are not virgins and are separated from them either by discord or death. Saturn in this position gives a wife late in life, a widow, or one seduced by another, or with children by another husband, or an object of scandal. Saturn allots a wife when he has finished his first orbit, or when he is in square aspect to the Moon, or when the Sun is in trine to him from Leo or Sagittarius. If Saturn allots a wife under these circumstances, she will be obedient to her husband and live with him in affection to the end of his life.

4. Under these same circumstances there will be offspring, and they will be prosperous if Jupiter is in aspect to the Moon in any way. If he is not, the native either never has children or loses them. When Saturn has again returned to Aries he indicates serious dangers and sharp hostility between brothers.

5. Those who have Saturn in Taurus obtain everything through their own efforts; but whatever they accumulate in early age will later diminish. In early life they are oppressed with various injustices, are subject to others and from necessity fawn upon powerful men. They will be needy in early life and also suffer from infected wounds; they will recover from long illnesses and live a long life.

6. They retain nothing of their father's or mother's fortune, but through themselves and other sources they will recover their possessions. Saturn thus located brings the mother close to beggary through loss of inheritance, unless Venus is in favorable aspect to Saturn. The Moon must also be in favorable aspect to Venus. These men through their own strength and merit attain the greatest good fortune, but are weighed down by misfortune until Saturn finishes his first orbit.

7. Dangers will come to them either from lawsuits, illness or travel. They will meet serious danger either in their 9th, 14th, 25th, or 32nd year. If in the time of danger they are under protection of a benefic planet, they will escape the threat of instant death and have a respite until the 43rd or 53rd year. In those years they will be in danger from plots, lawsuits or loss of possessions. Again, if they have the protection of a benefic planet they will be freed from all peril.

8. But Saturn never allows them to marry before the 32nd year and never are virgin wives given to them. If they do marry virgins, their children die, or they themselves are estranged from the love of their wives. They will be more fortunate if they take foreign wives or women seduced by another. But they will marry only when Saturn enters Cancer, or is located in Virgo or Capricorn.

9. Those who have Saturn in Gemini will encounter serious crises every seven or nine years up to their 23rd year. They will be especially susceptible to illnesses in these years, if Mars is in square aspect. There will also be danger in these years of riots, confrontations and great toil.

10. There will be no great inheritance either from mother or father. The native will gain everything through his own efforts and will be particularly oppressed with weight of toil while Saturn is crossing Cancer, Libra, and Aries. He will be successful when Saturn finishes his first orbit and is in Leo or Capricorn. Saturn in Gemini indicates afflictions, and important reverses, enemies, law suits, or quarrels of some kind. The native will meet losses of income and frequent conflicts until he reaches the last crisis of his life. After that he will be in charge of important affairs by order of someone in power and will be a friend of famous and powerful men. He will at last become famous and noble, travel a great deal, and move from one region to another.

11. But he will not be given a virgin for wife. If by chance the influence of Jupiter gives him a virgin for wife, he will be separated from her either by divorce or death. He will either be without children or will have one son. But when Saturn arrives at the sign of Scorpio, the native will be lucky, famous and rich. Then he will be allotted a widow for wife and will live with her without disagreement until his last day.

12. Many affairs will be entrusted to him; he will spend much, and will have many encounters with powerful men; from these encounters he will be in danger unless Jupiter helps him. For those who have Saturn in this position are always opposed to great and powerful men, always depend

for their protection on lesser men, and are often thrown into custody. They will grow their hair long (in mourning) because of some trouble in friendship or some kind of loss by death. But after they have been shaken by various crises, they will find increase and good fortune and achieve both praise and possessions and an unexpected inheritance. Then they acquire riches and control of very large estates.

13. Those who have Saturn in Cancer are involved in seditions, lawsuits, and reverses; they lose their paternal and maternal inheritances, but through their own efforts acquire great possessions. Their life is such that they always gain and lose again. They will face dangers or illnesses every seventh or ninth year until they are 23.

14. Up to that age they will be worn out by enormous perils. But if in the time of danger a benefic planet is ruler of time, or (well-located) is in favorable aspect to Saturn or to the ruler of the chart, the threat of danger is lessened. But even in this case there will still be deaths of parents or brothers, or losses from lawsuits; but the native himself will be freed from all physical danger. When Saturn is in his own houses, he indicates losses, storms, dangers, illnesses, constant lawsuits. In opposition to his own houses he predicts the same things.

15. But when Saturn is in Gemini he will disturb the native with a continuation of evils until he crosses to Cancer. When he comes to the tropical degrees of Cancer he indicates loss of inheritance and sets the native in such poverty that he must be maintained by a stranger's kindness. Also riots, revolutions, and various crises are indicated. But when Saturn has crossed the tropic degrees of Cancer, the aforesaid evils will be lulled to sleep and the native will be freed from anxieties and dangers.

16. The first marriage will not last nor will there be a successful outcome to the first marriage contract. For in early youth the native will marry a woman of low class or degenerate in some way, but afterwards will sensibly separate from her. But if Saturn in this sign either has the Moon with him or is aspected to her, he will deny children, or the children will be deformed by some blemish of color, be dark-colored with abundance of black bile, or suffer other bilious difficulties. They will be despaired of in their illness and will recover only with difficulty.

17. The natives who have Saturn in Cancer will be straight-forward, kind, merciful, helpful to strangers in trouble, gaining a livelihood from managing foreign investments. They will be fathers of foreign children; will have hidden afflictions, but will be endowed with such high office that they will seem to be masters of their brothers. They will be wealthy and always lead their lives in prosperity; known to powerful men; never in any servile occupations; of good and respectable character; but sluggish in all occupations and unwilling to be involved in public affairs.

18. Those who have Saturn in Leo will be objects of continual ill will. They will be strong in their early years; sometimes destined for famous

and glorious deeds from which they will gain great good fortune. Sometimes they will be removed from these occupations and even from all administration. They either receive nothing from parents, or lose what they get. In early youth they will be sluggish and endure hidden pains in the body. They will be involved in a variety of occupations.

19. They will never be able to marry virgins, but if they gain such wives through violence they will be separated from them. It will be useful for them to take wives who already have children. But as long as Saturn is finishing his first orbit they will have neither marriage, inheritance nor glory. Whatever they acquired before this time they, inheritance nor glory. Whatever they acquired before this time they lose. Saturn in this house indicates two wives. Those whom they know outside of this number they will either reject or get rid of.

20. But they will have grief from accidents to children, and if the Moon is either with Saturn or moving toward him they will get children with difficulty. Whenever Saturn enters tropical signs, he indicates difficulties. The same is true in Pisces and in Gemini. In other signs he indicates great fame; but in occupations and life there are many changes. The natives will sail great seas and rivers, make their way through deserts; they will dare what their parents never dared and accomplish it in the easiest way.

21. They will have many brothers either from another mother or another father, but they will be superior to all relatives and attain high office. They will be most prudent, benevolent but quick-tempered, of good counsel, upright, faithful, friends of many but hostile to foreigners; responsible in all dealings, putting their greatest effort into their work. They will have a scar on some part of the body and will frequently lose their high position and fall from the highest step to the lowest.

22. Income is acquired from a stranger's generosity, so large that they will be able to assuage the difficulties of others. They will be defenders of freemen and always protect the possessions of people in trouble. When all these things have been accomplished they will die after a long life and their spirit will be summoned to heaven by the gods. When Saturn is located in Leo he recalls to the sky—to their place of origin—the souls of those who have him thus in their charts.

23. Those who have Saturn in Virgo will suffer illnesses and difficulties in early life, but will be involved in more serious evils when Saturn makes a transit to Capricorn or to Taurus, or when he enters double signs. In these signs he indicates riots, losses, anxieties, griefs, sudden dangers and destruction. But when he is passing through other signs he indicates good deeds and occupations, fame and increase in income; or at least the natives will be freed from difficulties, toil and danger and get rest. That period of time will be considered joyful and glorious.

24. When, in the chart, Saturn comes into the sign of Virgo he indicates no good fortune. The natives will have more from their own efforts than from their parents; they will be sometimes in low positions and sometimes

in high. They will be constantly moved around from one place and from one business to another. Whatever they gain at first will be lost; but when lost it will be regained; but they will lose it again and never be able to attain the income they seek.

25. There will be trouble in connection with women in early life. Wives allotted in early life will not stay with them; the legal wives they take later will not agree with them and they will not have a happy life with them. They will not have virgins for wives, but women seduced by others, or who have already had children. But if they marry virgins, they quickly separate from them. They do not remain with one woman, but finally marry in the lower classes, and these wives they cherish with faithful affection.

26. They will be learned and wise, engaged in many activities, seeking many things. Whenever they attain any of these they will waste the substance of their possessions. They will sustain many losses on behalf of others, but will be deceitful even in these affairs. They will be involved in popular pursuits, known to all and familiar to all. If Saturn is located on an angle or in important houses, they will mourn for children, and waste their inheritance. Some are allotted relatives for wives.

27. They will have afflictions and pains in important places of the body. If Saturn himself is the ruler of time, dividing the time among the other planets, this indicates anxieties, injuries and journeys, but journeys which are unnecessary and difficult involving such dangers that they approach the state of crises. Some will encounter dangers from high places or precipices, or from wild beasts or quadrupeds, or from water; or they will see before their eyes such danger of death that they will think themselves reborn.

28. They will come to the attention of great and powerful men, and when they have been accepted by them will be freed by their help, and raised to great prosperity. They will be long-lived and achieve good fortune late in life. But they will only acquire possessions if Saturn is not ruler of the chart.

29. Those who have Saturn in Libra, aspected to benefic planets will have great resources. But if Saturn is bare of favorable influence they will have no livelihood; also they will lose whatever they inherit from parents. If Saturn is unfavorably aspected by a malefic planet, this indicates serious crises together with the aforesaid evils. If it is a seventh or ninth year, the dangers will be so much worse that they can escape them only with difficulty.

30. They will have such ill fortune and poverty that they will seek their daily bread from others. But if a benefic planet is in favorable position at the exact time the danger threatens, they will be released from all bad fortune. Still, whatever they accumulate in early age they lose, especially when Saturn has entered the sign of Cancer. For then they will suffer trouble, losses, accusations, illnesses, and prison.

31. When Saturn is found in a right square aspect, but also when he has

entered the first angles, then he indicates all kinds of bad fortune; proscriptions, loss of inheritance, beggary, grief to parents from accidents of children, poverty, anxieties, accusations, law suits. He indicates the same things when he has again entered his own house.

32. Saturn indicates the same in the charts of women. They will be intelligent, reserved, of good counsel, prudent, anxious for great learning, commanding, famous, glorious, involved in important affairs, in friendship with important men, holding high position in great states. They are quarrelsome, not easily deceived or cheated, study much and know much, quickly escape from danger. But they are seriously worn out from diseases of the nerves.

33. They will be in charge of public places, be helpful to others, and from others hold powers over men. They will control the property of strangers, and be outstanding in many ways; able to foretell the future. They get control of their own property and possessions and hand it down to their sons, and get wives for their sons according to the indication of their chart. When they die, freed from all danger and anxiety, their property will be divided among their sons, if a long space of life has been allotted them by the ruler of the chart. This you must carefully observe in all charts, as we have said.

34. Those who have Saturn in Scorpio are attacked in early youth by many disturbances and dangers, and have no control over paternal or maternal inheritance. If they have received anything from parents, they waste it in dissipation. The parents will be neither famous nor noble, but the natives themselves will be reared in greatest luxury, but afterwards will have severe trouble and have to earn their own living.

35. Similar dangers are indicated for every seventh or ninth year until the 43rd. But if the natives are protected in time of danger by a benefic planet they will escape the crisis. Nevertheless they will be disturbed by constant troubles. If Saturn aspects his own house in trine, especially when he is in Cancer, he indicates griefs, pains, journeys, and poverty.

36. But when Saturn comes to Leo and makes his station in that sign, then he will allow the beginning of good fortune; then he allots every kind of profit, high position, and the beginnings of famous activities. The moment he enters Leo the whole chart is transferred to good fortune. Pains, griefs and anxieties are put to sleep. But the natives do not continue with the first wife whom they had in Scorpio. Saturn in this house does not allot virgins for wives, but widows, or those who have been married to others. The natives will marry many women, but be separated either by death or divorce.

37. Illnesses and weaknesses in the extremities of the body and continual pains in hidden places are indicated by Saturn in Scorpio. If Jupiter from a favorable house is in beneficent aspect to Saturn, all these will be lessened. But if Saturn in Scorpio is in the house of children, he will be harmful and first sons will be lost in some way.

38. Afterwards the native will be gladdened by healthy offspring. But when Saturn has returned to this sign of Scorpio, they will be stronger, famous and powerful. These same things are indicated in charts of women. For, as we said in the book of principles, whatever is indicated in the charts of men is also true in women's charts.

39. Those who have Saturn in Sagittarius are involved in many dangers and illnesses, and never receive inheritance from fathers or mothers. They will gain possessions through their own efforts, but lose them again. Crises will occur throughout their whole lives every seventh or ninth year.

40. From these dangers they are easily freed. But when Saturn approaches the angles, that is when he enters the degree of the MC or the IMC, he produces a certain wandering of mind. He indicates riots, domestic quarrels, difficulties, losses, prison terms, lost law suits and griefs. But when he enters Pisces, he makes a beginning of good fortune, and when he makes his station in that sign he predicts fame and increase in income.

41. But when he arrives at Gemini and Cancer he is contrary to the native in every way. When he comes to Sagittarius, Capricorn and Aquarius, he indicates riots and revolutions. When he returns a second time to Pisces, he will make the native famous and restore the whole of what has been lost. But never will those who have Saturn in their chart have virgins for wives, and they will always have constant grief from misfortunes of children. If Jupiter is not in aspect to Saturn in Sagittarius, they will have neither wives nor children. They will have serious griefs because of women or through women, and will meet serious dangers in water or near water.

42. Those who have Saturn in Capricorn, that is in tropical degrees, will have their whole life and resources subject to constant reverses. They often reach the highest step of fortune and then slip back again, and are held captive by unjust ill fortune until Saturn completes his orbit, or as long as he is ruler of time.

43. These crises will endure while Saturn is crossing Gemini and Cancer. The natives may be expected to have great resources, but are hindered by domestic needs from having riches; their paternal and maternal inheritance is wasted. Whatever they accumulate they lose in various ways and are constantly diminishing their resources.

44. They will travel constantly, and have illnesses and encounter dangers on the fifth, seventh and ninth years, especially when those numbers are tripled. At that time they meet sickness, losses, riots, griefs and injuries. They will be submerged in deepest misfortune unless they are rescued by influence of benefic planets. These evils continue until Saturn enters his own houses in a right trine.

45. When Saturn begins in Capricorn and comes to Gemini and Cancer, he indicates all kinds of evils until he arrives at Leo. When he arrives in that degree of Leo in which he was in the chart in Capricorn, he

indicates great good fortune. But in this sign he does not allot a virgin as wife, but separates the native from her either by death or divorce. He does not allow the natives to marry the ones they were first betrothed to. They will be given wives seduced by others, will marry twice, have grief from death of children, or have no children altogether.

46. There will be pain and sickness in the extremities of the body or in hidden organs. Great storms of life and dangers occur when Saturn enters Cancer, but when he enters Leo, there will be smooth sailing. For then Saturn predicts rest, increase in income, health, happiness and a true order of life, with all misfortunes put to sleep.

47. Those who have Saturn in Aquarius will be unfortunate in early life and lose what they inherited from their fathers. Whatever they accumulate at first they lose, but gain it back again. They will have serious illnesses, but be cured of them. Crises will occur every seventh and ninth year until they are 43. At that time there will be unusual dangers— illnesses, lawsuits, terrors, journeys, poverty, and hard labor. The natives will be brought so low that their lot will be similar to that of captives or slaves. All these experiences will be like a wretched death. But after all crises are over, if Jupiter and Venus are well located in the chart there will be profit, fame, and high position. But they will have an affliction or illness, or a scar from fire or sword.

48. The lawful wives they are allotted will be unsatisfactory and the type who live contrary to the rule of law. But the natives only suffer until Saturn arrives in Leo. Before he arrives in Leo he lowers income, indicates loss of mental faculties, injuries, deaths in the family—such misfortunes that the natives will attempt suicide.

49. When Saturn is located on the angles he makes these same predictions so that evils grow from day to day. There will be grief from death of relatives, periods of freezing cold, and wretched poverty, especially if, while Saturn is on the angles, the natives reach their seventh or ninth year. For then the natives will be prisoners or beggars, unshorn and unwashed, especially if Saturn in Aquarius is the ruler of time.

50. They will carry out laborious tasks, especially in temples. They will also encounter different crises from their own acts and not easily be able to avoid them, and will find no road to happiness, but will lose everything in law suits. But if Jupiter is in important houses in these times of danger, flight and travels are eliminated from the prediction.

51. When Saturn has finished all this and the natives have spent the largest part of their lives in misfortune, then, little by little they will free their necks from bad fortune. All the sordidness will be washed away and they will rise to various high positions through their own planning. They will have all the insignia of the highest office and have such power over people and regions that their memory will be everlasting.

52. They will be friends of kings or powerful men, will receive rich gifts and priesthoods in temples. Their good fortune will comprise estates,

riches, servants, control over men and women; they will be so wealthy that they will maintain others. Their relatives will flourish through their protection. Finally, after a long life, they will die with a good reputation.

53. Those who have Saturn in Pisces will have neither paternal or maternal inheritance; whatever they have in early life they will lose. Through their own efforts they will win a new income. They will have great sickness and dangers, especially every seventh and ninth year until they are 33.

54. There will be illnesses, law suits, accusations without cause, riots, sudden uprisings, constant torments of mind, dangers caused by women or occurring in water. The wives they are first given are not profitable to them. Saturn in Pisces does not allot virgins as wives. When Saturn arrives at the angles of the chart, then he indicates the most serious troubles and reverses, especially when finishing his first orbit.

55. When Saturn reaches Cancer he predicts better times. When he enters Leo he straightens out their affairs and bestows fame, income and high position. All their activities turn out well, and the affairs of great men are entrusted to their management; from this administration they gain great increase in income.

56. But they will have great pains in the extremities or in hidden parts of the body and great scars from wounds by a weapon, also grief from accidents of children. But after Saturn has disturbed their early years, then he indicates happiness from children and marriage, according to the essence and measurement of the chart, as the other planets predict with their authority.

# IV

## [JUPITER IN DIFFERENT SIGNS]

1. Now that we have explained the predictions of Saturn, let us turn to those of Jupiter.

2. Those who have Jupiter in Aries will be disturbed in early life, until they have finished the reverses indicated in the chart. But afterward successful activities, prosperous times, important affairs are indicated. They will be friends of great and powerful men and will be entrusted with important administrative duties in royal houses. They will be gladdened by wives and children. Victory is predicted in all contests and law suits; and whatever they plan will be easily fulfilled.

3. Jupiter indicates the reputation of a good character. The natives have a certain mark around the mouth. They will be managers of other people's money, devout in worship of the gods, and responsible about keeping secrets. They will be appointed to high duties by powerful men or kings and appear commanding and strong. The first years will be difficult, but afterward everything will be completed successfully, by

constant help of the gods, especially if, in important houses, Saturn, Mars, the Sun, Mercury, Venus, or the Moon is in trine aspect.

4. Those who have Jupiter in Taurus will have great fame and power; but in early life they will encounter serious troubles: illness, law suits, even slavery, quarrels with the powerful, losses, toil, injuries. But after they have been thus oppressed they will find a fortunate outcome to all their affairs. They will have fame and the friendship of powerful men who will entrust their secrets to them.

5. They will sail great seas or rivers, or be attendants at sacred rites, but have encounters with criminals and disreputable men. Protection comes to them from women, as well as high position. They will be just, brave, and trustworthy friends. Their speech will be fluent; they will bravely defend friends. But they will be rash, brave in all contests, never desiring anything for themselves, but always for friends.

6. Their friends are often ungrateful; but after they have slipped away, they often return to them. They will be sons of two fathers—one by nature, the other by adoption—or of two mothers. They will at first have joy, then grief from wives and likewise from children. Their good fortune is a boon to many. But all these things are indicated according to the calculation of the chart.

7. Those who have Jupiter in Gemini will have great glory and power, and be known for their friendships; but whatever they seek they lose again, and their life is in a constant state of flux. In early life they will be involved in quarrels, troubles, losses, poverty, and illnesses, and will have constant grief from wives and children, until they are 45 years old. Up to that time they will lose whatever they accumulate.

8. But when that time is finished they will have possessions and fame. After quarrels with a wife in early years, later they will have a successful marriage; they will hold high public office. All this is indicated according to the computation of the chart and the combined aspects of the planets which you must observe and remember in all charts.

9. Those who have Jupiter in Cancer will be friends of the powerful and will faithfully preserve their secrets. When Jupiter becomes ruler of their time, they will have possession, high office and fame. But for them happiness and the trust of friends will not last. They will be unfortunate, especially when Saturn enters the important houses or when he arrives at Aquarius or Pisces. He indicates dangers, riots, losses, illnesses, quarrels with powerful men or relatives, false accusations and public slander.

10. These are alleviated if Saturn and Jupiter are found on the angles. If Saturn arrives in this sign and comes into conjunction with Jupiter, he is infinitely favorable, but more when he arrives in Leo. For when he reaches Leo in his second orbit he indicates good fortune, glory and high position; the natives have posts of command, overcome all adversaries, their reputation is universally good, and they have such power that they are able to maintain others.

11. But again they lose a part of their good fortune, according to the different indications of the chart. They will have joy from a woman or wife and offspring, will own buildings and movable wealth. After a varied and changeable youth they will arrive at prosperity and good fortune worthy of paradise, and become a source of wonder for their prosperity.

12. Trouble and weariness is indicated by Jupiter in Leo, until Saturn, having left Pisces, arrives in Aries. If Saturn is aspected in trine to Jupiter in Leo, this indicates fame and good reputation with the protection of powerful friends. Because of their training the natives win the greatest profit and all their activities have a prosperous outcome. But their first wives will not be satisfactory.

13. Their wives will not be virgins but will have been seduced by others. After their paternal inheritance has been lost, they will gain a fortune by their own efforts; they will be brave in spirit, generous and liberal, but will wickedly desire the possessions of others.

14. Those who have Jupiter in Virgo will be courteous, respected, well-bred, modest, successful, faithful, always cherishing friends with true affection. They will be talented, but competitive, powerful but hard-working; and they will not have a stable life until Saturn reaches the opposite of the sign in which he was located in the birthchart. When he arrives in Pisces he indicates storms, losses, griefs, illnesses, and anxieties.

15. When Saturn leaves Pisces, then he indicates glory and power, and chaste, amiable wives who serve the wishes of their husbands. There will be grief over children until the cycle of Saturn is completed, but then the indication is for high office and great power, according to the nature of the chart.

16. Those who have Jupiter in Libra will have disasters and riots in early life, especially if Saturn is found in opposition to Jupiter or to the Moon. Then the indication is for losses, domestic quarrels, grief, injuries, disgrace, law suits, journeys, insults, and loss of inheritance.

17. But when Saturn has crossed the point of opposition and Jupiter has begun to pass through favorable houses, the beginning of good fortune, fame and happiness are predicted. Jupiter joins the natives to powerful men, leaders or kings who entrust to them their secrets, affairs, and possessions.

18. Those who have Jupiter in this sign will be artisans or vineyard workers, and manage much property. They will have happiness from wife and children, but only after they are worn out with misfortune; all law suits will be decided in their favor, but only if they go to court unmarried. They will have control of foreign sources of income, be religious worshippers of the gods; the first period of their lives will have great difficulties but the last will be noted by honorable activities. There will be certain marks on their bodies.

19. Those who have Jupiter in Scorpio will be famous and powerful, especially when Saturn arrives at the sign of the summer tropical Cancer.

For when Saturn is in other signs, in the first quarter of the chart, there will be illnesses, riots, accusations, uprisings, lawsuits, quarrels, and losses. But when Saturn leaves the first quarter, that is when he makes his transit to Pisces, they will be with leaders and kings, keeping their secrets with silent fidelity.

20. They will sail great rivers and seas; through sterile or infamous men and women they will make their way in important affairs. They will be popular with the people, brave in mind as well as body and will acquire control of great income. Happiness will come from the affection of wives and children, but only after earlier difficulties. Though worn out in early life they will have a happy old age. But here it must be noted what we said about the sign of Aries.

21. Jupiter in Sagittarius will make the natives famous and powerful; rich, learned leaders, or friends of the powerful. But whatever they acquire they will lose again as long as Saturn is crossing the first house of the chart. At that time there will be disturbances, griefs, revolutions, and unfortunate outcomes to projects.

22. They will be in difficulties until Jupiter reaches his own house with a favorable aspect. Then, he predicts that all prosperity will arrive little by little, in proportion to the power of the houses. He indicates increase of income, joy and happiness, marriage and children. Those who have Jupiter in this location will have possessions abroad. They will be of good character and trained in every kind of courtesy.

23. In the first part of their lives they will be irresponsible and will quarrel with their wives. But when they arrive at middle age they will enjoy prosperity and good fortune. If Saturn is in opposition or square aspect to Jupiter in Sagittarius, they will not have either wives or children, especially if Jupiter is located in the terms of Saturn. But they will be generous, agreeable, friends of many, known to all, sophisticated, and respectable, especially if Jupiter, located in the first houses of the chart, aspects some other planets in trine.

24. Those who have Jupiter in Capricorn will be famous, friends of the powerful, keeping their secrets with silent fidelity. They will be lucky when Jupiter will have finished his second round. Before that time whatever office the native holds he will lose; he will be in poverty and serve low-class men as long as Saturn is crossing the second third of the same sign.

25. Before that time he will be involved in many griefs and losses, law suits and reverses, and will see deaths in his own family. He will have such misfortune that he will wish to be freed by death. But when Saturn has crossed the house we mentioned, all evils will be lulled to sleep and the greatest good fortune will follow, according to the strength and nature of the chart.

[There is a long lacuna here: The Sun, Venus and Mars are missing.]

## V

## [MERCURY IN DIFFERENT SIGNS]

1. Never make companions of those who have Mercury in the terms or decans of Mars, or entrust your secrets to their fidelity. They will deny and will persist in their impudence with wicked defense of their perjury. They will be prepared for every crime of infamy, especially if with Mercury thus located, Mars is found in the terms of Mercury or Mercury is located in unfavorable houses and Mars attacks him in square aspect.

2. In that case the natives will suffer from prison or exile or, fearing court sentence, will wander as fugitives far from their household gods. But if, when Mars and Mercury are in this position, the full Moon, either in square aspect or opposition, is moving toward Mars, and no benefic planets are in favorable aspect, especially Venus and Jupiter, the natives will suffer severely for these crimes.

3. If Mercury is found in the house or decan of the Sun in a diurnal chart, this will make the natives mediocre in mind and soul, but will have them work on obscure and evil writings. Or they will be chosen for public duties, be intelligent and inquiring, but involved in secret illegal activities and fruitless pursuits.

4. If it is a nocturnal chart, they will suffer mental illness or be impeded in speech or hearing. Afflictions or difficulties in life are indicated or continual bad repute. They never learn good judgment or forthright speech.

5. Mercury in the terms or decan of Venus indicates the same things in a diurnal or nocturnal chart: brilliant, elegant speech, friendship with kings or powerful men, good judgment, successful activities.

6. The natives will easily master all kinds of learning, including two languages; they will be in charge of athletic contests; be composers of music; follow the training of poetry; work with colors or perfumes; be merchants in precious gems; or carry on foreign trade. From these activities they will gain profit and high position. They will be highly sexed and tend to corrupt the marriages of others; from their vices a bad reputation will arise.

7. What Mercury indicates in the house of the Moon was told in the first part of this book.

## VI

## [THE MOON IN DIFFERENT SIGNS]

1. The Moon in her own house and decan in a nocturnal chart indicates great income and fame, and a position of power, especially if she is found on the first angles. She will make the natives successful, popular artisans, who earn a fortune through their own efforts. But in a diurnal

chart she makes travelling workmen involved in continual dangers, sickness or weakness, and torment of sharp pains. If in this position she occupies the ninth house then she predicts good fortune, riches, fame, high position, and great power.

2. If the full Moon is found in the terms or decan of Saturn, she makes the natives sluggish, cold in mind and body. They are lacking in all boldness, but have certain periods of rash fury. Their intestines are tormented by cold humors. But if the Moon is waning, activities and plans never turn out well, and all inheritance is lost. The natives are weighed down with poverty, slow in all their activities, and languid in mind and body. They suffer various pains from consumption, spleen, pains in the kidneys or hemorrhages.

3. The full Moon in the terms or decan of Jupiter will make the natives respectable, successful, always prosperous in their activities, seeking income through their own efforts. Some do business in foreign lands. But if the Moon is waning, she indicates misfortune from loss of parents and loss of inheritance. Also if she is found in signs of malefic planets, she indicates a mediocre life, some kind of demotion, or pains in the muscles.

4. If the full Moon is found in the terms or decan of Mars by day, the natives will be exposed or low-born, or will suffer illness and affliction, or be involved in dangers and accidents. But if it is a nocturnal chart, the parents quarrel and separate, or the mother is low-class. Some natives suffer from traveling, others from illnesses.

5. But if the waning Moon by day is in the degrees or decans we mentioned, this indicates wasted inheritance and dangerous occupations, and from those occupations, losses, quarrels, weakness, or illnesses. But a waning Moon by night will make the native successful in his occupations, brave, famous, entrusted with public duties, but in foreign regions.

6. The full Moon in the house or decan of the Sun will make the natives popular, successful in all affairs, entrusted with public duties. If she is found on the first angles, that is the MC, or the ascendant, and is in aspect to Jupiter, she will make powerful emperors or kings or governors with world-wide power.

7. But if the Moon is waning, they will be successful in no activities, ignoble in mind and in life, never persisting in any occupation. Or the mothers will be sickly with long continued illness, or the natives themselves will suffer an evil death.

8. The full Moon in the terms or decan of Venus will always involve the native in disreputable loves, incestuous desires, and abnormal sexual activities. But the waning Moon indicates good deeds, great increases in fortune, and marriage to a relative under favorable auspices.

9. If the full Moon is found in the terms or decan of Mercury, the natives will be untrustworthy, greedy, and obstinate. They refuse to return what has been entrusted to them. They will be malicious housebreakers or thieves, betrayers of their own people, despisers of the gods,

accustomed to cover their lies with the shadow of the truth. They will be tormented by necessity for constant labor and never enjoy the fruits of their toil.

10. But the waning Moon will make them malicious, wicked, consumptive, mentally disturbed, or insane. They willingly associate themselves with every kind of wickedness, defend evil men and evil deeds, and their depravity increases from day to day. But they are also hostile to men of their own kind. If Mars is in those degrees with the Moon, he puts these same men in company with bandits, involves them in various criminal charges, and finally brings them to prison. But if none of these is the case, then their income is diminished, their life humble and wretched with illness; weakness and a miserable death follow.

# VII

## [CONCLUSION]

1. These matters have now been explained to you in detail, my dear Mavortius, and nothing has been left out of the traditions handed down by learned men of old. But let us repeat what we have often called to your attention: be sure to collect the data on the entire force of the planets; the combination of all the signs; and the efficacy of the degrees as compared to the powers of the houses.

2. Do not try to explain the whole chart from the course of one planet; but compare the ascendant with the powers of the twelve houses; notice the effect of planet combined with planet; also which planets are aspected to the ascendant and in what way. Consider also to what extent the planets themselves lessen or increase their own influence, and what effect the natural quality of the signs and degrees has on individual planets, as well as what is indicated by the houses and angles. When you have collected all this information, inspect every detail and only after careful comparison give your interpretation.

3. Look carefully at the risings and anaforas of the signs. For Jupiter entering the house of Venus (the seventh house) does not always indicate marriage, any more than he assures offspring when he enters the house of children (the fifth house). He does this only when the whole essence of the chart has indicated wives and children. Mars moving around from the descendant does not always aspect the ascendant with threatening influence any more than Saturn coming from the degree of the ascendant always predicts a serious danger and horrors. These are true only when the whole essence of the chart indicates such things. These bad predictions are only true when the malefic planets start out from the anaforas of the signs and are rulers of time.

4. Therefore, as you have been so often advised, you must train your mind to obey the divine instruction and observe the combinations of

individual planets and the powers of the degrees. For frequently the hospitality of a bad sign changes Jupiter's beneficence, and the hospitality of a good sign weakens Saturn's malevolence. You must not necessarily look for danger from a bad house, when a helpful star is in aspect to that house; also the threatening influence of malefic planets are often reduced in effect by good houses. Thus the combination of houses, terms, signs, and planets shows all things in the charts of men. If you observe all these with a calm mind you will be able to set forth in truth the fates of men.

5. Our work must now turn to the principles of the sixth book. There I shall explain to you the true meanings of the combinations of the planets so that afterward we may continue to special interpretations.

# Liber Sextus

## I

### [THE HOUSES]

1. The work we are engaged in, my dear Mavortius, has had much to say about combinations of planets. We have emphasized that there is nothing more important in the principles of astrology or in the actual forecasts than the effects of a mixture of influences. We have especially noted that the first angles have one kind of effect, the second another.

2. The first angles are the ascendant and *Medium Caelum,* the second the descendant and *Imum Caelum.* From those four angles with their various significance the whole essence of the forecast is known. All the planets, according to the power of their own nature, predict differently when located on the first or the second angles.

3. Also the fifth and eleventh houses, that is, the house of Bona Fortuna and the Bonus Daemon, do not join in any aspect with the dejected houses, but associate themselves favorably with the ascendant. But a special kind of relationship—a third kind of influence—joins the third and ninth houses to the ascendant.

4. The second and eighth houses have no connection with the ascendant; the sixth and the twelfth houses are dejected and have no relationship to the ascendant.

5. As we explained before, the power of the planets varies with the difference in the houses. In the third book we set forth in detail what is predicted by the individual planets located in each house.

6. You should pray in every possible way that the chart you are working on should not have planets either malefic or benefic in the sixth or twelfth houses; or in the second or eighth. For these houses are always filled with hostile influences from all planets.

7. If a benefic planet occupies these houses it loses its salutary power;

182

if a malefic, its injurious influence is increased. In general, malefic planets in these houses together with the Moon indicate misfortunes without remedy; benefic planets enclosed in these debilitated houses lose their protective influence.

8. The predictions are changed by the condition of the planets — whether nocturnal or diurnal, as well as by the varying effects of the aspects — trine, square, and opposition.

9. From these combinations the whole power of the forecast is discovered. The planets oppose each other according to their nature and their condition and thus make up with their variety the fates of men.

10. Now I shall explain to you, my dear Mavortius, the effects of these combinations, so that I may set forth for you the full doctrine of the divine wisdom. But first I shall say a few things about the regal power of the bright stars.

## II
## [BRIGHT STARS]

1. In all the signs we find bright stars shining with awesome majesty, but regal ones in four — in Leo, Scorpio, Aquarius, and Taurus. I shall briefly show in what degrees of the planets you will find this awesome brilliance.

2. The fifth degree of Leo has a splendidly glowing star. If the waxing Moon is found in this star, if it is exactly on the ascendant or on the MC, this indicates the highest royal or imperial power.

3. The 20th degree of Aquarius is similarly adorned with majestic brilliance. If the full Moon rises in this star and holds one of the first angles, royal or imperial power is indicated in the same way. The 15th degree of Taurus and the 27th and the 30th also have a bright star, and the Moon in this star, if also on one of the first angles, indicates high position and power.

4. The Moon in the 27th degree of Taurus also predicts high position. She makes the natives maintain great peoples with their power. They donate whatever is demanded of them, such as magnificent temples, and gain great honor from these gifts.

5. The 30th degree of Taurus is also marked with divine splendor; if the Moon is found in this degree she predicts great power. If she is at the same time on the first angles, she indicates leadership, imperial or regal power, especially if she is waxing and Jupiter is in favorable aspect.

6. For then the natives by their own efforts gain domination over land and sea and lead armies successfully. The same is true of the seventh degree of Scorpio.

7. But the Moon in the seventh degree of Scorpio indicates together with high position fierce cruelty and capacity for inspiring immoderate terror. The one who has the Moon in this location will proceed against all

men with unbridled greed.

8. We have collected these few facts for you from our book on *Myriogenesis,* but now we must return to the work in hand. We must explain, as we promised, the combination of the planets. I shall have something to say in the last book about the bright stars in all the signs and their meaning.

## III

## [SATURN IN TRINE]

1. If all the planets, whether benefic or malefic, were in trine to each other, their predictions would be improved by that location. The evil of the malefic would be lessened and the helpful benefits of the good ones would be strengthened.

2. Thus, if Saturn is in trine to Jupiter and both are in signs in which they rejoice, avoiding debilitated houses; or if one of them in his own house aspects the other in trine; or they both are in aspect to the ascendant, this indicates infinite riches and great good fortune, especially if one of the two is also in aspect to the waxing Moon.

3. For then Saturn bestows endless wealth and dominion over large possessions, fertile fields, pastures, and forest. The native will attain great merit from building temples or shrines or earn high position as manager of the privy purse or of sacred treasuries.

4. The natives will be immensely superior to their fathers in position. According to the quality of the chart some will hold high government office, others will receive large inheritance, still others will win profit from foreign investments. In all cases, however, they will be attached with uncorrupted loyalty to great and powerful men.

5. But if, with Saturn and Jupiter in trine as we said, Mercury is in favorable aspect, the native will be involved in obscure religious rites or will carry on the business of kings or important states. Often they will head a famous legation.

6. But these men are worn out by excessive misfortunes concerning their children; they lose sons and are forced to raise the offspring of others; or after a time they receive back their children, brought up by others. This is the case only if the chart is diurnal without influence of Mars.

7. If Mars is in threatening aspect, or if it is a nocturnal chart, all the good predictions we have made are lessened. Mars indicates reverses and accusation from hidden hostility, so that whatever was good in the prediction is attacked by hostile influence.

8. If Saturn and Mars are in trine aspect to each other, in favorable houses, in signs or degrees in which they rejoice or are exalted, and also Jupiter and Mercury are in aspect, the natives will make great profit and have their activities turn out successfully.

9. They attain high position through their own efforts, become famous and honored, ruling great states. But they always suffer the death of elder brothers.

10. If Saturn is in trine to the Sun and both are in favorable houses in a diurnal chart, the natives will receive constant promotions and great fame. The parents also will attain a similar increase in honors, especially if Saturn and the Sun are in masculine signs. But if the chart is nocturnal, the parents' inheritance will be wasted and the natives will help them from their own resources.

11. Saturn in trine to Venus with both in favorable houses makes the natives' lives outstanding for moderation and mercy; they are known for good and modest behavior, removed from all unchastity, to the extent that their reputation arouses ill-will on the part of inferiors. But they marry late in life.

12. Those who have Saturn in trine to Mercury with both in favorable houses will be intelligent and talented, addicted to all kinds of learning, serious in character in early life. Their point of view is always supported by vigorous arguments. They will be in charge of public accounts or the privy purse and make a large income from these occupations. But we must remember that only the planet of Mercury rejoices in the twelfth house.

13. Those who have Saturn in trine to the full Moon with both in favorable houses will be close to kings, emperors, or powerful men and will gain fame from that connection. If the Moon is waning the good fortune is lessened. But we must also remember in the case of the Moon that she is favorable if found alone in the eighth house in a nocturnal chart, especially if she is full and in signs or terms in which she rejoices. For then she indicates, because of the power of that house, high position, large income, honors, and a position of rule. Located by day in this house she indicates the same, if Jupiter is in the eleventh house.

## IV

### [JUPITER IN TRINE]

1. If Jupiter is in trine to Mars and both are in favorable houses and unafflicted, they indicate high imperial position, successful activities, the highest government office, and honors conferred by royal command.

2. High position, riches, and fame are also indicated by Jupiter in trine to the Sun if both are in favorable houses. The natives will also win great joy from successes of children.

3. Jupiter and Venus in trine in favorable houses indicate great personal charm and pleasing appearance. The natives will always have loving relationships with their friends and their wives. They receive

promotions and increases in income through the protection of their wives.

4. Jupiter and Mercury in trine in favorable houses will make the natives clever and talented, supported by keen intelligence, able to bring all their activities to a successful conclusion.

5. Through their own merits they will be promoted over all others to positions of power and magnificence; in all their activities they will be praised and admired. They will be scribes or managers of public records or of the privy purse. Some will know the secrets of the stars.

6. Those who have Jupiter and the full Moon in trine in favorable houses will be famous and ennobled, of good reputation, but all this in proportion to the quality of the chart. Some will have high administrative posts, others will lead armies; still others will rule provinces. But all will be known for upright and incorruptible judgment.


## V

## [MARS IN TRINE]

1. Mars and the Sun in trine in favorable houses indicate the highest position and power, especially if it is a nocturnal chart and the Sun is located on the right side (i.e., in the direction of the diurnal movement of the heavens) of Mars.

2. But if Jupiter is in trine from another side and is located on one of the first angles, and the influence of the Moon is from a favorable house, then they indicate infinite power and position, either high government or military posts. This effect will be stronger if Mars, the Sun, and Jupiter are in masculine signs.

3. Mars and Venus in trine aspect and both in favorable houses indicate daily profit as a result of constant effort; also a prosperous marriage. The natives will have a good reputation, will be proud of their high position, and will have many marriages.

4. Those who have Mars and Mercury in trine with both in favorable houses will be intelligent and able to talk themselves out of all involvements. All their activities turn out well and they are always able to smooth away difficulties by good advice. They will cleverly and successfully carry on the work of record-keeping or literary duties.

5. Mars with the Moon in trine aspect and both in favorable houses, if the Moon is waning and if it is a nocturnal chart, indicates all good fortune and prosperous outcomes to all activities. The natives easily gain all they desire.

6. If aspect of Jupiter is added, the highest position, glory, and great power are indicated. But if the Moon is full the body is weakened with continual illness.

## VI

## [THE MOON AND SUN IN TRINE]

1. If the Moon and the Sun are in trine aspect and both in favorable houses, free of all debility, they indicate the rewards of good fortune if they have another benefic planet in favorable aspect and the Moon is waxing.

## VII

## [THE MOON AND VENUS IN TRINE]

1. The Moon and Venus in trine aspect with both in favorable houses, if the Moon is waning and in a nocturnal chart, indicate the greatest good fortune, glory, and great deeds. With this aspect maternal affection increases toward children, chaste fidelity preserves marriages unspoiled, and brothers cherish brothers. The forecast is for charm and physical beauty, happiness, fame, and power.

## VIII

## [THE MOON AND MERCURY IN TRINE]

1. The Moon and Mercury in trine aspect and in favorable houses indicate everything according to the variety of the signs. Some natives receive fluent speech, some success in famous skills, others as musicians, still others as painters; but all achieve distinction and fame in their arts.

2. This combination gives to some success in arms, to others in athletic training; still others delight the public by singing to their own accompaniment; all of these earn popular commendation. Still others carry on trade; but all these predictions are made in accordance with the influence of other planets, the signs, and the houses.

3. It was clearly explained in the second book what trine and square aspect are.

## IX

## [SATURN IN SQUARE ASPECT]

1. Now I shall explain to you the indications of square aspect. This is always a strong and menacing combination. From this aspect the force of malefic planets is increased and that of benefic hindered. Its power for evil is equal to that of opposition.

2. If Saturn and Jupiter are in square aspect and Saturn is above, holding the upper degree of a right square, but Jupiter lower, in a left square, they indicate difficulties in life, diminish possessions, distort all

plans, hinder activities; unsettle the mind with many kinds of dissension; attack fathers with various catastrophes, and waste paternal inheritance.

3. But if Jupiter is above and holds the right side while Saturn is located in the left square, the misfortunes are lessened, parents achieve distinction and fame, and daily profit is earned, all according to the measurement of the chart.

4. If Saturn and Mars are in square aspect with Saturn above in the right square and threatening Mars on the left, they make the natives sluggish in character and ineffective in all activities.

5. They indicate many kinds of illness with the body shifting between chills and fever. This combination also predicts loss of paternal inheritance and serious accident and death to brothers.

6. If Mars is above and holds the right side, an early death is predicted for the mother. But in this case all activities are successful; the previously described lack of motivation is reversed.

7. Nevertheless paternal inheritance is wasted, and the natives are enfeebled by continual losses and attacked by scandal through the ill-will of servants.

8. Saturn and the Sun in square aspect with Saturn above on the right square indicate demotion and loss of position; also contraction of the body from muscular deformity.

9. They also attack the parents with misfortune and make the father die before the mother. The natives suffer from different kinds of wrong-doing and unfortunate experiences; also serious illnesses from cold bodily humors. Their possessions and all occupations are ruined.

10. If the Sun is in the superior position, this indicates loss of paternal inheritance, serious hostilities among servants, and mental disorders which endanger all occupations. The plans of the native never turn out well and in early life he suffers from severe bodily fatigue and frequent illness.

11. If Saturn and Venus are in square aspect with Saturn above, the natives will lose all inheritance and be reduced to beggary. They have bitter experiences with women; there is no pleasure in love nor successful results from their desires.

12. But if Venus is in the superior position, she provides wives of respectable and chaste character who exercise the whole power in the home. They cherish their husbands with undivided affection and are equally loved by them. But both try to conceal their affection with some kind of dissimulation.

13. Saturn and Mercury in square aspect with Saturn in the upper position indicate exile from the first day of birth; they weaken all planning and thought processes and hinder activities by cold sluggishness of character. The natives will carry on administrative duties but in a position of subjection to the power of another. They wil suffer seriously from attacks of the envious.

14. Some will be tongue-tied and make babbling sounds; others will be deaf. These afflictions persist unless mitigated by aspect of Mars. If Mercury is in the superior position nothing good is indicated, but the evils described above are somewhat lessened.

15. Saturn and the Moon in square aspect with Saturn above wear out the body with evil humors and make the native unable to handle any activities because of sluggish torpor of character. This combination always dissipates maternal inheritance and makes children undertake hostile actions against mothers.

16. The Moon in the superior position indicates a miserable death for the mother. For the native, constant misfortunes are indicated: loss of position and of marriage, continual dangers, and death from malevolent humors. But if marriage is indicated through protection of other planets, the wife's mind will be unsettled by fierce hostility. The natives will be bereft of all help from friends and children.

# X

## [JUPITER IN SQUARE]

1. Jupiter and Mars in square aspect with Jupiter in the upper position indicate great fame, good reputation, and high position.

2. Some will be involved in military activities; others assigned to royal households with high government position. From these duties they will gain important promotions. But they are never able to preserve their paternal inheritance; they will have children late and suffer constant grief from accidents to children.

3. If Mars is in the superior place, this causes extreme mental anxiety. The natives will be involved in various kinds of errors and difficulties. They will suffer from royal or government actions and will be attacked by hostile accusations of dangerous enemies.

4. Jupiter and the Sun in square aspect with Jupiter in the upper position indicate high honor for the native and his father, promotions through great and good men, good reputation, and a well-deserved post in command of many persons.

5. But if the Sun is in the superior position, the father will have fame and distinction, but the native will lose his paternal inheritance in proscription and be persecuted by crowds of strong and evil enemies.

6. The combination of Jupiter and Venus in square aspect with Jupiter above is always associated with many friends. Through the protection of women occupations and profits will be conferred on the natives. They will enjoy high office all their lives and serve the rites of the gods with religious ardor.

7. But if Venus is in the superior position, she indicates illicit loves, also occupations having to do with clothing and care of the body. The

natives will show a desire for adornment, luxury, and pleasure. But whenever they attain prosperity and happiness these conditions turn to their opposites.

8. Jupiter and Mercury in square aspect with Jupiter in the upper position indicate occupations having to do with writing or literature. The natives will be in charge of records or figures and will gain a livelihood from duties as public prosecutor.

9. If Mercury is in the superior position, the natives will gain a satisfactory income but will hinder themselves in all their activities, avoiding good opportunities as if they were bad, with a certain timidity of mind. They will be the type that, if they attain whatever others desire with their utmost prayers, they will despise it. They do not wish benefits for themselves from others nor do they try to get anything good for themselves.

10. If Jupiter and the Moon are in square aspect with Jupiter on the upper degree, this indicates infinite riches for the mother and for the native himself. They attain the highest office and great fame and are deservedly promoted over their friends.

11. But if the Moon is in the superior place, this indicates the greatest good fortune, fame, and good repute with kings and powerful men. But this good fortune does not last through all time. For at some period loss of income and demotion are indicated. The natives will be overcome by sluggishness of mind and be estranged from their former high duties.

## XI

### [MARS IN SQUARE ASPECT]

1. If Mars and the Sun are in square aspect with Mars above, there is no variety of ill fortune which this combination does not predict. It attacks with malignant influence all journeys, meetings, promotions, and occupations.

2. But if the Sun is in the superior position, a miserable end is prepared both for the father and the native himself; a series of misfortunes is predicted. This combination stirs up revolutions and fights and excites fearful threats of public punishment.

3. It also destroys the bases of judgment and the power of the mind; to some it brings blindness. These dangers are stronger in a diurnal chart, especially if the combination of Mars and the Sun are also in threatening aspect to the ascendant, or if Mars from one of the angles aspects the waxing Moon.

4. Then the natives are destroyed by public torture and their torn limbs are denied burial, so that the punishment continues even after death. The same prediction is made by a nocturnal chart.

5. If Mars and Venus are in square aspect with Mars holding the

upper position of the right square,[72] aspecting Venus on the left square, all evils are indicated: the native will be involved in quarrels and accusations or cut down by accusations of a woman. But if this combination occurs in tropical signs, the bodies of men are made effeminate. Men experience desires suitable to women and are ruined by a reputation for depravity.

6. They lead their wives to adultery and force them to prostitute their modesty to the embraces of strangers. But if it is a woman's chart, she suffers with sharp grief prostitution of her body for the sake of a man.

7. If Venus is in the superior position holding the right side, this indicates the same things in the same way. But those who have Venus in this position practice their crime in secret, so that they cover the sale of their bodies by hiding their desires, especially if Jupiter is in conjunction with the ascendant or aspects it in trine.

8. If Mars and Mercury are in square aspect and Mars holds the superior part of a right square, this indicates a fearful outcome to all evils. It weakens the native with constant pains, attacks all his occupations with reverses, makes him the victim of evil rumors, and stirs up dreadful dangers of accusations, so that all these difficulties end in prison. These evils grow stronger in a diurnal chart but are lessened in a nocturnal.

9. But if Mercury holds the superior position and the right side, he makes the natives wicked and malicious, displaying poisonous desires, carrying on all kinds of fraud, and greedily devouring the goods of others. They pass from one victim to another, always rapaciously seeking what they can get; eventually they are made destitute by their wicked tricks and clever frauds and in the end lose all their possessions.

10. If Mars and the Moon are in square aspect and Mars holds the upper place in a right square, the native's mother will suffer widowhood, loss of strength, hemorrhage, or wretched death. The native himself will be fiercely attacked by demons so that his body is possessed by a malignant spirit.

11. This occurs especially if Mars is in the terms of Saturn, and the Moon in the terms either of Mercury or Mars. Often from the terms of benefic planets this evil is mitigated. In that case, when possessed in this way, they may escape the danger of attack and be freed through the help of some power.

12. But if the Moon holds the upper position, this makes the mother of low class, of ignoble family, and indicates a troubled and needy existence for the native. Fate destroys his possessions and, among these misfortunes, adds that of a wicked wife.

## XII

### [THE SUN AND MOON IN SQUARE ASPECT]

1. If the Sun and Moon are in square aspect, whether they hold the right or left sides, their predictions come from the influence of other

planets. When benefic planets are in aspect, great deeds, suitable income, fame, and prosperity are indicated.

2. But if malefic planets aspect the Sun and Moon without influence of favorable planets, the greatest dangers and misfortunes are predicted. If the full Moon is also moving toward Jupiter, or Jupiter aspects the waxing Moon, this indicates great unpopularity but with high office. But if the protection of Jupiter is lacking to this combination, the harmful effect of the malefic planets is stronger.

## XIII

### [VENUS AND MERCURY IN SQUARE ASPECT]

1. Venus and Mercury in square aspect make the same prediction, whichever of them holds the right square. This combination indicates great fame from the practice of some pleasing skill or some important doctrine. For these natives, because of the love of women, malignant tongues spread scandal.

2. Venus and the Moon in square aspect, with the Moon in the superior position, indicate great profit and riches. But they impose various losses or ill fame because of women.

3. But if Venus holds the upper position, she bestows great good fortune and constantly increases it; she makes occupation and life reputable, preserves for the natives the uncorrupted love of their wives, guarantees good and pure conjugal affection, happiness, rewards of famous skills, and high position. Nevertheless the natives constantly desire extra-marital affairs. Their mothers will be famous for chastity. But the wives, though pleasing to their husbands, will be freed slaves.

## XIV

### [THE MOON AND MERCURY IN SQUARE ASPECT]

1. The Moon and Mercury in square aspect with Mercury above, indicate wisdom, learning, fluent speech, and facility in oratory. But trouble often comes from popular uprisings.

2. But if, when Mercury is thus located, a malefic planet in a superior position is in unfavorable aspect to Mercury (so that he is in opposition to the Moon but square to Mercury), this indicates fearful crimes of falsehood and has the natives detected in these crimes, thrown into custody, and either killed in prison or exiled.

3. But if the Moon is in the upper position, the natives will be unstable in mind; their plans are inconsistent and their minds are not able to carry on a reasonable train of thought.

4. These are the indications of square aspect in men's charts. These forecasts you must diligently inspect in all your work especially when,

although the order of the planets is not changed, these square aspects make the forecasts change.

5. Now I shall set forth the meanings of the aspect of opposition. In the book of principles I have clearly explained what is meant by right and left squares.

## XV
### [SATURN IN OPPOSITION]

1. The aspect of opposition is always mutually hostile with the power of opposites. Like square it is a threatening aspect.

2. If Saturn and Jupiter are in opposition and attack each other mutually, they indicate many misfortunes and sharp grief from accidents to children.

3. But if Saturn is located exactly on the ascendant and Jupiter on the descendant in opposition to him, after severe misfortune in early life, old age will bring prosperity.

4. Saturn and Mars in opposition indicate serious crises, difficulties, and anxieties. The natives will be involved in wretched reverses and attacked by scandal; they will suffer want and constant illness.

5. These two planets always predict serious trouble in life: threat of fearful death, domestic hostilities, and frequent revolutions. They deny children, strike the father with an early death, and impose suffering on suffering.

6. If Saturn and Mars are in watery signs when in opposition, the natives will either be shipwrecked or drowned in storms at sea or in over-flowing rivers; or they will suffer illness from malignant bodily humors.

7. If one of the two is in a bestial sign this indicates danger from a four-footed animal or a wild beast. For others it means death through poison.

8. But if, while Mars and Saturn are in four-footed signs or at least one of them, in addition to the evils we have just described the natives will be crushed by collapsing ruins and they will either die or come close to death.

9. All these misfortunes grow worse if Jupiter is in no kind of favorable aspect. When Saturn and Mars are on two of the angles (in opposition) and the Moon is on another angle, either in opposition or square aspect, this indicates more severe misfortune—exile or public execution or the wretched burden of slavery.

10. But if Mars and Saturn when in opposition to each other are in the fifth, eleventh, ninth, or third house, then they extinguish all hope of good fortune and predict ruinous calamity. These misfortunes increase in middle life.

11. If Mars and Saturn are in sluggish or dejected houses when in

opposition, they are less harmful, but still they indicate grief and misery. But all these fearful crises are alleviated by favorable aspect of Venus and Jupiter; the malice of the bad planets is blunted by their favorable influence and the threats described above are resolved.

12. If Saturn and the Sun are in opposition and Jupiter is not in favorable aspect from any direction, either the father will be involved in hard labor and poverty or the native himself will suffer want and a life of toil. Some suffer from ill health.

13. But if they have any possessions, either they are destroyed while the natives are still living or are wasted after death. Also an evil death is indicated by this combination and the whole of life is endangered by evils and suffering. These misfortunes are worse if Mars and Saturn are in feminine signs.

14. Saturn and Venus in opposition will make the natives addicted to brothels and have them follow prostitutes with promiscuous desire. From this practice they become victims of serious scandal.

15. They are kept from marriage for the sake of lust. But if another part of the chart indicates marriage, then the native is allotted a wife lacking in chastity, or diseased, or polluted by slavery, or one who has associated with slaves in immodest desires. But to the natives themselves all pleasure in love is denied.

16. Saturn and Mercury in opposition hinder the tongue of the native so that his voice is impeded in his throat or his words are confused because he is tongue-tied.

17. These evils are stronger if Mercury is in a voiceless sign or if Mercury is hidden by the rays of the Sun. But if Saturn is also in opposition to the Moon as well as to Mercury, these misfortunes which we have described are stronger, unless Mars in some way has lessened the evil influence. Without the aspect of Mars the others indicate unending suffering.

18. But together with these evils the prediction is for a trained and intelligent mind and experience in various studies. But the natives are careless and their skills are ineffectual; they annoy others with an expression of mournful severity and are proud in spirit. These characteristics give rise to various anxieties day after day. The natives will be promoted over their brothers. They will be divided from their elder brothers either by death or long journeys. Also they lose their mothers in early life.

19. Saturn and the Moon in opposition first destroy the maternal inheritance; then they weaken the mother with various pains and illnesses or overthrow her mind.

20. But if all influence of benefic planets is lacking, then the mother's body is dishonored and she suffers constant losses. For the natives themselves various crises arise. But Saturn and the Moon indicate all this according to the nature of the signs.

21. If one of the two is located in a four-footed sign, this means danger from that kind of animal. But if they are in bestial signs, then death is predicted from wild beasts or from the bite of poisonous serpents. If they are in human signs the natives meet their end from plots of human beings.

22. But if they are in watery signs, danger is indicated from waves of the sea or from malignant humors; and if no benefic planet is in aspect, the appearance of the whole body will be changed by vicious illness and the sight of the eyes is lost. Others are forced by danger to desert their country.

# XVI

## [JUPITER IN OPPOSITION]

1. Jupiter and Mars in opposition indicate an unstable life and continual loss of possessions. Hostility of friends is stirred up, and there is the greatest danger from riots or rash activities.

2. If Jupiter and the Sun are in opposition, they waste the paternal inheritance and destroy all income. They cause demotion from former high office so that the natives are always in an inferior position. These misfortunes are less in a diurnal chart, stronger in a nocturnal.

3. Jupiter and Venus in opposition hinder all advancement and all hope of promotion.

4. The natives will not at any time have faithful affection from friends; their friends persecute them with fraud and treachery, never address them with true words, but are always trying to deceive them. Other friends, angry over rivalries, foment various kinds of quarrels with them. Wherever a benefit is bestowed it is repaid by hostility.

5. Nevertheless the natives will have an increase in good fortune in some directions; they will always have sufficient income. If Jupiter is found in the terms of Venus, they will always have a prosperous outcome to their desires, but in marriage will never have continued affection.

6. Jupiter and Mercury in opposition attack those who have had training in learned speech. Also they stir up fearful popular riots; the natives are often confronted with the wrath of the people; also they have bad relations with kings and powerful men because of those who envy them. They either suffer from death of brothers, are alienated from brotherly affection by quarrels, or encounter homicidal hatreds from blood kin.

7. If Jupiter and the Moon are in opposition, and if the Moon is full and the degrees of the Moon larger in number than those of Jupiter, this combination indicates high position, fame, and power. The natives will never be subject to the power of another, but with courage and steadfast character confidently resist other powers. But if the Moon is waning, none of the above are predicted but rather the greatest misfortune. The evils are greater in a nocturnal chart.

## XVII

## [MARS IN OPPOSITION]

1. Mars and the Sun in opposition in a diurnal chart strike down the father in a horrible death or at least blind his eyes. The natives themselves they cast down from high position or bring upon them unexpected peril. All occupations are hindered by serious reverses. In a nocturnal chart the strength of the body is broken and the mind is weakened. All inheritance is lost and the native is reduced to beggary.

2. If Mars and Venus are in opposition in a diurnal chart, the native will always be involved in wandering and wrong-doing and will be constantly ill. Venus and Mars thus placed attack marriage and children with harsh ill-will. If they are in tropical signs they indicate the same as we described above, especially if they are in opposition from Cancer and Capricorn and there is no influence of Jupiter.

3. Mars and Mercury in opposition indicate the greatest calamities. Either the natives will be apprehended for the crime of forging documents, or they are associated in evil knowledge with criminals, or they live a life of crime with wrong-doers and poisoners. Or they may be dragged to public judgment through pressure of debts.

4. Possessed by greed, they may corrupt the trade in religious articles, or refuse to return goods entrusted to them. For any of these crimes they may be brought to judgment. Some are sent into exile, especially if Mercury is in the terms or house of Saturn or in his own house and Jupiter is not in trine aspect.

5. Mars and the Moon in opposition make the natives short-lived or involved in continual dangers. They allow no marriage, or, if other planets decree a marriage, the wife dies a horrible death. The natives themselves suffer an evil death or are struck down by public punishment, especially if the Moon is full.

## XVIII

## [SUN AND MOON IN OPPOSITION]

1. The Sun and Moon in opposition change in many ways the life, status, and income of the native. After first accumulating wealth he falls into poverty but then regains new riches. He will have unpleasant disfigurements around his face and his body will suffer miserable contractions.

## XIX

## [VENUS AND THE MOON IN OPPOSITION]

1. Venus and the Moon in opposition indicate an unhappy marriage. They never allow the native any kind of good luck; either they do not

allow any children or those there are they strike down in wretched death. The natives themselves suffer many evils and injuries from their wives.

## XX

## [MERCURY AND THE MOON IN OPPOSITION]

1. If Mercury and the Moon are in opposition, they stir up attacks of the multitude and popular revolution. The natives are always persecuted in public meetings by the malevolent voice of the people. They display timidity in their character and in their words.

## XXI

## [SEXTILE ASPECT]

1. The planets in sextile aspect indicate the same things which we described in regard to trine aspect. But the effect of their portents is reduced, and in all charts this aspect has less power. You must remember this: that sextile aspects are blunted if they occur in tropical or mutable signs, and quite ineffectual if a fixed sign is in between.

## XXII

## [SATURN IN CONJUNCTION]

1. So that we may make plain to you, my dear Mavortius, the entire significance of the aspects, we have explained trine, square, and opposition in detail. Now we shall show the meaning of conjunction. When this is accomplished we may proceed to the individual predictions of the forecast.

2. If Saturn and Jupiter share the hospitality of one degree (conjunction), if they are in favorable houses and in signs or degrees in which they rejoice, they indicate the rewards of good fortune: increase in possessions, fame, uncorrupted virtue, and fortunate offspring, especially if it is a diurnal chart.

3. Then they add to the prediction the greatest positions of official control and power over the resources of others. But if Mars is in aspect to these planets from above, the whole of what we just described is changed by the hostility of Mars.

4. When Mars and Saturn are in conjunction and in favorable houses, they produce a balanced character and soften fierce aggression with milder traits.

5. The association with Saturn reduces the unthinking rashness and impatient ardor of Mars and blunts it with Saturn's cold sluggishness. Thus when Mars' heat warms Saturn's chill, and the cold of Saturn tones down the fires of Mars, from this combination of temperaments a sober,

well-balanced human being is produced.

6. Nevertheless activities are impeded by this combination, for one planet drives ahead while the other hinders. Those who have Saturn and Mars in this combination never attain what they want. They also suffer various illnesses, their bodies are fatigued, and they suffer from black bile.

7. Also an early death carries off their mother and father, their paternal inheritance is lost, and they themselves bring about an evil end for their brothers. Those who are first recognized as sons are either struck down by a wretched death or are bereft of all good fortune and forced to regard with humble awe the power and fame of a brother. The natives themselves suffer trouble and anxiety from serious wrongdoing.

8. All these predictions are stronger if Mars and Saturn are on any of the angles. For then the attitude of the natives is never amenable to reason. They withstand all toil and danger with firm courage unless Jupiter is on the first angles in signs in which he is exalted, in his own house or in favorable houses of the chart.

9. Saturn and the Sun in conjunction waste all paternal inheritance and indicate a wretched end for the father. These misfortunes are stronger in a nocturnal chart, whether Saturn is found in a morning or an evening rising. For then an accumulation of misfortunes attacks the father; the natives themselves suffer wretched crises and cruel death of brothers.

10. But if Saturn and the Sun are in the same sign but somewhat separated, so that Saturn has more degrees than the Sun, then in addition to his other calamities a wretched death is indicated for the father; all the other evils we described are also threatened, but also all possessions are lost or proscribed, and the native is thrown into extreme poverty. Fatigues, vicious humors, and wasted bodily strength are predicted. Some lose the sight of their eyes.

11. But this combination always produces types suited to agriculture, so that after a space of time they gain a livelihood from cultivation of the fields. They will always hold a humble position in life. But if the Sun and Saturn are located in the house of the Sun or of Saturn, this makes the father famous but bereft of all wealth. Thus placed, Saturn and the Sun turn the natives against their fathers in parricidal hostility. But they always attack the natives with the wretched events which we have described.

12. Saturn and Venus in conjunction always indicate misfortunes in matrimony and marriage with unworthy women. The wives are either sickly or sterile, have an affliction which deforms the whole shape of the body, or they are the objects of serious scandal. Because of these misfortunes there is no possibility of children.

13. The natives either have no children or have them late in life. They will always be frigid in love; their minds are unstable in various ways. In a

woman's chart the same things are indicated by Venus and Saturn.

14. These predictions are stronger if Saturn and Venus in conjunction are in Capricorn or Aquarius. For these signs always affect Venus badly, especially if she is in aspect to Saturn. For then the malice of his influence cannot be mitigated by the presence of Jupiter.

15. Saturn and Mercury in conjunction impede the sound of the voice with babbling confusion of the tongue, or they slow the speech and the expression of words, or they attack hearing in a serious illness. They never allow desires to be fulfilled.

16. In all occupations the natives will be destitute of credit. They will be hard in nature, rigid and obstinate, given to mournful hypocrisy. They conceal their plans in a deep, malicious silence. But they are intelligent and learned in many fields.

17. Saturn and the Moon in conjunction attack all thoughts and activities with witless weakness of fear. Also the maternal inheritance is lost. The mothers and the natives themselves are weakened by constant illness. But these evils are prevented if it is a diurnal chart, if the Moon is full and favorable planets are in aspect.

18. But in a nocturnal chart with a waning Moon the indication is for all misfortunes and evils. Even if Jupiter and Venus are in aspect, their helpful protection is despised and the calamities are more strongly indicated.

## XXIII

## [JUPITER IN CONJUNCTION]

1. Jupiter and Mars in conjunction indicate high position and great power. They make the natives governors of great states or great regions, holders of glorious powers among the most important peoples.

2. They will always attain their desires, especially if Jupiter and Mars are in favorable houses, or on the first angles in the fifth or eleventh houses, or in the houses of Jupiter or Mars. For then consular fasces and the greatest armies are entrusted to the natives and they attain high position and magnificent power.

3. If Jupiter and the Sun are in conjunction and Jupiter is hidden by the Sun's rays, this diminishes the whole fortune. But if Jupiter, freed from the Sun's rays and in a morning rising, is together with the Sun in the same sign, this indicates high honor and position. The natives will be born from respectable parents and from the day of birth all their parents' good fortune will be bestowed on them. They themselves will rejoice in fortunate offspring.

4. Jupiter and Venus together in the same degree or the same sign indicate the highest position and great personal charm. The natives are always associated in true friendship with great and good men. They are always known for good character and are devout in religious rites. They

will have great physical attractiveness and be joined in close friendship to kings and judges. They will always have a good reputation, and will attain high position and possessions through the protection of powerful women.

5. A happy and prosperous marriage is also predicted for those who have Jupiter and Venus in conjunction. They will have children unless a malefic planet prevents. But they are always driven by depraved desires to a series of love affairs. These same predictions are made by Jupiter and Venus in a woman's chart. But if Jupiter and Venus are in conjunction in fixed signs, favorably aspected to the Moon, and Mars from any direction is in unfavorable aspect, the relatives are objects of scandal.

6. Jupiter and Mercury in conjunction make the natives powerful, outstanding in counsel and oratory, trained in all fields of learning, and the objects of general admiration. They are particularly outstanding as orators for the fluency of their speech. Some because of their intelligence and learning will be in charge of royal letters and archives.

7. Jupiter and the Moon in the same sign indicate the greatest good fortune, especially if they are in the same degree. For then they bestow infinite riches and such marks of prosperity that the natives are always supesuperior to their parents. But if it is a nocturnal chart, and the Moon holds more degrees than Jupiter, this whole forecast is weakened and the good fortune lessened.

## XXIV

### [MARS IN CONJUNCTION]

1. Mars and the Sun in the same sign indicate for the father either an early or an evil death. But if they are on one of the angles or any anafora of the angles, then they indicate continual calamity for the father and loss of paternal inheritance. They harm some natives in the eyes or inflict wounds from iron or fire. Also they upset the stability of the mind and the true course of reasoning.

2. Mars and Venus in the same sign will make seducers and adulterers. Possessed by depraved desires and unconquerable lust, the natives break the bonds of other peoples' marriages by clever promises.

3. If Mercury is found together with Mars or Venus or if he is in aspect to them, these three indicate trouble from informers: accusations and law suits over these crimes, also riots and popular disturbances. But if Jupiter, in favorable houses, in his own signs or in his exaltation, is in favorable aspect, by his help the natives are freed from these charges.

4. But if Mars and Venus hold any angle without influence of Jupiter, and the waxing Moon is in aspect to them, or Saturn is in aspect to the waning Moon, then the natives suffer public punishment for adultery or incest. But if Mars and Venus are in tropical signs they indicate what we said is signified by tropical signs.

5. Mars and Mercury in the same sign will make the natives intelligent

and learned in great doctrine, but liars, adept at every evil deed. They use their intelligence for all kinds of trickery and meet every contest with malice and fraud.

6. But if Jupiter is in favorable aspect, he indicates fame in athletic contests. If Venus is in any kind of aspect, she drives the natives with depraved desires to the love of boys. But if, in addition, Saturn is in aspect, serious scandal ensues from what we have described.

7. If the Sun hides Mars and Mercury with his orb and they are all together on one of the angles and in aspect to the Moon on another angle, this will produce natives with criminal tendencies, involved in every wrongdoing; their speech is always stained with falsehood. Their criminal activities will be compared to the deeds of bandits; they also forge documents.

8. But if Jupiter is in favorable aspect, either in favorable houses, in houses or signs in which he rejoices, or in his own house, he conceals the crimes and provides great protection. If Saturn is in aspect rather than Jupiter, all the crimes are detected and great punishment ensues.

9. Mars and the Moon in the same sign make men clever and successful in all their undertakings, especially if the planets are on one of the angles. But they indicate either a short life or an untimely death.

10. For some the prediction is for affliction and illness, or fearful danger, or, if none of these, a mournful and wretched death by the sword.

11. This combination also indicates continual sickness for the mother. But if Jupiter is in favorable houses on the first angles, in his house or his exaltation, and in aspect to Mars and the Moon, all these misfortunes are lessened.

## XXV

## [THE SUN IN CONJUNCTION]

1. If the Sun and Venus are in same sign, they will make the native famous, easily obtaining his desires, but only if Venus is in a morning rising in a diurnal chart or in an evening rising in a nocturnal chart. She indicates, however, a miserable marriage or a difficult wife. She brings female slaves to the nuptial bed or deforms the face of the wife with a low-class appearance. For some she predicts wives who are paupers, or old, or sunk in misfortune, or polluted by foul experiences.

2. The Sun and Mercury in the same sign indicate duties subordinate to powerful men. The natives never shine in their activities. They are clever in council but always hide their thought in deep silence. They are also anxious in some way, worried over all the duties of life, filled with superstitious awe in all religious rites, suspicious of others, and hesitating even in small decisions.

3. But if Mercury is in a morning rising and preserving a straight course (i.e., not retrograde), he predicts a leading position in all affairs.

The natives will be able to give orders, be endowed with fluent speech, have good fortune, and succeed in all their desires. They will be able to foretell the future through divine inspiration, will be truly just and pious worshippers of the gods, often priests. Also from this conjunction fortunate offspring are predicted.

4. If the Sun and Moon are in conjunction in a diurnal chart, the native will be raised to great power, exercising the right of command with the greatest strength and mental stability. But if it is a nocturnal chart and the Moon is hidden by the Sun's orb, this will make the natives low-class, subject to the power of another.

5. When, however, the Moon leaves the vicinity of the Sun's orb and begins to renew her light, though still in the same sign with the Sun, then the natives carry on all their duties effectively and successfully and easily attain all high offices. If the Sun is in a masculine sign and the Moon in a feminine, this will make princes or heads of states, famous and splendid, noted for wisdom and good character. They always exhibit pure and steadfast affection for their friends and enjoy a chaste and modest marriage.

6. If the Sun and Moon are in opposition, then the parents are separated. But if the luminaries are in favorable aspect, that is, in trine, as we said before the parents live happily until the end of their lives. But if, when the Sun and Moon are in opposition, Mars or Saturn are between them with threatening aspect, this indicates constant quarrels and dissensions for the parents.

## XXVI

## [VENUS IN CONJUNCTION]

1. Venus and Mercury in conjunction make natives handsome and agreeable; they easily attain all their wishes, but are driven by depraved urges to bed with many women. They are trained in speaking so that they always delight the ears of their hearers, or they are successful musicians and singers or famous poets.

2. But if these planets are in their own signs and hold the first angles, or are found in their own terms in favorable houses, then these predictions are fulfilled more strongly. If they are found in dejected houses, they make musicians, but the kind addicted to pleasing the multitude.

3. If Mars is in aspect to Mercury and Venus located together, this indicates an early marriage but connected with some scandal. For then the natives also desire to bed with boys as well as women and seek depraved pleasures beyond measure.

4. But if Mars and Venus are in conjunction in the same sign as the ascendant, then divine talent is indicated for the natives, magnificent eloquence, and poems said to be written with divine inspiration. All these predictions are accompanied by increased good fortune if Mars and

Venus are in favorable houses, and Jupiter and the Moon, also in a favorable house, aspects them in trine.

5. The Moon and Venus together in the same sign indicate unusually high position. They make the natives handsome, agreeable, and distinguished. But their marriages are always unstable. No one who has Mars and Venus together continues in dependable affection of his wife or any steadfast relationship in love.

6. This combination estranges the natives from wives through their own vicious desires and drives them to bed with strange women. Likewise it forces the wives to become involved in love affairs and drives them to desire the same pleasures as the erring husband, so that the adulterous husband by his own teaching produces an adulterous wife.

## XXVII

### [THE MOON AND MERCURY IN CONJUNCTION]

1. The Moon and Mercury located together indicate all learning, together with the greatest power. For those who have the Moon and Mercury together easily learn whatever they study.

2. But if there is no influence of Jupiter, the Moon and Mercury make liars and men whose activities are unstable and changeable. The mothers also are intelligent but incur scandal from intercourse with inferior men. The Moon is better in the combination if she holds a smaller number of degrees and if Mercury is found with a larger number.

## XXVIII

### [THE MOON IN CONJUNCTION]

1. Now that we have finished all these discussions and before our work turns to the examples concerning the ascendant, we must briefly call to your attention that in all charts you should consider the planet to which the Moon attaches herself before the native is born. For if a benefic planet is either in conjunction with the rise of the Moon or in favorable aspect to her, this will make a good forecast for the one whom approaching birth is about to bring into the light. But if there is association with a malefic planet, a mediocre or obscure chart is indicated.

2. My dear Mavortius, we have explained to you all the effects of the combinations of the planets, what is accomplished by individual planets in trine or square aspect, and what they mean in conjunction or opposition, also what the lesser power of sextile signifies. But we shall point out all these things more clearly to you, confused as they are in every kind of forecast, when all the powers are brought together and joined; I shall explain all the secrets of the portents so that whatever we have described in general we shall show again in detail.

## XXIX

## [CHARTS OF ILL OMEN]

1. If the Moon and Jupiter are in conjunction and Saturn on a right square is in aspect to them and Mars is also in square aspect, but the Sun is in the sixth or twelfth house, that combination indicates a slave's chart; Jupiter, attacked from both sides, is not able to free the native from the necessity of slavery.

2. If the Moon is on the MC with Jupiter in the same place, and Mars comes into conjunction with the waxing Moon, but Saturn unfavorably aspects the conjunction of Mars and the Moon, this will produce good slaves but burdened with weight of misfortune.

3. If Mars and Saturn are in opposition to the Moon and no benefic planet is in favorable aspect to any of them, this combination will either make slaves or wretched orphans, deprived of the protection of parents.

4. If Venus and the Moon located in different houses are aspected by Saturn and Mars, in square or opposition, and there is no influence of Jupiter, the natives will be born from slave parents and burdened with continual slavery.

5. If Jupiter and Venus favorably aspect the degree of the ascendant and the Sun and the Moon are in any kind of aspect to this same degree, but Mars and Saturn are not in aspect, the native will be born and brought up in good fortune.

6. But if Saturn and Mars are in aspect to the ascendant without influence of benefic planets, or if one of the malefic planets is on the ascendant and the other in opposition on the descendant, the natives either die on the threshold of life, or vital nourishment is denied them at their first steps, or they are exposed by an obstinate mother. But if, as we said, malefic planets are located on the ascendant and Jupiter or Venus is in favorable aspect, the exposed infant will be picked up and nourished by a stranger.

7. If Jupiter is located exactly on the ascendant and Mars is in opposition to the ascendant with no other planet present, this combination indicates a mediocre forecast. But these natives are denied protection against enemies.

8. If Jupiter and Mars are located, as we said, with Jupiter on the ascendant and Mars on the descendant, and Saturn and Mercury are in aspect to Mars in any way, this will produce madmen or epileptics.

9. But if Jupiter is on the ascendant and Saturn is in opposition on the descendant in a diurnal chart with the full Moon moving toward Jupiter, this indicates riches, good fortune, and the highest degree of happiness. But if Venus is found on the descendant in opposition to Jupiter, this denies both brothers and children. Nevertheless riches and good fortune are predicted.

10. If Saturn is on the ascendant and Mars is in opposition on the

descendant or on the MC; and the Moon is full and moving toward Mars, or waning and moving toward Saturn, this combination indicates a wretched death. Either the natives are devoured by wild beasts, or they suffer a fall from a high place, or their bodies are crushed by ruins, or the one who has Saturn or Mars in this position is handed over to bandits to be destined to a bloody death, or is drowned in a fierce storm at sea.

11. But the end will be according to the nature of the signs. For if Saturn or Mars are located in bestial or rural signs they bring death at the teeth of wild beasts. In fixed signs falling buildings crush the natives. In watery signs the natives either perish in battle, their throat is cut by the sword of a bandit, or they are struck down by some punishing power.

12. In general, when Saturn is on the ascendant and Mars is on the descendant, a wretched death is indicated. If Mercury is in aspect the natives are executed by sentence of the court.

13. If Mars is on the ascendant and Jupiter is in opposition on the descendant, dangers, griefs, and anxieties in middle life are indicated, also threats of riots and revolution. In a similar way this indicates losses and law suits. But after many shipwrecks of life a happy period of old age is forecast. But wives are allotted who are either slaves, of advanced age, public prostitutes, or those who carry on the practice of some skill. All the brothers are not kept in one country, but they are separated by journeys or by death.

14. If the Moon is on any angle and Mars in opposition is in aspect to Saturn or in conjunction with him, or aspects the ascendant from any angle, but Jupiter is in the sixth, eighth, or twelfth house with the Moon, the native will live only as long as the Moon is in conjunction with Jupiter. As soon as the Moon has crossed out of the degree of Jupiter, the native will die.

15. If the Moon and Sun are synodic, and Mars is between the Sun and Moon with Saturn in square aspect, the natives will die oppressed by malignant humors, or will be captives of the fury of madness, or will die a wretched death in waves of the sea.

16. If all these planets, that is, the Sun, Mars, and Saturn, are in the eighth house, but all other planets are in the sixth or seventh house, they will produce epileptics or madmen whose minds are always disturbed by an angry or malevolent power. Their whole mind is in confusion and they suddenly throw out words without reason.

17. If in a man's chart the house of the Moon of the wife is found in the twelfth house, that is, the house of the *Cacodaemon,* and Mars is also found there, this will make the wife subject to all kinds of injuries from her husband and make her of such a temperate character that she patiently bears these injuries to the last day of her life.

18. If, on the other hand, the Moon of the husband is found in the *Cacodaemon,* you will predict that the wife will be adulterous and attack her husband with all kinds of injuries, so that charges of adultery may be

brought against her by the husband. But also in this case the husband bears patiently all his wife's injuries.

19. If the wife and husband in their charts have the Moon in the same sign, or if the woman's Jupiter aspects the husband's Moon favorably, or if, on the other hand, the man's Jupiter aspects favorably the woman's Moon, or if the Moon of both charts are in trine aspect, love will bind both of them with equal affection.

20. If Venus is found in earthy signs and in the seventh house or on the MC, or if she is in the twelfth house and in opposition to Saturn, this indicates a long widowhood.

21. If Venus in this location is in a morning rising, the widowhood will occur in early life. If in an evening rising, late in life. But this combination also drives some men to the incestuous bed of their daughters.

22. If the Moon and Venus are in conjunction in feminine signs on the descendant or the MC in a nocturnal charts, and Mars and Saturn are in aspect to them, they fill fathers with incestuous fire and drive them to illegal marriages with daughters.

23. If the ruler of the sign of marriage is on the descendant or the MC in a feminine sign, this drives virgins secretly to base desires. The nature of the corruption we discover from the difference in the planets. For if Saturn is ruler of the marriage sign, the virgin is seduced either by the father, paternal uncle, or step-father, or by an old man or a slave. If Mars is the ruler, the girl is raped. But if Venus is the ruler of the marriage sign, the seduction is accomplished spontaneously during nocturnal vigils of the mysteries. Mercury as the ruler has the girl give up her virginity in response to persuasive promises. But also this combination on occasion stirs up riots and revolutions. There are great dangers if Mars is found with Mercury.

## XXX

### [CHARTS SHOWING THE INFLUENCE OF VENUS]

1. If Jupiter and Venus are in conjunction in the sign of Saturn, and Saturn is in a near-by sign, that is, the second, so that he himself will next come into conjunction with Venus, and Mars is in aspect to the Moon and Venus; also Saturn is in aspect to the Moon; the Sun is on the MC, and the Moon and the ascendant are both in Cancer: in this case the natives, possessed by incestuous fury and removed from the protection of any celestial power, achieve intercourse with their own mothers or their step-mothers. But if it is a woman's chart, she is joined as in matrimony with her father or step-father. Tradition says that Oedipus had such a chart. For in that case the ascendant was in Cancer, the Sun in Aries, Saturn in Pisces, Jupiter and Venus in Aquarius, Mars in Libra, the Moon in the nebula of Cancer, and Mercury with the Sun.

2. If the Moon is found in the terms of Mercury and in a masculine

sign, especially if in Aquarius, and if Venus is not in trine to Jupiter, the native will have no children.

3. If the Moon on the ascendant is in equinoctial signs, that is, in Aries or Libra, but Jupiter and Mars are in conjunction on the MC or the descendant; and Venus and Saturn are in conjunction in either Capricorn or Aquarius in aspect to Mars and Jupiter, they will make the natives sterile and effeminate; or castrated eunuchs serving religious rites.

4. If Saturn and Mars are in conjunction in the house of Venus on the descendant or the IMC, and Venus is in opposition to them in a degree of the same number, this arrangement of stars shows us the chart of a eunuch.

5. If Mars and the Moon are in opposition, but Venus is in square aspect to them in a right square and Saturn, in opposition to Venus, aspects the Moon and Mars from a left square, with Mercury on the MC, this combination produces natives who are sterile, hermaphrodites, or eunuchs.

6. If Saturn and Venus are together on the MC in the sign or terms of Venus, and Mars is not in aspect to them, the native will either be a pauper or have a wife weighed down with age. If Jupiter is in trine to this combination or together with them, a widow is allotted as wife, but one who is extremely wealthy.

7. Venus in conjunction with Jupiter on the MC indicates a wife known for adultery. If Mercury is also in conjunction with them, the wife leaves the husband with whom she was living when accused of adultery and changes to another, either captured by love of a young man, or seeking the bed of a pauper or of a low-class husband, so that altogether she is allotted marriage with an inferior.

8. If the Moon is found exactly on the MC, the Sun on the ascendant, and Jupiter on the anafora of the ascendant in trine to the Moon, this combination indicates fame and high position.

9. If Venus is on the MC and separated from all malevolent influences, but Jupiter is in trine to her or together with her, great good fortune is indicated through protection of women or the beginning of fortune through some feminine occupation. In the last case the natives either accompany songs or play the lyre or the cithara[73] or dance gracefully.

10. Jupiter exactly on the MC always drives the native to depraved desire for low-class women. If Mars is found in the same degree, the wife will be carried off by violence. But, if the Sun is in square aspect to all of these, this indicates wicked intercourse with concubines of fathers or stepfathers. But when this depraved wedding is consummated, the woman flees and dissolves the marriage which was joined under impious omens.

11. If Mars is found on the MC, with the Moon and Jupiter exactly on the ascendant, the Sun on the descendant in opposition to Jupiter but in

square to Mars and the Moon, this indicates a marriage with unending conflict. For then a threatening sword inflicts severe wounds, famous battles are stirred up with savage heat; amid groans of the falling and sharp engagement of the fighters the nuptials are bloodied.

12. Paris Alexander (Paris of Troy) is said to have had such a forecast; from his marriage came famous battles and fabled destruction to his fatherland. The whole chart of Alexander was thus: the ascendant in Aquarius, the Sun and Saturn in Leo, the Moon and Mars in Scorpio, Jupiter in Aquarius, Venus and Mercury in Gemini.

13. If Saturn and Mars are exactly on the MC or aspect this place from other angles in square or opposition, and if their malice is not softened by protection of Jupiter or Venus, this combination will produce suffering paupers oppressed by weight of poverty and worn out by unending daily toil. If Mars is in aspect to this same place (the MC) in opposition, and Saturn is on the MC or the IMC or the ascendant, and there is no benefic influence of Jupiter, together with the aforesaid evils are included prison and iron chains. But if, with all these located as described, Jupiter aspects the full Moon, the natives are freed after much suffering and danger.

14. Mars exactly on the MC with Saturn in the second sign will produce suffering paupers who seek their livelihood by work of their hands. Also their faces are covered with a mournful expression. They never attain their desires.

15. The Moon on the cusp of Aries or Taurus or in Capricorn makes women shrews, and drives their husbands to all vices of lust. If Mercury and Mars are in the same degree with the Moon, but the Moon is moving away from Mars, the type of vice is discovered from the particular degree in which the Moon is. But if Jupiter is in trine to these planets, or in conjunction with them, the native is protected from the aforesaid vices and the wickedness is lessened.

16. If Venus is found with these planets without the influence of Jupiter, all vices of impurity and unchastity are indicated. For then men are driven by heat of desire to act as women. If it is a woman's chart, she becomes a prostitute, selling her body or attaching herself to the power of a pimp, even though she appears to be of good family.

17. If the Sun, the Moon, and the ascendant are located in the chart in such a way that they are not in aspect to each other in any way, the native is worn out by such a burden of poverty that he approaches the lowest level of beggary.

18. If the Sun, Moon, and ascendant are in feminine signs, and Mercury is exactly on the ascendant, the natives are forced to amputate their genitals with their own hands.

19. If the Sun and Moon are exactly on the ascendant, or one precedes the ascendant and the other follows, but they are nevertheless in the same sign with the ascendant, and Mars is on the anafora of the ascendant, and Saturn is in any aspect to Mars, the wretched burden of blindness is indicated.

20. The Moon on the MC and Venus in opposition on the IMC join sisters to brothers in incestuous union.

21. Venus in right square to the Moon will make men fitted for all duties of affairs; they seek the protection of many friends and cherish their wives with faithful affection as well as their friends. These predictions are stronger if Jupiter is in trine to Venus or to the Moon.

22. If the ascendant is in Virgo, and Mars, Mercury, and Venus are in conjunction in that degree, and Jupiter on the descendant in the sign of Pisces is in opposition to the three; and the Sun is in the anafora of the ascendant, that is, in Libra; and the Moon is in the fifth house in Capricorn, and Saturn is in the ninth house in Taurus—the native who has this combination will be an orator whose sentences issue like thunder; at his control the multitude if quiet are aroused, or if riotous are easily silenced. Such are his speeches that later ages will compete to learn them by heart to nourish their own talent. Such an orator persecuted Philip of Macedon, not with force of arms but by power of speech, as we shall explain. This chart inspired the divine genius of Demosthenes.

23. If Mars, Mercury, and Venus are in conjunction in Sagittarius in the terms of Venus and this is also the ascendant; and Jupiter from the descendant in Gemini is in opposition in a number of degrees equal to them; and the Sun is in Capricorn; and the Moon is in the fifth house in Aries in such a way that she is in the head of Aries (in these degrees she indicates blindness); and Saturn is in the ninth house, that is, in Leo—this chart makes a poet of heroic song. They write noble and famous songs about martial strife and fearful battles. Such a chart was that of the divine Homer, the author of the Iliad.

24. If the ascendant is in Aquarius, and Mars, Mercury, and Venus are in conjunction in that degree; Jupiter is on the descendant in Leo; the Sun is on the anafora of the ascendant in Pisces; the Moon is in the fifth house in Gemini, in trine to the ascendant; and Saturn is in the ninth house in Libra—this chart produces an interpreter of divine and celestial matters. He possesses a combination of learned speech and divine intelligence and is trained by some kind of heavenly power to give true expression to all secrets of divinity. This chart is said to have been that of Plato.

25. If the ascendant is in Libra; Mars, Venus, and Mercury are in conjunction on the ascendant; Jupiter is on the descendant, that is, in Aries, in opposition to Mars, Mercury, and Venus; the Sun is in Scorpio on the anafora of the ascendant; the Moon is in Aquarius in the fifth house; and Saturn is in Gemini in the ninth house—this chart makes an inspired lyric poet who writes choruses for religious poems in many rhythms. Such charts were those of Pindar and Archilochus, known for the divine inspiration of their sweet songs.

26. If the ascendant is in Aries in the terms of Jupiter; Mars, Venus, and Mercury are in conjunction on the ascendant, and Jupiter is on the descendant in opposition, that is, in Libra; the Sun is on the anafora of the

ascendant in Taurus; the Moon is in the fifth house in Leo; and Saturn is in the ninth house in Sagittarius—this chart produces inspired inventors of mechanical skills. This was the chart of our inventor of the sphere showing the course of all the heavenly stars—Archimedes of Syracuse,[74] my fellow citizen, who often conquered the Roman armies with his mechanical arts. The general Marcellus[75] in his victorious triumph among the rejoicing soldiers and the triumphal laurels wept for him with tragic grief.

## XXXI

## [COMPLEX ASPECTS]

We have told enough, my dear Mavortius, of the charts of famous men. Now we must return to the order of the work we have started.

1. If Saturn is in Libra in the terms or exaltation of Jupiter, and the ascendant is found in that same degree, but Venus on the descendant in Aries is in opposition; Mars and the Moon are in conjunction on the MC; the Sun and Mercury are in Gemini in the ninth house; and Jupiter is in Aquarius holding the fifth house and making his station (turning retrograde or direct); this indicates the most powerful kingly rule or high office and power.

2. If the Moon is in the twelfth house, that is, the *Cacodaemon,* and is in a sign which is said to be the triplicity of Saturn, that is, in Aquarius, Gemini, or Libra, with the Sun in the sixth house in opposition to the Moon with a like number of degrees; but Jupiter is in the eighth house; from this chart come toilsome poverty and wretched beggary.

3. If the Moon and Mars are in the seventh house, that is, on the descendant, and in the sign said to be the triplicity of Mars, that is, in Cancer, Scorpio, or Pisces; but Jupiter is exactly on the MC and the Sun in trine; this will make athletes who carry off the prizes in sacred contests.

4. If Venus is in a feminine sign, on the descendant; and Mars, the Sun, and the Moon are also in a feminine sign, the native will be a male prostitute.

5. If Saturn and Mars are in conjunction on the ascendant which is in a feminine sign; and Venus and Mercury are on the descendant, also in a feminine sign; or Mars and Saturn are on the MC in a feminine sign, or Mercury and Venus are on the IMC in a feminine sign; this chart will make male prostitutes or castrated eunuchs. If it is a woman's chart she will be a public prostitute.

6. If the Moon and Mars are in conjunction in the eighth house and Mercury is in opposition to them, this will produce bandits of immoderate cruelty. We discover the nature of their crimes from the variety of the planets. For if Mars and the Moon are in earth signs, the attacker will stain his hands with blood in deserted regions. If they are in water signs, they will be sheep stealers, threatening their pursuers with the sword. In fixed

signs the natives will be famous house-breakers who, armed with swords, threaten sleeping victims with loss of possessions and danger to life. But all these are caught in their crimes and suffer severe punishment. If Mars and Mercury are in conjunction on the IMC and the full Moon is in square aspect or opposition to them, this indicates the same in a similar way.

7. If Saturn and Venus are on the descendant and Mars is in the eighth house, and Mercury is with Mars, or with Saturn and Venus; and if Jupiter is not in favorable aspect to any of these; this will produce either slaves or castrates, but the type who display all kinds of impure vices.

8. If Mars is on the ascendant and Venus on the descendant, Saturn on the MC and the Moon on the IMC, this will make an unchaste man.

9. If Mars is on the MC in a feminine sign; Saturn and Venus in the eleventh house, but the ascendant with Jupiter, the Moon, and Mercury in the sign of Venus; the natives will corrupt with incestuous desire either their mothers, stepmothers, or mothers' sisters.

10. Venus with Saturn on the ascendant in any sign or degree allots wives who are either public prostitutes or advanced in age, especially if Jupiter is not in aspect.

11. Jupiter and Mars in conjunction on the MC makes natives marked by unusual goodness who always attain good fortune, especially if this combination is found in the house or terms of Jupiter.

12. If Mars is on the MC or in the house of the Moon, and Jupiter is in that house in conjunction with Venus and Mars, and if the full Moon is moving toward Jupiter, this indicates the greatest good fortune.

13. If Mercury, Saturn, Mars, Venus, and the Moon are in conjunction on the MC, they indicate miserable poverty; they make the natives doorkeepers driven to this service through poverty; death of children is also often indicated.

14. If Mars and Venus are in conjunction in the fifth house and the Moon is exactly on the ascendant, fame and high position are predicted and faithful affection from a king. Honors include consular rank, gold robes, and gold crowns. But these natives are allotted adulterous wives.

15. The ascendant in the twelfth house in the sign of a malefic planet will have the native destroyed by dogs. But if that malefic planet who rules the twelfth house is himself in the seventh house, that is, on the descendant, this indicates danger of death unless there is the protection of Jupiter and Venus.

16. If the Sun and Moon are in the triplicity of Mars, that is, in Cancer, Scorpio, or Pisces, and Mars himself is found on the MC or the descendant, difficulties and constant traveling are indicated; the natives will end their days in strange regions or on journeys.

17. If Mars and the ascendant are found in this triplicity, that is, in Cancer, Scorpio, or Pisces, with the Moon on the ascendant, and Venus with Mercury on the descendant in the same number of degrees, the natives will become murderers of their wives.

18. If Venus is on the ascendant and the ascendant is in the sign of Venus, but Mars and the Moon are on the descendant in the sign or terms of Mars, the mother of the native will be struck with a sword.

19. If the Moon is on the MC, and Saturn, Mars, and Jupiter are together on the IMC, the native will be dragged from his own country and sold into slavery.

20. If the Moon, Mars, and Saturn are in conjunction on the MC, they will make the natives either leaders or followers of base and lustful pursuits who gain a livelihood from these activities.

21. If Saturn is found in the sixth house and Venus and Mercury in the twelfth and if all of these, in opposition, hold an equal number of degrees, the natives will have intercourse with their daughters. The same is indicated by Venus, Mercury, and Jupiter in each other's houses.

22. If Venus, Mercury, Jupiter, and Saturn are all in conjunction in the eleventh house, they allot as wives women who have been the slaves of most powerful men.

23. When Saturn and Venus are exactly on the MC with Jupiter in no kind of aspect, if this is a woman's chart, she couples with eunuchs and sterile men in unsuccessful passion.

24. Venus and Jupiter in conjunction in the fifth or eleventh house with no benefic planet in aspect indicate marital difficulties and serious accidents from marriage; the couples are always involved in fierce quarrels and malevolent fights.

25. If Mars is in the same degree as the ascendant in the house of Jupiter, Saturn in trine to Mars and the ascendant, and the Moon in the last degrees of the ascendant, the natives have intercourse with their mothers or their stepmothers. If it is a woman's chart, she sleeps with her father or stepfather. She will have the vicious desires of a prostitute. If Saturn is in the fifth house and Mercury with Venus in the eleventh, marriage with a stepdaughter is indicated.

26. Saturn on an angle with Mercury in opposition denies all children.

27. The Sun on the ascendant with Mars and Saturn on the anafora of the ascendant indicates some kind of affliction of the right eye. If the Moon is on the ascendant with Mars and Saturn on the anafora, the affliction is in the left eye. Both of these must be in a nocturnal chart.

28. Blindness and weakness of body together with wretched beggary are indicated by the Moon on the IMC, with Saturn, the Sun, and Mars in the eighth house aspecting the Moon in trine. Blindness is also indicated by this combination if Saturn is in the twelfth house in trine to the Sun, Moon, and Mars.

29. The Sun and Mars in the eighth house with the Moon in opposition in a human sign, together with Saturn, also indicate blindness and weakness of body. And if Saturn is on the descendant and Mars on the ascendant, the Sun on the anafora of the ascendant and the Moon in the sixth house, in the course of time the blindness grows worse and is

accompanied with hemorrhage. Also if the Moon is on the ascendant and the Sun on the descendant in the seventh house, great affliction of the eyes is indicated.

30. If Mars is on the MC, Saturn in the eleventh house, the Sun on the anafora of the ascendant in opposition to the Moon in the eighth house, one eye will be extinguished but the other preserved.

31. If Mercury and the Moon are in conjunction and have Mars and Venus on the left side of a square, they either deform the body with a pointed head, disfigure the sight of the eyes, or make one shoulder twisted.

32. Dangerous blindness is also indicated by the Sun on the ascendant, Saturn on the IMC, and the Moon holding a right trine from the ascendant. If Saturn and the Moon are in tropical signs, or the Sun and Mars are in opposition to them, this combination always means danger to the eyes. But if Jupiter is on the MC in this combination, all difficulties of poverty are relaxed.

33. Saturn and the Moon on the MC with the Sun and Mars in the eighth house also indicate blindness. But if the Sun is found on the ascendant, Saturn on the anafora of the ascendant, the Moon on the MC, and Mars in the eleventh house, blindness is indicated. The same is true when the Sun is found on the ascendant, Saturn on the anafora of the ascendant, the Moon on the MC, and Mars in the eleventh house.

34. If the Sun, Moon, and Mercury are in conjunction in a tropical sign and the Moon is deprived of all light, they indicate the greatest wisdom, unusual intelligence, and knowledge of many things; but also with blindness and weakness of the body.

35. The Moon, Saturn, and Mars in conjunction in equinoctial signs make the whole body spotted with certain marks or make it blotched and white; on the other hand, either creeping impetigo will possess the whole body, or the native will suffer long-lasting scabies, or the disgraceful disfigurement of leprosy.

36. If Mercury, Saturn, and the Sun are in conjunction in the seventh house, that is, the descendant, and the Moon is in conjunction with Mars in the eighth house, they either amputate the hands or produce cripples or madmen who suffer from mental affliction.

37. Now, my dear Mavortius, I shall show you an amusing forecast. From this example you will be able to assess similar cases. That deformed and feeble Greek[76] whose misshapen body Homer described to us in his divine songs, whom the laughter of all wise men punished —he had a chart of this kind. The ascendant was in Aquarius, the Sun and Saturn in Capricorn (that is, the twelfth house), but Jupiter on the ascendant or on the anafora of the ascendant, and Mars with the Moon in the eleventh house in Libra; Mercury and Venus were on the ascendant (that is, in Aquarius). This forecast shows us the chart of Thersites. He was unwarlike, feeble, silly, always impatient, displaying garrulous wordiness. All

these traits the chart shows us.

38. Venus in Capricorn with Saturn in opposition makes natives hated by their wives in every way. Their bodies in heavy sweat give off an unpleasant goat-like odor. They will be despised in sexual relations and always be objects of scandal for their vicious desires. Jupiter lessens these difficulties to a certain extent if he is in trine to Venus, and he somewhat cleanses the odor.

39. The Moon, Saturn, and Venus in the seventh house, that is, on the descendant, make perverts with effeminate softness of body who dance on the stage and act in ancient fables, especially if Mars is in square aspect. For then he makes them addicted to all kinds of base vices; they also practice immoral kinds of intercourse with their wives. If to all these Jupiter is in square aspect from the IMC, together with all these vices he makes them lovers of boys.

40. If Jupiter, Saturn, and Venus are in conjunction on the MC, and Mars is in opposition on the IMC, this will make lovers of boys who pay for this vice with use of their own bodies.

41. If Jupiter, Venus, and Saturn are in conjunction in the seventh house, that is, the descendant, inheritance is acquired from the death of a wife. But the natives themselves suffer severe illnesses and get children only with difficulty. Mercury, Venus, Saturn, and Jupiter together on the MC indicate wives who are foreigners but extremely wealthy.

42. Saturn on the ascendant with Mercury and Jupiter in the seventh house denies offspring. But if the order of that combination is reversed so that Jupiter and Mercury are on the ascendant and Saturn is in opposition on the descendant, the prediction is the same.

43. If Mercury and Venus are on the IMC and Saturn is in square aspect to them on the MC, this indicates an old wife. Also the native will have impure sex relations with his wife. If Venus and Saturn are in conjunction on the MC and the Moon is in opposition to them on the IMC, either old or sterile wives are indicated, so that from that marriage children are never possible.

44. Mercury and Mars in conjunction in the fifth house indicate sisters for wives.

45. Saturn, Jupiter, and Mars together on the MC indicate every kind of grief from wives so that a happy marriage is never possible with this combination.

46. Venus on the descendant, that is, the seventh house, in an evening rising with Saturn on the MC will make men sluggish in love; it also makes women frigid, with no sexual desires.

47. If Mars, the Moon, and Venus are in conjunction on the MC and Mercury is in opposition to them, this will make public eunuchs in a man's chart, but women it turns into public prostitutes lost to all modesty.

48. A severe burden of grief from accidents to children is predicted by Saturn and Jupiter in conjunction on the IMC or in the seventh house.

But if Mercury and also Venus are with them, they make women sterile and men lose all sexual appetites. But if all these are in tropical signs, they make the woman's vagina closed to normal entry. But if Mars is also found with all these, they will make castrated eunuchs serving sacred rites.

49. If Mars and the Moon are in conjunction on the ascendant, Mercury on the MC, and Saturn on the descendant, this makes the children perish while still in tender years and crying in their nurses' arms.

50. If Mercury, Mars, Saturn, and Venus are in conjunction on the IMC, children will die a miserable death before being recognized by their fathers.

51. If Mars is on the IMC, Saturn on the descendant, and the Moon on the ascendant in square aspect to Mars and in opposition to Saturn, an early death is predicted for the wife.

52. If Jupiter is in the seventh house, that is, the descendant, and Mars and Mercury are in conjunction on the ascendant, offspring are denied. But if Mercury and Jupiter are on angles and in opposition to each other (one on the ascendant and one on the descendant, or one on the MC and one on the IMC), masculine children will perish in a horrible death.

53. If the ascendant is in tropical or mutable signs and Mars and Mercury are in conjunction on the ascendant but Jupiter is in opposition to the ascendant, this will produce epileptics or madmen.

54. Venus on the ascendant and Saturn in square aspect on the IMC produce servants in temples. These men are possessed by a divine instinct, though their minds are deranged, and they predict the future and from this gain a livelihood.

55. If Jupiter, Mars, Mercury, and Venus are located together on the ascendant, which is in Virgo, and Saturn is in Pisces in opposition to them, the Sun is on the anafora of the ascendant but the Moon is in Aquarius; and if all these are located in their own terms; this shows the chart of a most powerful emperor.

56. If Mars is on the ascendant and the Moon is moving toward him or away from him, the indication is for a humble life, afflictions of illness, serious dangers, and calamities. If Mars is on the descendant and the Moon is moving away from him, the prediction is the same.

57. If the Sun is in conjunction with the ascendant in Aries or Scorpio and Mars, Saturn, and Jupiter in favorable houses are in trine aspect, this makes tyrants—cruel, fearsome, but successful, who make their way with ferocious cruelty through deaths and wretched punishments of their victims.

58. If the Moon is found on the ascendant, and Saturn and Jupiter on the descendant (the seventh house) in opposition to her, the natives will be stained with knowledge of hidden homicide. But if the Sun, Mars, and Mercury are in conjunction on the descendant, that is, in the seventh house, in tropical signs, the native will be a bandit drenched with human blood, armed for every kind of cruelty. If Saturn is found with the other

planets, he shows us the kind of death. The native will be apprehended in his crimes, sentenced by the court, and raised on the cross.

59. If Jupiter is in the degrees of Pisces in which Andromeda is found, and the Moon, approaching Saturn, comes into conjunction with him, this indicates the greatest misfortune. If Mars is in opposition to the Moon thus located, this evil makes the natives apprehended in crime and crucified.

60. If Venus is in those degrees of Taurus in which the Pleiades are located, and Mercury and Mars are either in conjunction with the full Moon or in square aspect to her, the native will be captured by bandits and killed, struck by a sword.

61. If Venus is found in Taurus, on the ascendant in square aspect to the full Moon on the MC, this indicates the same as the above. If the ascendant is in Taurus and Mars is in Leo on the IMC in threatening aspect to the ascendant, the native will die by the sword. But if the ascendant is in Libra and Mars in Capricorn on the IMC in square aspect, the native will also be killed by the sword.

62. It must be noted that if the ascendant is in Aries or in Scorpio, and Mars is on the descendant, the MC, or the IMC, with little influence of the benefic planets, nothing bad is predicted, especially if it is a nocturnal chart. For Mars looks after his own house and when on the descendant never attacks it.

63. If the Sun is on the ascendant and Saturn is on the MC and the house of Saturn is on the descendant, the natives will die of dropsy. But if Mercury is on the MC they will die of poison. If Jupiter is on the MC, death will come suddenly among happy friends at a banquet from too much food or too much drinking. But if Mars and the Sun are on the MC, they will die by the sword or be burned in a fire. If the Moon is on the MC they will die of the sacred illness (epilepsy). But if Venus is on the MC they will finish their life from malignant humors or be drowned in waves of the sea.

64. Mars and Mercury in conjunction in the eighth house make wicked thieves, who with vicious avarice desire the goods of others.

65. If the Sun is on the ascendant, and the Moon on the descendant, and Saturn and Mars are either with the Sun or with the Moon, or one is with one of these while the other holds one of the angles, the native will be exposed.

66. If Mars is on the ascendant and Mercury on the MC in square aspect, this will make malevolent informers. But if Mercury is on the descendant and Mars, on the MC, this will produce bandits often stained with human blood.

67. If Mars is on the ascendant, and Saturn is on any angle, and the Moon and Jupiter are together in a dejected house, the natives will live only as long as it takes for the Moon to cross Jupiter's course. If the Moon is in firm aspect with Jupiter, they will live only as long as it takes Saturn to

cross the first angle which he meets. But if the rays of the Moon are unstable, they will live as many days as the Moon is found with Jupiter. But if Mars and Saturn are located as we said, and Jupiter is in a dejected house with the Moon on one of the angles, especially the ascendant, the natives will be short-lived and have an evil death.

68. If Saturn is on the MC and the Moon is in opposition on the IMC, but Mars is on the descendant or the MC in threatening aspect to the Moon, possessing equal degrees with the Moon, the native will meet death the minute he bursts from the uterus. But if the Sun is on the ascendant, the Moon on the descendant in opposition to Mars, and Saturn in conjunction with the Sun or with the Moon, or one is in conjunction and the other holding one of the angles, the native will be exposed.

69. If the Sun is found in the sixth house and Saturn in the twelfth house in opposition to him, but both the Moon and Mars are in conjunction with Saturn in the twelfth house and in opposition to the Sun, they make enfeebled paralytics whose whole body is deformed with dislocated muscles and broken strength.

70. If Saturn, Mars, and the Moon are in conjunction in the eleventh house and Jupiter is in trine aspect to them or in the third house or on the descendant with the Sun on the ascendant, this chart indicates a tyrant.

71. If Mercury, Venus, Saturn, and Mars are in conjunction in the eleventh house, they make the natives immoderately extravagant, reveling in sumptuous profusion and lascivious desires.

72. Mercury and Mars in conjunction in the fifth house with Saturn in square aspect to them from above, or in conjunction with them, will produce forgers who imitate legal tender with adulterating skills. If the Moon is in aspect they will later become bandits or murderers. But if Mars and Mercury are in the fifth house and the waning Moon is in opposition to Saturn, or the Moon is full, in opposition to Mars and Mercury, the forgers will be executed for their crimes or punished by a severe sentence.

73. If the Sun and Mercury are on the ascendant and Saturn and Mars are in opposition on the descendant, the forgers will be apprehended and crucified. The favorable influence of Jupiter is not able to soften this punishment; his helpful protection is despised and the threatening rays of the malefic planets indicate certain death.

74. If Saturn and Mars are in conjunction on the ascendant, and the Sun and Mercury are in opposition to them on the descendant, a hand or a foot will be amputated. After these lacerations the natives will suffer a wretched death.

75. If the degree of the ascendant is found in the same sign between Saturn and Mars, this shows a mournful case of dire misfortune. For the foetus of the native is impeded in birth and torn apart so that all its parts must be brought out with cruel artifice.

76. Epilepsy is predicted by the Moon on the MC in mutable signs with Saturn on the descendant and Mars on the IMC. But if the Moon is

synodic with the Sun and Mars is in conjunction with her, all of them on the MC; if Mars is in a morning rising and Saturn is on the descendant; this also produces epileptics who are changed in character by insane fury and lose the right path of life. But if with Mars, the Moon, and the Sun located as we have said, Saturn is on the IMC in opposition, the native goes mad and throws himself over a precipice. In general, Mars and Saturn in conjunction in double signs on the descendant produce this same effect. The same is true if the Moon is on the ascendant with Saturn and Mars in this situation.

77. Epileptics are also indicated by the Sun on the ascendant in Gemini, the Moon on the MC in Pisces, and Mars on the IMC in Virgo, so that all of these are in double signs.

78. If Jupiter is on the MC in a double sign, and Saturn and the Moon are in conjunction on the IMC, in opposition, the natives will be adopted by strangers who have no children of their own and will become their legal sons and heirs.

79. If Mars, Saturn, and Venus are in conjunction on the MC, and Mercury is in square aspect to them, this will produce prostitutes who sell their bodies for a living. If it is a man's chart, the natives will be involved in feminine vices with effeminate passion.

80. If the Sun and Mars are together on the ascendant, Saturn is on the IMC in square aspect to them, and the Moon is on the IMC in opposition to Saturn and in square aspect to the Sun and Mars, this always arouses murderous hatred of parents toward their sons.

81. If Mars is on the ascendant and Jupiter in the sixth house, but the Moon, Mercury, and Venus are in conjunction on the MC, this combination indicates fame and high position.

82. If Mars, Saturn, and Venus are in conjunction on the ascendant in Aries, and the Sun is in the same sign, the wife will be a slave, an old woman, or of low class. If Mercury is also present, the natives take prostitutes to the nuptial couch. But if with all these as we said the Moon is found on the MC, the natives are driven with mad fury and base desires to a daughter's bed.

83. Mars and the Sun in tropical signs on the descendant with Mercury in the same house make bandits who carry on their activities in foreign regions and are stained with human blood. They are detected in their crimes and suffer severe punishment.

84. If Mercury, the Moon, and Venus are in conjunction in the eleventh house in a feminine sign, and Mars is in trine aspect to them, they make musicians who sweetly play the cithara or the lyre.

85. Mercury, Mars, Venus, and the Moon together on the ascendant or the MC will produce dancers or pantomimers noted for grace and charm. If Jupiter is in favorable aspect, they will be famous and popular, especially if Saturn is also in favorable aspect.

86. If the Moon is synodic with the Sun in the eleventh house and

Jupiter in conjunction with them, and Mars and Saturn in diverse ways aspect the ascendant, one in square and the other in opposition, with one of these latter in an equinoctial sign, the prediction is for the disease of elephantiasis continued until the day of death.

87. If Saturn, the Moon, or Mars is located on a lower degree of Aquarius aspected in opposition by Saturn, children will be separated from parents.

88. The native will be blind if the Moon is found in the feet of Taurus, the nebula of Cancer, the mane of Leo, the forehead of Scorpio, from the eighth to the tenth degree of Sagittarius, in the horns of Capricorn, in the line of Pisces, or the head of Aries; and if either Saturn or Mars are in aspect. If she is on any angle in the signs and houses mentioned above, all use of the eyes is destroyed and wretched blindness ensues. But if the Moon is full or waxing she will not cause blindness but disfigures the face in an ugly way with an affliction, sickness, scar, or mark.

89. If Jupiter and Mars are found exactly on the MC, Mercury and Venus in conjunction in the third house, Saturn in the eighth, the Sun in Gemini, and the Moon either in her own house or her exaltation, this will produce brave, heroic, and murderous men who with their own right hand pile up heaps of dead.

90. If the ascendant is in one of the tropical signs, the Moon in the twelfth house, Jupiter and Mars in conjunction on the IMC, and Mercury and Venus in conjunction on the MC, this is the chart of a malicious prostitute who invites many to her bed for lovemaking. But she is forced to travel through many foreign places and is involved in frequent law suits and accusations. She will be in prison and will abort twin sons.

91. She will also sell her body to two brothers and will invite her father and son to her bed. These she will do both for passion and for gain. But when middle age arrives she will return to her own country and marry a young, unworthy, impoverished foreigner and will arrive at the last day of life chained to marriage with him and in dire need.


## XXXII

### [MEANINGS OF HOUSES]

1. We have now explained everything which is indicated by combinations of planets, my dear Mavortius, and this book hastens toward its end. But here is still something required for the full development of this work; and this I shall now point out to you. Otherwise, unless the whole foundation is laid, we may not arrive at the secrets of the *Mathesis* which the seventh book will contain and to the *Sphaera Barbarica* [77] which will be explained in the eighth.

2. Therefore we shall now show what you ought to seek, in which houses, and to what extent. For the fourth house does not in itself alone

show parents or the life of friends, nor the seventh marriage, nor the fifth children, nor the third friends, nor the sixth illnesses. Since we are now about to fulfill our promise, receive now the full, true account so that you may be able to observe all these phenomena diligently and not miss the true reasoning in generalities. Thus you will find the house of the father exactly in this way.

3. If you wish to investigate the house of the father exactly and if the chart is diurnal, compute from the degree of the Sun to the degree of Saturn, and when you have reached the sum divide these among all the signs beginning from the ascendant, giving 30 degrees to each individual sign. The sign in which the last degree falls is the house of the father. In a nocturnal chart compute from the degree of Saturn to the Sun and continue in the same way.

4. When by this customary computation you have found the house of the father, from the nature of this sign you will be able to discover the character and fate of the father. Note to what extent this sign is aspected by benefic planets. If benefic planets either are in this sign or in favorable aspect, good fortune for the father will be discovered. But if malefic planets are either in the sign or in aspect, all things will go contrary for the father.

5. Also notice whether this is in the house of a benefic or a malefic planet, where the ruler of the sign is located, in what sign or terms and whether on the first or second angles, in houses in which it rejoices or in sluggish and dejected houses. From all this information you will find the nature of the father.

6. Thus if the house of the father is in the sign of Jupiter, and if Jupiter is in his own house, or in signs in which he is exalted, or on the first angles; or in the fifth or eleventh house and in a straight course; if he is in a morning rising and in trine or sextile aspect to the house of the father; this means high position for the father. But if Jupiter is on second angles, in dejected houses, hidden by the rays of the Sun, or retrograde, this indicates a mediocre position for the father.

7. But if the ruler of the father's house is Venus, you must observe the house in which Venus herself is located. If she is in the father's house, or on the first angles, or in signs in which she rejoices or is exalted, or in the fifth or eleventh house and in a morning rising and in a straight course, and from these places aspects the father's house favorably, this indicates the highest position for the father and personal charm and grace. But if she is in dejected houses and in signs in which she is debilitated, or retrograde, or hidden by the rays of the Sun, this shows a mediocre father.

8. If the house of the father is found in the sign of Mercury, consider the house Mercury is in. If he is in the father's house, or in his own house, or his exaltation, or his terms, or in houses or terms in which he rejoices, or on the angles, and if he is in a morning rising and in a straight course, this will involve the father in many duties and negotiations from which he

will gain great profit; also he will love his children with gentle affection.

9. This will be a better forecast if a benefic planet is in aspect to Mercury. But if Mercury is in dejected houses, or in his debility, or on angles in which he does not rejoice, or is retrograde, or hidden by the Sun's rays, all the things we have described happen to the father but in a lesser degree.

10. If the house of the father is in the sign of Saturn, observe where Saturn is. If it is a diurnal chart and Saturn is found in the father's house, or in his own house or degrees, or in degrees or houses in which he rejoices; if he is in a morning rising and in a straight course, and Jupiter is in favorable aspect to him, this will make the father sober, modest, mature, fearsome with quiet severity, a cultivator of fields who gains great income from his crops and who wins many promotions.

11. But if it is a nocturnal chart and Saturn is in dejected houses or angles, in his debility, or is retrograde, or hidden by the Sun's rays, this makes the father low-class, hard-working, ill-kempt and mournful, always sluggish and hesitating, a slave, or given to servile habits and appearance.

12. If the father's house is found in the sign of Mars and Mars is in the house itself, or on the first angles, or in the fifth or eleventh house, or the ninth or third and in a morning rising, not retrograde, this will make the father severe, daring, short-lived, with monstrous sexual appetites, always involved in various troubles and crises.

13. Mars in square aspect or opposition to the house of the father means a violent death. But in a nocturnal chart, if Jupiter and Venus are in favorable aspect to the house of the father or of the mother, these predictions are to a certain extent mitigated; the father will be upright, soldierly, and severe, always pleased with arms and weapons. He will be a leader or a general according to the measurements of the chart.

14. If the house of the father is found in the sign of the Sun in a diurnal chart, observe the house or sign the Sun is in. For if the Sun is in the father's house, or his own house, his exaltation, or on the first angles, or in the fifth or eleventh house, the father will be supplied with riches and hold the highest position, bringing him fame and good fortune.

15. But if he is in dejected houses on the second angles, in his debility, or bereft of all good influences, and is attacked by malefic planets, all the predictions we have described are lessened, especially in a nocturnal chart; for then he strikes the father among other things with an early death.

16. If the house of the father is found in the sign of the Moon, notice in what house the Moon is located. If she is in the sign itself, or in signs in which she is exalted, or on the first angles, or in the fifth or eleventh house, and is full in a nocturnal chart, and benefic planets are in aspect, the father will be famous and rich, winning possessions and high position.

17. But if the Moon is in dejected houses, on the second angles, in her debility or bereft of benefic influence in a diurnal chart, is waning and

aspected by Saturn or full and aspected by Mars, all the things we have described are to a certain extent lessened, and the father either becomes an exile or dies a violent death. He will have an erratic character and be ignorant of the correct path of life.

18. But as we have said before, in the case of this house you must always carefully examine the combinations of the planets, their conditions and aspects, so that you may be able to put all the information together and explain the house of the father with true principles.

19. Carefully consider the degree itself and see who is the ruler of the degree and how he is located. He himself affects the house by his own nature. You should do this also in the houses of the mother, brothers, wife, and children, also in the houses of illness and affliction.

20. In other houses also we collect these same data. In general the Sun is placed in the house of the father, but we shall learn this better in detail.

21. If you wish to discover the house of the mother in a diurnal chart, begin from the degree of Venus, count the degrees to that of the Moon. Then begin at the ascendant and distribute the degrees among the signs. In whatever sign the last degree falls, that is the house of the mother.

22. In a nocturnal chart start from the degree of the Moon to Venus. Thus you will find the house with exact measurement. Look for everything we said in connection with the house of the father, that is, the aspects of benefic planets, powers of the houses and signs, also combinations of influences. All these you must put together with careful comparison and you will be able to explain the house of the mother.

23. If you wish to find the house of brothers in a diurnal chart, begin from the degree of Saturn and count to the degree of Jupiter. Then beginning from the ascendant distribute the sum of degrees among the signs. The sign in which the last degree falls is the house of brothers. In a nocturnal chart count from Jupiter to Saturn.

24. When you have found the house of brothers look to see whether any malefic or benefic planets are in aspect. Note also the powers of the signs and the house in which the sign is located.

25. If benefic planets are found in that same sign or in favorable houses, in signs in which they rejoice or in which they are exalted, or in their own houses, they indicate a number of good brothers. But if malefic planets are in the same locations with no benefic planets in aspect, the opposite is true.

26. But if malefic and benefic planets are equally in aspect, this both gives brothers and takes them away. But you will discover everything in accordance with the nature of the planets. Masculine benefic planets give brothers; feminine, sisters. Malefic planets remove them. Thus all things are fulfilled according to the power of individual planets. But in general, as we said in the book of principles, the third house shows the house of brothers. But let us investigate in detail.

27. If you wish to find the house of the wife, measure from the degree

of Saturn to the degree of Venus and, beginning from the ascendant, distribute the number among the signs. In whatever sign the last degree falls in a diurnal chart, that is the house of the spouse.

28. In a nocturnal chart begin from Venus and count to Saturn. Some count from the Sun to the Moon both in a diurnal and nocturnal chart and distribute from the ascendant both in a man's or a woman's chart. We have proved this method in many charts.

29. When you have found the house of the wife, first look at the sign, whether it is fixed, double, or tropical. Next observe in what house the ruler of the sign is located. Third, observe this same house: who is the ruler of its terms and to what extent it is aspected by benefic or malefic planets. For when benefic planets, located in favorable houses, with no debility, following the power of their condition possess that same house, they will join the natives in harmonious bonds with wives who are rich and famous.

30. They do not indicate marriage with many wives. Whatever wife is allotted, he remains with her to the end of his life in joy and delight. You may recognize the character of the wives from the nature of the signs. Also the kind of marriage.

31. If malefic planets are in aspect, they make all these the reverse. For then low-class and infamous wives are indicated; then there are quarrels and fierce struggles in marriage; and the wives are sterile and adulterous. All this you can explain according to the power of the planets.

32. If you wish to find the house of the husband in a woman's chart, if it is diurnal you must measure from Mars to Venus, in a nocturnal from Venus to Mars. Then from the ascendant distribute the number of degrees to the following signs and in whatever sign the last degree falls, that is the house of the husband. You can discover the kind of husband in the same way as the kind of wife. You must remember that in general Venus shows the wife and Mars the husband.

33. Venus and Mercury always show the house of children. Whichever of them is first in the chart, beginning from that one, count to the other. Then, beginning from the ascendant, distribute the degrees among the signs; in whatever sign the last degree falls, that is the house of children.

34. How one of the two planets is first we shall show by example. If Venus is in Taurus and Mercury is in Gemini, Mercury is first. Beginning from Mercury count to Venus. If Venus is first, count from her to Mercury.

35. But if they are in the same sign, begin from the one that is in the earlier part of the sign. If they are in the same degree, begin from the one that is in the earlier minute. If they are in the same minute, omit this and count from Jupiter to Mercury in a diurnal, and Mercury to Jupiter in a nocturnal chart.

36. Thus when you have found the house of children observe to what extent benefic and malefic planets are in aspect to this house. But also

investigate carefully the conditions of the planets and the nature and power of the signs. If benefic planets are in aspect in favorable houses, they grant children, according to the power of the houses and signs.

37. Malefic planets produce the reverse. But sometimes malefic planets, if the charts are of their conditions, indicate children: that is, Saturn in a diurnal and Mars in a nocturnal chart. The kind and number of children depends on the nature of the signs. You must remember that if the house of children is found in double signs there are children from two wives; if the sign is fixed, the man will have children from one wife, the wife from one husband.

38. But if benefic and malefic planets are equally in aspect to the house of children, they both give and take away children. If the power of the benefic planets is sufficient to grant children, then the children may have a certain weakness from the hostile rays of the malefic planets, or they will be suddenly separated from parents.

39. In the case of this house as in all others, you will carefully observe the combinations and modifications of the planets, the nature of the signs, and the powers of the individual houses. In general, the fifth house shows the house of children, but it is affected by the ruler of the sign, the nature of the sign itself, and the influence of good and bad planets.

40. If you wish to find the house of afflictions and illnesses, in a diurnal chart begin from Saturn and count the degrees to Mars; in a nocturnal chart go from Mars to Saturn; then from the ascendant distribute the degrees among the signs in order; the sign in which the last degree falls is the house of illnesses and afflictions.

41. In general the sixth house shows the house of afflictions. Thus in the first place you will define the kind of illness from the nature of the sign (in the book of principles we noted what parts of the body are controlled by individual signs); secondly, observe to what extent benefic or malefic planets are in aspect.

42. If the benefic planets in their own houses or exaltations are in favorable aspect to this house, they will free the natives from all attacks of illness. But if malefic planets are in aspect with threatening influence, they indicate bitter afflictions.

43. You will find these afflictions according to the nature of the signs and their power. Mars from his own house indicates bruises, small wounds in the body, falls from a height, and accidents from collapsing buildings; Saturn, spasms, trembling, blindness, attacks of malignant humors, dangers in water, and the like. These maladies are definitely attested if malefic planets are in aspect.

44. If the house is controlled by malefic planets and bare of all benefic protection, perpetual illness and endless calamities are indicated. Mars will bring illness within 15 years, Saturn within 30, and the Sun in 19 years. But if there are two who bring illness, measure the years of each and expect the attack of illness at both times. The type of illness is shown by the nature of the planet.

45. If you wish to find the house of sexual desires in a diurnal chart, count from the degree of the Daemon to the degree of the Part of Fortune and again from the ascendant. In a nocturnal chart, from the Part of Fortune to the Daemon in a similar way: again, beginning from the ascendant distribute the degrees among the individual signs; when you have found the house from the kind of sign and the influence of the planets you will discover the whole nature of sexual desires. (We showed in the fourth book how to find the Part of Fortune and the house of the Daemon.)

46. If you wish to find the house of necessity in a diurnal chart, count from the Part of Fortune to the Daemon; in a nocturnal chart from the Daemon to the Part of Fortune; when you have found the house, in the same way as the others you will learn all about this house from the quality of the signs and the planets.

47. If you wish to locate the house of honors, count from the ninth house to the Sun and, beginning from the ascendant, distribute the degrees; whichever sign receives the last degree is the house of honors. The type of honors you will learn from the nature of the signs and from the testimony of the planets.

48. If you wish to locate the house of military affairs, count from Mars to the Sun and again from the ascendant; and in whatever sign the last degree falls, that is the house of military affairs.

49. If you wish to locate the house of travel, always count from the Sun to Mars and again from the ascendant.

50. If you wish to locate the house of reputation, count from the Sun to the MC and proceed as before.

51. If you wish to locate the house of physical courage, count from the Moon to Jupiter and proceed as before.

52. If you wish to locate the house of possessions, always count from Mercury to Jupiter and proceed as before.

53. If you wish to locate the house of accusations count from Mars to Saturn and again from the ascendant and proceed as before.

54. If you wish to locate exactly the house of enemies, by day you will count from Mars to Mercury, by night from Mercury to Mars and again from the ascendant and proceed as before.

55. If you wish to locate exactly the house of friends, by day count from Jupiter to Mercury, by night from Mercury to Jupiter.

56. For the house of glory, count by night from Venus to Jupiter, by day the opposite. For the house of Nemesis, by night count from the Part of Fortune to the Moon; for the house of power, by night from Saturn to the Sun.

57. If you wish to locate the house of slaves, count always from Mercury to the Moon and again from the ascendant, and in whatever sign the last degree falls, this shows you the house of slaves; and you can determine the nature of the slavery from the nature of the sign and from the planets.

## XXXIII

## [SATURN AS RULER OF TIME]

1. We have begun, my dear Mavortius, to show you all the secrets of the *Mathesis* in the truest propositions and definitions; the seventh book will show you the fullest development of these so that you may find everything in the chart without any difficulty. But the following will be added to the present book that I may demonstrate to you what each planet signifies when it is ruler of time and when it has divided between itself and the other planets the whole ten years and eleven months which it controls. In the book of principles we have shown how to discover the ruler of time whom the Greeks call *Chronocrator*. Search out this matter diligently so that you may be able to find the kind and outcome of dangers.

2. If Saturn is the ruler of time, of all time, as we said in the book of principles, he allots to himself 30 months. Notice, therefore, how he is located in the chart, whether it is a nocturnal or a diurnal chart, whether Saturn holds the angles of the chart, and what he indicates from the nature of the signs or the power of the house. When you have collected all this information you will discover what Saturn signifies when he is ruler of time.

3. If dangers had been indicated by him, whatever he had indicated before will be more severe. If he had indicated orphanhood in the chart, then with cruel power he persecutes the wretched offspring. If he had decreed widowhood, then he breaks off marriage by death or dissension. If he had indicated accusations, then he stirs up riots of enemies. If he had indicated illnesses, then he inflicts calamitous afflictions. If he had decreed losses, then he endangers the entire income. But if he is well located and predicts anything prosperous in the chart, then, following the power of his condition, he bestows whatever he promised before, especially if he as ruler of time is well located in a diurnal chart.

4. From Saturn's own time he allots twelve months to Jupiter. If Saturn was badly located in the chart and through him danger, illness, loss, or other misfortune was decreed, then all threats are lessened by the powers of the helpful god. But if Saturn is well located in the chart and allots time to Jupiter, the greatest good fortune is indicated, especially if it is a diurnal chart and Saturn is in good signs or good degrees and is in trine aspect to Jupiter.

5. When Saturn is ruler of time he allots 15 months to Mars. When Mars receives this time all evil is put to sleep and he indicates a happy period. For contrary powers cancel each other.

6. Saturn allots 19 months to the Sun, and when the Sun receives them he stirs up law suits and quarrelsome confrontations. The law suits are largely over the ownership of houses and properties, especially in a nocturnal chart. The Sun also indicates danger to the father and loss of position for the native.

7. Saturn allots eight months of his time to Venus. When Venus

receives the eight months she will make a happy time, separated from all misfortune, so that she corrects the difficulties brought on by other planets. But if Saturn has indicated marriage, then the wife will have been a widow before.

8. When Saturn is ruler of time, from his ten years he allots to Mercury 20 months. When Mercury receives this time he stirs up old law suits and revives hidden quarrels.

9. When Saturn is ruler of time, he allots from his own ten years 25 months to the Moon. When the Moon receives these 25 months she will produce illness from vicious humors, inflict dangers from water, or stir up accusations and new litigations. In all her time she indicates various dangers and anxieties. But this happens when the Moon is full. If she is waning and in aspect to Saturn, she predicts even worse calamities.

## XXXIV
## [JUPITER AS RULER OF TIME]

1. When the rulership of time comes to Jupiter, ten years and eleven months are allotted to him. But he divides all this time in a similar way. Thus when he is ruler one must investigate how he is located in the chart, in what sign and what degrees, and whether on the first or second angles, in favorable or sluggish or dejected houses, and whether in a nocturnal or a diurnal chart.

2. From all these we find the efficacy of his decrees. What Jupiter in general indicates in a chart, this he brings about when he is ruler of time. But you must remember this also in the case of all the other planets. For whatever we have said of Saturn and Jupiter, this you must also observe in the cases of the other planets. Whatever all planets indicate, whether good or bad, will be carried out when they are rulers of time.

3. When ten years and eleven months are allotted to Jupiter, he himself takes twelve months. During these twelve months which he takes for himself he indicates good fortune, glory, and happiness in accordance with the nature of the chart, especially if he himself is the ruler of the chart. To whomever he had decreed marriage or children, he bestows them when he is the ruler of time if the age of the native permits. Also he brings glory, honors, and increase in income according to what the chart allows.

4. When Jupiter is ruler of time, he allots 30 months to Saturn. When Saturn receives them from Jupiter he will make the natives always torpid and hindered in activities so that they fail in all occupations from cold sluggishness. But this is the case only if it is a nocturnal chart and Saturn is not favorably located in the chart.

5. When Jupiter is ruler of time, from his own time he allots 15 months to Mars. When Mars receives these he changes the whole order of life and

occupations, and whatever was carried on before is transferred to another kind of life, so that the positions held before are lost; or Mars will be harmful with various kinds of crises.

6. Jupiter allots 19 months to the Sun. When the Sun receives these 19 months he makes public all the secrets of life, changes all activities in various ways, and leads the soul through many kinds of anxieties. For he scatters whatever was collected before, so that everything is disturbed and confused. But these misfortunes are less in a diurnal chart.

7. Jupiter from his own time allots to Venus eight months. When in a nocturnal chart Venus receives these, if she is ruler of the chart or if Jupiter is ruler, she makes marriages and indicates prosperous times and good fortune. But in a diurnal chart she predicts a mediocre fortune with continual illicit love affairs, especially if the nature of the sign or of the house affects Venus.

8. Jupiter from his own ten years allots 20 months to Mercury. When Mercury receives these he indicates occupations which will bring great profit, the protection of many important friendships, and promotions in all assigned duties, so that good fortune comes from all activities in every way.

9. Jupiter allots 25 months to the Moon. When the Moon receives these she indicates a period of serene tranquility and great increase in good fortune, according to the essence of the chart. Then the pains of preceding misfortune are soothed; then the exigencies of need are relaxed; then health cures the afflictions of illness; then fears of danger are overcome by favorable protection; then in all law suits decisions are handed down for the native; then grief is healed, anxiety is allayed, and a civilized time of good fortune approaches, wiping away the squalor of preceding bad luck, especially when Jupiter is in favorable aspect to the full Moon.

## XXXV

### [MARS AS RULER OF TIME]

1. When the rulership of time comes to Mars, that is, ten years and nine months, all this time is divided by him in the same way. But, as in the case of Saturn and Jupiter, you must carefully inspect the sign, the degree, the condition, the house, and the aspects, so that you may find out everything. Thus, when Mars is made ruler of time, he retains 15 months for himself. During these 15 months he indicates important occupations together with powerful disturbances, all in accordance with the essence of the chart. In the activities themselves, whatever they may be, dangers of various kinds arise, especially if Mars is ruler of the chart and it is a diurnal chart.

2. Mars allots 30 months of his time to Saturn. When Saturn receives these months he imposes a slow weight of sluggishness on all activities so

that all affairs are hindered; Saturn makes his time ineffectual, sordid, squalid, and inactive.

3. Mars allots twelve months to Jupiter. When Jupiter receives them he indicates all prosperity and makes all affairs turn out well. He bestows profit and high position, heals sickness, gives rest from suffering and security from anxiety, return for wanderers, an end of litigation, and abundance for those in need.

4. Mars allots 19 months to the Sun. The Sun indicates the greatest dangers and constant calamities; he disturbs the whole order of life with riots and revolutions; he also predicts pains in the eyes and continuing illness. Dangers will be inevitable unless resisted by favorable aspect of Jupiter.

5. Mars allots eight months to Venus. She makes a prosperous time freed from all danger. But hidden scandal is always brought to light in those months from promiscuous intercourse with many women. If Venus and Mars are in square aspect, she indicates adultery. This crime is concealed if Jupiter is in aspect, but the influence of Mercury and the Sun make it public with dangerous results.

6. Mars allots 20 months to Mercury. When Mercury accepts these months he rouses certain dangers from things written, or he inflicts loss from forgeries. But often he will have enemies destroyed in various ways. If Mercury and Venus are in conjunction, in square aspect, or in opposition, they indicate the crimes of forgery and counterfeiting, especially if Mercury is found in the house or terms of Saturn.

7. Mars allots 25 months to the Moon. When she receives them she produces the greatest dangers, especially if she is full. A dangerous period of time is indicated: exile, prison, fires, fevers, serious losses, and grave illnesses. But if Mars and the Moon are in opposition or square aspect without influence of Jupiter, then, without doubt, they produce cruel, fevered, or sudden death.

8. But if Saturn is found with the Moon, when the Moon has received time from Mars, then, with the preceding evils, a bitter death is indicated. These dangers are determined by the variety of the signs.

## XXXVI

## [THE SUN AS RULER OF TIME]

1. If the Sun is the ruler of time, you must inspect all things in the same way as before, so that you may find the order of the forecast. The Sun divides his time just as the other planets. He keeps 19 months for himself. In these 19 months we must expect nothing prosperous from him but all manner of misfortunes. All these are less in a diurnal chart, and are also counteracted by influence of Jupiter. But they are aggravated by the aspect of Saturn and Mars, especially if these two are unfavorably located.

2. The Sun allots 30 months to Saturn. When Saturn receives these in a nocturnal chart, he threatens pestilence and death, but in a diurnal chart he indicates the greatest increases in prosperity, in accordance with the nature of the chart, especially if he is favorably located.

3. The Sun allots twelve months to Jupiter. When Jupiter receives these, he indicates peaceful good fortune together with the happiest kind of life so that all traces of evil are washed away. Losses are made good, health is restored, and the natives are freed from difficulties.

4. When the Sun is ruler of time, he allots 15 months to Mars. When Mars receives them, whether in a nocturnal or diurnal chart, he indicates loss of income and extreme poverty; stirs up frequent law suits and quarrels; and also brings about pains in the eyes and serious dangers.

5. The Sun allots eight months to Venus. She brings prosperity in all affairs; but she excites the character of wives with a certain malevolent dissension, so that a concealing mind in the wife both betrays and then covers itself. Because of this lawsuits are stirred up, and small riots.

6. The Sun allots 20 months to Mercury, and when he receives them he indicates frequent business activities and continual profit, but the profit comes only after labor and danger.

7. The Sun allots 25 months to the Moon. At this time the whole life of the native is disturbed in a variety of ways; whatever he has collected up to that time he loses again; his life will be changeable so that he will be relieved of poverty by sudden riches, but will lose them again and poverty will follow.

## XXXVII

## [VENUS AS RULER OF TIME]

1. Venus also is allotted ten years and nine months. When Venus becomes ruler of time, you must investigate everything in the same way we showed in the case of the other planets. From this time she keeps eight months to herself. During these months she grants the greatest affect to the marriage couch, together with personal grace and charm. She brings happiness with great security, especially if she is ruler of the chart.

2. Thirty months of Venus are allotted to Saturn. When he receives these he stirs up serious quarrels with women. The natives are separated from their wives by death or dissension.

3. Venus allots twelve months to Jupiter; and he indicates a favorable and happy time, but he will stir up certain scandals.

4. When Venus is ruler of time she allots 15 months to Mars; he brings evils and frequent griefs. For he agitates the mind with various illicit loves and imposes grief from the harsh torment of love, so that frequent lawsuits ensue. Riots and dangers are stirred up by the worst kind of wives, or on account of them; or adultery is instigated, or impure love affairs.

5. Venus allots 19 months to the Sun. He always makes wives flee and also indicates danger to life and loss of possessions. If Jupiter is in favorable aspect, the natives are separated from their wives by necessary journeys.

6. Twenty months are allotted by Venus to Mercury, and he makes all business affairs turn out prosperously; he indicates joy and happiness, confers great profit and suitable income.

7. When Venus is ruler of time she allots 25 months to the Moon, who brings to light the disturbance of hidden jealousy. If the Moon is full, she will be harmful in important matters and stir up all kinds of misfortune.

## XXXVIII

## [MERCURY AS RULER OF TIME]

1. Mercury is also allotted ten years and nine months. You must study all the details in this case as in the others. When Mercury is ruler of time he keeps 20 months for himself. During this time all good things and constant prosperity are indicated. He brings a fortunate outcome to all activities, especially if he is ruler of the chart and well located.

2. Mercury as ruler of time allots 30 months to Saturn. Saturn in this time indicates deaths in the family from constant calamities; parents, relatives, patrons—all those who are of use to the native.

3. From his time Mercury allots twelve months to Jupiter. Jupiter promises a quiet time, free from all disturbances, but in this tranquility there are always great rewards of praise and happiness. But this happens only to those who have no children, if the chart permits.

4. Mercury allots 15 months to Mars, who stirs up enemies, brings in accusations, or instigates litigation from new denunciations. All these may be mitigated by favorable influence of Jupiter.

5. Nineteen months are allotted by Mercury to the Sun, who indicates great loss of inheritance and serious anxieties of mind.

6. Mercury allots eight months to Venus. She brings good fortune from constant prosperity, security, tranquility, and profit, according to the nature of the chart.

7. Mercury allots 25 months to the Moon. With her come the most serious illnesses and great afflictions of weakness. In accordance with the nature of the house and the sign, to weakness of body she will add cold sluggishness of mind; but these Jupiter mitigates if in favorable aspect.

## XXXIX

## [THE MOON AS RULER OF TIME]

1. The Moon is also allotted ten years and nine months, of which she keeps 25 months for herself. In these 25 months, if she is so located that she is losing light and is carried toward Saturn, or is full and moving

toward Mars, she indicates death in every way. But if she is full and aspected by benefic planets, she predicts a moderate increase in possessions after a struggle. The times controlled by the Sun and Moon always have a bad prediction, especially if they are in aspect to malefic planets.

2. The Moon allots 30 months to Saturn. If the Moon is waning at this time, Saturn indicates miserable death from malignant humors, from water or shipwreck. If the Moon is full, she gives the opportunity of avoiding these evils.

3. The Moon when she is ruler of time allots twelve months to Jupiter. If the Moon is full, Jupiter brings joy and happiness; for then dangers, fears, and illnesses are put to sleep and increase of prosperity can be expected, according to the nature of the chart.

4. The Moon allots 15 months to Mars. If she is full at the time, Mars indicates great riots and revolutions; and if the Moon is in square aspect or opposition to Mars, this will bring bloody catastrophes.

5. When the Moon is ruler of time she allots 19 months to the Sun, who indicates fires and illnesses with fever. These may be mitigated by favorable aspect of Jupiter.

6. The Moon allots eight months to Venus. If it is a diurnal chart, this brings sterility. But if it is a nocturnal chart, the indication is for great increases in possessions, especially if the Moon is waning.

7. The Moon allots 20 months to Mercury, and he brings chills and illness with weakness of the body.

## XL
## [CONCLUSION]

1. In this manner, my dear Mavortius, the sum of time is divided. But I do not wish individual sentences from this work to be quoted out of context. For often if a benefic planet receives the allotted time but has a malefic planet with him, or in square aspect, or in opposition, the favorable quality of his indications is lessened by the power of the malefic planet.

2. You will discover the same to be true in the case of malefic planets. For if a malefic planet receives the allotted time and is so placed that benefic planets are in aspect, the whole bad prediction is mitigated by the protection of a helpful star.

3. Now the whole of the discipline has been explained to you and there is nothing more to be sought. We have narrated in easy language all the things which we have to learn with our untaught minds. Now, initiated into the first ceremonies, we approach the threshold of the secrets. We must hear the rest with intent mind; our ears must not be too fastidious in rejecting these words, for we may instead ingest the propositions of false writings.

4. And so the sixth book has been completed and our attention must be transferred to the secrets of the seventh.

# Liber Septimus

## I

### [THE ASTROLOGER'S OATH]

1. When Orpheus[78] initiated strangers into his mysteries, he required nothing of them but an oath—an oath backed by the fearful authority of religion—that the rites once learned would not be betrayed to profane ears.[79] It is generally agreed that Plato also was concerned that the cherished concepts of his secret discourses should not be revealed to the untaught. Pythagoras,[80] too, and our Porphyry[81] believed that their ideas should be enshrouded in religious silence.

2. Therefore, following the rule of these men, my dear Mavortius, I beg you to take an oath by God, the Creator of the Universe, who has made and regulated everything under the control of everlasting Necessity, who has shaped the Sun and Moon, who arranged the order and courses of all the stars, who collected the waves of the sea between boundaries of land, who forever kindles the encircling divinity of the heavens, who maintains the earth balanced evenly in the middle of the universe, who has created with his majestic divine skill all men, beasts, birds, and every manner of living thing, who moistens the earth with ever-flowing fountains, who makes constant and ever-changing the breath of the winds, who has created all things out of the four contrasting elements, who initiated the rising and setting of the stars and the movements of the earth, who set up the stars as stations for the ascent and descent of the souls . . .

3. We beg you to take an oath that these revered doctrines will not be revealed to profane ears but that the entire teaching of divinity will be made known only to those equipped with pure splendor of mind, whom an uncorrupted soul has led to the right path of life, whose loyalty is above reproach, whose hands are free of all crime. Receive, therefore, the detailed account which with the greatest trepidation of spirit we have promised you.

233

## II

## [CHARTS OF EXPOSED INFANTS]

1. Whenever benefic planets do not aspect the ascendant, but the Moon is on any angle and Mars and Saturn are in the seventh house, that is, on the descendant, the natives will be exposed by their mothers. This is also true if the ascendant is in signs which have a shorter span of time, Mars in the seventh house, and the waning Moon moving toward Saturn, or full toward Mars.

2. Also if the ruler of Fortune, that is, the ruler of that sign which contains the Part of Fortune and the ruler of the sign in which the ascendant is hidden by the Sun's rays or in the signs we mentioned before, but Saturn and Mars are on the descendant, the native will be exposed at birth. If the Moon is found on the ascendant or the descendant with Mars and Saturn in opposition to her, or if one malefic planet is found in the orb of the Sun, the native will be exposed

3. If the Sun and Moon are on angles and in square aspect or opposition to each other, and each is in conjunction with a malefic planet, the native will be suffocated in a difficult birth and die. If these malefic planets are also in unfavorable aspect to the Moon, the mother in that birth will be in danger of death.

4. If the Sun is on the ascendant and the full Moon in any sign is moving toward Mars, with Saturn on any angle, the native will be exposed and die. But if the Moon is found with Mars on any angle in opposition to the Sun and Saturn, and all influence of Jupiter is lacking, the native will either be exposed or will die immediately with his mother.

5. If the Moon is found on any angle in opposition to Mars on another angle or in conjunction with him, and Saturn is on another angle or its anafora, the native will be exposed. If Jupiter is on any angle and is aspected from above by Mars, the exposed infant will be found and returned, especially if Venus is in any aspect to Mars.

6. If the Sun is found with Saturn on the ascendant, the Moon on the MC, and Mars on the IMC in opposition to the Moon, the native will be exposed. Also if the Sun is on the ascendant, the Moon on the MC, Saturn on the descendant, and Mars on the IMC, the native will be exposed and immediately perish or will die together with his mother. But always (there is general agreement about this) if Mars and Saturn are in opposition to the Sun and Moon on any angles, or one is in square aspect and the other in opposition, the natives will be exposed, or will perish at birth, or will die miserably together with their mothers.

7. If Mars and Saturn are on any angle, or one is on an angle and the other on an anafora or epicatafora of the angle, and the Moon is either in conjunction with one of them or in square aspect or opposition to one, the native will be exposed. But with all these thus located, if a benefic planet comes into aspect to the Moon moving toward it, the exposed will be

picked up and raised in place of the children of the finder.

8. If the Moon is on the ascendant, Mars is in the twelfth house, and Saturn is on the anafora of the ascendant in any aspect to the Sun, the fetus will be dismembered in the uterus and cut out by physicians. If in this case Jupiter is not aspected to the angles, the mother will die in that birth. If the Moon is so located that she has a malefic planet in the sign before hers and another in the sign following, and the one following is in any aspect to the Sun, the native will either be exposed or die at birth.

9. If the ruler of the chart or the ruler of the sign or the Part of Fortune is in the second, sixth, eighth, or twelfth house, and no benefic planet is in favorable aspect, nor the ruler of the chart in his own terms, the native will be exposed immediately at birth. If any malefic planet is in aspect to the Moon or the ascendant and there is no favorable influence of benefic planets, the exposed infants will be devoured by dogs.

10. If the ruler of the chart is in tropic signs in sluggish or dejected houses, in opposition to the Moon, and malefic planets are either in square aspect or opposition to the Moon in equal degrees with her, the natives will be thrown into a river or the sea and will perish immediately. But if benefic planets are in aspect to the Moon or in the ascendant, they will be nourished for a few days before being thrown into the water.

11. When the Sun and Moon hold the 30th degree of a sign, the native will have no time of life. If malefic planets are in square aspect to or in opposition to the Sun and Moon in the 30th degree, the native will be torn by dogs and perish. Also if the Sun and Moon are in the twelfth house with no benefic planets in aspect to them or to the ascendant, the native will be exposed. If malefic planets are in aspect, he will be devoured by dogs. If all are located as we said and in tropical signs, without aspect of favorable planets, the native will perish in water at birth.

12. The native will also be exposed if no benefic planets aspect the Sun, the Moon, the ascendant, or the Part of Fortune. If malefic planets are in aspect, the exposed infant will be devoured by dogs. The native will be exposed also if no benefic planet is with the Sun or Moon, nor on the ascendant nor the MC, nor in the third, fourth, fifth, seventh, ninth, or eleventh houses, but malefic planets are alone in these places.

13. If the benefic planets are hidden by this Sun's rays and the malefic are in morning rising, the native will be exposed. The same is true also if the Moon is synodic and loses all light and no benefic planet is in aspect. If a malefic planet aspects the Moon in this position, the native will either be born dead or be torn by dogs.

14. If all the planets with the Sun and Moon are in the sixth or twelfth house, the native will be exposed. But if a benefic planet is with them in these houses on any angle, the exposed infant will be picked up by a stranger. But this benefic planet indicates for him only a short space of life.

15. If the Moon is in conjunction with Mars in the same degree or in

opposition in equal degrees, and if Saturn aspects the Moon thus placed with Mars, with no benefic planet in aspect, the mothers will die together with the natives at birth. But if a benefic planet is in aspect to the Moon thus located with Mars, the infant will be dismembered and cut out and the mother freed from danger of death.

16. If the Moon is on the descendant and Mars is with her in the same degree or on the ascendant in a diurnal chart, the native will be exposed. But if Jupiter or Venus aspects them from another angle, protection will come to the exposed from a stranger who will pick him up and nourish him. But if the Moon is on the anafora of the ascendant with Saturn in aspect to her from the eighth house, and Mars is in square aspect to the Moon or the ascendant with no aspect of benefic planets, the native will be exposed and immediately die.

17. If the Moon is found in the same sign with Mars and Saturn in such a way that she is exactly between the two and no benefic planet is in aspect, the native will be exposed. But if both malefic planets are so located that they are close to the sides of the Moon, and no benefic planet is in aspect, the native will perish together with his mother at birth.

18. If the Sun is on the MC, the Moon on the descendant, and Saturn and Mars are so placed that one is close to the Sun and the other to the Moon, the native will be exposed. But if benefic planets are in aspect, the exposed will be picked up and nurtured. If Jupiter is on the anafora of the ascendant and himself aspects the Moon which is in square to Mars, the exposed will be nurtured but raised in slavery. But if the Sun is on the descendant and Saturn is with him or on the ascendant, Mars on the anafora or epicatafora of the ascendant, and if there is no benefic planet on any angle, the native will be exposed.

19. If the ruler of the sign containing the ascendant is in the anafora of the ascendant, and the ruler of the anafora is in the twelfth house, in a diurnal chart with the Sun, or in a nocturnal with the Moon, the native will be exposed. If all are placed as we have just described, but the Sun and Moon are in no aspect to each other, the exposed infant will perish immediately.

20. If the Moon is found in the third house, the Sun in the sixth or eleventh, and the ruler of the signs in which the Sun and Moon are found is in the eleventh, the native will be exposed. If the Sun and Moon are on the descendant, Mars and Saturn in the eighth, but the rulers of both their signs in the sixth house, the native will be exposed and torn by dogs. The same is true if the ruler of the sign containing the ascendant is on the MC and the ascendant is in conjunction with a malefic planet, not in aspect by any benefic planets.

21. If the sign of the Giver of Life is on the anafora of the ascendant or in the sixth house, and the Giver of Life himself is in conjuction with a malefic planet on the MC or the IMC, the native will be devoured by dogs. But if the Giver of Life is the ruler of the sign in which the anafora of the

ascendant is found, and the Giver of Life himself is in the sixth house, the native will not be nurtured. If the Giver of Life is found on the IMC and the ruler of the sign on the anafora of the ascendant or in the sixth house, and no benefic planet is on any angle, the native will not be nurtured.

22. If the Sun and Moon are so located that they are not in aspect to each other or to the ascendant, the native will not be nurtured. In general, one must note that natives who have all the planets either on the anafora of the ascendant or in the sixth house, or in the eighth or twelfth, will either be exposed or not nurtured.

23. If any planet, but especially the Sun by day or the Moon by night, is either on an angle or in the fifth house with the others, located as we have described above, the native will be nurtured but will be short-lived and unfortunate. But also if Mars and Saturn are in conjunction on the anafora of the ascendant and have in their own houses neither the Sun nor the Moon, the native will be exposed.

24. If the ruler of the sign in which the Part of Fortune is located is either on the anafora of the ascendant or in the sixth house, and the Part of Fortune is on the MC with no benefic planet on any angle, the native will not be nurtured. But if the Part of Fortune is found on the IMC and malefic planets are in aspect to this place, and the ruler of the sign itself is on the anafora of the ascendant or hidden by the Sun's rays, the native will not be nurtured.

25. If the Part of Fortune is found in the seventh house and the ruler of that sign is either in the sign itself or on the MC, hidden by the Sun's rays, the native will not be nurtured.

26. If the Part of Fortune is found in any sign, but the ruler of that sign is on the anafora of the ascendant or in the sixth house, not in aspect to the Part of Fortune, the native will not be nurtured. But if the Part of Fortune is found on the anafora of the ascendant and the ruler of that sign is on the MC, hidden by the Sun's rays, the native will not be nurtured.

## III
## [CHARTS OF TWINS]

1. If Jupiter and Mercury are in conjunction on the ascendant but the ascendant itself is in a double sign, with the Moon on any angle, and the Sun in a sign in which it has another planet with it, either the chart is that of twins or the native will have twin children.

2. It should be noted that no malefic planet from above should be in aspect to the planets mentioned. For if it is in aspect to one of them, whichever of the twins is conceived first will either die at birth or be premature. But also if the Moon is not found on any angle or in a double sign, but Jupiter and Mercury are in conjunction in double signs on the ascendant, and the Moon or the Sun in conjunction with another planet, twins will be born.

3. If the Moon is found either with Mercury or with Jupiter, and if the Sun is in aspect to any other planet while both are in double signs, and also if the ascendant is found in a double sign and has any planet in conjunction with it, twins will be born.

4. But if the Moon is found in the signs of Jupiter or Mercury, but Jupiter and Mercury are located on the ascendant or on the descendant, twins will be born. If the Moon is found in a double sign and the Sun on an angle in the second house from the Moon, or if the Moon is in a double sign with Mercury or with Jupiter, twins will be born or the native will have twins.

5. Whether the twins will be male or female we learn in this way: if the Sun and Moon are located on the ascendant and are in masculine signs and aspected to masculine signs, that is, to Jupiter, Saturn, or Mars, the twins will be male. But if Venus alone does the same, located in a feminine sign, the twins will be female. And if the Sun, Moon, and ascendant are in feminine signs, as we said, and are in aspect to each other in any way, the twins will be of different sexes.

6. If Mars and Saturn in their own houses aspect the Sun, Moon, and ascendant with no influence of benefic planets, the twins will either be premature or will perish at birth. But if, with all located as we said, there is no aspect of planets, benefic or malefic, the first born of twins will die.

7. If the Moon is found on any angle in a fertile sign and a benefic planet is with her, and the ascendant is in a double or a fertile sign, or with Jupiter or Mercury, either three or five will be born. If the ruler of the sign in which the house of children is found is in a double sign, and the fifth house is also in a double sign or in conjunction with her, twins will be born.

# IV

## [CHARTS OF SLAVES]

1. If Mars and Saturn are in opposition to the Moon, or one is in opposition and the other in square aspect a slave will be born, especially if the Moon is found either on the IMC or on the descendant. But if Jupiter is in favorable aspect, the slave will be freed.

2. If the Sun and Mercury are in conjunction on the MC and a malefic planet is in opposition to the Moon, located on the *Cacodaemon,* the native will be given to a slave woman. But if Jupiter is in favorable aspect, he will be given to a free woman. If the Part of Fortune is found in the sign of a malefic planet and Mars is found in this sign, it is the chart of a slave.

3. But if Mars in a morning rising is found in the sign of a malefic planet together with Saturn, the slave who is born will be unfortunate. Also if the Part of Fortune is in Leo, Libra, Sagittarius, Aquarius, or Gemini, and Mars is in the same sign, this will make slaves.

4. But if the ruler of the sign is found in the same sign with Mars, or

any benefic planet is so found, those born slaves will be freed.

5. If the Sun and Moon are found on the angles, and Mars and Saturn are either with them on the angles or in aspect from other angles, and no benefic planet is on any angle, a slave will be born. But if the Moon is found on the IMC or the descendant, with Saturn in square aspect to her, or Mars in aspect to both, either in square aspect or opposition, this will make slaves.

6. If Saturn is in aspect to the Moon in conjunction with Saturn and the Moon on an angle, this will produce slaves; if no benefic planet is in aspect to that conjunction, the result will be wretched and hard-working slaves.

7. If Mars and Saturn are in opposition to the Moon with no benefic planet in aspect to her, and the Moon is not in the same sign with a good planet, this will make slaves who are separated from their parents. If the Moon is on the IMC and Mars in any aspect to the Moon, slaves are born.

8. If the Sun and Moon are found in the twelfth house or in the sixth, and Saturn is in any aspect to them, and no benefic planets are in aspect to the Sun and Moon, this will make slaves. But if the Moon is found on the IMC and Saturn with her, but Mars in opposition or square aspect to them, this will make slaves.

9. But if the Sun is in the twelfth house and the Moon is on the anafora of the ascendant with no benefic planet on the angles, slaves are born. If the Sun is in the twelfth house and the Moon is in the eighth with no good planet in aspect, this will also produce slaves.

10. If the Moon in a nocturnal chart is on the MC, the Sun in the sixth house, and the rulers of both houses in the eighth house, this will make slaves.

11. But if the rulers of the houses in which the Sun and Moon are found are either on the ascendant or on the MC, with the other planets located as we said, a slave will be born but in early age will be freed. But if the rulers are located on the ascendant, the MC, IMC, or on the descendant, or in the fifth or eleventh house, the slave will be freed later in life.

12. If the Sun is on the IMC, the Moon in the sixth house, Jupiter on the MC, and Venus in unfavorable aspect to Mars or Saturn, or if they are located in dejected houses, the natives born in slavery will be freed. If the Sun and Moon are in the sixth house and other planets on the MC, the natives will be transferred from slavery to freedom.

13. If the Moon is in the sixth house and Mars in a higher degree in the sky in square aspect to the Moon; and the rulers of the signs in which the Sun and Moon are located are in the third house; but Saturn is located exactly on the ascendant, this will make slaves who will remain so to the last day of life.

14. If the Moon is found on the IMC, the Sun with Mars on the descendant, Saturn and Jupiter in the sixth or eighth house, this will produce unfortunate, hard-working slaves always oppressed by the

burden of slavery. If Jupiter is with the Sun in the sixth house, the Moon with Mars on the descendant, Venus on the IMC, and Saturn in the third house, slaves will be born.

15. If Saturn is in the twelfth house, Mars on the anafora of the ascendant, the Moon on the ascendant, Jupiter in the eighth house, and the Sun in the third, slaves will be born. If Mars is in his debility and the waning Moon is moving toward him, Saturn is in the third house, and the Sun on the IMC, but benefic planets are in the sixth house, the slaves who are born will be unfortunate.

16. If the waning Moon is in her debility in the seventh house with Saturn, Mars in the sixth house, and the Sun in the third, slaves will be born. But if a malefic planet is found with the Sun or on the IMC, the benefic planets are in their debility, and also the waning Moon, this will make slaves who are sickly.

17. If all these are located as we said but the Moon is with Mars in the twelfth house and Saturn on the IMC, the slaves will be born mad. But if the Sun is found with Mars or Saturn on the anafora of the ascendant, the Moon in the twelfth house, Saturn on the IMC, and benefic planets in the third house, the natives will be unfortunate slaves. But if all these are located as we have described and Jupiter is on the MC, after many years of slavery they will be freed.

18. If all the benefic planets are found in the sixth house, but the malefic are in the eighth or ninth, and the Moon in the third, slaves will be born who are wretched, retarded, and short-lived.

# V

## [NUMBER OF MASTERS]

1. If the Moon is found in the second, fifth, eighth, or eleventh house in a masculine sign, but the ruler of the sign in which the Moon is found is either in his debility or in dejected houses, and the Moon from above aspects Mars in square because Mars is in the fourth sign from the Moon, the native will serve four masters. But if another planet is found in the middle between the Moon and Mars, add another to the preceding number of masters.

2. However many signs the Sun is away from Mars in a diurnal chart, if dejected in sign or house, that will give the number of masters. In a nocturnal chart the number is the same as the number of signs the dejected Moon is away from Mars or Saturn. Count double signs for two masters.

3. If the Sun and Moon are dejected in the chart of a slave, but the rulers of the signs in which the Sun and Moon are found are on the angles, or in unaspected signs, or in their debility, the natives will be slaves of powerful masters. But if Jupiter favorably aspects those who we said are

located on the angles, the slaves will attain freedom and the greatest glory. If the Sun and Moon are either on the anafora of the ascendant or in the sixth house, or in eighth or twelfth, either together or separately, and are in their debility; and have malefic planets in the same sign, before them in degrees, they will make the slaves weak and blind and force them to maintain their lives by begging in public places.

# VI

## [PARENTS AS SLAVES]

1. When Jupiter and Saturn are on conjunction on the IMC; the Sun in the sixth house, say that the father has been a slave. If Venus is found on the IMC, and the Sun with Mars in the third house, this also shows that the father has been a slave. But if the Sun is found in the house of Saturn, and Saturn in the Sixth house, this also shows the father a slave.

2. If the Moon is in conjunction with Mars in alien houses on the ascendant, this shows the mother a slave. If the ruler of the sign in which the Moon is found is either in his debility or in alien houses, the mother is a slave. The same is true if the waning Moon is found with Mars on the ascendant and Saturn on the anafora of the ascendant.

3. Also if the waning Moon is found on the IMC in the same sign with a malefic planet, this will make the mother a slave; also if the Moon is on the IMC and the ruler of the house is found in the sixth house.

4. If you see the Sun and Jupiter in dejected houses, either together or separately, so that one is in the twelfth house and the other in the sixth, say that the father has been a slave. But if you see the Moon in a similar way with Venus in the dejected houses, either together or separately, or one in the sixth house and the other in the twelfth, say that the mother has been a slave.

5. If the Moon and Venus are found on the descendant in a tropical sign, and one malefic planet is in the sixth house and the other in the eighth; if Jupiter is not on the first angles or in trine aspect to the first angles, this shows that the mothers are slaves assigned to guarding doors.

6. If the Sun and Moon are in the sixth house and the ruler of that sign is together with them, the native's parents are oppressed by slavery and misfortune. But if benefic planets are on the angles, afterwards the parents obtain some good fortune.

7. If the Sun and Moon are in dejected houses and Saturn is in opposition or square aspect to Venus, on any angle or together with her, this produces slaves. Mars with Venus has the same effect.

8. If both the Sun and Moon are in dejected houses and malefic planets are in the same sign, or in the sign of the Part of Fortune, or on the ascendant, or on other angles, or on the anafora of angles, this makes slaves in a similar way. But if Saturn is in the eighth house or on the

anafora of the ascendant, the Moon is either on the anafora or the epicatafora, and Venus is hidden by the rays of the Sun or in the twelfth house, the natives will be captured and be made slaves.

9. If the Sun and Moon are in dejected houses with one of the malefic planets on an angle but the other on the anafora or epicatafora, this indicates slaves. But if all these are located as we said and benefic planets are in aspect to the waxing Moon, or on one of the angles, or the epicataforas of angles, the natives will be born slaves but be freed, or will be reared in place of sons by the master.

10. If the Sun and Moon are not in dejected houses but Mars or Saturn are on any angle, or one is on an angle and the other on the anaforas or the epicataforas of angles, and Saturn and Mars are both in any aspect to the Sun and Moon, the natives will be captives.

11. If with the preceding combination a benefic planet is on the angles or on the anafora of one of the angles in favorable aspect, the native will be freed from captivity by favorable protection. But if many benefic planets from above are in aspect to the waxing Moon, with all the others located as we said, the natives will be almost made captive but will escape.

## VII

## [CHARTS OF ANIMALS]

1. If the Moon is found in curved or bestial signs, that is, in Taurus, Cancer, Scorpio, Capricorn, or Pisces, and the ruler of that sign is in aspect to the Moon, and one of the malefic planets is in square aspect or opposition to the Moon or together with her, and the second malefic planet is on the anafora of the ascendant in aspect to the ruler of Fortune, quadrupeds will be born from quadrupeds, especially if the ruler of the ascendant and the ruler of Fortune are in the signs we listed.

2. But if the ruler of Fortune or the ruler of the ascendant are found in human signs in the sixth house with the others located as we said, a monster will be born from a human being. If malefic planets are located on the angles, together or on anaforas of the angles, but the Sun and Moon in opposition to them are also on the angles, and no benefic planets are on the angles or anaforas of the angles or hidden by the Sun's rays, either a quadruped or a monster will be born.

3. If Mars is in opposition or square aspect to the Sun or Moon on the ascendant, the quadruped which was born will be destined for public sacrifice. But if, with all as we described, Jupiter and Venus are located outside the angles in aspect to the Sun, Moon, or ascendant, what is born will either be reared by men or be consecrated in temples or shrines.

4. All these things are from our book which was written for you about the end of life and will be more clearly shown to you from triangles and right angles. In that work the system of triangles and right angles, which

seemed involved in obscurity to some Greeks, was explained in a clear and short argument.

## VIII

## [PHYSICAL INFIRMITIES]

1. If the Sun is found on the ascendant, the Moon on the MC, and the malefic planets divided so that one is on the anafora of the sun and the other on that of the Moon, and the benefic planets are alien to them, this will make the natives blind or with bad eyesight. But if the Moon is synodic to the Sun, and they are on the anafora or the epicatafora of the angles with Mars and Saturn on the angles, this indicates blindness.

2. In general, if the Sun and Moon are on the anaforas of malefic planets, afflictions of the eyes are indicated. If the Sun and Moon are synodic, located on one angle, and Mars in that same house, this indicates blindness.

3. But if the Sun and Moon are found on the ascendant, Mars in the fifth house, and no benefic planets are in aspect to the Sun or Moon, eyesight is afflicted. But if the Sun is on the ascendant in conjunction with Saturn, Mars in square aspect or opposition, eyesight similarly is affected.

4. But, with all these located in this way, if benefic planets are in favorable aspect from above, the blindness is cured either by protection of some divinity or by a physician. If Saturn is on the ascendant and the Moon in the eighth house, or if the Moon is on the ascendant and Saturn in the eighth house, the eyes will be running with a vicious infection.

5. If the Sun is with Mars or Mercury in the seventh house, this will make the natives one-eyed and in some way guilty of the crime of homicide. If the Sun is found exactly on any angle and either Saturn or Mars is on its anafora, the right eye will be afflicted. If the Moon is found on any angle and the Sun and Mars are on its anafora, the left eye is afflicted.

6. But if the Sun and Moon are both located on one angle, or on different angles, and are in opposition or square aspect, if malefic planets hold both anaforas, that is, of the Sun and Moon, this indicates blindness of both eyes.

7. If all are located as we have described, and Mercury is either on one of the angles or on the anafora or epicatafora of an angle, he makes the natives sickly and captives who will suffer a violent death. If, with all located as we said, Saturn or Mars are in aspect to Jupiter from above, the natives will be gladiators who come to this occupation as condemned men.

8. If Mars is found exactly on any angle and Saturn on its anafora or on another angle, and both are in opposition or square aspect to the Moon, or in conjunction with her, the natives will be lame or paralytic. If Saturn is on any angle and Mars on its anafora, but Mars or Saturn is in aspect to the Moon, the results are the same. The natives will be thrown

from a height, or fall from horses, or be involved in similar accidents and lose a part of the body.

## IX

## [DEATH OF PARENTS]

1. If anyone has the Sun badly located in his chart, or if the Sun is ruler of his chart, his father will die before his mother. If the Moon is in this condition, the mother will die first. We will explain how this comes about. If the ascendant is in Aries, the Sun in Aquarius, and if Saturn is in Pisces, and is also the ruler of the sign the Sun is in, the native's father will die first because the Sun has fallen into the sign of a malevolent killer. If this happens to the Moon the mother will die first.

2. If, with all located as we said, Mars is in square aspect to Saturn, the father will die a violent death by the order or anger of a prince. But with all located as we said, if Jupiter is on one of the angles, the misfortunes of the father are mitigated if, in a diurnal chart, Jupiter is in aspect to the Sun, or in a nocturnal chart, to the Moon. If what we have described happens to the Moon in a nocturnal chart, the mother will die first. Also the evils are stronger if, with all located as we said, the benefic planets are in dejected houses or hidden by the Sun's rays.

3. If Mars is in square aspect or opposition to the Sun on any angle, or in conjunction with him, the father will die a violent death by order of the prince. But if Saturn is in aspect in the same way as Mars was to the Sun in this position, the father will die from water, or from bodily humors, or from poison. If the Sun is found on the anafora of the ascendant and Mars is in square aspect to him, the father will die vomiting up blood.

4. But if the Sun is found in the sixth, third, or twelfth house, and malefic planets are in square aspect or conjunction with him, an evil death is indicated for the father. But if Saturn is in square aspect to the Sun thus located, or together with him, the father will die of a hidden or secret illness, that is, dysentery, consumption, or something of this kind.

5. But if the Sun is on the descendant and Mars and Saturn are on the IMC, they affect the father in the same way. But if the Moon is in the condition we described for the Sun and attacked by malefic planets, the mother will have a similar death. In all these combinations we must carefully observe the influence of the benefic planets.

6. For if Jupiter and Venus are on the angles or in favorable houses and in aspect to the Sun (with all else as we described), the misfortunes of the father are alleviated; if they aspect the Moon, of the mother. But if, with a helpful benefic planet located as we said, the ruler of the sign in which the benefic planet is found is with malefic planets or with the Sun, the aforesaid misfortune of the father and mother will be worse.

7. Often when Jupiter approaches Mars or is in square aspect to him, death comes to the father. The same is true if Saturn is ruler of time and

aspects the Sun in square or opposition. If Saturn is in this situation with the Moon, the mother will die. This is not always the case but only when the arrangement of time has demanded it, according to the rulership of the planets which we treated before.

8. If you wish to learn more about this matter in detail you must turn to my *Myriogenesis,* where many obscure things are discussed. If the chart is diurnal, count the number of signs from the Sun to the Moon, then begin again from the ascendant, and if the last sign is masculine the father will die first, if feminine, the mother.

9. In a nocturnal chart this same thing is done in reverse. That is, count the signs from the Moon to the Sun and proceed as before.

10. But if both the Sun and Moon are found in masculine signs and the ascendant is in a masculine sign, and Mars or Saturn on the MC, the father will die first. If the Sun, Moon, and ascendant are in feminine signs with Mars and Saturn on the MC, the mother will die first. This has been proved by us and many others; the computation we have outlined definitely predicts the death of parents.

# X
## [HOSTILITY TO PARENTS]

1. If Mars or Saturn is found in the seventh house and the Sun in the eighth, the native will either be estranged from his father or will have serious quarrels with him. The same is true if Mars is on the anafora of the ascendant or on the anafora of the MC, also if Mars is found exactly on the ascendant or the MC, with the Sun on the descendant or the IMC.

2. If this combination of malefic planets occurs with the Moon instead of the Sun, the quarrels are stirred up with the mother, especially if Saturn is in aspect to the Moon. If the Sun is in the terms of Mars in a diurnal chart, of Saturn in a nocturnal, and Mars by day is in opposition or square aspect to the Sun, or Saturn the same by night, with no benefic planet in favorable aspect, the sons will kill their own father; if the Moon is found in this situation instead of the Sun, they will kill the mother.

3. If the Sun is in the terms or houses of malefic planets in the sixth or twelfth house, and a malefic planet is in square aspect or opposition to the Sun, the children will be disinherited by their father. But if a benefic planet is in aspect to the Sun in any way, the severity of the father's punishment is lessened. But if the Sun is found on the anafora of the ascendant or in the eighth house, not only is the native disinherited by his father, but he will in some way waste his father's possessions.

4. If the Sun is located as we said and benefic planets are in aspect to him, only a few of the father's resources will be destroyed. The Moon has the same effect in regard to the mother and the maternal inheritance. The maternal inheritance is more definitely wasted if the Moon is in the 15th

or 17th degree of a tropical sign, and a malefic planet is in square aspect or opposition to her.

5. But if a benefic planet is in aspect to her something is saved. If the Sun and Mars are together on any angle in a tropical sign, they indicate dissipation of the father's possessions. If a benefic planet is in aspect to them, something is preserved. The Moon accomplishes the same thing for the maternal estate.

## XI
## [ORPHANS]

1. When the seventh house is in a double sign (the double signs include Libra) and Venus is on any angle, the parents will be removed by death and the children left alone. But if a double sign is found on the descendant, the ascendant also in a double sign, Saturn on one of the angles, the Sun and Moon in the houses of malefic planets and in dejected houses, both parents will die an early death.

2. But if the Sun is located as we said, only the father will die; if the Moon, the mother. But these events are found only up to the 15th or 16th year of the native's life. The planets announce the death of parents within that time. You will find the time of the deaths when Saturn as ruler of time has arrived at the houses we mentioned above.

3. If the angles are in double signs; the Sun and Moon on the descendant or the MC; the ruler of the chart either on the descendant or on the IMC, the parents will die in the children's early years. If the MC is in a masculine sign the mother is allotted two husbands; and the native is born from the second. If the MC is in a feminine sign, he will be born from the second wife of the father, especially if the MC is in double or tropical signs.

4. If Venus is in Gemini, in signs in trine to Gemini, or in Pisces or Taurus, the native will be adopted. The same is true when she is on the angles, even if not in Pisces or Taurus.

5. To find the number of brothers and sisters, count the signs from Saturn to Jupiter. This shows the number of brothers and sisters. If malefic planets are in aspect to this house, the brothers will die, or be enemies, or suffer for a capital crime. If benefic planets are in aspect, they will prosper.

6. If Saturn is found exactly on the ascendant in his own terms, all the brothers will die in their early years. Some astrologers count the number from Mercury to the Sun and again from the ascendant, and thus define the house of brothers, making the same prediction from this house. This method also has great success in forecasts.

## XII

## [NUMBER OF MARRIAGES]

1. In all charts, if Saturn is found with Venus in the same sign and if Saturn has more degrees, this means one wife; if Venus has more degrees, many wives. You will find this true also in the charts of women. Venus located on the descendant indicates a wife seduced by others; or they will live together without marriage tablets. If Mars is in aspect, the natives will take wives known for adultery. But if Venus is in Taurus or Libra she will provide well-born wives; in other signs, low-class.

2. To find the house of the wife in a man's chart, count from Saturn to Venus if it is a diurnal chart; in a nocturnal chart, the reverse. You compute the house of brothers from Saturn to Jupiter and again from the ascendant. If the house of the wife falls together with that of brothers, computed as we said, sisters or relatives are allotted as wives. You will find a similar effect in a woman's chart.

3. Also Venus in conjunction with the ruler of the chart gives sisters or relatives as wives. But if the house of the wife, computed exactly, is found in maternal or paternal signs, observed exactly, the natives will take mothers, stepmothers, or nurses as wives. You will find a similar effect in the charts of women, especially if Mars, Venus, and Mercury are in aspect to these same houses.

## XIII

## [INCEST]

1. We must now pass over other things and repeat what we have begun about incestuous marriage. If Saturn is found in the sign or terms of Jupiter, and Venus is in the house or terms of Saturn; Mars and the Moon are in square aspect to Jupiter, Venus, or Saturn, the natives sleep with their mothers or stepmothers. If Mercury is also in aspect, they sleep with sons, daughters, or sons-in-law.

2. If the Moon is found with Jupiter, Saturn, or Mars in the house of Saturn, the natives will cohabit secretly either with the mother, stepmother, or the father. But if all these planets are found in the sixth house, after the father's death the native will be given the mother as wife, or after the mother's death the daughter will marry the father. If Mercury is found with the other planets, women will marry their own sons, fathers their own daughters.

3. If the Moon is located in the first degree of Cancer and is moving toward Jupiter, Venus is in the first degree of Saturn, and Saturn is in the house of Venus, the indication is the same.

4. In all charts, if Venus is found in double or tropical signs and the rulers of the sign in which Venus is found is also in a double or tropical sign, men will have many wives, women will have many husbands. But if Venus is located neither in double nor tropical signs, and the Moon is in aspect to her, a man will have one wife, a woman one husband. But if the Moon is in aspect to Venus in double or tropical signs, men will have many wives, women many husbands.

## XIV

## [KINDS OF MARRIAGES]

1. If Venus is in the house or terms of Mars, and Mars is in the house or terms of Venus, aspected in opposition to the full Moon in her own house or terms, husbands kill their wives with their own hands. If Mars is on one of the angles, they kill them with a sword. But if in a woman's chart Mars is in his own house or his terms, on the MC and in opposition to Venus, husbands are killed by their wives. This only happens if there is no influence of Jupiter.

2. If the house of the wife, found as we showed in the last book, is in the house of Jupiter, the husband will be separated from all illicit desires. If Jupiter is in aspect to this house (his own), or if he is found in this house, the husband's chastity is even stronger. But if the house of the wife is in the house of Saturn, this will make the native lustful. If Saturn is in aspect to this house, this makes men austere toward their women.

3. If the house of the wife is found in the sign of Mars, and Mars or Jupiter is in aspect to this house, or one of them is in the house itself and another is in aspect to it, this will make husbands cherish their wives forever with true affection. But if the house of the wife is found in the house of Mercury, and Mercury is in it, or in aspect to it, this will make passive lovers. The Sun will make them royal, the Moon pleasing and lovable.

4. If the Moon is with Mars in the house of Mars, and Saturn is in opposition or square aspect to them, the natives will be impotent and consumptive, without wives or children. If Jupiter is found with Venus on the descendant, men freely cohabit with older women and women with old men. But if Jupiter is found with Venus on the ascendant, men sleep with younger women and women with youths.

## XV

## [LOVERS OF BOYS]

1. Mercury and Mars in conjunction on the ascendant make lovers of boys. If the two are in an alien house the indication will be stronger. Also if

Venus is in the house of Mercury, and Mercury is badly located, the natives are driven with monstrous desire to the bed of boys. To be exact: this occurs when Venus is in the house of Mercury and Mercury is on the IMC or the descendant, or in the sixth, eighth, ninth, or twelfth house, or on the anafora of the ascendant, or in his debility.

2. If the house of marriage, exactly computed, falls in the house of Mercury, and Mercury is on an angle in a masculine sign, this will make lovers of boys who never wish for intercourse with women. And if Mars and Mercury change houses so that Mars is in the house of Mercury and vice versa, this will still make lovers of boys, especially if the two thus located are in the house of Mars.

3. If Mercury is in the house of Mars and Mars is in opposition or square aspect to him, this makes lovers of boys. Likewise, if Mars is in the house of Mercury and Mercury is in opposition or square aspect to him, this indicates the same lustful vices. If the Moon is in the house or terms of Mercury, and Mercury is in the house of the Moon, this will have the same effect.

## XVI

## [NUMBER OF WIVES]

1. One wife is indicated if Venus is on the MC in trine aspect to the Moon with favorable influence of other planets. But if she is in any other house, you will find the number of wives by counting the signs from Venus to the house of marriage. In women's charts you will find the number of husbands this way. Let others verify this method: it has not been proved by us.

2. Venus with Mars in the sixth house will make men and women adulterers. If they are in the house of Saturn and are in conjunction with Saturn himself in his house, in a woman's chart this makes public prostitutes; in a man's chart they either have prostitutes for wives or are joined in impure lust with homosexuals.

3. If you locate the house of marriage exactly, and the ruler of that sign is in the sign itself, marriage is indicated when the first years of that sign are completed. But if the ruler of that sign is so located that he is not in aspect in any way to the house of marriage, that is, to his own sign, and if another planet is located in that sign, marriage is indicated to take place when the first years are completed of the planet which is found in the house of marriage. If no planet is in that sign, marriage will occur after the anafora of that sign.

4. There is another more subtle way of discovering this: count the degrees of all the planets, add them all up and, beginning from the house of marriage, divide the number of degrees among the signs, allotting thirty degrees to each. In whatever sign the last number falls, the

marriage will occur when Jupiter reaches that sign.

5. If the native marries before this time the marriage will be dissolved, either by divorce, or death with no issue, or they quarrel in various ways.


## XVII

## [MURDER OF SPOUSES]

1. If Mars, Venus, and Jupiter are found on the descendant, and the ruler of the sign in which they are located is on the MC, the husband kills the wife. If Mars is found alone on the descendant and Venus on the MC, and the full Moon is on the ascendant or on the IMC, the wife will be killed by the husband's own hands.

2. In a man's chart, if Jupiter and Mars are in any house and the rulers of the houses in which they are located are placed, one on the descendant and one on the IMC, a similar death is indicated for the wife. The same is true if Venus is on the IMC and Jupiter on the descendant. It is also true if Venus is on the descendant, and the ruler of the sign in which Venus is found is on the IMC.

3. Death is indicated for the wife if Venus and Jupiter are in the seventh house, and the ruler of that sign is on the IMC or on the descendant with them. If, with these located in this way, the Sun, Saturn, and Mars are in either the sixth or eighth house, the wife will die by the husband's own hands.


## XVIII

## [KINDS OF MATES]

1. Men will marry old women or women old men if Saturn and Venus hold equal degrees but in different signs, or if they are in conjunction in the sign of the wife, or if Venus is in the terms of Saturn and vice versa, and if they are not in aspect to each other, though in each other's terms.

2. If Jupiter, Venus, and the Moon are in conjunction in any sign or in opposition or square aspect to each other, especially if Jupiter is in the terms of Venus and vice versa, and both are in opposition to the Moon, this indicates a wife from the mother's family. If the Sun is with Venus or with Jupiter and in the same relationship we described for the Sun, a wife is indicated from the father's family.

3. If the Sun and Moon are in conjunction, and Venus and Jupiter are with them or in square aspect to them in such a way that Venus is in the terms of Jupiter and vice versa, brothers marry sisters.

4. If Saturn and Venus are in conjunction or in square aspect or opposition but have the same degrees, and if the Moon is in any aspect to them or together with them, but Jupiter is in the terms of Venus and in

any aspect to her, they bring together mother and son in marriage.

5. If they are as we have just described in a woman's chart, and if the Sun is in the house in which we put the Moon, daughters marry fathers. If Venus is in the terms of Jupiter and vice versa and Mars is in opposition or square aspect to them, this compels daughters to have intercourse with fathers.

6. If Jupiter and Venus are located on angles, holding equal degrees and in square aspect to each other, and the Moon is in opposition or aspect to them, the natives marry their stepmothers. Women marry their stepfathers if Venus and Jupiter are situated in this way and the Sun is in aspect instead of the Moon.

7. If Venus, Jupiter, and the Moon are in conjunction on the angles, or if, located on the angles, they are in opposition or square aspect to each other, and Saturn is so placed that he aspects all of them in any way, this makes the native cohabit with his mother or daughter. But if Saturn is in aspect only to Venus and the Moon, the crime is committed secretly. But if he is in aspect to all three, the wives are allotted publicly.

8. In a woman's chart, if the Sun is found where we placed the Moon in a man's chart, the woman has intercourse both with a father and a son. If Mercury is in the terms of Venus and vice versa and, thus situated, they aspect each other in square or in opposition, and if Jupiter is in square aspect or opposition to them, this makes sons an object of desire to their fathers.

9. If Mars and Venus are in conjunction, or if Mars is in the terms of Venus and vice versa, and they aspect each other in any way, this makes adulterers. If Mercury is in square aspect or opposition to them, holding equal degrees with them, they will be discovered in their crime. But we have often spoken about this topic in the preceding books.

## XIX

### [CHILDREN]

1. If the Sun and Moon are in masculine signs, but Saturn is on the descendant or on the IMC, women will not bear children, especially if the ascendant is in Leo, Virgo, Capricorn, Pisces, Scorpio, Cancer, or Taurus. But if a benefic planet is on one of the first angles, one or two children will be raised.

2. If the Moon is in a masculine sign, certainly if in Leo, Virgo, or Capricorn, and the Sun is also in a masculine sign, but Saturn is on the angles or in the twelfth house, children are indicated neither for a young girl nor a woman. But if Jupiter is on the first angles and in favorable aspect, one child is allotted.

3. If the Sun and Moon are in feminine signs and the ascendant in a feminine sign, Saturn in the seventh house or on the MC, and no benefic

planet on an angle, children are not indicated.

4. The same is true if Saturn and the Moon are located on angles, have the same degrees, and are in square aspect to each other, and are also in double signs, and Jupiter is not in aspect in any way or located on the angles. This is also true if Jupiter and the Moon are together in the seventh house or on the IMC, and Saturn aspects them from an angle in square or opposition.

5. If Venus and the Moon are in conjunction, and Saturn from his own terms aspects them in square or opposition; if the influence of the Sun is added to this, Saturn in a morning rising in a diurnal chart and Venus on the angles in masculine signs, or in a nocturnal chart in an evening rising, the natives never marry.

6. But if all are located as we have said and Saturn, the Moon, and Venus are in Leo or Virgo, the natives will never have intercourse with women. The same is true if no planet is in aspect to Venus in the terms of Saturn, but the Moon is in Leo, Virgo, or Capricorn in the terms of Saturn.

## XX

### [MENTAL DEFICIENCIES AND OTHER AFFLICTIONS]

1. If the Sun and Moon are in double signs and on the angles, and Mars and Saturn are in square aspect to them, this will make imbeciles and lunatics. If Mars is on the ascendant and Saturn is on the MC, and the Moon is either together with them or in square aspect, the effect is the same. This is also true if Saturn is on the MC and Mars on the IMC.

2. If the Sun and Moon are in conjunction and aspected by Mars and Saturn, the affliction of imbecility or madness appears in the first years. But if Mars is found alone, blindness is inflicted by some violence. If Saturn is alone it comes from a running of the eyes. The same is indicated if Mars and Saturn are in square aspect to the Moon.

3. If Saturn and the MC are in the twelfth house, and Mars is in conjunction with him or on the anafora of the MC, the light of one eye will be extinguished. But if both, that is, Mars and Saturn, are in the eighth house and are retrograde and in square aspect to the Moon, this makes the native both feeble and blind. If they aspect the Moon from the right side, they blind the right eye and weaken the right side of the body; from the left, they have the same effect on the left side.

4. If a malefic planet is found in the middle between the Sun and Moon, or in conjunction with the Sun, or in the same sign, or if the Sun and Moon are in different houses and a malefic planet is in the house midway between them, this indicates blindness. If a benefic planet is in favorable aspect to them, the misfortune is lessened. Whoever has the Moon in the third degree of Sagittarius, the 16th of Leo, the 14th of Cancer, or the fifth of Taurus will be sickly.

5. If Mars is in the seventh house and the Moon is in the eighth, part of the body will be amputated or broken, according to the nature of the sign in which Mars is found. If the Moon is in tropical signs—that is, in Aries, Cancer, Libra, or Capricorn—and Mars is in square aspect to her, this will amputate either a hand or a foot.

6. With all these placed as we have said, if the Sun is in square aspect and Saturn either in opposition or square aspect, or if one of the luminaries is in the seventh house, or Saturn is in that house, this causes stomach trouble. But also if the Sun, Moon, Mars, and Mercury are in the sixth house and Saturn is in square aspect to them, or if they are in the seventh house and Saturn is on the ascendant, this will make lunatics of strange appearance and impeded speech.

7. If Saturn is in the seventh house and Mars in square aspect to him, this will produce madmen. But if Mercury is on the ascendant and Mars on the descendant, and Saturn is either on the descendant or the MC, this will make madmen who are at times homicidal. If Mars and Saturn are found together in Capricorn, Pisces, Aries, or Taurus, they will amputate a part of the body according to the nature of the sign.

8. Saturn and Mars together in any sign bring pains in hidden and secret places. But if they are in fixed signs and in square aspect to each other, or if one is on the ascendant and one on the descendant, or one on the MC and the other on the IMC, this will make epileptics. If they are in tropical signs and aspect each other, they make epileptics who can never be cured in any way.

9. If Saturn and Mars in double signs are aspected as above, in addition to the afflictions we described, they make the natives impious and cruel; they will be made captive. If a benefic planet is in aspect to them, the captives are returned to their fatherland. But if malefic planets are in the signs with Mars and Saturn, the misfortunes are greater; if benefic, the misfortunes will be less.

10. Saturn and Mars on angles in opposition to each other, in aspect to the Moon on another angle, in square aspect, or in opposition (especially if in the last degree of Libra, Capricorn, or Aries) weaken the native's feet. If Mars is in alien signs on the ascendant, this will be harmful either to the genitals or to the ears. Mars and Saturn in tropical signs in square aspect to the Moon make cases of dropsy.

11. Mars and Saturn in opposition to each other produce vomiting of blood. Mars in Scorpio, Capricorn, Pisces, or Cancer, if he is in opposition to the Moon, brings on impetigo, leprosy, and jaundice. If Saturn is in opposition to the Moon, when she is not in her own house or in the house of Saturn, this will make hemorrhoids or boils. Mars has the same effect located on the angles if he is in opposition to Venus.

12. If Mars, Venus, and the Moon are in tropical signs and in opposition to each other, and Saturn aspects them by night from Leo, Taurus, Pisces, or Sagittarius, this will produce gout; if by day, elephantiasis. If the

Moon is found in Taurus and Saturn in Scorpio or vice versa, with no benefic planet in aspect to the Moon, the native will suffer from elephantiasis.

13. If Mercury in Virgo or Pisces is exactly on the ascendant, and Saturn and Mars are in square aspect to him, they will produce madmen. Mars and Saturn on the anafora of the ascendant or in the eighth house will make a flow of blood from the nose, mouth, or anus. If Mars and Saturn are so located that one of them is on the MC, the other on the IMC, they indicate an illness from malignant humors.

14. But if Mercury is in square aspect to them, health is restored through help of the gods. But Mars and Saturn in conjunction in these houses produce madmen. If they are in their own terms, or Saturn is in the terms of Mars and vice versa, in the houses we have mentioned, the natives will be freed from insanity when fifteen years of Mars or thirty of Saturn have been completed.

15. Jupiter and Mars in a similar way make epileptics if they are in aspect to each other. If they are in their own terms, or Jupiter is in the terms of Mars and vice versa, the natives will be freed in the beginning of the affliction, but only when the first times of the planet have passed, that is, fifteen years of Mars or twelve years of Jupiter. If Mercury is in opposition or in square aspect in the same degrees, he will make the native able to give responses in temple.

## XXI

## [PHYSICAL INFIRMITIES]

1. When the Moon is on the angles and in signs which are without hair or in Sagittarius, and the malefic planets are in fixed or tropical signs in the house of illnesses and afflictions, the native will be bald. The same is the result of Venus in her own house on the MC. But Saturn between the Sun and Moon will make them gray at an early age.

2. If Mars is in Cancer, Scorpio, Capricorn, Pisces, or Taurus and in his own signs on any angle, or if he is in opposition or square aspect to the Moon or with her, this will make the natives hunchbacked, deformed, lame, or paralyzed in part of the body.

3. If Mars and Saturn, or one of them, is found in the sixth or twelfth house and that house is either a double or a tropical sign, or the sign in which the Part of Fortune is located, afflictions both of body and mind are indicated, especially if Mars and Saturn are in aspect to the Sun and Moon, either in opposition or square. But if thus located they aspect the Moon alone or are in conjunction with her, they cause afflictions from malignant humors or they make epileptics or madmen.

4. Always, if malefic planets are in opposition or square aspect to the Moon in the sixth, seventh, ninth, eleventh, or twelfth house or are

together with her, they make the natives deformed or spastic, or they twist the face in various ways, especially if the ascendant and the Part of Fortune are located in signs of the malefic planets. This combination indicates stomach trouble, epilepsy, madness, dropsy, impetigo, leprosy, consumption, or elephantiasis.

5. If a benefic planet is in favorable aspect, these afflictions are alleviated. But if there is no benefic planet and the malefic ones are in strong aspect to the house of illness, located in a fixed sign, the afflictions are more serious. But if benefic and malefic have equal power, the afflictions grow worse.

6. But if the benefic planet is stronger and in aspect to the Moon, the natives are freed from those illnesses by a certain divine power. If the malefic planets are stronger in influence, but the benefic are in conjunction with the Moon, through some power there is a temporary respite in the illness.

7. But if, when the benefic planets are stronger, the Moon is moving toward Mercury and coming into aspect with him, then the natives are freed by incantations, medicine, or amulets. But if Mars is in any aspect to Mercury and the Moon, the afflictions will be cured by medicine. If Saturn is in the seventh house and aspected in any way to the Moon on an angle, hidden places of the body will be operated on by physicians.

8. If Jupiter is alien to the angles and aspects the waning Moon in any way, the natives will die in the operation. But if Mars is in aspect to Mercury, and in tropical signs aspects in any way the Moon and Saturn, this will make epileptics and madmen. But if all this is the case and Jupiter from above is in aspect to Mercury and the Moon, the natives will be freed from an abscess by an operation.

9. If Mars is in the sixth or twelfth house and the Sun and Saturn are in aspect to him thus located, this indicates illness and afflictions followed by dreadful calamity. But if Mars in this position in a masculine sign is in square aspect to the Sun and Moon, from above, this will make the affliction more serious. In a woman's chart the indication is for serious difficulties from abortion and childbirth; the child will be cut out or a premature birth will cause continual pain to the mother.

10. If Jupiter is on the ascendant and Mars in opposition to him and in aspect in any way to the Sun and Moon, this will produce madmen or lunatics. If the Moon is in conjunction with the Sun, or is full on the angles and in aspect to Mars and in square aspect or opposition to Saturn, the same afflictions are indicated.

## XXII

## [ROYAL CHARTS]

1. If the Sun and Moon are in masculine signs on the first angles, and benefic planets are so located that in a morning rising they protect the Sun

in a diurnal chart (in an evening rising, the Moon in a nocturnal chart), this will make powerful and fearsome kings, subjugating great regions and states. If the Sun and Moon are on the MC, these kings will subdue outside tribes and faraway regions with infinite power and courage.

2. But, with this combination, if Mars is found on the anafora of the Sun, and the Moon and Saturn on another angle, the natives are cast down from their power and subdued by others. But if Jupiter from above is in favorable aspect to Mars and Saturn, and receives the light of the waxing Moon, after captivity they will again be returned to power and gain a greater accumulation of honors and good fortune.

3. If the Sun is exactly on the MC in a masculine sign, the Moon on the anafora of the Sun, and a benefic planet in a morning rising protecting the Sun, kings are born in the same way. But if in this combination Mars is found on the MC and Jupiter on the IMC, the kings will be involved in dangers, but be successful and feared, holding mastery of the whole world.

4. If the Sun is on the first angles in a masculine sign and the Moon is in important houses in a feminine sign, the natives will be famous, honored, and powerful, entrusted with the government of states. If the influence of Jupiter is added, imperial command is entrusted to them.

## XXIII

## [VIOLENT DEATH]

1. The natives will die a violent death if the full Moon is on the angles, or on the anafora or epicatafora of the angles, and Mars with her; or if Mars is in opposition or square aspect to her when she is waning, and if Saturn is on the anafora or epicatafora in opposition or square aspect to either Mars or the Moon, or if Saturn is in opposition or square aspect to the Sun.

2. Violent death is also indicated if Saturn and Mars are in opposition or square aspect to the Moon in any other house without influence of benefic planets, also if Mars is found on the angles, the Moon on the anafora of the angles, but Jupiter alien or hidden by the Sun's rays, Saturn on the angles, or on the anafora of the angles, or aspecting the Sun in any way.

3. In a similar way violent death is indicated by Mars on the angles or on the anafora of the angles aspecting the waxing Moon from above with no benefic planet in aspect. The kind of death is determined by the nature of the signs, as we have so often said. In human signs death is inflicted by the sword, either by bandits, or in a fight, or in some display of power. In earth signs death occurs in desert places or in various kinds of natural catastrophes.

4. In watery signs the native drowns in storms, shipwrecks, whirlwinds, or floods, but always by water. In fixed signs he falls off a cliff or from some kind of height. In fire signs he is handed over to the flames, or exposed to accident, or to someone's power. In watery signs death comes from stomach upset, consumption, black bile, hemorrhage, or inflammation.

5. If Mars is found on any angle, or in the eighth or eleventh house, and Saturn is in opposition to him, or if with Mars thus placed Saturn is in the seventh house, after many dangers the natives will die a violent death, especially if Jupiter is not in aspect to Mars from above and is not found with him. But the kind of death is determined by the signs.

6. If in this combination, without influence of Jupiter, Mercury is with Mars and Saturn, or if they are in opposition or square aspect to him, or the Moon is on an angle or on the anafora or epicatafora of an angle, this makes falsifiers, counterfeiters who are seized for their crimes and severely punished.

7. If Saturn is in the fourth or eleventh house, and Mercury is with him or in square aspect to him and Mars is with them in opposition or square aspect to them, and Mars is in the house of Saturn in square aspect or opposition to the Moon on the angles, this indicates the same crimes as the preceding.

8. But if Jupiter from above is in favorable aspect to Mars or is with him and receives the rays of the full Moon, the natives accued of these crimes are freed by the court. If the Moon is on the descendant and Mars and Saturn, or one of them, is exactly on the ascendant, and if another malefic planet is on the MC, the native will die a violent death.

9. If the Moon is found on any angle, Mars and Saturn are in conjunction with her or in opposition or square aspect to her, but one of them from above is in square aspect or opposition to Mercury, also on an angle or the anaforas or epicataforas of angles, this will make a violent death. The evil is greater if Mars or Saturn is in opposition or square aspect to the Sun.

10. If the Sun is found in watery signs, and Mars or the Moon is with him in the same house, or if the Sun is with the Moon in the sixth or twelfth house in opposition to Saturn on the ascendant, this indicates a violent death. They will die suspended from a noose or drowned in water. If the Moon is in conjunction with Saturn in the eighth house and no benefic planet is on an angle, death will come from a hemorrhage.

11. If there is a benefic planet on an angle, the natives, though despaired of, will be cured by physicians. But if the Moon is with Mars in the seventh house, the natives will die of hemorrhage. In general, Mars by night and Saturn by day in the seventh house produce hemorrhage, that is, a flow of blood. If the Part of Fortune is found in the seventh house, this indicates an affliction from cutting with a knife.

12. If all are located as we have just described and a benefic planet is in

favorable aspect, though cut with a knife, they will be cured. But if both Saturn and Mars are in the seventh house and the Part of Fortune is either on the ascendant or in the signs of Mars or Saturn, or if one of them (Mars or Saturn) is in the seventh house and the other is in opposition or square aspect, the native will die in an operation by physicians.

13. If the Moon is on the descendant, and Mercury and Mars are in conjunction on the MC, the natives will be homicides and parricides, or in wicked rage they will be stained with a brother's blood. They suffer severe penalties for their crime.

14. If the Moon and Mars are in the ninth house, and the Sun and Mercury in the third, this makes impious despoilers of temples who also suffer severe penalties for their crimes. If the Sun is with Saturn, Mars and Mercury are in the eleventh house, and the Moon is in the third without aspect of Jupiter, the natives suffer a violent death.

15. If the Sun is on the ascendant, and Mars and Saturn are in conjunction in the twelfth house in opposition to the Moon in the sixth, the natives will be slaves who will suffer a violent death. If the Sun is on the ascendant and Mercury is in conjunction with him, and Saturn and Mars are in the seventh house, they will make epileptics who die a violent death.

16. If the Moon is on the MC, Mars is on the ascendant, and Saturn is on the anafora of the Moon, this will cause a violent death. Also if the Moon is with Mercury in the eighth house, and Mars is with Saturn either in the fifth or twelfth. The same is true if Mars and Saturn are in square aspect to each other, Mars on any angle, and one of them in opposition or square aspect to the Moon or together with her.

17. If the Moon is found with Mars in the eighth house, the Sun in the seventh, and Saturn on the MC or any angle, this will make a violent death. If Mars and Saturn are in the eleventh house, or if one of them is in this house but another is with the Moon or in square aspect to her, and Mercury is in any aspect to Mars, this will produce epilepsy, insanity, and a violent death. This will be worse if Mars is in the eleventh house and Saturn in the fifth.

18. The Sun in the eighth house and the Moon on the MC, the ascendant or the Part of Fortune in the sign either of the Sun or the Moon—this will make madmen who suffer a violent death. If Mars and Saturn are found in the house of desire and the house itself is on any angle, and Mars and Saturn are in aspect in any way to Venus, the natives will die of gonorrhea; but in aspect to the Moon they make madmen. If both Mars and Saturn are in aspect to Mercury, the natives will be seized for forgery and counterfeiting and will die a violent death. But if Jupiter is in aspect they are freed.

19. Mars and Saturn on the ascendant with the Moon on their anafora make the natives lose their sight and suffer a violent death. If the Moon or the Sun is on the ascendant and Mars and Saturn on the anafora, the same is true. If the Moon is with Mars on the ascendant and Saturn is with the

Sun on the MC, this will produce epileptics, spastics, or madmen, and the prediction is for a violent end. This kind of death is also indicated by the Sun and Moon found on the angles, and Mars and Saturn together with them or on any other angles.

20. If Mars or Saturn is found in the Part of Fortune and in conjunction with the Sun, in the fifth or eleventh house, this makes for a violent death, as does Mars located with the Moon in the twelfth house, and Saturn and the Sun in the second, that is, in the anafora of the ascendant. These natives often die at birth, being cut from the mother, especially if all these planets are found in the same degree.

21. If the Moon is on the MC or the IMC; one malefic planet is on one angle, and another is in opposition to the Moon or to the ascendant; or if she is found in the fifth or eleventh house—this makes a violent death. The natives in this case will fall from a height or die as suicides. But according to the nature of the planet which is in opposition and according to the nature of the signs, different kinds of death are indicated.

22. If the Moon is in the eighth house; Mars in his own house on the ascendant, and with him Venus, Mercury, and the Sun, all in neighboring degrees, and Mars and Saturn in aspect to the Moon, the natives will die devoured by beasts. If the waning Moon is in the eighth house and Saturn is with her or in aspect to her in any way, this will make a violent end such as drowning.

23. If the Moon is on the descendant, Saturn is in the sixth house, and the Part of Fortune is in the house of Saturn or of the Moon, the natives will die of dysentery. If the Moon is on the ascendant but Saturn is with Mercury in the seventh house, the natives will be stupid, slow, silly, and epileptic. If Mars is on any angle, they also suffer a violent death.

24. If Saturn is in the third or ninth house and in aspect to Mars in square, the natives will be in charge of great affairs and great deeds but their inheritance will be wasted. They will also have serious illness and be compelled to suffer much evil in foreign places. Their parents will be sickly and suffer a violent death. But if Mercury is found with one of them (Mars and Saturn) or the Moon is with them or in opposition or square aspect to them, the natives become impious despoilers of temples, leaders of bandits, and suffer an evil end.

25. If the Sun, Saturn, and Mercury are on the MC, there is danger of accusations from hidden writings; public documents are forged or money is counterfeited. If Mars is in opposition or square aspect to these planets or is found with them, the natives become bandits, homicides, exiles, and fugitives.

26. If in addition to this combination Jupiter is on any angle, after a time the natives are freed from calamities and given great power. But if the Moon is on any angle or on its anafora or epicatafora, after all this they die a violent death.

27. If Mercury and Saturn are in the sixth or twelfth house, the natives

are put in charge of miserable and unsuccessful affairs, and they do everything in a slow and sluggish manner. But if Mars is in square aspect or opposition, this makes criminals, bandits, perjurers, informers, betrayers of their own people. Some are taken into custody because of slaves or condemned men, especially if Mars is in any aspect to the Moon.

28. If Saturn is in the eighth house or on the anafora of the ascendant, the Moon on the anafora or the epicatafora of the ascendant, and Mars in the seventh house, the native will have no care for religion. If Saturn and the Moon are in opposition or square aspect to each other, they become despoilers of temples and are publicly punished for this crime. But if Venus is found together with them and also Jupiter, the natives become priests, prophets, or temple attendants, but they suffer a violent death.

29. If the Moon is found with Mars on the descendant but in such a way that Mars is higher in degrees, and Saturn and Mercury are on the IMC, they indicate a violent death. The kind of death is recognized by the nature of the signs. In tropical or water signs they die of dropsy or are drowned in seas or rivers. In double or fixed signs they become epileptics and die a violent death. If Venus and Jupiter are in any aspect, the danger of these misfortunes is lessened.

## XXIV

### [COURT SENTENCES]

1. If the house of necessity is in the house of Mercury but the Moon is in the house of Mars or Saturn; and either Mars or Saturn is in opposition or square aspect to Mercury, or if they are with him on any angle or on the anafora or epicatafora of angles, or if they are on the ascendant, in the Part of Fortune or in the house of necessity; the native will be condemned in some way.

2. But if the house of necessity is found in the house of Mercury or of the Moon, Mars, or Saturn, and the house itself is on any angle; and of all the planets we have just mentioned, if one is on the anafora or epicatafora of the angle, in a similar way the native will be condemned. The sentence, however, will be exile, gladiatorial games, or public mines.

3. The condemnation will be just if the house of necessity is in the houses of the planets we mentioned, with some of them on the angles, and some on the anafora or epicatafora of the angles. But if Jupiter on the MC is in favorable aspect to the malefic planets, the chance of condemnation will be lessened. After a certain space of time the natives are freed from accusations by judgment of the emperor and restored to their position and their country. But if the influence of Jupiter is not present, the natives are justly condemned and suffer severe punishment.

4. If the ruler of the sign of the house of necessity is located in the house of Mars, Saturn, or Mercury, with one on the ascendant and one in

the house of necessity itself, the sentence will be carried out. The same is true in the aforesaid houses if the sign of the house of necessity has its own ruler in it.

5. This is also true if the house of necessity is found in the house of Mercury, and Mercury is on any angle, but Mars and Saturn are on the anafora or epicatafora of the angles. But if all these are in this position, and the Moon is on any of the angles or the anafora or epicatafora of an angle, the condemned will suffer a violent death.

6. The sentence also will be carried out if the house of necessity is found in the house of Mercury, if Mercury is in the house of Saturn or on the anafora or epicatafora of an angle, and Jupiter is not in aspect.

7. If the house of necessity is in the Part of Fortune, or the ruler of the Part of Fortune is found in the house of necessity, or the ruler of the house of necessity is found in the Part of Fortune, the condemnation is just and will be carried out.

## XXV
## [HOUSE OF SEXUAL DESIRE]

1. If the Sun and Moon are in feminine signs, either together or in different houses, Venus is in a feminine sign on any angle, and the Moon and Mars are together on another angle, they will make eunuchs or hermaphrodites. If the Sun and Moon are in masculine signs and Venus is also in a masculine sign in a woman's chart, women will be born who take on a man's character and desire intercourse with women like men.

2. If Venus is in the house of Mercury and vice versa, or if they are in each other's terms, the Moon in Virgo, Capricorn, Taurus, or Leo, and the other masculine planets are in feminine signs and the feminine in masculine, hermaphrodites will be born.

3. If Mercury and Venus are in conjunction in the 19th degree of Aries, they make the native impure of mouth. If Venus and the Moon hold the 30th degree of any sign and are in square aspect or opposition to each other, they will exercise these vices secretly. But if the rulers of those signs in which the Moon and Venus have the 30th degree are in any aspect to these signs, they exercise these vices publicly, without shame.

4. Mars and Venus in conjunction in a morning rising and in a masculine sign make women shrewish and sterile. In an evening rising in feminine signs, in a man's chart, if Saturn is in any aspect, they make perverts who serve in temple choirs. If this combination is found in Aries or Capricorn, these same afflictions are indicated. But if Venus is in opposition or square aspect and there is no influence of Jupiter, women will be born with masculine character, but men will become castrates or eunuchs or male prostitutes.

5. If the Moon is in opposition to Saturn, but Mars is so placed that he is in square aspect to them and in opposition to Venus, and all these four

are in each other's houses, this combination makes women sterile and shrewish, and makes men male prostitutes. Saturn in conjunction with the Moon will produce male prostitutes.

6. The same is true of Venus and the Moon in conjunction, also the Sun and Venus in the eighth house, Mercury and Venus in the houses of malefic planets, with Mars and Saturn in the house of Venus.

7. I shall briefly show how you may observe this more accurately: count the signs from the Moon to Venus and the same amount from the ascendant. If the number falls in a feminine sign, and the Moon is in a feminine sign from the 25th to the 30th degree, you will find male prostitutes who exercise their vice secretly; in a woman's chart the indication is for prostitutes.

8. But count the signs from Venus to the Moon and again from the ascendant, and if the number falls in a feminine sign, say that men will be detected in their practices. You will say the same in women's charts. If Venus and the Moon are located in feminine signs in the first degrees of these signs, the women perform their practices with public scandal.

9. If Venus is not with the Moon but is in an evening rising located in the first degree of a feminine sign, aspected to the Moon also in the last degrees of a sign, this makes both men and women prostitutes, both of whom hide their practices. But if, with all as we have described, Saturn in a feminine sign is in square aspect to Venus or the Moon, this will make degenerates who are deformed and poverty-stricken.

10. If all are located as we have said, and Mars is found with Saturn, he makes castrates. If Venus is in the last degrees of her sign and in aspect to Saturn and Mars, the degenerates will have good fortune and be entrusted with duties in temples; in a woman's chart they will be noblewomen involved in prostitution.

11. Mars, Mercury, Venus, and the Moon together in tropical signs, either in conjunction or in square aspect to each other, produce prostitutes, but their motivation varies according to the nature of the signs. If they are in feminine signs, this makes prostitutes, but in masculine signs, shrews.

12. If the Moon is on the ascendant with Mars and Venus, the Sun in the twelfth house, Saturn in opposition or square aspect to the ascendant, this will make castrates, but only if all influence of Jupiter is lacking. If Venus and Saturn are together, or in square aspect to each other, or are hidden by the Sun's rays, and the Moon and also the ascendant are in feminine signs, this makes secret degenerates.

13. But if Saturn and Venus are in a morning rising, they make these vices public. If Mars is in an evening rising in opposition or square aspect to Saturn and Venus, he will make public perverts. But if all are located as we have said and Mars is on any of the angles, this will make castrates. If it is a woman's chart and all are located in masculine signs, they make her lustful and a shrew.

14. In general if the Moon, Sun, and ascendant are in the face or back of Capricorn, Aries, Taurus, or Leo, they indicate all kinds of sexual impurities together with extreme effeminization of the body. In all charts, if the Moon is found in the tail of Leo it will produce homosexuals who serve as tympany players to the mother of the gods.[82] But if Venus is found in the face of Leo, or of Capricorn, Aries, or Taurus, she drives both men and women to all kinds of vices.

15. If the Moon is in the signs mentioned above, Saturn and Venus in the seventh house in square aspect to the Moon, this makes perverts; also if Mars is in any aspect to the Moon, and if Mars and Saturn are in any aspect to Venus in Taurus, Leo, Virgo, or Capricorn.

16. If the moon is in the sixth or twelfth house in a nocturnal chart, or the Sun by day in these houses and the Moon by night, or the Sun by day in the terms of Venus, Venus in the seventh house or on the IMC in her own terms, degenerates are born. But if Mars is in opposition or square aspect, he will make castrates. In all this look for the influence of Jupiter, for he to a certain extent mitigates or conceals these vices.

17. Eunuchs are produced if the Moon is in sterile signs, Saturn in conjunction with her, Venus in any aspect to them, but Saturn in the terms of Venus and vice versa, and Jupiter not in aspect to the Moon. But if the Moon is with Venus in earth signs, and Venus exchanges terms with Saturn, still with the influence of Jupiter lacking, eunuchs will be produced, but they will have intercourse with women.

18. Now I shall show you the house of sexual desire so that you may be able to find all vices and lusts. Count the signs from the Moon to Saturn, and again from the ascendant, and in whatever sign the last number falls, that is the sign of vices and the house of desire.

19. If the house of sexual desire falls in a feminine sign, if a malefic planet aspects this house in square or opposition, and if Venus is located on any angle, degenerates are born but their vice is hidden. And if the house of desire has been exactly computed and found in dejected houses in a feminine sign, the native will be polluted by all impurities. But if it is located as we said and the Moon is in the first degrees of Pisces, Capricorn, or Leo, or in the last degrees of Taurus, the natives will be involved in all vices.

20. If the house of desire is located in dejected houses and attacked by influence of malefic planets, and the Sun and Moon are in dejected houses in signs of malefic planets or in their humiliation, they make public perverts engaged in all vices. These vices grow stronger if the house of desire is in Capricorn, Aries, or Taurus.

21. If Venus is ruler of the chart and is together with Mars in a feminine sign and in dejected houses, but Saturn in a masculine sign is in trine to the ascendant in his own sign or his own terms, and the Moon is in a dejected house, degenerates will be born. If the Moon, Venus, Mars, and Saturn are in feminine signs in dejected houses and are either together or in

square aspect to each other, they make male prostitutes. But if one of these is well located the natives will exercise their vices secretly.

22. If Venus and Saturn are in feminine signs in the seventh house but the Sun, Jupiter, the Moon, and Mercury are in dejected houses, this without doubt will make degenerates. And if all are located as we said and Jupiter alone is on the first angles, this will indeed make male prostitutes, but they will have the highest position, and glory and royal offices will be entrusted to them. If in this combination the Moon is found on the first angles, this will make them wealthy as well.

23. Venus and Mars in tropical signs, if they are in opposition or square aspect to each other in feminine signs, make perverts, but secret ones. Located as we said, without influence of Jupiter, they make women prostitutes and men homosexuals.

## XXVI

## [HOUSE OF OCCUPATIONS]

1. If Mercury and the Sun are in conjunction, and the Moon is not in aspect to them or not on the ascendant, the natives will be men trained in literature.

2. Jupiter in the terms of Mars in any sign and Mars in the terms of Jupiter, if they are on the angles and in opposition or square aspect to each other in a diurnal chart, with the Sun in dejected houses (the Moon in nocturnal charts)—this will produce famous gladiators.

3. If Mars is in the terms of Mercury in any sign and vice versa, with Venus in aspect to both, athletes will be born. If Mars and Mercury are on the angles, the athletes will be victors in all contests. If the influence of Venus is lacking, the natives will be gladiators, wrestlers, or trainers who never engage in sports themselves.

4. If there is any aspect of Venus when Mars and Mercury are in each others' terms, the natives will be boxers; if Venus alone is in aspect she will make runners. But these indications are stronger if the Part of Fortune and the house of occupations are found on angles and joined to Mars, Mercury, and Venus.

5. If Mercury is found in his own terms or in those of Mars and is in dejected houses, and Mars is in aspect to him from the house or the terms of Mercury, the natives will be orators or lawyers. If Mercury is located in this way in a diurnal chart in dejected houses, and Mars in favorable aspect from an angle, the orators will be great and famous.

6. If Mars and Venus are in square aspect to each other and in aspect to the house of occupations, physicians will be born. But if Mars and Venus exchange their terms the physicians will be very talented. If there is no influence of Mercury the natives will be cooks.

7. Mercury with Venus by night or day, in the terms of Venus or his own terms, will make musicians. The same is indicated by Mercury in the

terms of Venus and vice versa. But if Venus is in the terms of Mercury and Mercury in an alien sign or in alien terms, the natives will have a musical voice but will be humble or low class in some way.

8. In all degrees observe the Part of Fortune, then the house of occupations if it is located on the anafora of the Part of Fortune. When you have found the house of occupations, observe who is the ruler of the sign and in what house he is located. Also inspect the ruler of the sign in which the Part of Fortune is, see what house he is in, whether favorably located, and what planets are in the sign; if both the rulers are in one house, see which one falls more fortunately.

9. If they are not in the Part of Fortune, note if they are in the house of occupations; if they are, see which falls more favorably; if not, observe whether they are in aspect to the ascendant or on an angle. From this you will be able to determine the type of skill.

10. If Venus is in this position she will make painters, plasterers, goldsmiths, silversmiths, or musicians, according to the variety of the signs; but Jupiter makes businessmen, farmers, money-lenders, ship-owners, and the like, according to the variety of the signs. Mars makes physicians, barbers, and men who make a living from iron or fire; Mercury, those who carry on the business of oratory, speech, or who play the flute. Saturn makes hard-working dyers or sailors. These last are oppressed in many ways. But all this, as we said, is according to the quality of the signs.

11. I shall show briefly whether the natives will persevere in their skills. Note the sign Mercury is in and observe the ruler of the sign, and see if he is located well. If he is located well, they continue with their skills and gain a profit from their own efforts. If he is badly located, they will labor at their skills without profit and eventually will be worn out and desert their occupations.

12. My dear Mavortius, we have explained these things in detail to you so that all divine secrets may be clear to you. Now that these have been discussed the work turns to the exposition of the *Sphaera Barbarica*.

# Liber Octavus

I

## [THE ASTROLOGER'S CREED]

1. We should have no concern in this short life, my dear Mavortius, other than to give back to God our Creator our divine souls uncorrupted by crime, purged of all earthly stain, with all ties, or at least most, cut away. Otherwise we may lose our souls if they are forgetful of their divine creation, become entrapped in vicious desires, and are finally cast over the precipice.

2. This is what the earthly body works for day after day—to snare the divine soul in depraved desires, deceive it with sweet blandishments, so that the soul is so submerged and weighed down that it can never find its source but will be forever cast down into the shadows and the mire.

3. We must concentrate our thoughts on nothing earthly, especially since we know that God our Maker has so fashioned us with his divine skill that when the idea of the body has been separated from all downward tendencies, we see nothing but the Sun, Moon, and planets; also the fairest of all these things—their immortal home, namely, the universe.

4. Nature has so created other living things that they are bound to the earth. They cling with body and spirit to earthly experiences. But it has made us in such a way that of necessity one part of us belongs to the fragile body, another to the divinity of the immortal soul. The body which we seem to have in common with the beasts must always serve the spirit of divinity and be subject to its control.

5. Therefore we must contemplate the principles of our origin and strengthen our soul by the protection of its majesty. Thus we may find the true path back to our source and not with erring steps fall back into eternal error.

6. And so, my dear Mavortius, look with wide open eyes at the heavens, and let your soul contemplate the most beautiful fabric of the divine

creation. This is the way to free our souls from the depraved snares of the body and to put off the dangers of mortality. They will then hasten to their maker with accelerated pace, seeking nothing other than divine things through all the moments of all the hours.

7. These principles of the *Mathesis* will give us a small intimation of divine knowledge and lead us to the secrets of our source. Occupied with this holy doctrine we turn our souls toward heavenly powers and initiate them into divine rites.

8. This study will most successfully bring us to the point where our souls will despise everything which is considered either evil or good in human affairs. For when we learn of the approach of difficulties, we despise the threat of evils because we have learned from our doctrine about things to come. We do not shrink from dangers once foretold.

9. By recollection of its majesty, our souls have formed themselves to withstand these things; we are not overcome by bad fortune nor elated by promise of high office. Thus fortified by stable reason we cannot be oppressed by ill fortune nor overjoyed at the expectation of good.

10. Therefore I shall explain in this last book what remains of our theory. I have reserved for another time the explanation of the *Myriogenesis*. In the beginning we shall tell what signs see each other and which hear each other and which neither see nor hear. This matter pertains to the *Sphaera Barbarica*. [83] We shall also explain the measurement of the degrees and add which degrees are to be seen in the bodies of the signs; also what the 90th degree signifies, the one which the Greeks call *enenecontameris*. [84] From all this we will continue on to explain the *Sphaera Barbarica* and the power and effect of the famous stars.

## II
### [THE NINETIETH DEGREE]

1. First I shall discuss the *enenecontameris,* that is, the 90th degree. The use of this degree seems to be unknown to many and it is only lightly treated by a few writers. The tract of Petosiris on this subject seems to me to display a kind of hostile prejudice and an attempt to conceal the concept. In all charts the 90th degree must be carefully observed. From this degree can be discovered the nature of death for the native, his misfortunes, dangers, good fortune—the whole essence of the chart.

2. To find the 90th degree begin from the ascendant and count 90 degrees. When you have found the 90th degree observe the sign it is in, also the ruler of the sign and how he is located in the chart. Then see whether malefic or benefic planets are in aspect to the 90th degree.

3. Individual planets aspect that degree with the whole force of their nature; if they are malefic they bring ruin; if benefic they indicate the highest good fortune. If both kinds are in aspect they moderate the

influence of each other. Observe therefore the ruler of the degree and in what terms that ruler is located. Thus you may discover everything from the nature of the planet and the power of the house. For all things both good and bad are shown by the 90th degree, according to the nature of the sign in which it is found.

4. Similarly observe the Moon: setting out from the degree in which the Moon is located, count 90 degrees. Note everything in the same way: the kind of sign, the kind of degree, who is the ruler of the sign, the house, and the degrees in which he is located, and what planets are in aspect to the degree.

5. If the Moon is waxing observe whether Mars or Saturn is in aspect to the 90th degree; similarly if the Moon is waning. Thus you will find the kind of death, the order of life, the whole essence of the chart.

## III

### [SIGNS WHICH SEE AND HEAR EACH OTHER]

1. Now I shall explain which planets see and hear each other:[85] Aries does not see Leo but hears him. Leo sees Aries but does not hear him. Aries sees Cancer and also hears him. Cancer does not see Aries but hears him. Taurus both sees and hears Leo and similarly Leo, Taurus. The Gemini see Virgo and hear her slightly. Virgo sees the Gemini slightly but hears them fully. Cancer both sees and hears Libra. Libra does not see Cancer but hears him. Leo neither sees nor hears Scorpio. But Scorpio both sees and hears Leo.

2. Virgo regards Sagittarius obliquely but does not freely hear him. Sagittarius both sees and hears Virgo. Libra both sees and hears Capricorn and also is seen and heard by Capricorn. Aquarius does not see Scorpio but hears him. Similarly Scorpio does not see Aquarius but hears him. Sagittarius neither sees nor hears Pisces but Pisces both sees and hears Sagittarius. The Pisces do not see the Gemini but hear them. Capricorn and Aries neither see nor hear each other. Aquarius and Taurus neither see nor hear each other.

3. The Gemini both see and hear Libra. Similarly Libra sees and hears the Gemini. Sagittarius and Leo both see and hear each other. Virgo sees Capricorn but does not hear him. Similarly Capricorn sees Virgo but does not hear her. Libra sees Aquarius but she herself is not seen by Aquarius. Nevertheless they hear each other.

4. Scorpio sees the Pisces but does not hear them. The Pisces see Scorpio but do not hear him. Sagittarius and Aries are so located that they are not able to see or hear each other. Capricorn and Taurus are not able to see or hear each other. Aquarius and Gemini see each other but are altogether separated as to hearing. The Pisces and Cancer do not see, but hear each other.

5. We have discussed these secrets so that you may understand the order of the stars and know how they are located in the circle of the zodiac. For the twelve signs are not located in a definite order, or in equal steps, nor are they so placed that those that rise in a later position always are in aspect to those that precede or follow. So that I may show you not in argument but in the thing itself, I have appended this extract from the Book of Abraham[86] so that our writing may show you this matter in a clear interpretation.

## IV

### [INDIVIDUAL DEGREES]

1. I shall show what degrees you should look for in the signs. All the 30 degrees are distributed through all the bodies of the signs. So that you may know where the first degree is, and where the second, and the others, I shall give a whole list briefly. The first and second degrees of Aries are located in the horns; the third, fourth, and fifth in the head; the sixth and seventh in the face; the eighth, ninth, and tenth in the mouth; the eleventh and twelfth in the breast; 13th, 14th, and 15th in each shoulder; 16th and 17th in the heart; 18th and 19th in the right arm; 20th, 21st, and 22nd in the left arm; but the 23rd in the belly, and also the 24th and 25th; the 26th and 27th are in the feet; the 28th and 29th in the kidneys, and the 30th in the tail. This is the way the 30 degrees are distributed in the body of Aries.

2. The first and second degrees of Taurus are in the horns; the third, fourth, and fifth are in the face; the sixth and seventh in the neck; the eighth, ninth, and tenth in the forehead; the eleventh and twelfth in the heart; the 13th, 14th, and 15th in the shoulders; the 16th and 17th in the front feet of Taurus; the 18th, 19th, and 20th in the belly, the 21st in the knees; the 22nd, 23rd, 24th, and 25th in the back feet but the 26th and 27th in the genitals; the 28th and 29th in the hips; the 30th in the tail. Thus the degrees are distributed in the whole body of Taurus. But the *Sphaera Barbarica* makes another order of the degrees.

3. In Gemini the first and second degrees are in the head which turns toward the North; the third, fourth, and fifth in that same face; the sixth and seventh in the heart of that twin; the eighth, ninth, and tenth in the breast; the eleventh and twelfth in the hands; the 13th, 14th, and 15th in the feet. But first we must note that the space between the twins has the 16th and 17th degrees; the 18th, 19th, and 20th are in the head of the southern twin, the 21st, 22nd, and 23rd in his face; under the belly the 24th, 25th, and 26th; in the knees the 27th, 28th, and 29th, and in the feet only the 30th.

4. The degrees of Cancer are divided thus: the first and second degrees are in the head, the third, fourth, and fifth in the neck; the sixth and seventh in the jaws; and we find the three following degrees in the

eyes. This is what we often call the *nebula* (cloud) of Cancer. The eleventh and twelfth are in the back; the three following on the belly, stretching to the breast; the three following in the arms of Cancer; the seven following in the right feet; the 26th and 27th in the left feet; on the ends of the feet the 28th and 29th, and only the 30th in the tail.

5. The degrees of Leo are divided thus: the first and second degrees in the head; the three following in the face and nostrils; three more in the mouth of Leo; the same number in the heart; three in the shoulders and three in the feet; two in the belly; the 20th, 21st, and 22nd in the back; 23rd and 24th in the breast; three on the knees; the 28th in the genitals, the 29th in the kidneys, and the 30th in the tail.

6. The degrees of Virgo are distributed thus: the first and second degrees are in the head; the next three in the face; the sixth and seventh in the hands; the three following in the spine; the eleventh and twelfth in the shoulders; the three following in the heart and the 16th and 17th in the right breast; the three following in the right foot; the next three in the left breast; the 24th, 25th, 26th, and 27th in the left foot; the 28th and 29th in the kidneys, and the 30th only in the genitals.

7. The degrees of Libra are divided in this way: the first and second degrees are in the head; the third, fourth, and fifth in the left side of the balance; the sixth and seventh in the right side of the balance, . . .the eleventh and twelfth on the left part of the beam, the three following on the right part of the beam; the 16th and 17th in the heart of Libra; the four following on the right hand; the 22nd and 23rd in the breast; the three next in the kidneys; the 27th and 28th stretch to the tips of the feet, the rest of the body takes up the 29th and 30th. From these last degrees the Earth is said to have been formed.

8. The degrees of Scorpio are distributed thus: the first and second degrees are in the head; the three following on the forehead; the sixth and seventh in the face; the following three in the neck; the next two in the back; three in the belly; the three following in the right hand; two on the left hand; the next two on the right feet and the next three on the left feet; but in his sting, which stretches toward the North, the last five are located.

9. The degrees of Sagittarius are divided thus: in the head the first and the second; the three following in the face; two in the mouth; three on the shoulder; two following on the left hand; three others on the bow; two on the feet but the next three on the back; two in the belly of the horse, and on the back feet to the hooves the three which follow; the 26th and 27th in the genitals; the next two on the right hand, and the 30th only in the tail.

10. The degrees of Capricorn are distributed thus: in the horns the first and second; three following in the head, the sixth and seventh in the face; the three next in the mouth. In those degrees which are in the mouth of Capricorn, if the Moon is in one with benefic influence, it will make men impure in the mouth and will stain women with lustful desires. The

eleventh degree is in the heart of Capricorn; the twelfth and 13th in the neck; the two following in the shoulders; the three following in the right hand; the two next in the back; the three next in the belly; the four that follow on each side; the last three following to the end of the tail.

11. The degrees of Aquarius are divided thus: in the head the first and second are located; the three following in the face; the sixth and seventh in the back; the three next on the breast; on the right hand the eleventh and twelfth. The three which come after this are in the water of Aquarius; the 16th and 17th on the left hand; the two which follow on the sides; two others in the belly; the three following stretch to the feet; another three in the kidneys, and the last three in the vase.

12. The degrees of Pisces are distributed thus through the body. We must note that one fish turns to the South, the other to the North. The first and second degrees are located in the mouth of the southern fish; the third, fourth, and fifth in the head of the same fish; the next two in the jaws; the three following in the neck; the eleventh, twelfth in the end of the spine; the following three the fish has in his back; the 16th, 17th, and 18th we find in the fish line of the Pisces.

13. But in the fish which turns to the North the 19th degree is in the head; the three following in the breast; three next in the neck, and two in the tail. The three last degrees of Pisces are between Aries and Pisces, hidden in a mist. For this reason, if anyone has either the Sun or Moon in those degrees, without influence of a benefic planet, he will be oppressed either by constant blindness or a wretched weakness of the eyes.

14. When you begin to look for the house of afflictions and illnesses you will be able to find it most easily from this division of degrees. The divine Nechepso tried very carefully to locate this house and with his divine intelligence he explained it clearly. At another time I shall take care to show you, my dear Mavortius, the interpretation of his books.

15. Now I shall discuss the meaning of individual degrees. From this interpretation you will be able to find the whole measurement of the zodiac. Also I shall explain to you the magnitude of the signs so that you may know how the divine mind arrives at divine secrets.

16. The immortal soul, remembering the principles of its mine secrets.

17. The immortal soul, remembering the principles of its majesty, does not learn these things but knows them. Therefore what is said of one sign, he will figure for all the twelve. When you have done this, the whole measurement of the zodiac will be known to you. One degree of one sign has 21,040[87] stadia. For thirty degrees this makes 631,200 stadia.

## V

### [SIGNS NEAR THE ZODIAC]

1. You will now hear, my dear Mavortius, the fullest teaching of this doctrine. It is unknown to many Greeks and all Romans and even to this

day no intelligence has inquired into it. For even those divine men, the supporters of the divine religion, Petosiris and Nechepso (one of whom held the reins of government), when they explained everything pertaining to their art were not able to discover what we are about to divulge. Therefore let our writing not extend itself. I shall tell you briefly the secret of the promised work.

2. The circle of the zodiac, as we said in the book of principles, has twelve signs. To the sides of these signs cling other stars. But they never desert their own path in an erratic course but hold space assigned to them and turn always with the immutable revolution of the universe. These are located in the neighboring regions of the signs, rise with the twelve and set with them, keeping always an unchanging course.

3. To these stars antiquity gave names from fables. In Greek the most learned poet Aratos[88] traced the number of these stars and in Latin, Caesar[89] and Tullius, the model of eloquence. These men published the names of the constellations and their risings but not the significance for forecasting, so it seems to me that not the science of astrology but poetic license motivated them.

4. We have investigated all kinds of forecasting and we have found that these stars may claim for themselves great importance in human charts. Therefore, in order to fulfill our promise to explain everything, we shall tell their location and names, what the planets then indicate if they occupy the ascendant or descendant if in a morning rising.

# VI
## [ARIES]

1. The Ship Argo[90] rises on the right side of Aries, that is, in the fourth degree of Aries. If anyone is born with this degree rising, if his birth occurs at the point of its rising, he will be a pilot, ship-owner, or ship's captain. All his life he will wish to be involved in marine occupations.

2. Orion[91] rises on the left side of Aries, that is, in the tenth degree. If Orion is found either on the ascendant or on the MC he produces men outstanding for movement and speed of body; but their minds are always heated with sleepless anxieties. They will always be changing homes and will flit from one threshold to another in morning greetings.

3. Auriga, the Charioteer, rises in the 15th degree of Aries toward the North. Anyone who is born in this star's rising will be a charioteer, a tamer of horses, or one who crosses from one chariot to another in a leap, or standing on the backs of horses sustains himself with wonderful balance, or carried on the leading horse trains military maneuvers. Both Salmoneus and Bellerophon[92] are said to have been born when this star was rising.

4. Haedus[93] (a small double star in the hand of the Charioteer) is in the 20th degree of Aries toward the North. He is the one Auriga carries.

Those who are born when this star is rising promise one thing from the front but hide another in their thoughts. They have a severe face, large beard, stubborn forehead, and seem to imitate the appearance and character of Cato. But their whole appearance is a lie. For they are petulant, lascivious, always involved in depraved and vicious desires.

5. They will be separated from all practice of virtue, often be half-witted idiots, and be terrified of all danger of battle. They are involved in monstrous loves and are forced to commit suicide. Also from this star are born shepherds who make sweet songs to rustic pipes.

6. The Hyades (the Rainers)[94] rise in the 27th degree of Aries. Whoever is born with this star rising will be restless and riotous, always stirring up popular dissent and revolution, inflaming the minds of the people with furious quarrels, an enemy to quiet and peace, always madly desiring civil and domestic wars. But various ways of making money occur to him along with constant anxiety. This star also makes cowherds, keepers of oxen or of sheep.

7. Capra, the She-goat (Amalthea),[95] rises in the 30th degree of Aries. The poets said she was the fabled nurse of Jupiter. Those who are born when this star is rising will be over-anxious in mind and body and will be attacked by constant tremors. They are afflicted with slight tics and shake with terror at trivial messages. They will be curious about all things and have impatient eagerness to hear anything new.

8. We have told what these stars signify in their rising; now we must say what they indicate in their settings. For just as shadows are contrary to light so is death the opposite of life. Life therefore will be found in the rising and death in the setting. If the rising is on the ascendant, as we have often said, the setting is in the seventh house.

9. If the Ship (Argo) is in its setting, or if the descendant falls exactly on the Ship, and if malefic planets are either in opposition or square aspect to this point, severe dangers of shipwreck are indicated. If Saturn is in the star that is in the Ship, the natives will die of drowning in rivers or the sea.

10. If Orion is found on the descendant the natives will have minds disturbed by various kinds of anxiety. They will die miserably on a journey, sent by their fellow citizens. They will receive solace in the underworld because perpetual honors, images, titles, and statues will be decreed to them.

11. If Auriga is found on the descendant and attacked by malefic planets, the natives will be thrown from a chariot and suffer miserable death with a broken body; or, struck by a thunderbolt, they will be crushed to death; or they are crucified and their legs broken by public sentence.

12. If Haedus, whom Auriga carries, is found on the descendant and Saturn is in opposition or square aspect to him the natives die in the first

minute of life or are strangled on the very threshold of life; or a bitter end comes to them with swelling jaws. But if Mars is found with that star on the descendant and all influence of benefic planets is lacking the natives will be sacrificed on the altar of a fearful religion.

13. If the Hyades are on the descendant, aspected by malefic planets, this indicates sudden and unexpected death. The natives will be overcome in riots or seditions, torn apart by the hands of the people, so that the authors of their death cannot be found in any way.

14. If Capra the Goat is found on the descendant, the native will have an opportunity for income from booty. But they will suffer severe ill will because of insults to religion. They will also have an income from shipwreck or from goods found in a river.

## VII

## TAURUS

1. The Pleiades[96] are found in the sixth degree of Taurus. Those who are born when these are rising are always involved in luxury and lust. They are always drenched in perfumes, given to too much wine drinking, impudent in speech, so that in banquets and love-making they attack their companions with a sarcastic wit. They are addicted to all crimes of passion and are the kind who raise laughter by their biting tongues.

2. They will always be well-groomed and well dressed. They twist their hair in ringlets and often present a fictitious appearance by using another's hair. They soften their whole body with various cosmetics; pull out their body hair and wear clothes in the likeness of women; they walk softly on their tip-toes.

3. But the desire for flattery torments them; they seek it so constantly that they think that from flattery they attain virtue and good fortune. They will always be in love, or pretend that they are, and it pains them that they were born men. If a malefic planet is in aspect to this place they will be struck with sudden blindness.

4. When the Pleiades are descending in the sixth degree of Taurus, if this degree is attacked by malefic influence, the natives will perish in a shipwreck. But if benefic planets aspect this place equally with malefic, a pleasant death will come to them, either in sexual pleasure or at banquets or drinking parties, without grief. If the ascendant is in the split of the hoof of Taurus and one of the benefic planets is in aspect to this place, as well as malefic with equal influence, they will make a painter who acquires honor from his occupation. But if only malefic planets are in aspect, famous gladiators will be born. After taking many palms and prizes they will die fighting with the sword in the favor and applause of the spectators.

## VIII

## GEMINI

1. Lepus, the Hare, rises in the seventh degree of Gemini. Those who are born when this star is rising will be of such lightness of body that when they begin to run they seem lighter than birds. If Mars is in aspect to this point, he makes runners of races; but if the Moon is with Mars, they will be boxers or sword-fighters; if Mercury, either jugglers or javelin throwers; if Venus, pantomimists or actors of farces. But if Mercury and Venus are in conjunction, they will acquire new arts with the greatest diligence, especially if Jupiter helps them with favorable aspect.

2. If Saturn is in opposition or in square aspect to this place, he will make fugitives who in a spirit of hostility desert their own hearths and migrate to far-away regions. If Lepus is on the descendant and influenced by benefic planets, the natives will seek their livelihood with great toil. If only malefic planets are in aspect, they will die torn and devoured by wild beasts.

## IX

## CANCER

1. The three stars in Orion's belt (the Iugulae) rise in the first degree of Cancer. The one who is born when these are rising will be irreligious and treacherous, passionately devoted to hunting. He will capture wild beasts in nets, take them in pits, or chase them with various iron weapons, or follow the secret pleasures of the forest with dogs. If the native is a woman, she will have the same characteristics and the attitude of a shrew. But she will only do this if Mars together with benefic planets is in any aspect to this place.

2. If Saturn is in aspect to this place, the natives will be enthusiastic fishermen and will capture marine beasts in carefully chosen places. If the Iugulae are on the descendant and benefic planets are in aspect, the native will die in his sleep. If Mars is in aspect he will incur all kinds of danger but will be strangled in his sleep.

3. Procyon (the Foredog), a constellation which rises before the Dog-star, rises in the 20th degree of Cancer. Those who are born at his rising will not themselves enjoy hunting but will manufacture weapons for hunting; that is, nets, hunting-spears, arrows, and whatever pertains to that sport. They will also raise dogs to be used in hunting.

4. If this star is on the descendant and Mars is in opposition or in square aspect, and if influence of Jupiter is lacking, the natives will die from the bite of a mad dog. Imitating the dog's rage they will avoid water, dread all drinking from cups and die with burning jaws; or they will be torn apart by beasts when they are laying snares for wild animals.

## X

## LEO

1. In the first degree of Leo rises Canicula, the smaller Dog-star whom the Greeks call *Sirios.* Whoever are born with this star rising will apply a maddened brain to every kind of monstrous crime. They will be separated from all human feelings and seek out violent deeds. They will be raving, wrathful, fearsome, and threatening, and be both hated and feared by everyone.

2. They will also be lively and fluent in speech, stirring up new, unheard-of reasons for quarrels; their hearts beat wildly, their voice in burning jaws is like the barking of a dog when, moved by rage, they gnash their teeth.

3. If Mars is in aspect to this place the characteristics we have described are even stronger. These men never fear the secrets of the forest and despise the teeth of wild beasts; often they run into danger from fire or wild animals.

4. If malefic planets are in aspect to this place and the Moon is in aspect to Saturn, hunters will be born who work with slings in the arena and fight with beasts in sight of the public. Also they become gladiators. They will be so swift of body that they can catch rabbits.

5. If Canicula is found on the descendant and Mars in conjunction or in threatening aspect to it, the native will be eaten by dogs, wolves, or other wild beasts.

6. Cratera (the Bowl) rises in the 30th degree of Leo. Those who have this star rising will love well-watered fields, rivers, fountains, or streams, and will divert them from their channel to another place. They will be lovers and cultivators of vineyards who graft fertile shoots on infertile trees, or who trim bushes into the shape of beasts, or bend vines into green porticos. They drink wine freely without mixture. But if the influence of a benefic planet indicates it, they will do business in merchandise connected with water.

7. If Cratera is found on the descendant without malefic aspect, the native will die in middle life at a banquet or drinking bout. If a malefic planet is present, he will be drowned either in a keg of wine or in a well, river, lake, swamp, or the sea; or he will be found in a fish-pond or in a bath tub.

## XI

## VIRGO

1. Corona (the Crown) rises in the fifth degree of Virgo. Whoever is born with this star rising will spend his life in a variety of pleasurable pursuits. He will be involved in feminine arts such as making crowns or

wreaths, gardening, designing unguents, perfumes, and aromatics. He decks his own body with adornments and secretly carries on love affairs or adultery, hastening to the bed of boys or girls.

2. If Corona is found on the descendant, or if Saturn is with it or in threatening aspect to it, the native will die in early youth. He will be sentenced by the court, thrown out unburied, and devoured by dogs.

3. Spica (Ear of Grain) rises in the tenth degree of Virgo. Whoever is born in the rising of Spica will always be involved in rural occupations and will cultivate the fields with patient toil. He will store many crops in warehouses for his subsistence. This star, according as it is influenced by other planets, always makes millers of grain, pastry-cooks, and the like.

4. If this star is found on the descendant, the natives will be stricken with fever, or suffer imprisonment, or hostile attacks. If Saturn is in threatening aspect, they will be oppressed by weight of poverty so that throughout their whole life they will be almost naked and dressed in rags. To the last day of their lives they will be demanding food from public mercy so that from torment of body and mind they do not live out their allotted life span.

5. If Mars is in aspect they will be torn apart at the hands of the people because of stolen taxes or investments fraudulently appropriated.

## XII

### LIBRA

1. Sagitta (the Arrow) rises in the eighth degree of Libra. The one who is born in this sign will be a shooter of arrows. He hits flying birds with unique skill or spears fish with a three-pronged spear. But if this star is found on the descendant and malefic and benefic planets aspect it equally, the native will be drafted into the army, placed in line of battle, and will die amid flowing blood and heaps of enemy dead.

2. If Mars alone or with Mercury is in aspect or in conjunction with this place, the natives will be sold as gladiators and die from loss of blood for the pleasure of the spectators. But if Saturn is in aspect, they become gladiators by sentence of the court. The River Styx is said to be in this degree.

3. Haedus rises in the 15th degree of Libra. The one who is born when this star is rising will be indecisive in mind and anxious in thoughts, involved in a variety of plans, never enjoying anything in quiet security. He will be assigned to the service of magis!trates or carry out the duties of a public recorder or a public tax-collector. But he will have monstrous desires and lascivious habits; be addicted to wine and banquets. He will put the pleasure of guests before public affairs; he will be adept at dancing and theatrical arts.

4. If this star is found in its setting and the malefic planets are in

aspect, the natives either perish from being thrown over a precipice or leap to their death in a dance; or, in breaking into a girl's house in the darkness of night, through too much impatiemce they are caught by the husband and thrown over a cliff. If benefic planets are in aspect they die of shortness of breath.

## XIII

## SCORPIO

1. Ara (the Altar) rises in the first degree of Scorpio. Those who are born when this star is rising with influence of benefic planets will be priests, prophets, temple attendants, ministers of the most sacred religions, or diligent interpreters of divine doctrine.

2. But if this star is at its setting and Mars and Saturn are in threatening aspect, the natives are sentenced for some kind of sacrilege. If Jupiter is in aspect, they are either sacrificed to the gods or killed in some religious rite.

3. Centaurus rises in the twelfth degree of Scorpio. The one who is born with this star rising will be either a charioteer, or a breeder and trainer of horses, or certainly a mule trainer, a mule doctor, or a horseman of some sort. If Mars is in favorable aspect, he will be a cavalry soldier. But if Mercury is in aspect, this will make him a gardener who will collect herbs for curing the herds.

4. If this star is found in its setting and malefic planets are in aspect, he will either die being thrown from a height, or from an attack of quadrupeds, or from the kick of a horse, or from being thrown from a horse, or, from an overturned chariot, dragged to death by the horses.

## XIV

## SAGITTARIUS

1. Arcturus (the Bear-Keeper) rises in the fifth degree of Sagittarius. The one who is born with this star rising will guard the secrets of friends in faithful silence. The resources of kings will be entrusted to him, or the treasury of public temples. But if malefic planets are in aspect, he will be a door-keeper to kings and have the duty of admitting and saluting guests.

2. If this star is found in its setting and Saturn and Mercury are in aspect, the native will be accused of serious crimes, handed over to die in prison by torture.

3. Cygnus (the Swan) rises in the tenth degree of Sagittarius. The one who is born with this star rising will either capture or trade in birds or with human voice will cleverly imitate the sound of birds, or will raise doves. If this star is found in its setting, the natives, although provided with income by others, will be captured by the enemy or suffer public punishment because of theft of the spoils of war.

## XV

## CAPRICORN

1. Ofiuchus (the Serpent-Holder) rises in the first degrees of Capricorn. Those who are born with this star rising will be snake charmers who soothe poisonous snakes. But if this star is found in its setting and malefic planets are in aspect, they will die from the bite of a poisonous snake.

2. Delphinus (the Dolphin) rises in the eighth degree of Capricorn. Whoever has this star rising will have swimming as a hobby. If Saturn is in aspect he will be a diver; with aspect of Mars and Mercury a juggler, rope-dancer, tumbler, or be conspicuous for agility in nautical races. But if this star is found in its setting and Saturn is in unfavorable aspect, he will be drowned in storms on a river or the sea.

3. Lyra (the Lyre) rises in the tenth degree of Capricorn. Those who are born when this star is rising will be just, upright, and miserly, trained for all duties of the court, avengers of crimes, in charge of public courts and inquiries. But if Saturn is in aspect they will be torturers and executioners who persecute evil men with zeal. If this star is found in its setting, the natives will be publicly tortured, burned in fire, or die on the wheel, especially if Mars and Saturn are in aspect.

4. Cepheus[97] rises in the 15th degree of Capicorn. Those who have this star rising will be serious, austere, feared for their severity, always assuming the countenance of upright characters who follow with zeal the Stoic philosophy. Such among the ancients were the Catos; and another was Tullian[98] in our time, who deservedly through his severity attained the rank of regularly-elected consul.

5. If Venus and Mercury are in aspect, the natives will be writers or performers of tragic dramas. But if this star is found in its setting they will at some time incur dangers and death on certain rocks or they will perish immediately at birth; or will be publicly punished for incest with a new and unheard-of death.

## XVI

## AQUARIUS

1. Aquila (the Eagle) rises in the twelfth degree of Aquarius. Those who have this star rising will make their living from the slaughter of men and the spoils they win. They will also capture wild beasts and tame them. They will be especially brave soldiers who by their courage overcome fearful attacks in war. They will despise death and attack the enemy with bared breast.

2. If benefic planets are in favorable aspect to this place, the natives will liberate their fatherland, found other states, and conquer or subju-

gate other peoples. But if Mars is in aspect, or Saturn, this will make officers, administrators or emperors, or followers of kings, to whom the custody of the empire and its armies are entrusted. But if this star is found in its setting they will be suffocated at birth.

3. Cassiopea[99] rises in the 20th degree of Aquarius. Those who are born when this star is rising will be goldsmiths, makers of jewelry, plasterers, or pearl-setters, carrying on all these arts with talent and skill. From their art they will earn a large income. But if this star is found in its setting, the natives will perish from falling ruins or from sickness.

## XVII

## PISCES

1. Andromeda[100] rises in the twelfth degree of Pisces. Whoever is born with this star rising will always attack men with brutal ferocity. He will be either a minister of public punishment, or a jail warden, or an executioner.

2. If both benefic and malefic planets are in aspect, the natives will be in charge of work houses or mines. If this star is found in its setting and malefic planets are in aspect, the natives will be killed by wild beasts or crucified. If benefic planets are also in aspect, they will be assigned to the gladiatorial games or be held in prison.

3. Equus (the Horse) rises in the 21st degree of Pisces. Whoever has this star rising will be an especially famous charioteer, driver, horseman, or courier of scouts; he will not be a physician but will make medicines out of herbs for men and animals. But if this star is in its setting with malefic planets in aspect, he will be killed by kick of a hoof or a fall from an overturned chariot.

4. Ingeniculus (the Kneeler, i.e., Hercules) rises in the last degrees of Pisces. It is called in Greek *Engonasis*. Those who are born with this star rising will be wise, clever, trained in various tricks, liars who deceive people with different kinds of plots; they are always aggressive and display unbridled hostility. With aspect of Mars or the Moon they will be rope-dancers or tightrope walkers. Those who are born when this star is setting will be in danger from various plots. If Mars is in aspect they will be burned alive.

5. In the last degrees of Pisces on the left side rises Belua whom the Greeks call Cetus (the Sea Monster). Those who are born with this star rising will be fishermen, but of large fish. They will catch sea-dogs, sword-fish, tunnies, and crocodiles. They will make a living from salt, or salted fish, or fish sauces. But if this star is in its setting and Mars is in aspect, the natives will be eaten by crocodiles while swimming in a river; or on land by dogs or some wild animals.

6. Septentrio (the Big Dipper) rises between Pisces and Aries, that is, between the beginning and end of the world; it is fixed in one place and at the vertex of the universe turns the axis of the world with constant speed. Those who are born when this star is rising will be kind to wild beasts, will associate with beasts, bulls or lions, as if they were people. But if Septentrio is found in its setting with Mars in aspect they will be killed by wild beasts.

7. Anguis (the Eel) is the last constellation and is between the two Bears and winds with sinuous bends in the manner of a river. Those who have this star rising will be snake charmers and prepare medicine from poisons and pigments of herbs. But if this star is found in its setting, they will die by the bite of poisonous snakes or from drinking poison.

8. Lygnus is also part of this constellation. Those who have this star rising will be finders of metal who seek for hidden veins of gold or silver and other metals. They will also be minters of money. But if this star is found in its setting and Mars is either in conjunction, opposition, or square aspect, they will either be burned when their house is consumed or they will be given to avenging flames by public sentence.

9. One should note that if the hour in which birth is completed has either an earthquake or a thunder storm, the natives will always be unstable with trembling bodies and shaking steps; through all minutes of the day they will fear the fall of threatening ruins.

10. Their eyes will flash, they will shrink from everything; they will not be able to keep a definite order of words but the sound of their voice will be impeded, and they will hiss with a tremulous murmur; or between clenched jaws their words will die on utterance. They will always think it is going to thunder or that the earth is about to move and that everything is falling. By these fears the correct order of their speech is disturbed.

11. There, my dear Mavortius, are the principles of the *Sphaera Barbarica;* this is the teaching of the Chaldean theory.


## XVIII

## [THE MYRIOGENESIS]

1. Now I shall come to the following parts of the *Sphaera Barbarica* which in every way are like the theory of the *Myriogenesis*. For whatever *Myriogenesis* says about individual minutes we shall say about individual degrees. Therefore the entire measurement of the chart must be located so that the true degree, discovered with the accustomed computation, will make the forecast trustworthy. If the measurement is not correct the promised forecast will be shadowed with vicious lies. Now, beginning from Aries, let us set forth the meaning of the individual degrees according to the *Sphaera Barbarica*.

## XIX

## ARIES

1. Those who have their ascendant in the first degree of Aries if a benefic planet is in aspect will be born kings or generals and always lead armies successfully. If it is in the second degree of Aries, they will be persistent thieves who always attack their victims with monstrous fury; they make their homes in foreign regions. If Mars is in opposition or square aspect to the Moon, these predicted crimes will be detected and punished.

2. Those who have their ascendant in the third degree of Aries will be deaf, one-eyed, and stupid. If it is in the fourth degree they will be thieves who will be caught in their crimes and punished by death. The one who has it in the fifth degree will be ruler of a great people, will judge important cases, and hold high office through his own merits. He will be just, upright, sober, and hold his native religious rites in veneration. He will die universally respected for good character.

3. The man who has his ascendant in the sixth degree of Aries will be a friend of kings and of the most powerful judges, himself holding high office. One will be known for an outstanding skill, another will hold high military office. These die at their appointed time. The ascendant in the seventh degree of Aries, with influence of Jupiter, will make an athlete; with that of Mars, a hunchback who dies a violent death.

4. Those who have the ascendant in the eighth degree of Aries, if malefic planets are in aspect, will be athletes ennobled by their own virtue, but after winning many prizes they will die a violent death. If benefic planets are in aspect, they will be prophets showing great divinity of soul. The ascendant in the ninth degree indicates a violent death early in life.

5. In the tenth degree it makes natives who are treacherous, irreligious perjurers who die in early life from various illnesses. The eleventh degree, if Jupiter is in that degree or in trine aspect to it, will make a high official, a friend of kings or powerful men, possessed of great wealth and lands, or a famous general. He will die at his appointed time.

6. If Venus and Jupiter are in the twelfth degree of Aries and in trine to the Moon, whoever has the ascendant in that degree will be rich and honored in every way. He will die in old age. Those who have the ascendant in the 13th degree will be sterile, with no children. They die in middle life.

7. Whoever has the ascendant in the 14th degree of Aries will be a businessman with great riches, a money lender or investor in public funds, collecting great income and known to all. This degree also makes weavers of purple wool; they die of old age. The 15th degree will involve the native in disgraceful sexual desires or make him a notorious male prostitute. If it is a woman's chart, she will be marked by a similar disgrace.

8. Those who have the ascendant in the 16th degree of Aries will be

tortured by constant intestinal pains and will die of them. If it is a woman she will die in childbirth. The one who has the ascendant in the 17th degree will be a bird-catcher, or a hunter and breeder of birds or animals. If Mars is in aspect, the native will be torn by dogs or wild beasts and die.

9. The 18th degree of Aries will make the native a mule-driver or a mule-herder; he will die from a small animal such as a scorpion or a spider. The ascendant in the 19th degree will make the native die on the threshold of life.

10. The man who has the ascendant in the 20th, 21st, or 22nd degree of Aries will be rich, have many famous children, and the protection of many brothers, provided Jupiter is in favorable aspect or in that degree himself. He will be a friend of kings or powerful men, a worshipper of the gods, a benevolent man, long-lived. He will be fortunate in old age and die at his appointed time.

11. The ascendant in the 23rd degree of Aries will give the native scrofula, ulcerous spots, or elephantiasis.

[The 24th degree of Aries is missing].

The one who has the ascendant in the 25th degree will be a goldsmith, a maker of bracelets, or a worker in marble. The ascendant in the 26th degree will make the native so timid that every minute of the day he will shake with empty fears.

12. The ascendant in the 27th degree of Aries will make the native a wool-worker, dagger-maker, or weaver. The 28th will make cleaners of latrines and of sewers, or they will be condemned to public work by the court. The 29th degree makes barbers. Those who have the ascendant in the 30th degree of Aries, that is, in the tail, will be epileptic, insane, and short-lived.

## XX

### TAURUS

1. Whoever has the ascendant in the first degree of Taurus will be an inspired seer, accustomed to prophesy in temples. If in the second degree, he will carry manure or clean latrines and sewers. In the third degree he will be a farmer or a plowman. In the fourth degree, a famous actor who will win prizes in contests.

2. Whoever has the ascendant in the fifth degree of Taurus if Mars is in aspect will die, sentenced for serious offenses. Those who have the ascendant in the sixth degree of Taurus will be adolescent perverts, diseased, with running noses, addicted to every vice, objects of serious scandal. The ascendant in the seventh degree will make *haruspices*, augurs, or jugglers. The ascendant in the eighth degree will bring the native new and unexpected honors but he will die suddenly.

3. Those who have the ascendant in the ninth degree of Taurus will be

base, scandalous, polluted by every vice. If it is in the tenth degree, they will be evil, malevolent, shaken by bad fortune; these always die a violent death. Those who have the ascendant in the eleventh degree will swell with malignant humors and die of dropsy.

4. Whoever has the ascendant in the twelfth degree of Taurus will die in a fire. In the 13th he will be in charge of athletic contests or master of a wrestling school. Whoever has the ascendant in the 14th degree will have a fetid odor, exuding poison like a goat. The 15th will make liars, separated from all dependable truth; they will also be voracious gluttons, serving the pleasures of the stomach.

5. The ascendant in the 16th degree of Taurus will pollute the natives with every vice. The 17th degree will make iron forgers; the 18th, slaves or millers of the lowest class. Those who have it in the 19th degree will be sterile. But if Mars is in that degree they will die by falling from a height or into water.

6. Those who have the ascendant in the 20th degree of Taurus will be male prostitutes serving base desires. If it is the chart of a woman, she will be a public prostitute. If they have the ascendant in the 21st degree, they will die from a lance wound. In the 22nd they will be hunchbacked clowns and die a violent death.

7. Those who have the ascendant in the 23rd degree of Taurus will be pimps with harsh voices or vicious male prostitutes. If benefic planets are in trine aspect or in the degree itself, they will be actors of tragedy or comedy, or heralds. Those who have the ascendant in the 24th degree will be musicians. If malefic planets are in aspect they will die a violent death.

8. If the ascendant is in the 25th degree they will be fullers or barbers. In the 26th they will be blind in one eye. In the 27th they will be actors in pantomime or male prostitutes. Those who have the ascendant in the 28th degree will have great possessions and infinite riches will come to them; but in very old age they will be miserable.

9. Whoever has the ascendant between the horns of Taurus will be a king or a general. If it is on the right horn, he will be a prince or a general; great, famous, a leader of navies or infantry; he will conquer some states and liberate others. But offspring are forever denied him. Also in this place fortunate eunuchs will be born, entrusted with the care of the state; they will do many things for many people, and statues and titles will be decreed for them. But later they will offend the monarch and die an evil death.

10. Navis (the Ship) rises with Taurus. Those who have the ascendant there will be businessmen, joyful and happy. If a benefic planet is in aspect, they will be powerful ship-owners. But if Mars and the Moon are in aspect, they will lead an army, both cavalry and infantry, over land and sea. They will die from the anger of a prince. In general those who have Navis on the ascendant will be sailors, pilots, merchants, or ship-builders.

## XXI

## GEMINI

1. Those who have the ascendant in the first degree of Gemini will be powerful men, the first in their own provinces, feared and honored by their fellow-citizens, but only if Saturn is in that degree or in aspect in any way. These men will die from the anger of a superior.

2. Whoever has the ascendant in the second degree of Gemini, and Jupiter is in that place with Saturn, especially if the Moon in a favorable house is moving toward them, will be a general of cavalry and infantry and also of naval power. He will conquer many unknown regions and will be given power even in far-away places. He will be just, pious, a benefactor of many, and will die after his sons.

3. Those who have the ascendant in the third degree of Gemini will be priests, religious leaders, or sacred kings. Those who have it in the fourth degree will have unusual bodily beauty, which will commend them to kings to such an extent that kings are always burning with love for them. The fifth degree will make the natives noble, proud, and over-confident.

4. The ascendant in the sixth degree of Gemini will make inspired seers, The seventh degree makes prison guards. Those who have the ascendant in the eighth degree will be musicians if the degree is in the house of Mercury; if in the house of Mars they will be trumpeters, and they will die in war. If the ascendant is in the ninth degree with Mars present, they will be porters, worn down with constant misfortune.

5. Those who have the ascendant in the tenth degree of Gemini will die of pain in the lungs. In the eleventh they will be heavily-armed fighters. In the twelfth, if Mars is present, they will die of a spear-wound; if women, they will die in childbirth. In the 13th degree they will die of dropsy; in the 14th, with Mars present, they will die of a fall from high places.

6. Those who have the ascendant in the 15th degree of Gemini will be common servants or bath attendants. In the 16th they will be actors in pantomime who are loved by many for their bodily beauty. Those who have the ascendant in the 17th degree will be outstanding for both size and beauty of body. They will be modest and, because of this, the friends of kings.

7. Those who have the ascendant in the 18th degree of Gemini will be trainers of athletes, always assigned to duties around the wrestling field. Those who have it in the 19th, with Mars present, will die from the wound of an iron weapon. If Saturn is in that degree they will have constant toil drawing water. But if the full Moon in scaly signs is moving toward Mars or waning toward Saturn, they will suffer from elephantiasis. Those who have the ascendant in the 20th degree of Gemini with Mars present will rule the people, and the popular courts will be entrusted to them, but they will die a violent death.

8. Those who have the ascendant in the 21st degree, if Saturn is in that place and the Moon well located, will be immensely wealthy, friends of kings, fathers of few sons, or brothers of few brothers. They will die of old age.

9. Whoever has the ascendant in the 22nd degree of Gemini will be a lute-player; from this profession he will gain great fame and the friendship of kings, but he will die a violent death. Whoever has it in the 23rd degree will be strong in virtue, noble in war, and have a favorable reputation from these characteristics. He will die without children.

10. Those who have the ascendant in the 24th degree of Gemini will be runners, worn out with constant toil. Those who have it in the 25th, if Mars is in the degree or in opposition or square aspect to it, will die from a fall or be eaten by wild beasts.

11. Those who have the ascendant in the 26th degree of Gemini will be priests, *haruspices,* prophets, and friends of kings. But if Saturn is in that degree, he will make male prostitutes who die from the anger of a king. The 27th degree will make guardians or keepers of temples, ritual attendants, or temple servants.

12. Those who have the ascendant in the 28th degree of Gemini will be epileptic, mentally deficient, or short-lived. In the 29th degree they will be addicted to legal quarrels and involved in lawsuits. If Mars is in that degree, or in opposition or square aspect to it, they will die, torn by dogs, and without children.

13. Those who have the ascendant in the 30th degree of Gemini with the Moon in that degree will be noble and famous but will die in early youth. If the ascendant is in the first line of Gemini and Mars is in that place, they will be attacked by wild beasts or serpents and lose a foot or a leg.

## XXII

### CANCER

1. Those who have the ascendant between the eyes of Cancer will be blind or one-eyed. Those who have it in the first degree of Cancer, if the Moon is in that degree, will be well-born men of affairs; if Saturn is in aspect they will be sailors, fishermen, inn-keepers or shop-keepers and the like, but always low-class. Those who have it in the second degree of Cancer will be extremely noble and powerful, and through violence and greed will possess the goods of others. They will travel endless journeys but will die suddenly.

2. Those who have the ascendant in the third degree of Cancer will be hard-working businessmen, never settling in one place. Those who have it in the fourth degree always attack their enemies in every way and are superior in every contest. Those who have the ascendant in the fifth

degree of Cancer will have their eyes wounded by small stones. If in the sixth degree they will be cross-eyed.

3. Those who have the ascendant in the seventh degree of Cancer will have lumps on their heads. If the Moon is moving toward the ascendant they will be clever but irreligious. But if the Moon and Mars are both in aspect to the ascendant, they will be aggressive with cruel ferocity. These men are either crucified or punished by some other public sentence.

4. The ascendant in the eighth degree of Cancer makes the natives blind. This degree is between the eyes of Cancer. In the fourth degree is the *nebula* (cloud, of which we have often spoken). Those who have the ascendant in the ninth degree will be sailors or pilots who steer ships through every type of sea with their skill. Those who have it in the tenth degree will fill every office with success . . . .
[The eleventh through the 24th degrees of Cancer are missing.]

5. Those who are born in the 25th degree of Cancer will attain every good fortune if the Moon is present or in aspect. But these men are guilty of adultery; their adolescence is praiseworthy but their later life is scandalous. The same is indicated for women with this chart.

## XXIII

### LEO

1. Those who have the ascendant in the first degree of Leo will be pimps with loud and filthy mouths. This is true of all degrees which are in the mouth of Leo. Those who have the ascendant in the second degree of Leo will be powerful kings. But whenever Mars or Saturn come to that space, they arouse danger of war. In this degree is the bright star we spoke of before.

2. Whoever has the ascendant in the third degree of Leo will be king of a double kingdom, dominating many provinces by his courage. In this degree the same bright star shows his influence. He who has the ascendant in the fourth degree of Leo will be a hunter. In the fifth he will be master or oiler of athletes.[101] The one who has the ascendant in the sixth degree of Leo will be born an athlete.

3. Whoever has the ascendant in the seventh degree of Leo will be a writer of hymns. In the eighth he will be famous for some skill or art if benefic planets are in aspect; but if malefic are in aspect he will be a pervert or pantomimist. Women with this chart will sell their modesty as prostitutes. Those who have the ascendant in the ninth degree of Leo will be midwives and raise another's children. If the waxing Moon is on the ascendant and benefic planets are in aspect, they will raise the sons of kings or powerful men. He who has the ascendant in the tenth degree of Leo will be a noble leader or a bowman. If Mars is in aspect to the Moon and the ascendant, he will be a gladiator . . . .
[The eleventh to the 30th degrees of Leo are missing.]

## XXIV

## VIRGO

1. Whoever has the ascendant in the first degree of Virgo will be conspicuous for his high position, provided the Moon is full or is in favorable aspect. He will become a friend of a king or queen for his literary qualities and will have many in his power. But if Mars is in aspect he will be a male prostitute and he will die in humid places. Those who have the ascendant in the second to the sixth degree of Virgo will be priests, prophets, or *haruspices,* conspicuous for high position.

2. Those who have the ascendant in the seventh degree of Virgo, together with a waxing Moon or one located on the ascendant, will be priests or *haruspices;* they will be powerful and always overcome their adversaries with their authority. But if Jupiter and Mars are in aspect to this spot, they will be generals who lead armies against the barbarians and die on the expedition. If Mercury is in aspect they will be in charge of treasures or be money-lenders.

3. But whenever Saturn approaches this spot they will be in great poverty. If Jupiter alone is in this degree, all kinds of good fortune are indicated. If the waxing Moon is in aspect to Jupiter, the natives become fast friends of the powerful through their own merits and their good looks. But if Venus is in that place she will make prostitutes of women. If Spica, the star, has the ascendant under her, the natives will be successful millers. But if the ascendant is next to Spica, they will be miserable paupers.

4. Those who have the ascendant in the eighth degree of Virgo, that is, in Spica itself, will be religious and just, conspicuous for their magnificent office, immensely wealthy, and rejoicing in many offspring. They die of old age. Those who have it in the ninth degree will be fighters who win wreaths and prizes in all contests. In the tenth degree they will be bandits always filled with unbridled greed.

5. Whoever has the ascendant in the eleventh degree of Virgo will gain fame and honor as an athlete, will be rich, and the husband of a wealthy woman; but he will die a violent death. With the ascendant in the twelfth degree he will be religious, just, and in high position. He will be a prophet, priest, or a ruler of great temples, states, or provinces. Often he will be in charge of public courts. But he will have great grief from misfortunes of children.

6. Those who have the ascendant in the 13th degree of Virgo will be lute players or hymn-writers. If in the 14th, they will also be musicians; if in the 15th, they will be gentlemen of fashion and will seek the bed of virgins. They will have an affliction of the hip and be disturbed by malignant humors, together with dried blood. Those who have the ascendant in the 16th degree will carry on important affairs but will die a violent death.

7. Whoever has the ascendant in the 17th degree of Virgo will be a gladiator assigned to public games. If in the 18th degree, they will be important priests, learned friends of kings, and always loved by women. But if Mars is in that spot or on the descendant, the natives will be punished by public death for the sake of women.

8. Whoever has the ascendant in the 19th degree of Virgo will be an architect, a builder of walls, or a worker in marble. In the 20th degree he will be a lute-player or singer of sweet songs. These men become clients of patrons who are always providing flattery for themselves through their attendants. Those who have the ascendant in the 21st degree of Virgo, that is, in the toe, will be involved in important affairs. Some will have courts entrusted to them or be friends of judges . . . .

[The 22nd to the 29th degrees of Virgo are missing.]

Whoever has the ascendant in the 30th degree of Virgo, that is, in the last line, will be tempted by a demon. But if Mars is in that degree of the descendant he will be captured by pirates and killed at sea.

## XXV

### LIBRA

1. Whoever has the ascendant in the first degree of Libra will be handsome, charming, and lovable. If Saturn is in that degree he will be unblemished in every part of the body. There are many stars in the second degree of Libra, some masculine, some feminine. Whoever has the ascendant in masculine stars will be noble and a writer of hymns to whom the secrets of the gods are entrusted. But if the ascendant is in feminine stars, he will be a male prostitute always conspicuous for charm and sophistication.

2. Those who have the ascendant in the third degree of Libra will be just, long-lived priests. In the fourth degree they will be lute-players or singers. In the fifth degree they will be immensely rich but always involved in lawsuits. In the sixth degree they will be wealthy and carry on great affairs.

3. Those who have the ascendant in the seventh degree of Libra will be captured by pirates and die a cruel death or will be torn by wild beasts, if Mars is found in that degree. Those who have the ascendant in the eighth degree will be bath attendants or common servants. If in the ninth degree they will be famous players at dice. This degree also produces skilled writers.

4. Those who have the ascendant in the tenth degree of Libra will be male prostitutes, objects of public scandal. In women's charts they will be prostitutes. Those who have it in the eleventh degree will die of dropsy. In the twelfth they will be famous and experienced in law courts. In the 13th degree they will be pious and just, in charge of public courts, friends of

kings. They will die of old age.

5. Whoever has the ascendant in the 14th degree of Libra will be a brilliant sculptor who makes images of the gods. The one who has it in the 15th degree will be a short-lived queen, without offspring, who will die a violent death. The 16th will produce a businessman who carries on foreign trade.

6. Whoever has the ascendant in the 17th degree of Libra, that is, in the northern degree, if the full Moon, well-located, is moving toward benefic planets, will become a writer or scribe of kings; he will have a high position and be entrusted with the duties of dictating. He who has the ascendant in the 18th degree will be crucified by command of the emperor or will be tortured or hanged in the presence of the emperor, but only when Mars is found in that degree.

7. Whoever has the ascendant in the 19th degree of Libra will be captured in a sudden attack of the enemy. Those who have it in the 20th degree, that is, in the northern part, will be famous physicians. But if Mars is in that degree they will die in a fall from a height and have no children. If the ascendant is in the 21st degree, they will be short-lived geometers.

8. Those who have the ascendant in the 22nd degree of Libra will die in a fall from a height if Mars is in that degree. If in the 23rd degree, they will be kings or queens. They die by the sword and leave many children. In the 24th they will be businessmen carrying on foreign trade in ships. But if Mars is in that degree or on the descendant, they will be captured by pirates and killed.

9. Whoever has the ascendant in the 25th degree of Libra will be a worker in iron or other metals. In the 26th degree he will be a weaver or textile worker given to fits of insanity. Whoever has it in the 27th degree will be a painter or a maker of incense. Those who have it in the 28th degree will be wealthy priests.

10. Those who have the ascendant in the 29th degree of Libra will be pious, just, benevolent, adorned with every virtue. Those who have it in the 30th degree will be verbose liars, inflated with fluent speech. If benefic planets are located in that degree they will be great physicians who travel much and die a violent death. Those who have the ascendant in Boötes will be divine astrologers, skilled in the Chaldean art.

## XXVI

### SCORPIO

1. Whoever has the ascendant in the first degree of Scorpio will be a magician who lessens hidden pains by the power of words. Whoever has it in the second degree will be debased and often a reputed prostitute. Those who have it in the third degree will be dwarves, hunchbacks, or clowns. In the fourth degree they will be hunchbacks assigned to the pleasure of kings or emperors.

2. Those who have the ascendant in the fifth degree of Scorpio will be noble, pious, and just, and have distinguished friends. They will have many children. They will have their livelihood from the office of magistrate or interpreter; or will be scribes of kings. Those who have the ascendant in the sixth degree will be wealthy priests and will have many children. But often they will die from the anger of kings.

3. Whoever has the ascendant in the seventh degree of Scorpio will die from the attacks of wild beasts. In the eighth degree they will be snake charmers. They will die from an asp or a viper. Whoever has the ascendant in the ninth degree of Scorpio will be a gardener. In the tenth he will die at an early age. In the eleventh he will be an inspired priest giving responses to those who ask for them.

4. Whoever has the ascendant in the twelfth degree of Scorpio will be a temple servant or involved in some way in sacred duties. If he has it in the 13th degree, if the Moon is on any angle, he will be an honored judge, debating the opinions of other judges, holding power of life and death.

5. But they hold this power only between the ages of 30 and 35. They will have wives and children. In their 27th, 42nd, and 58th years they will have difficulties and dangers. They will have such dangers in the 66th year that they will die. They will have some kind of illness but will die suddenly from water or an iron weapon . . . .
[The 14th and 15th degrees of Scorpio are missing.]

6. Those who have the ascendant in the 16th degree of Scorpio will be millers. But if the Moon is in the sign of a bright star they will be judges with great power. If, however, Mars is in dejected houses they will be spies beheaded by the sword. Those who have the ascendant in the 17th degree will be goldsmiths, jewelers, or workers in gold-leaf.

7. Those who have the ascendant in the 18th degree of Scorpio will be eaten by wild beasts. In the 19th degree, if the Moon is favorably located, they will attain high position and good fortune and have the greatest power of life and death. But if Jupiter is in aspect in any way to the ascendant their power will be almost imperial.

8. They will be elated by too much good fortune and be involved in plots to gain imperial power; will be bold and rash and will die by fire, and will leave surviving sons.

9. Whoever has the ascendant in the 21st degree of Scorpio in the first right foot of Scorpio will be a fisherman, but one who collects sponges. The one who has it in the second foot will die from another beast or quadruped. Whoever has the ascendant in the third foot will be a gardener; in the fourth foot he will be a pervert; if a woman, a prostitute.

10. Whoever has the ascendant in the 22nd degree of Scorpio in the first left foot will be a gardener; if it is in the second left foot he will die from wild beasts; in the third foot he will be a barber; in the fourth foot he will be killed by pirates or eaten by beasts in wet places. Whoever has the ascendant in the 23rd degree of Scorpio, if the Moon, Venus, and Mars

are in that degree, will be rich, powerful, and long-lived; his honors will increase late in life. He will also have many offspring.

11. Those who have the ascendant in the 24th degree of Scorpio will kill their brothers from greed and homicidal rage, but they themselves will die a violent death. Those who have it in the 25th degree, if Mars is in that degree or opposition or square aspect to it, will be burned by fire.

12. Those who have the ascendant in the 26th degree of Scorpio will be orators, lawyers, or physicians ennobled by their talents in their professions. With influence of benefic planets, legations of the fatherland will be entrusted to them. But they will die from offense to the king. Those who have the ascendant in the 27th degree, if Venus and Jupiter are present, will be wealthy, just, lovable, long-lived, and loved by many women. In process of time they achieve increases in fortune. They will attain great fame and glory in their own country.

13. Those who have the ascendant in the 28th degree of Scorpio will be squint-eyed but their eyes otherwise will be beautiful. They will be careless in their habits. If Mars is in that degree they will suffer hemorrhages. Some will have elephantiasis, others will be mad. Those who have the ascendant in the 29th degree will be learned lawyers. If a benefic planet is found in that degree, they will be sent as ambassadors to an emperor and will accomplish everything entrusted to them. They will gain high rewards but will have an affliction in an important part of the body.

14. Those who have the ascendant in the 30th degree of Scorpio will be snake-charmers, poisoners, and killers of men; they sell poisons to kill men. They will be malevolent liars. But if Mars is found in that degree they will be hunters and die a violent death. Next to Scorpio on the right side are Ofiuchus and Vulpes (the Fox), on the left side Cynocefalus (the Dog's Head) and Ara. Those who are born in Ofiuchus will be daring and be possessed by a god; they will have divine knowledge of the future.

15. Those who are born in Vulpes will be clever, forgers of documents; but they will make a living from cultivation of the soil. If Saturn is in that place they will be guardians of monuments. These will die through trickery. Those who are born in Cynocefalus will be sickly, short-lived, and without children. Those who are born in Ara will be priests who make a living from sacrifices, but they also are perjurers and die an evil death.

## XXVII

### SAGITTARIUS

1. Whoever has the ascendant in the first degree of Sagittarius will be noble, pious, just, and attain the highest rank of glory. If a benefic planet is found in that degree they will be kings or officials near the king; they will fulfill all their duties successfully. Those who have the ascendant in the second degree will be bad-tempered sacrilegious perjurers. Those who have it in the third will lose an eye in some way.

2. Those who have the ascendant in the fourth degree of Sagittarius will be guardians of tombs. In the fifth degree they will be impure and unchaste and wretched objects of scandal. In the sixth degree they will be bow-legged, have varicose veins, and die a violent death. Those who have the ascendant in the seventh degree will be considered pious and just and will be entrusted with judgeships, such that they pass on the opinions of other judges.

3. Those who have the ascendant in the eighth degree of Sagittarius, if Jupiter is found in that degree, will be long-lived, pious, and the first among their relatives to have children. They will be interpreters for kings or master scribes. In process of time good fortune will come to them and they will die a good death. Those who have the ascendant in the ninth degree of Sagittarius will be inspired astrologers, worshippers of the gods. In the tenth degree they will be athletes who fight in full armor.

4. Whoever has the ascendant in the eleventh degree of Sagittarius will die in war. If in the twelfth degree he will be rash, involved in dangers, attracted to every crime. Whoever has the ascendant in the 13th degree of Sagittarius will kill a parent in a fit of parricidal fury and will himself die a violent death. If in the 14th degree, he will be a musician with a weakness of the eyes.

5. Whoever has the ascendant in the 15th degree will also die in war. In the 16th, if Mars is found in that degree, he will be a mechanic who makes engines of war, and will die from a lance; if a woman, she will die in childbirth. Whoever has the ascendant in the 17th degree will be an athlete; if Mars is in aspect, he will be a hunter; if Jupiter, a horse-breeder.

6. Whoever has the ascendant in the 18th degree of Sagittarius will be a malevolent thief and perjurer; he will die a violent death without children. Whoever has it in the 19th degree will be a successful athlete, also without children. In the 20th degree he will be a hunchback, a cripple, or a clown; in the 21st degree he will be fond of eating and will be prejudiced against foreign habits.

7. Those who have the ascendant in the 22nd degree of Sagittarius, if Jupiter is in that degree, will be great and powerful, possessing infinite territory; armies, both foot and horse, will be entrusted to their command, often navies also. They will fight in many wars, conquer barbarians, restore some states and destroy others. They will have wives and children but their wives will have afflictions and scars in important parts of the body. They will die fighting in foreign countries. Those who have the ascendant in the 23rd degree of Sagittarius will die in a desert or hidden places from wild beasts.

8. Whoever has the ascendant in the 24th degree of Sagittarius will be a trainer of horses or a charioteer. If Jupiter is in that degree he will be a royal mule-trainer or driver and gain great glory from his profession. If Mars is present he will die a violent death. Whoever has the ascendant in the 25th degree will be an unsteady alcoholic, especially if Mars is in that

degree. But if Venus is in aspect he will be a pervert ruined by scandal; if a woman she will be a prostitute.

9. Those who have the ascendant in the 26th degree of Sagittarius will be polluted by vice; women will be shrews or prostitutes. If in the 27th degree they will die in desert places. But if Mars is found there they will be unfortunate, short-lived, and die of pestilence.

10. Whoever has the ascendant in the 28th degree of Sagittarius will be a hard-working muledriver. In the 29th degree he will be a hunchback, a cripple, or a captive. In the 30th degree he will be consumptive and an envious, unpleasant character; his death will come from wild beasts. If Mars is in that degree he will be short-lived and without children.

11. If the ascendant is found in the last line of Sagittarius, that is, in the tail, the natives will be potters. If the ascendant is below the tail they will be one-eyed and squinting but fast couriers, always in another's power, and have an affliction of the blood. They will have a pleasant appearance and be killed by quadrupeds.

12. The Ship Argo rises on the right side of Sagittarius; Canis, the Dog, rises on the left. Whoever has his ascendant in the Ship will be a ship-owner, a pilot, or be a businessman who trades with the East. If Mars is in aspect to that place, he will be killed by pirates returning to the East. Whoever has the ascendant in the Dog will be fond of noisy litigation. If Mercury is found in that place, he will be a distinguished lawyer and a friend of kings. Whoever has the ascendant in the mouth of the Dog will have a depraved life and a foul mouth but he will be proud of his fluent speech.

## XXVIII

## CAPRICORN

1. Whoever has the ascendant in the first degree of Capricorn will be a king or emperor. Those who have it in the second degree will be army doctors, learned in military tactics, entrusted with the arrangement of battles. They will die a violent death. Those who have it in the third degree of Capricorn, if Mars is in that degree with the Moon, will have great power of the sword, but they will exercise their power severely and cruelly. They will be clever, bold, cruel, and kill many men. They will lead armies and will die in battle.

2. Those who have the ascendant in the fourth degree of Capricorn, if Mercury is found in that degree, will be musicians or skilled artisans but they will pursue the love of women with monstrous appetites. They will be careless, but if the Moon is well placed they will be well-known scribes, entrusted with important affairs. They will be wealthy, just, pious, and will die of old age. Those who have the ascendant in the fifth degree will be degenerate and addicted to every vice.

3. Those who have the ascendant in the sixth degree of Capricorn will

have elephantiasis. If in the seventh degree they will be patient artisans, known for the excellence of their work, friends of kings. Also they may be physicians.

4. Those who have the ascendant in the eighth degree of Capricorn will hold the highest positions if Venus is found in that degree. If the Moon is well located, they will carry on much important business and some will be in charge of public taxes. Those who have it in the ninth degree, if Mars is found there, will die an early death. If Mercury is in aspect, they will be wealthy money-lenders and will die because of money.

5. Those who have the ascendant in the tenth degree of Capricorn, if Mars is in that degree, will be adulterers but have grace and personal charm. They corrupt their friends' wives but are never detected in their crimes. They earn a great income from some skill but they are allotted wives who are known for adultery. They die a sudden death. Those who have the ascendant in the eleventh degree will be goldsmiths; in the twelfth, athletes who die a violent death.

6. Those who have the ascendant in the 13th degree of Capricorn, if Mars is found in that degree, will approach all crimes for the sake of profit. They will be snake-charmers who raise serpents for their poison, which they sell. Through them many will die. They will be perjurers, adulterers, or pimps. They will be able to sing with pleasant voices, deceive all men with pretended simplicity, but they are really noisy and foul-mouthed and have no pleasure in wives or children. In time they will be lame in the feet. But they sometimes make a living from commerce or from public office.

7. Those who have the ascendant in the 14th degree of Capricorn will be ministers of kings, entrusted with great affairs, if Jupiter or Venus is found in that degree. They will be leaders among their own people but will be careless and fond of banquets. But if Mercury is found in that place they will have even higher positions and attain the friendship of kings. Those who have the ascendant in the 15th degree will be hunchbacks, cripples, or clowns.

8. Those who have the ascendant in the 16th degree of Capricorn will have six fingers and be hunchbacked. Whoever has the ascendant in conjunction with the spine and the neck of Capricorn will be long-lived, friends of kings, and parents of noble children, if Mars is present and the Moon favorable. But they will die a violent death. Whoever has the ascendant in the 17th degree will die of a puncture of the spine.

9. Whoever has it in the 18th degree will kill his wife and be punished by the court if Mars, Venus, and Mercury are in that same sign or in that degree. Whoever has the ascendant in the 19th degree will be a scribe of kings if Mercury is found in that degree. He will die in humid places or be eaten by beasts.

10. Whoever has the ascendant in the 20th degree of Capricorn will be devoted to the study of records and the law. In the 21st degree he will be a

friend of kings, much rewarded from the imperial largesse, beloved by the people, quick to anger, indulging his anger with the great force of his power. (But his position will only be conferred on him in middle life.) Misfortune will come to him from accidents to children. He will die a suicide. . . .
[The 22nd and 23rd degrees of Capricorn are missing.]

11′. Those who have the ascendant in the 24th degree of Capricorn will be sluggish in mind and senses, often threatened by insanity. In the 25th degree they will die consumed by beasts. In the 26th degree they will be pantomimists, outstanding for grace and charm. In the 27th degree they will be just men, powerful friends of kings, judges who pass on the decisions of other judges. But great grief will come to them from the misfortunes of children.

12. Whoever has the ascendant in the 29th degree of Capricorn will be a cruel tyrant, armed for every crime, involved in dangers, and rash, dealing death to multitudes by his own hand. . . .
[The 28th and 30th degrees of Capricorn are missing.]

## XXIX

### AQUARIUS

1. Whoever has the ascendant in the first degree of Aquarius will be a king—great, famous, long-lived, possessing the entire earth, if Jupiter and Saturn are found in that degree, or if they aspect the ascendant in trine, and if the Moon is well located. The greatest powers are indicated for him over a period of time, but he will die in water. Whoever has the ascendant in the second degree of Aquarius will have a skill which has to do with painting or ornamentation; he will die leaving surviving sons.

2. Whoever has the ascendant in the third degree of Aquarius will be great and powerful and possess much land if Jupiter is in that degree or in any aspect to the ascendant. But he will lose his possessions and gain great income through his own efforts. He will make war on his own people and be guilty of every crime of cruelty, rejoicing in the slaughter of many men. He will have sons from a slave woman but will lose them at an early age.

3. He will never be sad but will be generally disliked, and will alienate everyone so that all his friends will avoid him. He will be gluttonous, eat too much, and hold much land. In process of time he will obtain high position. But when he has entered the threshold of old age he will cultivate his land with a weakened body. Whoever has the ascendant in the fourth degree of Aquarius will be just, a worshipper of the gods, a judge handing down decision on the opinions of others. But he will die a violent death.

4. Whoever has the ascendant in the fifth degree of Aquarius will hang himself. In the sixth he will lead a wretched life drawing water. He

will become a well-born athlete. . . .

[The seventh degree of Aquarius is missing.]

Those who have the ascendant in the eighth degree of Aquarius, if Venus is in aspect in any way, will be long-lived, wealthy, and just. They will be prosperous in old age and will die with children surviving.

5. Whoever has the ascendant in the ninth degree of Aquarius will be a builder, a sculptor, or an architect. In the tenth degree if Mars is in aspect he will be a bath attendant and will die at an early age. If in the eleventh, he will die in watery places. If the ascendant is on the vertex of the urn they will be physicians. If Saturn is in any aspect they will be corpse-washers or undertakers, entrusted with the duties of burial.

6. Whoever has the ascendant in the twelfth degree of Aquarius will be a fisherman making his living from the sea. In the 13th degree they will be gardeners or cleaners of sewers. If Mars is in aspect they will be bath attendants, if Saturn, drawers of water. Those who have the ascendant in the 14th degree, if Mars is in aspect, will be hard-working divers or sailors. In the 15th degree they will be workers at laborious tasks living in watery or humid places.

7. Whoever has the ascendant in the 16th degree of Aquarius will be a degenerate pervert who exercises his vices secretly. In the 17th degree, if Mars is in any aspect, he will die from the stroke of a lance . . . [The 18th degree of Aquarius is missing.]

8. Whoever has the ascendant in the 19th degree of Aquarius will have pains in the lungs. In the 20th degree he will die of dropsy. In the 21st he will be a goldsmith. Whoever has the ascendant in the 22nd degree of Aquarius will be beautiful of face and figure, pleasing in body, but will die in early life. Whoever has the ascendant in the 23rd degree will be a wealthy painter.

9. Whoever has the ascendant in the 24th degree of Aquarius if Jupiter is in any aspect will be handsome with a large body, pleasing, and lovable. If Venus is in any aspect he will be a friend of the king, loved for the beauty of his body, but he will die young. Those who have the ascendant in the 25th degree will be sterile, without children, but always burning with abnormal sexual desires.

10. Those who have the ascendant in the 26th degree of Aquarius will make a living from cultivation of the soil or herbs but will be oppressed by continual toil. They will be long-lived and useless in old age. Those who have the ascendant in the 27th degree will be temple servants; they serve in temples and sing hymns in sacred rituals.

11. Whoever has the ascendant in the 28th degree of Aquarius will be gouty. In the 29th degree he will be devoured by beasts in desert places. If Mars is found in that place or in conjunction, he will be lamed falling off a cliff; if Saturn is in aspect, he will die from the fall.

12. Those who have the ascendant in the 30th degree of Aquarius, if Saturn is in any aspect to the Moon, will be long-lived and in process of

time obtain a high position. Some will cross the great sea for commerce. They will be without children of their own and will have stepchildren in their place.

13. Outside of the degrees of Sagittarius rise Falcis (the Sickle), Lupus (the Wolf), Aquarius Minor, and Ara (the Altar). Whoever has the ascendant in Falcis will be a plowman who cultivates the soil and reaps a large harvest. Whoever has it in the mouth of the Wolf will be a dancer; if Mars is in aspect, he will be eaten by dogs. Those who have the ascendant in the Wolf itself will be tricky thieves, cruel and homicidal, who persecute strangers with cruel ferocity. They themselves will die a violent death and be thrown out unburied. Those who have the ascendant in the left foot of the Wolf, if Mars is in aspect, will be attacked by bandits and dislocate their feet. If on the right foot of the Wolf, they will go mad and die at an early age.

14. Whoever has the ascendant in the head of Aquarius Minor will have much experience in desert places and will often lose his way on journeys in such spots. If the ascendant is on the right of Aquarius Minor, they will be masters of the horse. If benefic planets are in aspect, they will be charioteers or mule-drivers for the king. Whoever has the ascendant in the belly of Aquarius Minor will be a gardener or a hard-working money-lender; he will die a violent death. If on the right foot, he will die in watery or humid places.

15. Those who have the ascendant in Ara will make a living from sacrifices; they will die of burning. If anyone has the ascendant in the pouring water of Aquarius, he will be rich in early life and an owner of property, but will waste his paternal inheritance. He will be generous but many will be ungrateful to him. Over a period of time he will attain a great increase in income and position and will see all his enemies subjugated in every way.

## XXX

## PISCES

1. Whoever has the ascendant in the first degree of Pisces will be a diligent composer and be granted a living from royal resources. He will have children from the seduction of sisters or relatives. Whoever has the ascendant in the second degree of Pisces will be shrill, suspicious, and jealous. In the third degree he will be involved in impure vices, a prostitute whose life is always a public scandal.

2. Whoever has the ascendant in the fourth degree of Pisces will have the effeminate habits of a pervert. If it is a woman she will prostitute her body. In the fifth degree the native will be rich, noble, long-lived, and have a living from some skill, if Mercury and Venus are in aspect in any way. He will be a friend of the king, live to an old age, and die leaving surviving children.

3. Whoever has the ascendant in the sixth degree of Pisces will die eaten by wild beasts. In the seventh degree, if Mars is found in that degree, he will be eaten either by beasts or in the water by fish. In the eighth or ninth degree if Mars and Venus are present, they will be just, long-lived, pious, and involved in literary activities. They will be scribes and familiars of kings and will die leaving surviving children.

4. Whoever has the ascendant in the tenth degree of Pisces, if the Moon is well-placed and Venus on the ascendant, will be great, powerful, well-known to all, and a friend of kings; he travels over many lands and sails great seas; naval commands will be entrusted to him. He will be a victor in battle, have great pleasure in love; he will be just and pious but always impatient with desire around women; demanding and obtaining many things. He will die from the anger of the king. Whoever has the ascendant in the eleventh degree of Pisces will be castrated by beasts in desert or humid places or will die a violent death in early youth, leaving no children.

5. Whoever has the ascendant in the twelfth degree of Pisces will be mad and a fisherman, and die in early life. In the 13th degree, if Venus and Jupiter are present, he will have his livelihood from some skill and be rich and famous. If Mercury is in any aspect he will be a businessman dealing in paints, rich and fortunate. He will die leaving surviving children.

6. Those who have the ascendant in the 14th degree of Pisces will attain high position. They will die in humid or watery places from pirates. Those who have it in the 15th degree, if Mars is present, will travel through the deserts of the earth and sail unknown seas. They will be tossed about much of their life on ships. The one who has the ascendant in the 16th degree of Pisces will be rich and long-lived, first among his relatives.

7. Those who have it in the 17th degree will be singers of sweet songs. If Mars is found in that degree they will hang themselves. Whoever has the ascendant in the 18th degree of Pisces will be bold, fond of food, and will live to an old age. In the 19th degree he will be an orator or a lawyer, endowed with fluent speech. If a benefic planet is in aspect, he will be in the royal house, giving or controlling everything soberly, serious in habit, and always honest.

8. Those who have the ascendant in the 20th degree of Pisces will die strangled in early life. In the 21st degree they will be fishermen laboriously bringing up sponges and will die in early life. In the 22nd degree they will wander through many lands and peoples. If Mars is in aspect they will be made captive in early life.

9. Whoever has the ascendant in the 23rd degree of Pisces will be a bird-catcher making his living from birds. In the 24th degree he will die in the sea. In the 25th degree he will be a goldsmith, an engraver, or a painter. In the 26th degree, if Mars and Saturn are in aspect, they will be

bath attendants, common servants, or sailors; they will be unfortunate and will die a violent death. They will have the duties of caring for some kind of musical instrument.

10. Whoever has the ascendant in the 27th degree of Pisces will be a fugitive, wandering through many lands. He will die from a wound in the spine. Whoever has the ascendant in the 28th degree of Pisces will be torn to pieces by beasts or die in watery places if Mars is found in that degree. If Jupiter and Venus are in the 29th degree and the Moon well located, the native who has the ascendant in that degree will be wealthy and fortunate all his life. He will die at his appointed time.

11. Whoever has the ascendant in the 30th degree of Pisces will have a life at sea and will always be involved in toilsome occupations. If Mars is in aspect, he will be a snake-charmer and magician, and die a violent death. Whoever has the ascendant in the tail, that is, in the line which divides Pisces from Aries, if Mars is on the line, will be a castrate who has lost his virility.

12. To the north of Pisces rise Cervus (the Deer) and Lepus (the Hare), in the East Cetus, that is, the Sea Beast. Whoever has the ascendant in the horns of the Deer will lead armies, will fight fiercely, and die in battle if Mars is in that degree. Those who have the ascendant in the mouth of the Deer will die a violent death. Whoever has it in the feet of the Deer will wander much and die violently.

13. Those who have the ascendant in Lepus will be experienced helmsmen. Those who have it in the tail of Cetus will be torn by beasts if Mars is in that degree. Those who have it in the second degree of Cetus, if Venus and Mercury are in aspect, will be subject to powerful men and gain great prosperity from this relationship. Some will be slaves who arrive at high position through their good character. Those who have the ascendant in the third degree of Cetus will sail to many lands. If Mars is in that degree, they will be killed by pirates.

## XXXI

### [BRIGHT STARS]

1. We said in the sixth book that there are many bright stars[102] in many signs shining with royal majesty. I shall explain what is indicated by the ascendant in those degrees in which the bright stars are found.

2. A bright star is in the eleventh degree of Aries. Whoever has the ascendant in this star, if Jupiter is with it or in trine aspect to it, will be a great, powerful leader, a friend of kings, holding important land. He will die at the appointed time.

3. There is a bright star in the horns of Taurus. Whoever has the ascendant in the horns of Taurus will be a king or general. The one who has it in the right horn will be a great leader of naval and infantry forces,

fearsome and hard-working, who frees many states from the sieges of war. This man will be an only child and will have no children of his own. Titles and statues will be decreed to him by the people, but afterwards he will die from having offended kings. The sixth book shows you in what star of Taurus these things are decreed.

4. A limpid star is found in the second degree of Leo. Whoever has the ascendant in this star will be a powerful king holding a double kingdom, but whenever Mars and Saturn approach that star great wars are stirred up.

5. A bright star is in the 13th degree of Scorpio. If the Moon is in that degree the native will be great and powerful, entrusted with a large part of the empire, and will hold the power of life and death.

6. In the 19th degree of Scorpio there is a bright star. Whoever has the ascendant in that degree will be powerful if the Moon is well located. If Jupiter is in favorable aspect he will be next to the king in honors; he will be of outstanding character, but careless. Death will come to him from the king's anger.

7. There are limpid stars in the 22nd degree of Sagittarius. Whoever has the ascendant in these stars, if Jupiter is with them, will be great and powerful and hold much land; he will lead armies both horse and foot; he will also be in control of the imperial navy. He will be a victor in battles and conquer the barbarians. He will restore some states and overthrow others, but he will have a wife with an affliction in her genitals. He will die in battle but will leave surviving children.

8. A bright star is in the third degree of Capricorn. If Mars is in that sign and the Moon is well placed, the native who has that star on the ascendant will be great and powerful, holding the power of life and death. But he will be cruel, rejoicing in slaughter, and will die in war.

9. In the first degree of Aquarius is a bright star. Whoever has that star on his ascendant, if Mars and Saturn are in favorable aspect and the Moon well located, will be a great king, glorious, just, pious, and long-lived; as life goes on the greatest possible powers are conferred on him.

10. A bright star is in the tenth degree of Pisces, that is, in the East. If Venus is in that star on the ascendant and the Moon well located, whoever has that star on his ascendant will be great and powerful, a familiar of kings; he will travel many lands and sail the great sea. He will lead navies, be a victor in battles; will be beloved by all, be just and pious. But he will be involved in love affairs with many women. He will be outstanding in many areas and will always obtain his desires. He will die from the anger of the king.

## XXXII

## [NECESSITY OF ALL DATA]

1. The doctrine of the *Sphaera Barbarica* teaches these things about the

individual degrees. But it is not able to explain the chart entirely unless all the data are brought together, the combinations and aspects of the stars compared as you remember we have often said. For the cold of some stars is opposed to the fire of others, the ice of cold is tempered with the burning heat, and a mixture of temperaments is accomplished.

2. Therefore the whole data must be collected concerning the power of the houses and the planets. For a planet suffers loss of its own power when it is in dejected houses or in its debility, and it is allotted the greatest power of forecasting when it gains authority, either from the house or the exaltation. Planets rejoice, as we have often said, in the first place when they are located in their exaltation, and secondly in their own terms, thirdly in their own houses.

3. Therefore when all these data have been meticulously collected we must inspect the whole body of the chart, so that judging the fates of men from the power of all the planets, we can interpret in true propositions whatever has been decreed.

## XXXIII

### [CONCLUSION]

1. Receive now, my dear Mavortius, what we promised you with the utmost mental trepidation: seven books composed in the number of the seven planets. For the first book contained only the defense of the theory. In the other books we translated for the Romans the theory of the new discipline.

2. It is for you to remember the sanctity of your oath: guard these books with a pure mind and soul and do not reveal this science to inexperienced ears or sacrilegious minds. The nature of the divine prefers to be hidden in diverse coverings; access to it should not be easy nor its majesty open to all.

3. This is what we would like to accomplish with our book, that it should be open to the religious but denied to the profane. In this way we will not pollute the revered theories of the ancients by publishing them for the sacrilegious. Therefore hand this book down to your sons, since you have brought them up from early years in the practice of virtue; give it to your friends, but only those who are closest to you, whom you know follow virtuous examples.

4. It is enough for us that for you alone we have produced this book which you ordered. You alone as true interpretor, you as faithful guardian, you as pious high-priest will be able to adorn with your virtues this work which we have prepared with sleepless diligence, with toil of mind as well as of body, with the greatest anxiety and fear.

## Book I

1. Firmicus's patron, Quintus Flavius Maesius Lollianus Egnatius, surnamed Mavortius, held a series of high offices in the fourth century, as noted by a number of inscriptions. He is mentioned twice by the late fourth-century historian Ammianus Marcellinus.

2. A lake near Mt. Aetna, now known as Lago Naftia or Lago die Palici; in ancient times it had two spectacular geysers which were worshipped as brothers apparently from the early Bronze Age. It is mentioned by a wide range of authors from Aeschylus to Ovid.

3. The famous Syracusan scientist constructed two models of the movements of the heavenly bodies (orreries) and wrote about his method of construction in a book now lost. The spheres were brought to Rome after the conquest of Sicily in the Punic wars (212). Cicero saw them and describes them in his *Republic*. Firmicus has led his introduction, under pretense of praising Lollianus, to the movements of the heavenly bodies and then to a description of his native land and its most distinguished citizen, also connected with the stars.

4. In Plato's *Republic* the nine spheres represent the fixed stars, the seven planets and the unmoving Earth. Cicero copied Plato in the end of his Republic, in the passage called the "Dream of Scipio." But Cicero and Firmicus after him were being literary, not scientific. For even Aristotle in *De Caelo* had distinguished something like 55 spheres. Firmicus must also have known the complicated system of Ptolemy. But this introduction bristles with literary allusions and serves, as was the style, for a display of his wide reading.

5. The earth as sphere was commonly divided into five zones, two polar, two temperate, one equatorial (Cf. Pliny, *N.H.* II, 68, 173 and Strabo, II, 23). Achilles Tatius (*Isaoge*, 29) attributed the five zones to five planets—Saturn and Mercury to the north and south polar, Jupiter and Venus to the north and south temperate, Mars to the torrid. These zones should not be confused with the "climates," ranging from five to twelve but usually numbering seven, which began to be distinguished as soon as it was known that there were differences in length of days in different latitudes.

6. The "Great Year" was a concept often described in ancient times, but especially by Stoics. It usually means the time when all the planets will return to their original places and would be marked by the destruction and renewal of the universe. Plato in the *Timaeus* has the Demiurge (the Creator) set the celestial machinery in motion for the first time, saying that the perfect number is that in which all the eight revolutions of the spheres will have accomplished their courses. There were many estimates of the length of the Great Year. Firmicus's number 1461 is the number of the "Sothic Year" in Egypt, starting from the rising of the star Sothis (Sirius) about the end of July, the beginning of the Egyptian year which ran for 365 days. The extra quarter day over a period of years threw off the entire calculation until it came round again in 1460 years, i.e., four times 365.

7. It was a tendency of Greek writers, growing stronger in Hellenistic and Roman times, to trace their lore back to the Ancient East, and thus writers on astrology traced their doctrine to Babylonian or Egyptian sources. There was a

semi-legendary basis for both. Chaldean star-lore (their observations go back to Hammurabi but horoscopes appear only in the fifth century B.C.) was supposedly transmitted to the Greeks by Berossos, a real author of the third century B.C. of a history of Babylon, and founder of a school for astrologers on the island of Cos, where his methods of observations were combined with Greek mathematics to form individual aspectual astrology. This new science was much practiced in Hellenistic Alexandria and therefore called Egyptian. The ancient Egyptians had a star-lore of their own, allotting small periods of the day and night to various divinities, but they did not have a natal astrology. The notion of *dekans* is probably from ancient Egypt. The most quoted handbook of astrology at Rome was a product of Hellenistic Egypt, probably of the second century B.C., but given the names of the Pharaoh Nechepso and his scribe, Petosiris.

8. The term *consul ordinarius* originally meant a regularly-elected (i.e., not appointed) consul. But in the time of Constantine there were many consuls, with much reduced duties, throughout the year, but only one at Rome appointed by the emperor. This was the *consul ordinarius* who gave his name to the year.

9. The bulk of Book I is concerned with refutations of well-known arguments against astrology and fatal determinism, which had taken strong root in Stoic philosophy, especially from the time of Posidonius (135–50 B.C.), and had thus become the object of attack by other schools: the New Academy, the Epicureans, Skeptics, and sometimes the Peripatetics. Most of the arguments appear to stem from a widely known attack by the New Academician Carneades (214–129) against the Stoic Chrysippus. Carneades left no written remains, but there are numerous references to his savage oratory against fatal determinism. He was followed by Cicero's teacher Panaetius, Philo of Alexandria, Favorinus, the Gallic orator of the second century A.D., Sextus Empericus ca. A.D. 200, and St. Augustine (354–430).

10. This term, meaning learning in general, first came to be used for the mathematical sciences, then for astrology.

11. Aristides, the fifth century Athenian statesman and soldier, was exiled in 482 B.C. by a vote of ostracism. The ballots were pottery sherds with names scratched on. Plutarch recounts (*Aristides,* VII, 5–6) that an illiterate peasant asked Aristides to mark his ballot "Aristides" for him, and that Aristides complied; this is one of the incidents contributing to his nickname of "the Just." Actual sherd ballots, some bearing the name of Aristides, have been recovered in the excavation of the Athenian Agora (cf. M. Lang, *The Athenian Citizen,* 1960, fig. 27).

12. Plotinus was the second-century founder of Neo-Platonism, the philosophical school most prevalent in the (pagan) third and fourth centuries. His life, written by his disciple Porphyry, does not contain the detailed account of Plotinus's illness which Firmicus describes. There may be a lost source, or Firmicus may be embroidering in his rhetorical style (Paul Henry, "Plotin et l'Occident," *Specilegium Sacrum,* Louvain, 1934).

13. This account of Sulla's career, a blood-curdling masterpiece, was formerly believed to have been written by the Roman historian Sallust (85–35 B.C.). Analysis of the language, however, suggests that it may have come from a lost epitome of Livy.

14. *Himarmene* is a Greek term also meaning what is fated. Firmicus uses the term for a school which accepted the control of Fate over birth and death, but left the

rest of human life to free will. Firmicus is the only Latin writer who uses the word in this way, although the philosophical position is well known. It is connected with the Middle Platonists and Maximos of Tyre, and with the author called "Pseudo-Plutarch" of a tract "Against Fate."

15. This section is similar to the end of an astrological poem of the first century A.D. by Manilius, a passage which was intended as a panegyric of Tiberius. The "Hymn to the Sun" is reminiscent of Cicero in the "Somnium Scipionis." From the time of the Emperor Aurelian (215–275 A.D.) Sol Invictus had been the recognized head of the Roman Pantheon and was addressed in terms taken over from the old religion.

## Book II

16. This writer has not been identified. The name might, however, be a corruption of Fonteius Capito (on the analogy of Navigius—Nigidius, Note 20), a member of the group of Nigidius and Varro who followed Antony to Egypt and who was known to have written on astrology.

17. See Index of Ancient Writers on Astrology.

18. Some have assumed that in mentioning Julius Caesar, Firmicus is referring to a book *de Astris* mentioned in Pliny, *N.H.* XVIII and Macrobius, *Saturnalia*, I, 16, 39. It is more generally agreed, however, that that work was an astral calendar put together by Caesar's Egyptian informant Sosigenes, who helped him with calendar reform. Firmicus is probably referring to the translation of Aratus's *Phaenomena* by Germanicus Caesar (Tiberius's nephew), especially since he follows with a reference to Cicero, who also translated the same poem.

19. The term "antiscia" is a neuter plural occurring, though rarely, in both Greek and Latin, and meaning "opposite shadows" or "shadows on the other side." Used as an astrological term it is unique in Firmicus. But Firmicus seems to imply that he has learned the term as well as the doctrine from the sources he quotes (see Note 45).

20. There is general agreement that this misspelling refers to Nigidius Figulus, a religious philosopher, Neo-Pythagorean, and friend of Cicero a religious philosopher, Neo-Pythagorean, and friend of Cicero and Caesar.

21. See H. G. Gundel, and R. Böker, *Zodiakos*. München, 1972.

22. Before the first century A.D. there were presumed to be twelve divisions of the zodiac but only eleven signs. The one now called Libra was considered to be the claws of the crab. This was also true of the Babylonian zodiac. Geminus, a writer of the first century B.C. (see Index of Authors), is perhaps the first to use the complete list of twelve signs. Manetho (see Index of Ancient Writers on Astrology) writes, "The Claws, for which holy men have changed the name and call the Balance, because it stretches out on both sides like the sides of a balance." Firmicus in VII, 5 says that Libra must be added to the double signs, i.e., he always thinks of it as a human holding a scale.

23. The allotment of signs as houses of the planets is closely related to the concept of the *Thema Mundi* (Book III, 1) where the universe begins with each planet in its own (preferred?) house. It is possible that originally each planet had one sign each (as is true now with the expanded number of planets). In this case some nativity charts would have untenanted signs and therefore be less meaningful. The awkward arithmetic (seven into twelve) was solved by giving the Sun and Moon

one sign each. Firmicus's remark in III, 3, "for this reason the Babylonians wanted those signs in which the planets are exalted to be their houses," may indicate that the Babylonians had a one-house system.

24.  The names Firmicus gives us are the familiar Greek names and not, of course, Egyptian. They came into use in the second century B.C. in Alexandria and began to fall into disuse about the first century A.D.. As folklore developed the *Phaeno* set of names was often thought of as Chaldean instead of Egyptian. Vettius Valens (second century A.D.) says the Babylonians called Kronos (Saturn) *Phaenon*. Pre-Ptolemaic Egyptians referred to Venus as the star of Isis, Jupiter as Osiris, and Saturn as Horus. Plato in the *Republic* (Book X) knew of five planets but not their names. In the *Timaeus* he says that the planets have no names but should belong to the gods. In a dialogue called *Epinomis*, probably by one of Plato's pupils, the planets are all named after the gods, showing that in the generation after Plato the Greeks learned to name them Aphrodite, Zeus, etc. The Romans hardly used the *Phaenon* list of names; they are not mentioned by Manilius or Pliny, and only once by Cicero. It is likely that this list fell into disuse because the names of the gods were easier to remember and because the seven-day week with its divine names began to be used from the time of Augustus.

25.  Ptolemy in his *Tetrabiblos* does not give any particular degrees for the exaltations and falls, but simply the entire sign. Porphyry in his *Commentary* on the *Tetrabiblos* offers further explanation: the day-time planets are exalted, he says, according to their trines, and the nocturnal according to their sextiles, since the latter have weaker rays. The Sun with a house in Leo has an exaltation in Aries, the trine of Leo, but the Moon has its exaltation in Taurus, the sextile of Cancer. Mercury, he adds, is the only one with the same houses for exaltation and fall because he is tired from his constant risings and settings. As time went on the exaltations and houses of the planets began to be confused. Manetho (IV, 20–26), for instance, called the exaltations of Saturn his "houses."

26.  The decans are of pre-Ptolemaic Egyptian origin. As early as the Middle Kingdom (ca. 2000–1700 B.C.) there were images and names for the decanal constellations which follow each other in heliacal rising in periods of ten days, and thus provide a star clock for the houses of the night. Since the Egyptians had early adopted a calendar of 360 days with five intercalated days, there were roughly 36 decans, though the number varied from place to place. They all belong to the zone of the sky more or less parallel to and south of the ecliptic. (Wilhelm Gundel, "Dekane und Dekansternbilder;" *Studien der Bibliothek Warburg*, XIX, Gluckstadt-Hamburg, 1936, passim.) The decans were personified by the Egyptians and in Greek and Latin were called "faces," "thrones," "guardians," "soldiers," or "daimons," and easily passed into the astral mysticism of Neo-Platonists and Gnostics. Ptolemy does not mention the decans in the *Tetrabiblos*, but Porphyry in his commentary says "the zodiac, which is divided into twelve zodia, the ancients divided differently into 36 parts which they called decans, and these were allotted to the zodia in part of ten degrees, which is why they are called *dekanoi*."

27.  Firmicus says that some divide decans into three parts which are called *munifices* or *liturgi*. These are Latin and Greek terms, respectively, originally meaning those who performed a public service or duty, then ministers or attendants. In a fragment of the Hermetic writings which goes under the name of Stobaeus (*Corpus Hermeticum*, ed. A.J. Festugiere, Paris, 1945–54) the decans are

called "guards" or "sentinels," and they have subdivisions called "soldiers" or "sub-liturgi."

28. A degree, Firmicus says, is as much as the Sun accomplishes in one circuit, i.e., one day. He assumes there are 360 days in one year, corresponding to 360 degrees in twelve signs of 30 degrees each (the equal signs theory). The Moon probably was included by mistake.

29. Ptolemy in the *Tetrabiblos* has a lengthy discussion of the "terms" (Greek *oria*), which he shows can be computed in different ways. The method Firmicus uses Ptolemy calls the Egyptian. His criticism is that the allotment of degrees is arbitrary in this system. The number of degrees is supposed to be in proportion to the years of life each planet determines when it is "ruler of the chart." Ptolemy believes the terms should be based on the houses, triangles, and exaltations. He knows a simpler arrangement which he calls the Chaldean, and which he claims to have found in an old manuscript. As it turns out, the malefic planets have only 119 degrees in Ptolemy's systems, as against 123 in Firmicus's.

30. *Crios* is the Greek for Aries, the Ram. It is Firmicus's idea to derive it from *crinein,* which means "to judge" in Greek.

31. This lacuna in the descriptions of the signs could be reconstructed, for instance from Paulus Alexandrinus (see Index of Ancient Writers on Astrology) as follows:

THE SECOND SIGN is Taurus, feminine, solid, a Spring sign; house of Aphrodite, exaltation of the Moon in the third degree, fall of none, in trine with Aphrodite by day, with the Moon at night. It lies in the climate of Babylon and is influenced by the South Wind.

THE THIRD SIGN is the Gemini, masculine, double-bodied, a Spring sign, human-shaped, the house of Hermes, exaltation of none, fall of none. It lies in the climate of Cappadocia and is influenced by the South-West Wind.

THE FOURTH SIGN is Cancer, feminine, tropical, belonging to Summer, house of the Moon, exaltation of Zeus in the 15th degree, the fall of Ares in the 28th degree, in trine to Aphrodite by day and to Ares by night. It lies in the climate of Armenia and is influenced by the North Wind.

THE FIFTH SIGN is Leo, masculine, solid, belonging to Summer, the house of the Sun, the exaltation and fall of none, in trine to the Sun by day, to Zeus by night. It lies in the climate of Asia and is influenced by the East Wind.

THE SIXTH SIGN is Virgo, feminine, double-bodied, belonging to Summer, the house and exaltation of Hermes around the 15th degree, the fall of Aphrodite around the 27th degree. It lies in the climate of Greece and Ionia and is influenced by the South Wind.

THE SEVENTH SIGN is Libra, masculine, tropical, belonging to Autumn, the house of Aphrodite, the exaltation of Kronos in the 20th degree, the fall of the Sun around the 19th degree, in trine to Aphrodite by day and by night to Hermes. It lies in the climate of Libya and Cyrene and is influenced by the South-East Wind.

THE EIGHTH SIGN is Scorpio, feminine, solid, belonging to Autumn, the house of Ares, the exaltation of none, the fall of the Moon in the third degree, in trine to Aphrodite by day and to Ares by night. It lies in the climate of Italy and is influenced by the North Wind.

THE NINTH SIGN is Sagittarius, masculine, double-bodied, belonging to Autumn, the house of Zeus, the exaltation and fall of none, in trine by day to the Sun, by night to Zeus. It lies in the climate of Cilicia and Crete and is influenced by the East Wind.

THE TENTH SIGN is Capricorn, feminine, tropical, belonging to Winter, the house of Kronos, the exaltation of Ares in the 28th degree, the fall of Zeus in the 15th degree, in trine to Aphrodite by day, by night to the Moon. It lies in the climate of Syria and is influenced by the South Wind.

THE ELEVENTH SIGN is Aquarius, masculine, solid, belonging to Winter; the house of Kronos, the exaltation and fall of none, in trine to Kronos by day and to Hermes by night. It lies in the climate of Egypt and is influenced by the South-East Wind.

32. This section of Firmicus on the rising time of the signs in different latitudes or *klimata* shows a good many obvious errors even after the numbers have been adjusted by recent editors. Firmicus either copied too hastily or did not understand the material (Ernst Honigman, *Die Sieben Klimata,* Heidelberg, 1929, 56 ff.). Hipparchus first mentions the *klimata* in his Commentary on Aratus, and Strabo gives an extended account (II, 5, 34). Pliny the Elder has a long description (*N.H.* VI, 33) which he attributes to Nigidius Figulus.

33. The idea of connecting the signs of the zodiac with the winds is reminiscent of Ptolemy who bases his whole case for astrology on the meteorological argument and who has much to say about the warm/dry, moist/cold concept.

34. Greek, the Libyan wind (Cf. Aristotle, *Meteorologica,* II, 6.).

35. The system of duodecatemoria is another way to extend the influence of the planets in the zodiac. There are two methods of computing them, of which Firmicus uses the more usual, that of multiplication. This method is used by Haephestion of Thebes, Paulus Alexandrinus, and to a certain extent by Manilius (see Index of Ancient Writers on Astrology). Firmicus, however, makes a mistake in his calculations. He begins by aas assuming that the Sun is in Aries in the fifth degree and five minutes. This multiplied by twelve gives 61 degrees, but in distributing the degrees around the circle he forgets that he started with the Sun in five degrees, five minutes and goes back for his start to the first degree of Aries. Paulus remedies this situation by multiplying by 13 instead of twelve, thus taking one more time the degrees in which the planet is located.

36. It would have been logical for Firmicus to discuss the *cardines* (angles) before the eight houses since it is obvious from the description in Manilius that the eight houses were based on the four quadrants which result from the four angles. The system of eight houses would have been incompatible with the aspects, or would invariably have given pessimistic forecasts, since it allows only square aspect and opposition. Perhaps for this reason it was superseded by the twelve-house system. Manilius gives a long description of the eight-house system (II, 808, ff.) where he says the spaces between the angles refer to the four periods of human life. This is a division which does not occur elsewhere, although the idea that the entire 360 degrees represent human life is not strange. Ovid *(Metamorphoses* XV) attributes to Pythagoras the idea that the four seasons of the year equal the four ages of man. There was also a tendency to equate the twelve-house system with human life, but with the difficult question of where to put death, at the descendant or at the Imum Caelum. Only Porphyry allots the period from the Imum Caelum to the Ascendant to the period after death—which to the Neo-Platonist is also the preparation for re-birth.

37. Both sets of terms mean Good Luck (feminine) and Good Spirit (masculine). The same is true of Bad Luck and Bad Spirit (II, 17, 1).

38. Firmicus introduces the concept of "aspects" with the term *mathematicum,* the mathematical relationship. He also frequently uses *radiatio.* The Greek writers call them *schemata* or *schematiskoi.* This is probably the most truly Greek contribution to

astrology. Firmicus lists four types of aspects—opposition, trine, square, and sextile—and the condition of being unaspected, which he calls *ableptum,* from the Greek *ablepton* (not seen or blind). The more usual Greek expression is *asyndeton* (unconnected).

Although the term aspect (from the Latin *aspicio,* to regard) is not used until the Middle Ages, Firmicus's use of *ableptum* indicates that there was a tendency to think that the signs "regarded" or "looked at" each other when they were geometrically related. Sextus Empiricus (*ad Mathematicos,* V, 39) says, "They are said to look toward one another and to agree with one another when they appear in the form of a triangle or square." Firmicus and the classical Latin writers never use the Latin *aspicio* or *aspectus* in the astrological sense. When Horace says (*Carmina,* 11, 17), "Seu Libra seu me Scorpio aspicit" (Whether Libra or Scorpio regards me), he is probably not using the term in a technical sense.

Firmicus occasionally translates Ptolemy's *blepo* (to regard) as *testimonium perhibere,* relying on the original meaning of *testor* (to witness with one's own eyes).

For *ableptum* (unseen) Firmicus also uses *pigrum* (sluggish), *aversum* (turned away), and *alienum* (alien).

Most writers earlier than Firmicus listed only three types of aspect, as for instance Geminos (see Index of Authors), 1, 9, who cites opposition, trine, and square. Sextus Empericus mentions only trine and square. But Ptolemy (*Tetra,* 1, 13) lists four and gives exact degrees. Firmicus in Chapter XXII lines up the aspects only according to the signs, i.e., *platice.* In XXIII, he lines them up more exactly, by degree, *partiliter.*

39. This is doctrine known to the Greeks as *melotheia.* It belongs strictly to a branch known as iatroastrology—diagnosing and healing illness by the stars. Firmicus's system is zodiacal melotheia which connects the signs with different parts of the body. It is also possible to have planetary melotheia. Sextus Empericus combines both. Ptolemy describes the planetary form with Saturn ruling the right ear, spleen, bladder, phlegm, and bones; Jupiter the touch, lungs, arteries, and semen; Mars the left ear, kidneys, veins, and genitals; the Sun sight, brain, heart, muscles, and all right-hand parts; Venus the sense of smell, the liver, and the flesh; Mercury speech, thought, tongue, bile, buttocks; the Moon taste, drinking, stomach, womb, and all left-handed parts.

40. The idea that every subdivision of time has its special divine ruler can be traced back to Egypt of the Middle Kingdom (ca. 2000–1700). In the Greek world Hesiod (*Works and Days,* 765 ff.) first mentions the idea of lucky and unlucky days. These were calendar computations based first on phases of the Moon and later on the Sun, and this is why the luminaries have first importance in most systems of rulerships of time.

41. The number of days of the year allotted to each planet add up to 361. The ruler of the sign which begins the year, that is, the sign on the ascendant, receives his days first, and so on. This distribution of good and bad days cuts across all boundaries of signs, terms, and decans.

42. See Index of Ancient Writers on Astrology.

43. Ibid.

44. Ibid.

45. Maximus (see Index of Ancient Writers on Astrology) lists parts of signs which "see" and "hear" one another, and the poet Manilius not only describes "seeing" and "hearing" of the signs but introduces emotional relationships as well:

Aries loves Taurus, who tricks him, Gemini love Pisces, etc. Firmicus is concerned here only with the "seeing" relationship, and this is what he calls the antiscia (see Note 19). But he breaks them down to individual degrees. Perhaps the elimination of the 30th degree was necessary in order to pair odd numbers with odd and even with even—a Neo-Pythagorean idea which might have come from Nigidius

Figulus (Bouche-LeClerq, *l'Astrologie grecque,* Paris 1899). In Firmicus the planets act through their antiscia partners just as they would in other aspectual relationships. It is simply as if they had been plugged into another circuit. It extends the possibilities of the forecasts (see Note 19).

46. In the lengthy exposition at the end of this chapter Firmicus demonstrates how the use of antiscia caa change a forecast. He remarks that his patron, Lollianus, knows to whom the chart belongs. In 1894 Theodore Mommsen pointed out that this chart would fit the story of Ceionus Refus Albinus, *praefectus urbis* of the year 336/337 ("Firmicus Maternus" in *Hermes,* XXIX, 1894, 468–72). Otto Neugebauer demonstrated that the astronomical data would be suitable for the dates of this candidate ("The Horoscope of Ceionus Rufus Albinus," *AJP,* LXXIV, 1953, 418–20). Albinus and his father were both well-authenticated holders of public office and Albinus was interested in literature, as Firmicus points out, and was the patron of Servius, the commentator on Vergil. It had formerly been believed that Lollianus himself was the subject of the chart until Mommsen pointed out that the details would not fit. The two men would have known each other, however, and perhaps the fact that the career of Ceionus could not have been predicted without the use of antiscia had already been discussed by Firmicus and his circle of friends.

47. *Haruspices* are Etrusco-Roman diviners who examine the livers of sacrificed animals.

## Book III

48. Firmicus claims he learned of the *Thema Mundi* from Petosiris and Nechepso to whom it had been transmitted by Aesculapius, Hanubius, and Mercury. Mercury here refers to Hermes Trismegistus, the name translated from the Egyptian "all-powerful Thoth" (the Egyptian god of learning), the supposed author of a series of Hellenistic tracts known as the Hermetic Corpus. Aesculapius is often used for Imhotep, Egyptian sage of the Early First Kingdom, and Hanubius is probably Anubis, the Egyptian deity (Wilhelm and Hans Georg Gundel, *Astrolegumena,* Wiesbaden, 1966). Numerous Egyptian gods such as Isis, Osiris, Ammon, and Horos are mentioned as teachers of astrological lore.

The idea of a birthday of the universe was very popular in the ancient world, stemming perhaps from the New Years' festivals of Egypt and Babylon. It came into prominence with the growing popularity of the Stoic doctrine of continual destruction and renewal of the world. (Note, for instance, Vergil, *Georgics,* II, 336.)

The Egyptian year began with the rising of Sothis (Sirius) in Cancer, but the Babylonian and Roman in the spring. From the time of Posidonius, Aries was generally accepted as the first sign of the year. Eudoxus had placed the spring equinox in the middle of Aries; Hipparchos, who is credited with the discovery of the procession of the equinoxes, at the beginning. Ptolemy separated the real from the fictitious zodiac and kept the beginning of the year in Aries.

49. Predictions derived from individual degrees. Firmicus attributes it to Aesculapius, which probably means Hellenistic Egyptian in origin. He also says (VIII, 1, 10) that he has written a book on the subject.

50. See Note 6.

51. The concept of the Part of Fortune appears first in Manilius, who gives the same account as Firmicus. Both probably derived from the Petosiris handbook. Ptolemy counts in reverse around the circle but achieves the same result.

52. The ancients did not know that Mars cannot be in opposition or square aspect to the Sun.

53. Firmicus, like all the other ancient writers, did not know that Venus cannot be in opposition to the Sun, since she is never more than 48 degrees away.

54. It was necessary to watch over the dead to keep away evil spirits and witches who would mutilate the corpse. Cf. Apuleius, *Golden Ass,* 11, 23 ff.

55. See Glossary, under semi-voiced signs.

56. Put out on a hillside, as infants, to die or to be picked up.

57. See Note 51.

## Book IV

58. See Note 48.

59. As god of healing, Aesculapius might naturally be involved in the transmission of astrology, particularly iatroastrology. But the name is often used to indicate the ancient Egyptian wise man Imhotep, builder of pyramids and legendary founder of medicine.

60. Abram or Abraham may refer to the Hebrew patriarch in an attempt to ascribe astrological teachings to ancient wise men. Or, as Gundel believes (*Astrolegumena,* p. 52), there may have been a real author of a Hellenistic tract who either was an Abram or who took the name. He is mentioned again in Book IV, 18, and Book VI, 18.

61. In Book VII, 1, he is spelled *Orpheus.* He was a legendary Greek musician and seer, founder of a mystical sect.

62. See Index of Ancient Writers on Astrology.

63. This term refers to the changing distance of the Moon from the Sun as it passes from the dark of the Moon (conjunction) to full (opposition) during the month.

64. Stars and constellations outside the Zodiac, considered a non-Greek system of astrology. For a comprehensive discussion see Franz Boll, *Sphaera,* Leipzig, 1903/1955.

65. According to H.G. Gundel, (op. cit.) this Achilles is an astrological writer of the second century A.D., not the Achilles Tatius who wrote a commentary on Aratus in the third century A.D..

66. The Part of the Daemon should be opposite to the Part of Fortune, as is shown by Paulus Alexandrinus (n. 31), where he counts from the Moon to the Sun in a diurnal chart and the Sun to the Moon in a nocturnal. Thus the Part of Fortune can be considered as belonging to the Moon and that of the Daemon to the Sun as, Firmicus tells us, Abraham taught. Firmicus (or his manuscript) was confused and gave the same directions for both.

67. As Firmicus points out, there were a number of methods for determining the

ruler of the chart. Many ancient authors simply prefer the planet closest to the Sun. Firmicus definitely rules out the Sun and Moon as rulers of the chart since they have power in general in every chart.

68. This character is unidentified. The name is not a Roman one, but a descriptive one signifying "mousy."

69. The idea that some degrees have no power may perhaps have come from observations of the constellations and the spaces between the stars. Manilius (*Astronomica,* IV, 411 ff.) lists degrees in the signs which he calls "bad" (*damnandae*), either because they have an excess of cold or heat, or of dryness or moisture. Haephestion of Thebes has a set of bright (*lamprai*) degrees which are especially favorable. Neither of these lists correspond with each other or with those of Firmicus. What is interesting is the names Firmicus gives to his "full" groups. Most of them are variants of Egyptian names for decans, but some are Greek or Persian. For a full discussion of the names see A. Bouche-Leclerq, *L'Astrologie grecque,* Paris, 1899.

## Book V

70. Here Firmicus speaks of the creator god in Neo-Platonic terms. But the notion of a bisexual god, "father and also mother," belongs to the Sol Invictus of Elagabalus. Cf. Gaston H. Halsberghe, *The Cult of Sol Invictus,* Leiden, 1972, p. 85 ff.

71. See Note 59.

## Book VI

72. See Book II, 22, 6.

73. The cithara is a lyre-like instrument, but with a deeper sounding board.

74. See Note 3.

75. The Roman general who captured Syracuse in the Second Punic in the Second Punic War, 211 B.C.

76. *Iliad* II, 212 ff.

77. See Note 64.

## Book VII

78. See Note 61.

79. In this passage Firmicus speaks of the knowledge of astrology as if it were one of the mystery religions, mentioning secrecy, oaths, etc. However, in other passages of the *Mathesis* and in the *de Errore,* he strongly attacks the mysteries.

80. Semi-legendary philosopher-mathematician of the sixth century B.C., supposed leader of a mystic cult, revived in first century B.C., supposed leader of a mystic cult, revived in first century B.C. by Neo-Pythagoreans, especially Nigidius Figulus.

81. Neo-Platonist, 232–305 A.D. Here Firmicus calls him "our Porphyry," although he attacks him in *de Errore.*

82. The castrate priests of Cybele, Mother of the Gods, sang and danced for her in processions and at ceremonies. See Homeric hymn, "To the Mother of the Gods," XIV.

## Book VIII

83. See Note 64.

84. The importance of the 90th degree is connected with a widespread belief that the years of human life are measured by degrees of the zodiac (cf. Pliny, *N.H., VII,* 160). The most usual method was that of Firmicus, to begin life with the ascendant and end with the MC. The oblique zodiac would not always put the MC at the 90th degree, but Firmicus may have been influenced by the older Egyptian configuration which made the circle of the decans near the equator.

85. Firmicus presented his antiscia as purely mathematical relationships (see Book II). But other writers described parallel relationships as "seeing" and "hearing," sometimes with emotional overtones, as Manilius (op. cit., II, 489 ff.). Usually the signs which "see" each other are on horizontal parallels, and those which "hear" each other, perpendicular. This scheme of Firmicus in Book Eight does not lend itself to any general rule. It is, says Bouche-Leclerq (op. cit., p. 159, 1) the most unreasonable, and consequently the most "revealed" theory he has encountered in the history of astrology. This theory is ascribed to "Abraham" who is also mentioned in connection with the Part of Fortune and of Daemon in IV, 17, 2 and IV, 18, 1.

86. Probably the same Abraham or Abram mentioned in IV, Proemium 5; IV, 17, 2; and IV, 18, 2.

87. According to Franz Boll (op. cit., p. 394, 3), this number does not occur elsewhere. Perhaps the first number is an approximation of 6 x 60 x 60 (21,600).

88. See Index of Ancient Writers on Astrology.

89. See Note 18.

89. The ship, Argo, is named after the ship of Jason and the Argonauts who sailed after the Golden Fleece.

91. A giant hunter, already identified with the constellation by Homer *(Iliad* 18, 486; *Odyssey* 11, 572 ff.).

92. Salmoneus and Bellerophon are both heroes connected with horses. Salmoneus was thrown from his chariot by a thunderbolt of Zeus *(Aeneid,* 6, 585 ff.). Bellerophon slew the chimaera while riding on Pegasus *(Iliad,* 6, 155 ff.).

93. Usually in the plural, Haedi, a small double star in the head of the Charioteer.

94. "The Rainers" were said by Eudoxos to rise at rainy times of the year. In mythology, they were either nurses of Dionysus, or sisters who cried themselves to death.

95. The Goat, Amaltheia, is supposed to have suckled the infant Zeus. The poet who told the story is Manilius (op. cit., V, 132), whom Firmicus closely follows in this whole account but does not mention as a source.

96. The Pleiades were seven stars supposed in mythology to be seven daughters of Atlas or seven doves fleeing from the hunter Orion. They were known to Homer and Hesiod.

97. Cepheus was the husband of Cassiopea and father of Andromeda, and was placed with them among the stars.

98. Tullianus Symmachus Valerius, Consul 330 A.D..

99. Cassiopea was the wife of Cepheus; her daughter Andromeda was punished for her pride.

100. Andromeda, daughter of Cassiopea and Cepheus was tied to a rock and rescued by Perseus. The whole family became stars.

101. The oiler of athletes was quite an important position. Oil was the soap and water used by athletes for washing, and was scraped off.

102. Firmicus's "bright stars" are mostly those mentioned by Ptolemy. Only two have not been identified, the one in the 19th degree of Scorpio, and that in the first degree of Aquarius. Cf. Boll, op. cit., p. 410 ff.

# INDEX OF OCCUPATIONS
Numbers refer to book, section, and paragraph.

Account-keeper: **III** 3.15, 10.1; **IV** 14.1; *for kings,* **III** 3.8; **IV** 21.9; *recorders of loans and interest,* **IV** 14.6

Actor: **VI** 31.39; **VIII** 20.1; *of farce,* **VIII** 8.1; *of tragedy or comedy,* **VIII** 20.7

Actress: **III** 6.23, 12.17

Administrator: **III** 3.10, 3.15, 5.5, 5.6, 13.9; **V** 2.15, 2.17; **VIII** 16.2; *of states and important affairs,* **III** 3.3, 5.14, 7.6, 7.24, 11.2, 11.5; *of laws,* **III** 12.3

Agent: *of government or privy purse,* **IV** 14.6; *for King,* **III** 3.8, 7.6; *of powerful men,* **III** 9.2, 9.10.

Ambassador: **III** 12.5; **IV** 19.25, 19.28; **VIII** 26.12

Architect: **VIII** 24.8, 29.5

Archivist: **VI** 23.6

Arms, in charge of: **IV** 14.11

Army doctor: **VIII** 28.1

Astrologer: **III** 2.18, 7.6, 7.19, 8.3, 12.16; **IV** 9.8, 19.25, 21.9; **V** 2.15; **VIII** 25.10, 27.3

Astronomer: **III** 7.9, 7.19, 8.3; **IV** 19.25, 21.9 and 10; **V** 2.13, 2.15

Athlete: **III** 11.6, 11.18; **IV** 11.4, 13.11, 14.11; **VI** 31.3; **VII** 26.3; **VIII** 19.3 and 4, 23.2, 24.5, 27.5 and 6, 28.5, 29.14; *who fight with the sword, or fully-armed,* **IV** 10.3; **VIII** 21.5, 27.3

Athletes, Masseur of: **VIII** 23.2

Athletes, Master of: **IV** 13.1; **VIII** 23.2

Athletes, Trainer of: **VII** 26.3; **VIII** 21.7

Athletic contests, in charge of: **V** 5.6; **VIII** 20.4; *sacred contests manager,* **III** 10.3

Augur: **III** 7.19, 8.3, 10.8, 12.16; **VIII** 20.2

Bandit: **III** 4.20, 4.23, 11.10; **IV** 11.5, 14.7, 24.8; **VI** 31.6, 31.58, 31.66, 31.72, 31.83; **VII** 23.25, 23.27; **VIII** 24.4; *leader,* **VII** 23.24

Barber: **VII** 26.10; **VIII** 19.12, 20.8, 26.9

Bath-attendant: **VIII** 21.6, 25.3, 29.5 and 6, 30.9

Beggar: **IV** 10.2 and 3; *naked,* **III** 9.2; *unshorn and unwashed,* **V** 3.52

Bird-catcher: **III** 7.12; **IV** 14.14; **VIII** 14.3, 19.8, 30.9

Bird-seller: **VIII** 14.3

Bodyguard: *of emperors and kings,* **III** 12.1; *of noble families,* **IV** 13.1

Botanist: **III** 9.2; cf. *Herbalist*

Bowman: **VIII** 23.3

Boxer: **VII** 26.4; **VIII** 8.1

Bracelet-maker: **VIII** 19.11; cf. *Jeweler, Pearl-worker, Goldsmith*

Builder: **IV** 14.14; **VIII** 29.5; *wall-builder,* **VIII** 24.8; cf. *construction work*

Businessman, Business Overseer, Manager: **III** 10.1; **IV** 14.1, 19.29; **VIII** 19.7, 20.10, 22.2; *engaging in foreign trade,* **V** 5.6; **VIII** 25.5; *ibid., in ships,* **VIII** 25.8; *who trades with the East,* **VIII** 27.12; *traveling for commerce,* **IV** 9.3; **V** 2.20

Butcher: **III** 11.18

Caretaker (Business Manager): *of governors of states,* **V** 2.15; *for noble families,* **IV** 13.1; *for women,* **III** 6.19; *ibid., rich,* **III** 7.15; *for women and children,* **III** 10.4

Caterer: **IV** 11.2; **IV** 13.2

Cavalryman: **VIII** 13.2

Census, Master of the: **III** 9.10

Charioteer: **VIII** 6.3, 13.3, 17.3, 27.8; *for King,* **VIII** 29.13
Composer: **III** 12.1; **V** 5.6; **VIII** 30.1; *for stage or public performance,* **III** 12.17
Construction work, in charge of: **III** 7.3, 7.13
Consul, Consular, Proconsul: **III** 3.10, 5.34, 13.9 and 10; **IV** 10.7
Cook: **III** 8.7; **IV** 14.13, 21.6; **VII** 26.6
Corpse washer: **III** 15.23; **IV** 13.7, 14.14; **VIII** 29.5
Corpse watcher: **III** 9.3
Courier, Messenger: **VIII** 27.11; *of kings,* **III** 11.18; **IV** 14.5; *or scouts,* **VIII** 17.3
Cowherd: **III** 5.23; **IV** 13.7; **VIII** 6.6; *cf. Ox-herd*

Dagger-maker: **VIII** 19.12
Dancer: **III** 12.1; **IV** 14.17; **VI** 30.9, 31.39, 31.85; **VIII** 29.13
Dice-player: *famous,* **VIII** 25.3
Diver: **IV** 13.6; **VIII** 15.2, 29.6
Diviner: **III** 2.18, 10.3, 12.16
Door Keeper: **VI** 31.13; *to kings, admitting and saluting guests;* **VIII** 14.1
Dove breeder: **VIII** 14.3
Drawer of water: **VIII** 21.7, 29.4, 29.6; *from deep wells,* **IV** 13.6, 14.14
Dream interpreter: **III** 6.7, 8.3
Druggist: **IV** 13.2; *cf. Herbalist, Medicinal drugs*
Dwarves, Hunchbacks, Clowns: *Often referred to, not clear whether as a condition or an occupation. Assigned to pleasure of kings or emperors,* **VIII** 26.1
Dyer: **III** 6.3 and 4, 11.18, 12.11; **IV** 11.2, 13.1, 14.13; **VII** 26.10

Embroiderer: **III** 6.4
Emperor: **III** 2.20, 4.30, 5.2, 13.9 and 10; **IV** 17.10; **VI** 31.55; **VIII** 16.2, 28.1
Engraver: **VIII** 30.9
Estate Manager: **III** 9.3
Eunuch: *Often referred to, not clear whether as condition or profession. But: serving religious or sacred rites,* **VI** 30.3, 31.48; *entrusted with care of state,* **VIII** 20.9
Executioner: **III** 11.12, 11.18; **IV** 11.4, 14.14; **VIII** 15.3, 17.1; *public,* **III** 5.20; **IV** 14.10
Exorcist: **III** 4.27, 8.9
Exotic pleasures and delights, provider of: **IV** 13.2

Farmer or Plowman: **III** 7.3; **IV** 19.32; **VII** 26.10; **VIII** 11.3, 20.1, 29.13
Feather worker: **III** 11.18
Fisherman: **III** 3.11, 10.8; **IV** 13.6, 14.14; **V** 2.14; **VIII** 9.2, 22.1, 29.6; *of large fish,* **VIII** 17.5; *mad,* **VIII** 30.5
Fish sauce, making living from: **VIII** 17.5
Flute-player: **VII** 26.10
Forger: **III** 7.26; **IV** 14.6, 14.9; **VI** 31.72; *Counterfeiter,* **VII** 23.6
Fuller: **III** 8.7, 10.8; **VIII** 20.8
Furrier: **IV** 14.13, 14.20

Gardener: **III** 3.11, 5.25, 9.3; **VIII** 11.1, 26.3, 26.8 and 9, 29.6, 29.14; *arbor-maker,* **VIII** 10.6; *grafter of trees,* **VIII** 10.6; *poor,* **IV** 13.6; *topiary specialist,* **VIII** 10.6; *veterinarian herbalist,* **VIII** 13.3; *worker in gardens,* **IV** 14.14

General: **III** 2.20, 3.8 and 9, 4.8, 4.28, 5.34, 11.2, 13.9; **IV** 13.8, 14.13, 19.15; **VIII** 19.1, 19.5, 20.9, 21.2, 24.2, 31.3

Geometer: **III** 7.1, 7.9, 7.24; *short-lived,* **VIII** 25.7

Gladiator: **VII** 8.7, 26.2; **VIII** 7.4, 8.1, 10.4, 12.2, 23.3; *assigned to public games,* **VIII** 24.7

Gold-leaf worker: **IV** 21.6; **VIII** 26.6

Gold miner: **III** 7.7

Gold-plater: **IV** 21.6

Goldsmith: **III** 3.14, 3.23, 7.7, 12.9; **IV** 21.6; **VII** 26.10; **VIII** 16.3, 19.11, 26.6, 28.5, 29.8, 30.9

Gold-thread garment adorners: **III** 3.14

Government worker: *In obscure and wretched job,* **III** 8.1; *in laborious task,* **III** 10.14

Governor: **III** 2.10, 4.8, 5.21, 5.34, 13.9 and 10; **IV** 14.18; **V** 23.1; *of Asia,* **IV** 21.5

Grain market, in charge of: **III** 9.5; *cf. Granary or Storehouse*

Grammarian: **IV** 15.8; **V** 2.13

Granary or Storehouse, in charge of: **III** 7.13, 9.5, 10.1

Haruspex: **III** 7.9, 8.3, 12.16; **IV** 19.25, 21.9; **V** 2.15; **VIII** 20.2, 21.11, 24.1 and 2

Healer: **III** 7.6

Helmsman: **VIII** 30.13

Herald: **III** 11.18, **VIII** 20.7; *royal,* **III** 3.15

Herbalist: *For men and animals,* **VIII** 17.3; *prepares medicines from poisons and pigments or herbs,* **VIII** 17.7; *cf. Botanist, Gardener, Snakecharmer*

Herdsman: **III** 5.23; *in charge of king's herds,* **III** 6.3; *cf. Cowherd, Shepherd, Ox-herd, Swineherd*

Horse breeder: **VIII** 27.5; *and trainer,* **VIII** 13.3

Horseman: **VIII** 13.3, 17.3; *circus rider,* **VIII** 6.3

Horse tamer, Horse tender, Horse trainer: **III** 5.23; **IV** 13.7; **VIII** 6.3, 13.3, 27.8

House-breaker: **III** 11.12; **IV** 7.3, 14.9; **V** 6.9; **VI** 31.6; *cf. Thief*

Hunter: **III** 11.18; **VIII** 9.1; 23.2, 27.5; *of four-footed animals,* **IV** 11.5; *of wild beasts,* **IV** 14.14; *who work with slings in wild-beast fights in the arena,* **VIII** 10.4; *hunters and breeders of birds and animals,* **VIII** 19.8

Hunting dog breeder: **VIII** 9.3

Hunting gear maker: **VIII** 9.3

Hymn-writer: **III** 5.33, 10.3; **VIII** 22.3, 24.6, 25.1

Image carrier: **III** 9.9, 10.3, 12.2

Incense maker: **VIII** 25.9

Informer: **III** 7.12, 7.26, 11.18; **IV** 14.14; **VI** 31.66; **VII** 23.27

Initiator: *those who initiate men into cults,* **III** 10.3

Inn-keeper: **III** 6.4; **IV** 11.2, 21.6; **VIII** 22.1

Interpreter: **III** 7.12, 10.8; **VIII** 26.2; *of divine doctrine,* **VIII** 13.1; *of emperors,* **III** 7.1; *of the gods,* **III** 3.17; *for kings,* **VIII** 27.3; *of law,* **III** 3.6; *of philosophy,* **IV** 19.29; *of words,* **IV** 14.1

Inventor: **III** 9.10; **IV** 21.10; *of mechanical skills,* **VI** 30.26; *of theories,* **III** 6.21

Jailer: **III** 5.26; *care of prisons,* **IV** 14.1; *warden,* **VIII** 17.1; *cf. Prison guard, Prison official*

Javelin-thrower: **VIII** 8.1

Jeweler: **III** 11.18, 12.10; **IV** 11.2; **VIII** 16.3, 26.6; *cf. Pearls, Precious stones, Bracelet-maker, Goldsmith*

Judge: **III** 3.6, 4.33, 5.8, 5.10, 7.3, 10.1, 13.2; **IV** 10.3, 14.6, 21.9 and 10; **VIII** 26.4, 26.6, 27.2, 28.11, 29.3

Judge's assistant: **III** 4.15

Juggler: **III** 7.15; **VIII** 8.1, 15.2, 20.2

King: **III** 2.10, 4.30, 5.2, 5.5 and 6, 5.21, 5.34, 8.1; **IV** 21.9; **VII** 22.1; **VIII** 19.1, 20.9, 21.1, 23.1, 25.8, 27.1, 28.1, 29.1, 31.3 and 4, 31.9

Language scholar: *of obscure languages,* **III** 9.10; *skilled in difficult writings,* **III** 7.4

Lathe-turner: **IV** 13.2

Latrine-cleaner: *and sewer-cleaner,* **VIII** 19.12, 20.1

Lawyer: **III** 5.25, 7.1, 9.1; **VII** 26.5; **VIII** 26.11 and 12, 27.12, 30.7; *law writer,* **III** 12.1

Leather-worker: **III** 8.7, 10.8, 11.18; **IV** 14.13

Legislator: **III** 3.6

Linen-worker: **III** 11.18; **IV** 14.13. *cf. Tunic weaver, Weaver, Wool worker*

Literary man, man of letters: **III** 5.37, 7.24, 9.10, 12.1; **IV** 19.28; **V** 2.15

Longshoreman, Porter: **IV** 14.2, 15.7; **VIII** 21.4

Lute-player: **VIII** 21.9, 24.6, 24.8, 25.2

Lyre or Cithara player: **VI** 30.9, 31.84

Magician: **III** 2.18, 7.6, 7.20, 10.3, 12.16; **VIII** 30.11; *experienced,* **III** 12.6; *and healer,* **VIII** 26.1

Magistrate: **III** 2.10; **VIII** 26.2

Male prostitute: **III** 9.1; **VI** 31.4 and 5; **VII** 25.5, 25.7, 25.9, 25.21 and 22; **VIII** 19.7, 20.6, 7, and 8, 21.11, 24.1, 25.1, 25.4, 30.1

Manure-carrier: **VIII** 20.1

Master of the Horse: **VIII** 29.14

Mathematician: *discoverer of mathematics,* **III** 7.15; *learned in computing and calculating,* **III** 7.7; *mathematics and machines,* **III** 10.4; *writer in mathematics,* **III** 12.1

Mechanic: *Machinist,* **III** 12.10; *mechanic who makes engines of war,* **VIII** 27.5; *artificer or mechanic of subtle and intricate arts,* **V** 2.12

Medicinal drug discoverer: **III** 12.10; **IV** 14.17; *cf. Druggist, Gardener, Herbalist*

Merchant: **VIII** 20.10; *cf. Businessman, Shopkeeper; of metals,* **IV** 11.2

Metal worker: **III** 11.18, 12.10; *of mediocre talent,* **IV** 14.20; *brassworker,* **IV** 14.15; *in iron or other metals,* **VIII** 25.9; *in charge of metals,* **III** 9.5

Midwife: **VIII** 23.3

Miller: **III** 8.7, 10.8; **VIII** 24.3, 26.6; *lowest class,* **VIII** 20.5

Mines, in charge of: **VIII** 17.2; *cf. Gold miner, Metal prospector*

Mint worker: **VIII** 17.8

Money-changer: **III** 7.3, 7.13

Money-lender: **III** 7.3 and 4; **IV** 15.8; **VII** 26.10; **VIII** 19.7, 24.2, 28.4, 29.14; *recorder of loans and interest,* **IV** 14.6

Money manager, Banker: *Foreign investments manager,* **V** 3.17; *manager of others' money,* **III** 7.4; **IV** 14.6; *investor in public funds,* **VIII** 19.7; *cf. Treasury, in charge of*

Mosaic worker: **III** 3.23

Mule-driver: **VIII** 19.9, 27.10; *for King,* **VIII** 29.13

Mule-trainer: **VIII** 13.3; *royal* **VIII** 27.8

Musical instrument maker: **IV** 19.18; *those who care for musical instruments,* **VIII** 30.9

Musician: **III** 6.1, 12.1, 12.10; **IV** 13.1, 15.8, 21.6; **V** 2.10, 2.12; **VI** 8.1, 26.1; **VII** 26.7, 26.10; **VIII** 20.7, 21.4, 24.6, 27.4, 28.2; *discoverer in music,* **III** 7.15; *public,* **III** 6.21; *crowd-pleaser,* **VI** 26.2; *song accompanist,* **VI** 30.9

Notary: **V** 2.17

Nurse, children's: **VIII** 23.3

Officer: **III** 4.29, 5.8; **VIII** 16.2

Ointment dealer: **III** 12.10; *cf. Druggist, Perfume*

Orator: **III** 4.27, 6.1, 7.1, 7.24, 9.2, 9.10, 12.1; **IV** 7.1, 9.8, 13.2, 14.16, 15.8, 19.24, 19.26, 21.9; **V** 2.13, **VI** 23.6, 30.22; **VII** 26.5; **VIII** 26.11

Organist: **IV** 14.17; **V** 2.12

Ox-herd; **IV** 13.7; **VIII** 6.6; *cf. Cowherd, Herdsman*

Paint: *dealer in paints,* **VIII** 30.5; *discoverer of paints or colors,* **IV** 14.17; *inventive worker in colors,* **III** 6.4; *worker in colors,* **V** 5.6

Painter: **IV** 11.2, 13.2; **VI** 8.1; **VII** 26.10; **VIII** 7.4, 25.9, 29.8, 30.9; *artist in paint,* **III** 6.4; *who paints the whole figure,* **IV** 19.18

Pantomimist: **IV** 14.17; **VI** 31.85; **VIII** 8.1, 20.8, 21.6, 23.3, 28.11

Pastry-cook: **VIII** 11.3

Pearl-dealer, -worker, -setter: **III** 9.5, 12.10; **IV** 11.2, 13.1; **VIII** 16.3

Perfume: *in charge of,* **III** 9.5; *designer of unguents, perfumes, and aromatics,* **VIII** 11.1; *manufacturer,* **III** 6.3

Perfumer: **III** 11.18; 12.10; **IV** 11.2, 13.1, 14.20, 21.6

Philosopher: **III** 2.18, 7.1, 12.6

Physician: **III** 7.19 and 20, 8.3, 9.2; **IV** 10.3, 13.1, 15.8; **V** 2.17; **VII** 26.6, 26.10; **VIII** 25.7, 25.10, 26.11, 28.3, 28.5

Pilot: **VIII** 6.1, 20.10, 22.4, 27.12; *cf. Helmsman, Sailor, Sea-captain*

Pimp: **III** 5.24; **VIII** 20.7, 23.1, 28.6; *or master of prostitutes,* **IV** 13.4; *and whoremaster,* **III** 7.14

Pirate: **III** 4.23, 11.10, 13.2; **IV** 24.8

Plasterer: **IV** 13.2, 14.13; **VII** 26.10; **VIII** 16.3

Poet: **IV** 14.16, 19.22, 19.24; **V** 2.12 and 13, 2.20; **VI** 26.1; *of heroic songs,* **VI** 30.23; *lyric,* **VI** 30.25

Potter: **VIII** 27.11

Precious stones: *worker in,* **IV** 14.17; *polisher of,* **IV** 14.20; *dealer in,* **V** 5.6; *those who paint gems with different colors,* **IV** 14.20

Pretorian Prefect: **III** 2.20, 4.8

Priest: **III** 3.17, 5.27, 7.6, 7.19 and 20, 8.3, 12.5, 12.16; **IV** 14.5; **VII** 23.27; **VIII** 13.1, 21.1, 21.11, 24.1 and 2; 24.5, 24.7, 25.2, 25.9, 26.2 and 3; *chief priest,* **IV** 14.19; *ibid., robed in purple and gold,* **III** 6.1; *high priest of the provinces,* **IV** 21.5; *priest of a powerful religion,* **III** 13.5; *who makes his living by sacrifices,* **VIII** 26.14; *in charge of great religions,* **III** 11.2

Priestess: **III** 6.8

Prison guard: **III** 5.26; **IV** 11.5, 14.10; **VIII** 21.4

Prison official: *trained to beat prisoner with whips,* **III** 5.26

Prophet: **III** 6.7, 9.9, 12.5; **IV** 14.5; **VII** 23.27; **VIII** 13.1, 19.4, 21.11, 24.1, 24.5; **VIII** 20.1; *unkempt,* **III** 6.19; *cf. Temple prophet*

Prospector: **VIII** 17.8

Prostitute: **III** 5.24; **VI** 30.7, 31.80, 31.90; **VII** 25.7, 25.11, 25.23; **VIII** 24.3, 25.4, 26.8, 27.8 and 9, 30.2; *hidden,* **VII** 25.9; *public,* **IV** 13.3; **VI** 31.5, 31.47; **VII** 16.2; **VIII** 20.6

Prostitution, house of, manager: **III** 6.23

Publican: **III** 11.3; *cf. Inn-keeper, Tavern-keeper*

Public prosecutor: **VI** 10.8; **VIII** 15.3 *(implied)*

Public works, in charge of: **III** 10.9


Queen: **VIII** 25.5, 25.8


Record-keeper: **III** 9.10, 10.1; **IV** 21.10; **VI** 5.4; *of public records,* **IV** 12.4, 14.6; *manager of public records,* **VI** 4.5

River-bank Inspector: **III** 4.8

Rope-dancer: **VIII** 15.2; *and tightrope walker,* **VIII** 17.4

Ruler of the Games: **IV** 21.5

Runner: **VII** 26.4; **VIII** 8.1, 21.10


Sacred rites: *in charge of,* **III** 6.7, 12.2, 12.5; *ritual attendant,* **VIII** 21.11; *cf. Haruspex, Image carrier, Priest, Sacrificer,* and *Temple Attendant.* Also *Hymn-writer, Musician, Singer of Holy Songs,* and following entries

Sacred statue dresser: **III** 9.9, 12.5

Sacred teachings: *discoverer of,* **IV** 19.18

Sacred writings: *men skilled in,* **III** 7.1

Sacrificer: **III** 5.27

Sacrificial animal breeder: **III** 5.27

Sailor: **III** 12.9; **IV** 13.6, 14.14; **VII** 26.10; **VIII** 20.10, 22.1, 22.4, 29.6, 30.9

Salt: *making a living from,* **VIII** 17.5

Salt fish: *making a living from,* **VIII** 17.5

Scribe: **III** 9.1, 9.10; **VI** 4.5; **VIII** 28.2, 30.3; *of kings,* **III** 10.14; **VIII** 25.6 *(who dictate),* 26.1, 28.8; *learned in the law,* **III** 5.25; *legal,* **IV** 14.10; *master scribe,* **VIII** 27.3; *of powerful men,* **III** 10.1; *of the Senate,* **III** 10.14; *put in charge,* **III** 7.13

Sculptor: **III** 7.12, 10.8; **IV** 13.2, 14.20; **V** 2.12; **VIII** 29.5; *in brass or iron,* **III** 11.18; *popular,* **V** 2.14; *of images of the gods, or sacred images,* **III** 9.5; **IV** 14.20; **VIII** 25.5; *cf. Stone*

Sea-captain: **III** 12.9; **IV** 9.3; 14.14; **VIII** 6.1; *of great ships,* **III** 13.1

Secret and illegal: *arts, skills or writings, man skilled in, scholar and teacher of,* **III** 8.4, 9.4; **IV** 9.8, 12.4; *those who delight in obscure writings of secret religions,* **IV** 19.28

Secret writings: *discoverer of,* **III** 7.15; **IV** 12.4

Secretary: **III** 10.14

Seer: **III** 2.18; **VIII** 21.4

Servant: **III** 5.15; **VIII** 21.6, 25.8, 30.9

Sewer cleaner: **VIII** 29.6; *and latrine cleaner,* **VIII** 19.12, 20.1; *and well-cleaner,* **IV** 13.6

Sheep-stealer: **VI** 31.6

Shepherd: **III** 5.23; **IV** 13.7; **VIII** 6.6, 19.9; *pipe-playing and singing,* **VIII** 6.5

Ship-builder: **VIII** 20.10

Ship-owner: **IV** 9.3, 14.14; **VII** 26.10; **VIII** 5.1, 20.10, 27.12

Shoe-maker: **III** 10.8; **IV** 14.13

Shop-keeper: *low-class,* **VIII** 22.1

Shorthand-writer: **III** 5.25

# INDEX OF ANCIENT WRITERS ON ASTROLOGY

**ANTIOCHUS of ATHENS.** Author of a prose introduction to Astrology used by Rhetorius (q.v.) and Porphyry (q.v.). Formerly placed in second century A.D. (W. Kroll, *RE*, Suppl. IV, 32 ff.), he is now considered to belong to the first century B.C. Mentioned by Firmicus II, 29, 2. E. Boer, *Der Kleine Pauly I*, (1963) 662; F. Cumont, "Antiochus d'Athenes et Porphyre," *Melanges Bidez*, Bruxelles, 1933. 150 verses attributed to him are probably by Dorotheos of Sidon (Kroll, *loc. cit.*). Fragments, *CCAG*, I, 108, A. Olivieri.

**ANUBION.** First century A.D. writer of astrological handbook in elegiacs, quoted by Antiochus (q.v.), Hephaestion (q.v.), and Rhetorios (q.v.). Mentioned by Firmicus as Hanubium (III, 1, 1) together with Aesculapius and Mercury. Possibly Firmicus confused him with the Egyptian god Anubis, since he puts him in divine company (W. Kroll, *RE*, Suppl. I, 87, s.v. "Anubion"; Bidez-Cumont, *Les Mages Hellenisés*, II, 310).

**ARATUS of SOLI.** 315-240/39 B.C. Poet, worked at the court of Antigonus Canatas and Antiochus of Syria. Author of *Phaenomena*, a poem on the heavenly bodies, based on researches of Eudoxos of Cnidos. Commented on by Hipparchas and many others, translated into Latin by Cicero and Germanicus. E. Maass, *Phaenomena*, Berlin, 1898; rept. 1958.

**ANONYMOUS of 379.** Egyptian living at Rome (using *klima* of Rome), who dates himself by the consuls of that year. Influenced by Ptolemy and Vettius Valens; writes on the meaning of the bright stars. *CCAG*, I, 195 ff., F. Cumont.

**CENSORINUS.** Roman grammarian of the third century A.D. Author of *De die natali*, containing much calendar lore, which he probably derived from Varro and Suetonius. Ed. E. Hultsch, Leipzig, 1868.

**CRITODEMOS.** One of the earliest Greek writers on astrology, perhaps of the third century B.C. Mentioned by Pliny (*N.H.*, VII, 193) as a disciple of Berossos; by Vettius Valens (III, 12) as the author of a work called *Horasis;* by Firmicus (*Math.* IV, proe.), after Nechepso-Petosiris, Abram and Orpheus, all more or less legendary.

**DOROTHEOS OF SIDON.** Lived before Balbillus (Nero's astrologer), 65 A.D. Writer of astrological lore in verse. Mentioned by Firmicus, *Math.*, II, 29. Much quoted by Arab astrologers, according to V. Stegmann, *Quellen und Studien zur Geschichte und Kultur des Altertums und des Mitelalters*, Reihe B, Heft I. V. Stegmann, *Die Fragmente des Dorotheos von Sidon*, Würzburg, 1937; also by A. Koechly, Leipzig, 1858.

**FRONTO.** Mentioned by Firmicus (*Math.* II, prae.), together with Hipparchus, Ptolemy and Navigius (Nigidius?) as sources of the antiscia theory. Called unknown by all commentators on Firmicus, but the name might possibly be a corruption of Fonteius Capito, a member of the group of Nigidius and Varro, who followed Antony to Egypt and was known to have written on astrology. Stefan Weinstock, "C. Fonteius Capito and the Libri Tagetici," *Papers of the Br. Sch. at Rome*, XVII, N.S., V 1950, 44–49.

**GEMINOS of RHODES.**     ca. 50 B.C. Author of "the oldest existing work on astronomy from the ancient world" (Gundel, *Astrolegumena*). Gives the basic concepts of mathematical astrology as well. Of his many writings, one on astronomy remains. Chapter II is on astrology. Ed. C. Manitius, Leipzig, 1898.

**HEPHAESTION of THEBES.**     Fourth century A.D. writer from Egyptian Thebes who gives many details about Egypt, including the Egyptian names of the decans. Includes a horoscope dated 381 A.D. It has been suggested that he was a Christian, but his discussion of gods, temples and decans indicates not. Ed. A. Engelbrecht, Wien, 1887; also, *CCAG,* VIII, I, 146 ff., F. Cumont.

**HIPPARCHUS.**     ca. 190 to after 126 B.C. One of the greatest of the Greek astronomers. Attributed to him is the discovery of the procession of the equinoxes. In his commentary on Aratus (q.v.), he corrected many observations of Eudoxos. Also is reputed to have written on astrology which, as Neugebauer points out (*Exact Sciences,* p. 168), was perfectly reputable for his day. Mentioned by Firmicus as one of the discoverers of the antiscia (*Math.* II, prae.). D.R. Dicks, *Geographical Fragments of Hipparchus,* London, 1966; O. Neugebauer, "Notes on Hipparchus," in *Studies in Honor of Hetty Goldman,* Philadelphia, 1956.

**MANETHO.**     Author of a work called *Apotelesmata* from the time of Hadrian. It is not known whether this was his real name or whether he took the name of the Egyptian priest of Hellenistic times who wrote the famous history of Egypt in Greek. His extant writings consist of six books in verse showing the influence of Dorotheos of Sidon. Ed. A. Koechly, *Manethonis Apotelesmaticorum qui feruntur libri VI,* Leipzig, 1858.

**MANILIUS, MARCUS.**     Otherwise unknown author, of the time of Augustus or Tiberius, of a poem in five books called the *Astronomica.* This contains star lore, but omits any discussion of the planets, either because he did not finish the poem, or because he left them out on purpose, so as not to be accused of writing an astrological manual. Ed. A. E. Housman, Cambridge, 1937.

**NAVIGIUS.**     Mentioned by Firmicus, *Math.,* II prae, as one of the sources of his antiscia theory. Generally assumed to mean Nigidius Figulus, Pythagorean philosopher, astrologer, contemporary of Cicero. Known to have written on the *sphaera barbarica* (stars outside the zodiac), and perhaps on the *sphaera graecanica* (stars in the zodiac). Ed. A. Swoboda, *P. Nigidii Figuli Operum reliquiae* (Vienna, 1889; reprinted Amsterdam, 1964); Adriana della Casa, *Nigidio Figulo,* Roma, 1962.

**NECHEPSO-PETOSIRIS.**     Handbook of astrology, compiled perhaps about 150 B.C. in Alexandria, named after an Egyptian pharaoh of the seventh century and his high priest. Mentioned frequently by Firmicus and others, it was undoubtedly an important source of the doctrine. "Nechepsonis et Petosiridis fragmenta," ed. Ernst Riess, *Philologus,* Suppl. 6, 1891-93.

**PAUL OF ALEXANDRIA.**     End of fourth century. Wrote in Alexandria a handbook, which is a very complete account of the astrological methods of his time. Heliodorus, an Athenian disciple of Proclus (475–509), wrote a commentary on it. Paul had an important influence on Indian astrology. Ed. A. E. Boer, Leipzig, 1958.

**PORPHYRY.** Neo-Platonic philosopher who wrote, among his other many works, a very informative commentary on Ptolemy. *CCAG*, V, 4, S. T. Weinstock.

**PTOLEMAEUS, CLAUDIUS.** fl. 127–148 A.D. The great astronomer who produced the *Syntaxis (Almagest)*; also wrote a work on astrology known as the *Tetrabiblos* to provide a scientific basis for the art. Mentioned by Firmicus (*Math.*, II, prae.). Eds. F. Boll and A. E. Boer, *Claudii Ptolemaei opera III, 1 Apotelesmata*, Leipzig, 1940; see also the Loeb edition by F. E. Robbins, 1940.

**RHETORIUS.** A practicing astrologer who worked in Constantinople under Anastasios I (491–518). Ninety chapters survive of his lengthy compilation entitled *The Thesauros. CCAG*, I, 140–164, F. Boll.

**SEXTUS EMPIRICUS.** Physician and skeptical philosopher who included much interesting material in his book against astrology: *Adversus Mathematicos V*. Ed. J. B. Bury (Loeb Classical Library, 1949, 1961).

**TEUKROS of BABYLON.** Probably first century A.D. Wrote on *sphaera barbarica*. Great influence on Arab astrology. Modern scholars who favor Egyptian origins for astrology would like to make this Babylon a small town on the Nile. Ed. F. Boll, *Sphaera*, Hildesheim, 1967. *CCAG*, VII, 194 ff.

**VETTIUS VALENS.** Practicing astrologer, probably of the second century A.D. One of the very few whose work, a lengthy casebook, has almost entirely survived. Ed. W. Kroll, Berlin, 1908.

# BIBLIOGRAPHY

## Ancient Sources

Aelius Aristides, *Hieroi Logoi*; ed. W. Dendorf, 1829, rep. 1964.

(Aetna) *Incerti auctoris Aetna*, ed. F. R. D. Goodyear, Cambridge, 1965.

Albohazen. Ali ibn Abi al-Rijal al-Shaibani, abu al-Hassan, Albohazen Haly filii Abenragel, *Liber de ludiciis astrorum*, Basle, 1551.

(Abu Ma'shar) Albumasaris, *de Revolutionibus nativitatem*, ed. D. Pingree, Leipzig, 1968.

Alexander of Aphrodisias, *Praeter commentaria scripta minora*, ed. Ivo Bruns, Berlin, 1892.

Ammianus Marcellinus

Ammon. Maximos et Ammon, texteausgabe von A. Ludwich, Leipzig, 1877.

Antiochos of Athens. *Catalogus Codicum Astrologorum Graecorum*, I, 140 ff., Bruxelles, 1898.

Apuleius, *Apologia. Metamorphoses.*

Aratos, *Phaenomena.*

Aristotle, *De Caelo. De Anima. De Meteorologica. De Mirabilibus auscultationibus. Physiognomica.*

Augustine, *De Civitate Dei.*

Aulus Gellius, *Noctes Atticae*, ed. C. Hosius, Leipzig, 1903.

Censorinus, *De die natali*, ed. E. Hultsch, Leipzig, 1867.

Cicero, *De fato. De republica. Tusculanae disputationes. De divinatione. De natura deorum.*

Chalcidius, *In Platonis Timaeum.*

Diodorus Siculus

Diogenes Laertius

Dorotheos of Sidon. Ed. H. Koechly. Leipzig, 1858. Ed. V. Steigman. Leipzig, 1939.

(Eusebius) *Eusebii Caesariensis opera, Vol. I, Praeparationes evangelicae libri* I–X. Ed. G. Dindorf, Leipzig, 1867.

Firmicus Maternus. *Matheseus libri VIII.* Ed. W. Kroll, F. Skutsch, K. Ziegler. Leipzig, 1897–1913.

Firmicus Maternus. *De errore Profanarum religionum.* Ed. K. Ziegler, Leipzig, 1953.

Geminos. *Elementa astronomiae.* Ed. C. Manitius, 1898.

Hephaestion of Thebes. Ed. A. Engelbrecht. Wien, 1887.

(Hermes Trismegistos) *Corpus Hermeticum.* Ed. A. J. Festugière, Vol. I–IV. Paris, 1945–1954.

Iamblichos. *De Vita Pythagorika liber.* Ed. A. Nauck. Amsterdam, 1965.

(Isidorus) *Isidori de natura rerum.* Ed. G. Beeker. Amsterdam, 1967.

Julian. *The Works of the Emperor Julian.* Ed. and Trans. W. C. Wright. 3 vol. Loeb. Cambridge (Mass.) 1913.

(Lydus) *Joannes Lydus de Mensibus.* Ed. R. Wuensch. Leipzig, 1898.

Macrobius. *Commentarii in Somnium Scipionis. Saturnalia.*

(Manetho) *Manethonis Apotelesmaticorum qui feruntur libri VI.* Ed. A. Koechly. Leipzig, 1851.

(Manilius) *M. Manilii Astronomicon.* Ed. A. E. Housman. Cambridge, 2nd ed., 1937.

Nechepso. "Nechepsonis Petosiridis fragmenta magica." Ed. E. Riess, *Philologus. Suppl.* VI, 1891. 325–94.

Nigidius Figulus. *P. Nigidii Figuli opera.* Ed. A. Swoboda. Wien, 1899. Amsterdam, 1964.

Nonnus. *Dionysiaca.*

Ovid. *Fasti. Metamorphoses.*

Paulus of Alexandria. Ed. E. Boer. Leipzig, 1958.

Petosiris. V. "Nechepso."

Philo Judaeus. Ed. L. Cohn and P. Wendland. Berlin, 1896–1916.

Plato. *Republic. Timaeus.*

Pliny. *Naturalis Historiae.*

Plotinus. *Enneades.*

Plutarch. *De facie in urbe lunae. De Iside et Osiride. De superstitione. De defectu oraculorum. De tranquilitate animi.*

(Polemon) *Polemonis Periegetae fragmentae.* Ed. L. Preller. Leipzig, 1838. Chicago, 1967.

Porphyry. *Isagoge.* Ed. Stefan Weinstock. *Catalogus Codicum astrologorum Graecorum, V.* 4. Brussels, 1940. 187–228.

Proclus. *In Platonis Timaeum Commentarii.*

(Ptolemy) *Claudii Ptolemaei Tetrabiblos.* Ed. F. Boll and E. Boer. Leipzig, 1940.

Pseudo-Aristotle. *De mirabilibus auscultationibus.*

Pseudo-Plato. *Epinomis.*

Pseudo-Plutarch. *De fato.*

Quintilian. *De institutio oratoria.*

Rhetorius. *CCAG VIII,* 5. Ed. F. Cumont. Brussels, 1935.

Seneca. *Quaestiones naturales.*

Sextus Empiricus. *Adversus mathematicos.*

Silius Italicus. *Punica.*

Strabo

Varro. *De lingua latina.*

Vergil. *Aeneid.*

(Vettius Valens). *Vettii Valentis anthologiarum libri.* Ed. W. Kroll. Berlin, 1908.

(Vitruvius). *Vitruve de l'Architecture livre IX.* Ed. Jean Soubiran. Paris, 1969.

## Modern Sources

Amand, David, *Fatalisme et Liberté dans l'antiquite grecque,* Louvain, 1946.

Arnim, Hans Friedrich Auguste von. *Stoicorum veterum fragmenta.* Colegit Joannes ab Arnim, Leipzig, 1903–1905.

Barb, A. A. "The Survival of the Magic Arts," in *Conflict between Paganism and Christianity in the Fourth Century,* ed. Arnaldo Momigliano, Oxford, 1963.

Bickerman, E. J., *Chronology in the Ancient World,* Ithaca, 1968.

Bidez, Joseph, *Eos, où Platon et l'Orient,* Bruxelles, 1945.

Bidez, Joseph. "Les écoles chaldéennes sous Alexander et les Seleucids," *Melanges Capart,* Bruxelles, 1935.

Bidez, Joseph and Franz Cumont. *Les mages hellenisés,* Paris, 1938.

Bidez, Joseph. *Vie de Porphyre, le philosophe neo-platonicien,* Ghent, 1913.

Boll, Franz. *Kleine Schriften zur Sternkunde des Altertums,* Leipzig, 1950.

Boll, Franz. *Sphaera,* Leipzig, 1903, 1965.

Boll, Franz, Karl Bezold und Wilhelm Gundel. *Sternglaube und Sterndeutung,* Leipzig, 1931, 1966.

Boll, Franz. *Studien ueber Claudius Ptolemaeus,* Leipzig, 1894.

Boll, Franz. *Die Sonne in Glauben und in der Weltanschauung der alten Voelker,* Stuttgart, 1922.

Bouche-Leclerq, A. *L'Astrologie grecque,* Paris, 1899, 1963.

Bousset, Wilhelm. "Die Himmelreise der Seele," *Archiv fur Religionswissenschaft* I, V, 1901. 136–169.

Bowersock, G. W. *Greek Sophists in the Roman Empire.* Oxford, 1964.

Brehier, E. *Les idées philosophiques et religieuses de Philon d'Alexandrie.* Paris, 1926.

Burckhardt, Jacob. *The Age of Constantine the Great.* Trans. by Moses Hadas, New York, 1949.

Carcopino, Jerome. *Cesar.* Paris, 1936.

Cary, Max. *Geographical Background for Greek and Roman History.* Oxford, 1949.

*Catalogus codicum astrologorum Graecorum (CCAG),* I–XII. Bruxelles, 1898–1953.

*Corpus Inscriptionum Latinarum.*

Courcelle, Pierre. *Les lettres grecques en Occident.* Paris, 1943.

Cramer, Frederick H. "Astrology in Roman Law and Politics." *Memoirs of the American Philosophical Society.* XXXVII. Philadelphia, 1954.

Cumont, Franz. *Astrology and Religion among the Greeks and Romans,* London, 1912.

Cumont, Franz. *L'Egypte des Astrologues,* Bruxelles, 1937.

Cumont, Franz. "Fatalisme astrale," *Revue d'histoire de litterature religieuse,* N.S. III, 1912. 513–543.

Cumont, Franz. "Les noms des planetes et l'astrologie chez les grecques," *L'Antiquite classique,* IV. 1935. 1–43.

Cumont, Franz. *Oriental Religions in Roman Paganism.* Chicago, 1911.

Cumont, Franz. "La plus ancienne geographie astrologique," *Klio* IX, 1909. 263–73.

Cumont, Franz. *Recherches sur le symbolisme funéraires des Romains.* Paris, 1942.

Dessau, Hermann. *Inscriptiones Latinae Selectae.* Berlin, 1892–1955.

Dicks, D. R. *Early Greek Astronomy to Aristotle.* Ithaca, 1970.

Dicks, D. R. *Geographical Fragments of Hipparchus.* London, 1960.

*Dictionnaire des antiquités grecso et romaines.* Ed. par Ch. Daremberg et Ed. Saglio. Paris, 1877–1919.

Dill, Samuel. *Roman Society in the last Century of the Roman Empire in the West.* London, 1905.

Dodds, E. R. *Pagans and Christians in an Age of Anxiety.* Cambridge, 1965.

Duhem, Pierre. *Le Systeme du Monde.* Paris, 1913, 1959.

Eriksson, Sven. *Wochentagsgotter, Mond un Tierkreis. Laienastrologie in der roemischen Kaiserzeit.* Stockholm, 1956.

Evans, Elizabeth. *Physiognomics in the Ancient World.* American Philosophical Society Transactions. Philadelphia, 1969.

Ewbanks, W. W. *The Poetry of Cicero,* London, 1933.

Farrington, Benjamin. *Greek Science.* London, 1949.

Festugière, A. J. and A. D. Nock. *Corpus Hermeticum.* Paris, 1945–1954.

Festugière, A. J. *Personal Religion among the Greeks.* Cambridge, 1954.

Festugière, A. J. *La Revelation d'Hermes Trismégiste. I L'Astrologie et les sciences occultes.* Paris, 1944.

Friedrich, Theodorus. *In Julii Firmici Materni De Errore Profanarum Religionum Libellum Questiones.* Diss., Bonn. 1905.

Gagé, Jean. *Basileia.* Paris, 1968.

Grant, Frederick C., ed. *Hellenistic Religions.* New York, 1953.

Guido, Margaret. *Archeological Guide to Sicily.* New York, 1969.

Gundel, Wilhelm, and Hans Georg (Gundel). *Astrolegumena.* Wiesbaden, 1966.

Gundel, Wilhelm. *Beiträge zun Entwicklungsgeschichte der Begriffe Ananke und Heimarmene.* Giessen, 1914.

Gundel, Wilhelm. *"Dekane und Dekansternbilder," Studien der Bibliothek Warburg,* XIX. London, 1936 (Glueckstadt-Hamberg, 1936).

Gundel, Wilhelm. *Sternglaube, Sternreligion und Sternorakel.* Leipzig, 1933, Heidelberg, 1959.

Gundel, Hans Georg and R. Böker, *Zodiakos,* München, 1972.

Halliday, W. R. *Greek Divination.* Chicago, 1967.

Heath, T. L. *Aristarchos of Samos.* Oxford, 1913.

Heath, T. L. *History of Greek Mathematics.* Oxford, 1921.

Heath, T. L. *The Works of Archimedes.* New York, 1953.

Henry, Paul. "Plotin et l'Occident," *Specilegium Sacrum Lovaniense.* Louvain, 1934.

Hone, Margaret. *Applied Astrology.* London, 1970.

Hone, Margaret. *Modern Textbook of Astrology.* London, 1970.

Honigmann, Ernst. *Die sieben Klimata.* Heidelberg, 1929.

Housman, A. E. "Manilius, Augustus, Tiberius, Capricorn, and Libra," *Classical Quarterly,* VII, 1913. 109–114.

Jones, A. H. M. *The Later Roman Empire.* Norman (Okla.), 1964.

Jones, A. H. M. "The Social Background of the Struggle between Pagans and Christians in the Fourth Century," in Arnaldo Momigliano, *Conflict between Paganism and Christianity in the Fourth Century.* Oxford, 1963.

Kahn, Charles. "On Early Greek Astronomy," *Journal of Hellenic Studies,* XC, 1970. 99–116.

Koster, W. J. W. "Le mythe de Platon, de Zarathrustra et des Chaldéens," *Mnennosyne,* Suppl. III, 1951. 59 ff.

Kroll, W., F. Skutsch and K. Ziegler. *Praefatio to the Mathesis.* Stuttgart, 1968.

Laistner, M. L. W. *Thought and Letters in Western Europe,* A.D. *500-900.* New York, 1931.

Laistner, M. L. W. "The Western Church and Astrology during the Early Middle Ages," *Harvard Theological Review,* XXXIV, 1942. 251–75.

Laroche, E. "Les noms grecs de l'astronomie," *Revue de Philologie,* LXXIII, Third ser. 20, 1946.

Le Grand, Louis. *Publius Nigidius Figulus.* PKKRIS, N.D.

Lindsay, Jack. *Origins of Astrology.* New York, 1971.

Ludwig, W., D. Pingree. "Manfred Erren: Die Phainomena des Aratos von Soloi. Untersuchungen zum Sachund Sinn Verständnis." (review). *Gnomon,* 1971. 346–54.

Maas, Ernst. *Commentariorum in Aratum reliquiae.* Berlin, 1898, 1958.

MacMullen, Ramsay. "Social History in Astrology," *Ancient Society,* II, 1971.

Momigliano, Arnaldo. "Popular Religious Beliefs and the Late Roman Historians," *Studies in Church History VIII,* 1971. 1–18.

Mommsen, Theodore. "Firmicus Maternus," *Hermes* XXIX, 1894. 468–72.

Moore, Clifford H. *Ancient Beliefs on the Immortality of the Soul.* New York, 1931.

Moore, Clifford H. *Greek and Roman Ascetic Tendencies.* Boston, 1912.

Moore, Clifford H. *Julius Firmicus Maternus der Heide und der Christ.* Diss. München, 1897.

Neugebauer, Otto. *Egyptian Astronomical Texts.* London, 1960–1969.

Neugebauer, Otto. *The Exact Sciences in Antiquity.* Providence, 1957.

Neugebauer, Otto and H. B. van Hoesen. Greek Horoscopes. *Memoirs, American Philosophical Society,* Philadelphia, 1959.

Neugebauer, Otto, "The Horoscope of Ceionius Rufus Albinus," *American Journal of Philology,* LXXIV, 1953. 418–20.

Neugebauer, Otto. "Notes on Hipparchus," in *Studies in Honor of Hetty Goldman.* Philadelphia, 1965.

Neugebauer, Otto. "On Some Astronomical Papyri and Related Problems of Ancient Geography." *American Philosophical Society Transactions.* Philadelphia, 1961. 251–60.

Nilsson, Martin P. "The Rise of Astrology in the Hellenistic Age," *Historical Notes and Papers.* Lund, 1943.

Nilsson, Martin P. *Geschichte der griechischen Religion,* Vol. II. Munich, 1961.

Nykl, A. R. "Libro conplido en los Juizios de las Estrellas," *Speculum, a Journal of Medieval Studies.* Cambridge (Mass.), 1954. 35–68.

Pauly-Wissowa et al. *Real-Encyclopaedie der klassischen Altertumswissenschaft.* Stuttgart, 1894 ff.

Reese, Gustave. "Musical Compositions in Renaissance Intarsia," *Medieval and Renaissance Studies, Proceedings.* 1966. 74–93.

Reitzenstein, R. *Poimandres.* Leipzig, 1904.

Robbins, Frank Eggleston. "A New Astrological Treatise," *Classical Philology* XXII, 1927. 1–35.

Sachs, S. J. "Babylonian Horoscopes," *Journal of Cuneiform Studies,* VI, 1942. 151–56.

Saumaise, Claude de (Claudius Salmacius). *De annis climacteris.* Leyden, 1648.

Schanz-Hosius. *Geschichte der römischen Literatur. Handbuch der Altertumswissenschaft.* Munich, 1914, 1959.

Schmekel, A. *Die Philosophie der Mittleren Stoa.* Berlin, 1892.

Schnabel, Paul. *Berossos.* Leipzig, 1923.

Sittl, K. "Firmicus Maternus," *Archiv fur lateinische Lexographie,* IV. 1887. 610–32.

Skutsch, F. "Firmicus Maternus als Syrakusaner," *Hermes* XXXI, 1895. 645–57.

Souter, Alexander. *Glossary of Later Latin to 600 A.D.* Oxford, 1949.

Stahl, William H. *Commentary on the Dream of Scipio.* New York, 1952.

Stahl, William H. *Martianus Capella and the Seven Lively Arts.* New York, 1971

Stahl, William H. *Roman Science.* Madison, 1962.

Tannery, Paul. *Pour l'histoires de la science Hellène.* Paris, 1887.

Taylor, A. E. *A Commentary on Plato's Timaeus.* Oxford, 1928.

Thorndike, Lynn. "A Roman Astrologer as a Historical Source: Julius Firmicus Maternus," *Classical Philology,* VIII, 1913. 415–35.

Van der Waerden, B. L. "Das grosse Jahr und die ewige Widerkehr," *Hermes,* LXXX, 1952. 129–55.

Van der Waerden, B. L. *Science Awakening.* Oxford, 1953.

Volkmann, Richard. *Die Rhetorik der Griescher und Romer.* Leipzig, 1885.

Weinstock, Stefan. "C. Fonteius Capito and the Libri Tagetici," *British School at Rome, Papers,* XVIII, N. S. 5, 1950. 44–49.

Weinstock, Stefan. "Martianus Capella and the cosmos system of the Etruscans," *Journal of Roman Studies* XXXVI, 1946. 101–29.

# GLOSSARY OF ASTROLOGICAL TERMS

**ABSCONSAE** (Latin adjective *absconsus*) – Hidden, as by the Sun's rays.

**ACRONYCTAE** (Greek *akronyktos*) – At nightfall, at sunset.

**AFANEIS** (Greek *aphanes*) – Unseen.

**AGATHE TYCHE** — Greek for *Bona Fortuna,* Good Fortune; name for the Fifth House.

**AGATHOS DAEMON** – Greek for *Bonus Daemon,* Good Spirit; name for the Eleventh House.

**AIR SIGNS** – Three of the twelve signs when they are classified according to the four elements: Gemini, Libra, Aquarius.

**AMFICYRTOUS** (Greek *amphikyrtos*) – Convex on each side, gibbous.

**ANAFORA** – The rising of a sign; the sign about to rise after the one on the Ascendant. Used especially of the angles. Also the name of the Second House, the one about to rise. See Book II, 17, 1.

**ANATOLE** – Greek for rising, Ascendant.

**ANTISCIUM, pl. ANTISCIA** – Sometimes known today as Mundane Parallax. Relation between degrees or signs equidistant from the MC or the IMC. A rare kind of aspect especially favored by Firmicus, who seems to have invented this term for it.

**APPLICATION, APPLYING TO** – Approach of one planet toward aspect with another. In Firmicus, used only of the Moon.

**ASCENDANT** – The degree which appears on the horizon when the birthchart is cast; sometimes applied to the whole rising sign.

**BENEFIC** – Planets, signs, or relationships which have favorable predictions. The particularly benefic planets are Venus and Jupiter.

**BONA FORTUNA** – Good Fortune, the name for the Fifth House.

**BONUS DAEMON** – Good Spirit, the name for the Eleventh House.

**CACODAEMON** (Greek *Kakos Daemon*) – The Malus Daemon, Evil Spirit; name for the Twelfth House.

**CARDO, pl. CARDINES** – The angles, the four cardinal points of the astrological chart; sometimes the entire First, Fourth, Seventh, and Tenth Houses, known as the Ascendant, Mid-Heaven (*Medium Caelum*), Descendant, and Nadir (*Imum Caelum*).

**CATAFORA** – Point or house risen before the point or house on the Ascendant.

**CENODROMON** (Greek *kenodromon*) – Running through a vacuum. Used in Firmicus for the Moon moving toward or applying to nothing.

**CHART** – The astrological map of the Heavens taken at the moment of birth; nativity, geniture. Today sometimes known as the horoscope.

**CHRONOCRATOR** (Greek chronokrator) – Ruler of Time. Each of the planets controls a certain period of time in a subject's (native's) life. In a diurnal chart, the Sun rules the first span and passes the rulership to the other planets in turn. In a nocturnal chart, the Moon does the same. See Book IV, 20, 2.

**CONDITION** – Quality of being diurnal or nocturnal. Planets follow the condition of the Sun or the Moon in being either diurnal or nocturnal.

**CONJUNCTION** – Relationship of planets very close together. Strictly speaking, they should occupy the same degree. Today a distance of seven degrees is usually accepted.

**DAEMON** – See *Bonus* and *Malus Daemon.*

**DEA** – Goddess; name for the Third House.

**DEBILITY** – Fall; the opposite of Exaltation.

**DECAN** – A subdivision of signs. Each sign has three decans of ten degrees each. See Book II, 4.

**DEFLUXION** – Movement of the Moon away from Conjunction.

**DEGREE** (Latin *pars*) – A 360th part of the circle of the Zodiac.

**DEUS** – God; name for the Ninth House.

**DESCENDANT** – Point opposite the Ascendant; the entire Seventh House.

**DICHOTOMOUS** (Greek *dichotomos*) – Cut in half; half Moon.

**DIURNAL CHART** – One taken in the daytime.

**DOUBLE SIGNS** – Also called Two-bodied or Mutable: Gemini, Virgo, Sagittarius, Pisces.

**DUODECATEMORION,** pl. **DUODECATEMORIA** – A point on the chart of special importance for a planet. Found by multiplying by twelve the number of the degree in which the planet is found.

**DYSIS** – Greek for *Occasus,* Descendant.

**EARTH SIGNS** – Taurus, Virgo, Capricorn.

**EMPTY AND FULL DEGREES** – According to Firmicus, in each sign some degrees are ineffective, i.e., empty. See Book IV, 22.

**ENENECONTAMERIS** – The 90th degree in the chart, one with special powers. See Book VIII, 2.

**EPICATAFORA** – Opposite to the Anafora. The Eighth House.

**EQUINOCTIAL** – Referring to the points on the Sun's path where the length of day and night are equal. Equinoctial signs are Aries and Libra.

**EXALTATION** – Also known as Dignity. Planets are said to have special powers in certain degrees outside of their own houses. The opposite of this point is Fall or Debility, where they lose power.

**FAENO** (Greek *Phainon*) – Early Greek name for Saturn.

**FAETHO** (Greek *Phaethon*) – Early Greek name for Jupiter.

**FALL** – Opposite of Exaltation; point where planet loses power.

**FEMININE SIGNS** – In Firmicus every other sign is feminine: Taurus, Cancer, Virgo, Scorpio, Capricorn, and Pisces.

**FIRE SIGNS** – Aries, Leo, Sagittarius.

**FIXED SIGNS** – Also known as solid signs: Taurus, Leo, Scorpio, Aquarius.

**FOSFOROS** (Greek *Phosphoros,* light bringer) – Early Greek name for Venus.

**GENITURE** – Birthchart, nativity. Map of the Heavens at the moment of birth.

**GIVER OF LIFE** – The planet which measures the length of life. In Book II, 25, Firmicus says this is the same as the Ruler of the Chart. In other places, for instance Books III, 2, 23; and IV, 1, 8, he seems to indicate that they are different.

**HOUSE** (Latin *locus,* Greek *topos*) – One of a set of divisions of the Zodiac which are stationary, through which the signs rotate. Firmicus notes an earlier Eight House system in Book II, 14, but prefers the usual twelve. Each house represents a phase of human life, such as Health, Marriage, Children, Death, etc.

**IMUM CAELUM** – The IMC. Now known (with corrupt Latinity) as Imum Caeli. The Nadir.

**LITURGI** (Greek *litourgos*) – Thirds of decans; also called munifices.

**MALA FORTUNA** – Bad Fortune; name for the Sixth House.

**MALUS DAEMON** – Evil Spirit; name for the Twelfth House.

**MASCULINE PLANETS** – In Firmicus, every other planet is masculine: Aries, Gemini, Leo, Libra, Sagittarius, and Aquarius.

**MATHESIS** – Greek for science, knowledge. In post-Augustan Latin, the science of astrology.

**MALEFIC** – Planets, signs, or relationships which are especially unlucky. The malefic planets are Saturn and Mars.

**MEDIUM CAELUM** – Mid-Heaven; now called Medium Caeli.

**MENOIDES** (Greek *Menoeides*) – The new Moon.

**MESURANIMA** – Greek for Mid-Heaven.

**MOVING TOWARD NOTHING** – Used in Firmicus only for the Moon when void of course.

**MUNIFICES** – Thirds of decans. See Liturgi.

**MUTABLE SIGNS** – Also double or two-bodied: Gemini, Virgo, Sagittarius, Pisces.

**MYRIOGENESIS** – Theory concerning forecasting from individual degrees.

**NATIVITY** – Chart taken at moment of birth.

**NATIVE** – The one born, the subject of the nativity or birthchart.

**NOCTURNAL CHART** – Chart taken at night.

**OECODESPOTES** (Greek Oikodespotes) – Planet which is Ruler of the Chart.

**PART OF FORTUNE** – An especially important point in the chart which has the same relationship to the Ascendant as the Moon to the Sun.

**PART OF THE DAEMON** – Like the Part of Fortune, but measured from the Sun to the Moon.

**PLANET** – From the Greek *planetai,* wanderers. In ancient times only five were known: Saturn, Jupiter, Mars, Venus, Mercury. Together with the Sun and Moon they were the most important bodies in the forecast.

**PYROIS** – Greek for fiery. An early Greek name for Mars.

**REJOICE** – A planet is said to rejoice in its Exaltation (q.v.).

**RETROGRADE** – In the ancient earth-centered view, planets appeared sometimes to go backward.

**SEMI-VOICED SIGNS** – Sometimes called Signs of Small Voice: Leo, Sagittarius.

**SEXTILE** – Aspect of 60 degrees.

**SIGNS** – Twelve divisions of the Zodiac, each considered to consist of 30 degrees. They are named after, but do not coincide with, constellations. The twelve are: Aries, Taurus, Gemini, Cancer, Leo, Virgo, Libra, Scorpio, Sagittarius, Capricorn, Aquarius, and Pisces. Signs are classified in various ways: Cardinal (tropical), fixed, and double (mutable), q.v.; air, fire, earth, and water; masculine and feminine, q.v.; diurnal and nocturnal; human and bestial; voiced, semi-voiced, and unvoiced, q.v.

**SOLSTITIAL** – Referring to the points on the sun's path where the Sun appears to stand still, i.e., the longest and shortest day. Solstitial signs: Cancer and Capricorn.

**SPHAERA BARBARICA** – Stars and constellations outside the Zodiac. Non-Greek systems of astrology.

**STATION** – Points where, in the ancient Earth-centered view, planets appear to pause and turn retrograde.

**STILBO** – Early Greek name for Mercury.

**SYNODICAE** (Synodicus) – In conjunction with the Sun.

**TERMS** (Latin *fines,* Greek *oria*) – Degrees outside of their own houses in which planets have special powers or dignity. No longer much used.

**THEA** – Greek for Dea (q.v.).

**THEOS** – Greek for Deus (q.v.).

**TROPIC SIGNS** – Cancer and Capricorn. Also used for all four cardinal signs.

**TRINE** – Aspect of 120 degrees.

**TYCHE** (Latin, *Fortuna*) – Fortune.

**UNASPECTED** – Not in any aspectual relationship, therefore, in general, unlucky. Firmicus often calls planets in this relationship "sluggish" or "alien."

**UNVOICED SIGNS** – Cancer, Libra, Scorpio, Pisces. Libra is probably in this list, because she is a late-comer to the signs, and was formerly considered the claws of the Crab.

**UPOGEON** – Greek for underworld or under-Earth. Imum Caelum, Nadir.

**VESPERTINE** – Setting after the Sun.

**VOID OF COURSE** – Moving toward nothing. Not coming into aspect. Firmicus uses this term only of the Moon.

**VOICED SIGNS** – Aries, Taurus, Gemini, Virgo, Aquarius.

**WATERY SIGNS** – Cancer, Scorpio, Pisces.

**ZODIAC** – A set of twelve signs named after the constellations which lie along the ecliptic, the Sun's path.